S0-AHD-577

Life Care

Life Care

A Long-Term Solution?

Robert D. Chellis
and
Paul John Grayson

Lexington Books
D.C. Heath and Company/Lexington, Massachusetts/Toronto

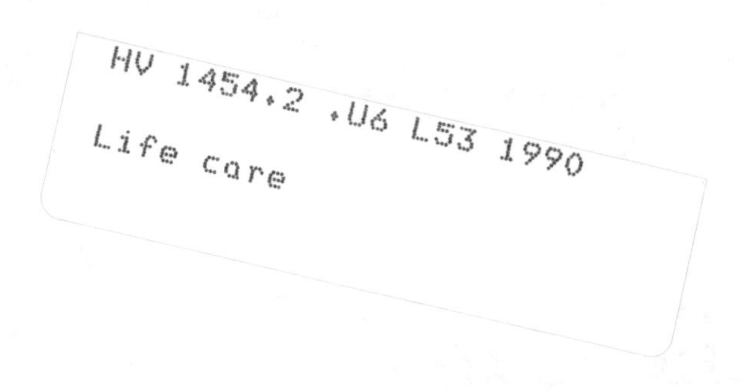

Library of Congress Cataloging-in-Publication Data

Life care : a long-term solution? / edited by Robert D. Chellis, Paul John Grayson.
p. cm.
Papers drawn from the Second Farnsworth Trust Symposium held in Cambridge, Mass., Mar. 7–8, 1988.
Includes bibliographical references.
ISBN 0-669-19937-0 (alk. paper)
1. Life care communities—United States—Congresses. I. Chellis, Robert D. II. Grayson, Paul John. III. Farnsworth Trust Symposium (2nd : 1988 : Cambridge, Mass.)
HV1454.2.U6153 1990
362.1′6′0973—dc20 90-31415
CIP

Published simultaneously in Canada
Printed in the United States of America
International Standard Book Number: 0–669–19937–0
Library of Congress Catalog Card Number: 90–31415

The paper used in this publication meets the minimum requirements of American National Standard for Information Sciences—Permanence of Paper for Printed Library Materials, ANSI Z39.48–1984. ∞™

Year and number of this printing:

90 91 92 10 9 8 7 6 5 4 3 2 1

Sandy Adams and Beatriz Grayson,
our patient wives,
who have been true pals
during the preparation of this volume.

Contents

Figures

Tables

Acknowledgments

This work, drawn from the Second Farnsworth Trust Symposium, on life-care organization, development, and management, would not have been possible without the generous support and encouragement of the Harvard Medical School and the Farnsworth Trust.

In 1930, Charles H. Farnsworth left a bequest to help frail, elderly people in Massachusetts and across the nation. Under the enlightened stewardship of the State Street Bank and Trust Company of Boston, and Trust Officers, Deborah Robbins, Vice President, and George G. Robbins, Senior Vice President, the First Farnsworth Trust Symposium, "Congregate Housing for Older People—A Solution for the 1980s" was held some eight years ago at the Harvard School of Public Health. It too resulted in a book.

The Second Farnsworth Trust Symposium: "Life Care—A Long Term Solution?" was held in Cambridge, Massachusetts. Its goal was to explore the current status, best models, and potential directions of life care in the United States and abroad.

Harvard Medical School and the Program for the Analysis of Clinical Studies, under the direction of Jerry Avorn, M.D., Associate Professor of Social Medicine & Health Policy, provided cosponsorship and administrative support.

Our special thanks go to Margaret Zusky of Lexington Books for her encouragement and support, to Susanne Bellavance for her superb administrative efforts on behalf of the Harvard Medical School, and to Judith G. Willett, who provided invaluable assistance before and during the Symposium.

Acknowledgments

Introduction

As our population ages, more Americans are becoming aware that preparation for the unpredictabilities of a long old age is a necessary, prudent, and fiscally sound planning approach. The United States is one of two nations in the developed world that as yet has no universal health program to protect its citizens against the potential of catastrophic illness and the eventual depletion of their savings, home, and possessions.

In the absence of such protection, each of us is on our own. Most of us will do our best, using our savings, our pensions, individual health and accident insurance, along with various combinations of Medicare plus "Medigap" to manage to age in place, at home. But too often there is a limit to this, for when we can manage no more, due to frailty, lack of services, or the need for extended care through placement in a nursing home or other form of institution, we will be forced to relocate under duress and at considerable emotional and psychological cost.

This book is about an option that could be made available to perhaps 50 percent or more of those older Americans who have the good fortune to own their own home, or have available other assets that can be used to qualify for residence in a life-care community. This option is the full-service, insurance-based, "life care" version of the continuing-care retirement community (CCRC). It is an approach that appears, at this time, to offer the best opportunity for a secure, comfortable, active, and health-care-protected future for one's golden years. It does this by providing housing, services, social programs, health care, and insurance in one package. Even more people can be covered if new life-care communities are encouraged to support some percentage of lower-income elders with internally generated funds.

Life care offers more benefits and support systems for old age than any other option available today in the United States. Life-care communities with their continuum of care are ideal living arrangements for those elderly who can understand the benefits of this style of life, can afford it, can make such a major decision, and can find such programs in an area where they wish, or are willing, to live.

Life Care: A Long-Term Solution? has been assembled to provide you, the reader, whether you are a potential sponsor, developer, investor, builder, architect, banker, lawyer, service provider, or interested and concerned potential resident, an opportunity to learn all about life care. This volume has been organized to provide, particularly for those interested in the development and management of such facilities, a broad-based sequential view of the procedures, including the ways and means of researching, planning, designing, financing, marketing, and managing successful projects.

We also explore, through the presentation of an eminent physician and ethicist, critical health policy and ethical issues in the United States today, and suggest new ways to apply humane therapies for the severely ill and those unable to make life or death decisions. We conducted and include a survey on the consumer preferences and interests of current life-care residents. This report provides valuable lessons for the future planning, development, marketing, and evaluation of retirement communities.

With an awareness that for many years housing, housing product, and appliance design and research has been a priority in other industrialized countries, we look at significant developments outside our borders. This look at trends, innovative technology, design research, and various approaches and attitudes is intended to excite the imagination and stimulate further thought and interest in creating enabling environments. Our objective is to cause a rethinking of environmental design so that elderly or disabled individuals can be as independent as possible and can age in place with dignity and self-esteem, be it in a life-care center or an institutional or home setting.

Life care at home the subject of one of our chapters, which was written by a distinguished innovator in the field, is a subset of the life-care community model, and is presented as an option that permits access to services and amenities similar to those of a life-care community, while the participating senior lives at home. Ideally, this would be an extension of the life-care campus' services for the larger community.

As mentioned previously, the full life-care concept involves an insurance-based group program that pools the health-care risks of the life-care community's residents. This notion of insurance protection is fundamental to a life-care community, and actuarially based planning is essential to its survival. To provide the reader with an in-depth understanding of the insurance aspects and implications for the life-care industry and the public, two leading experts present their views on this important subject.

To conclude our volume, we restate our view that the notion of life care, with its variants and subsets, is indeed a viable and flexible long-term solution for this nation's elder care needs, and we include our thoughts on future options and trends. We trust you will find your time spent with *Life Care: A Long Term Solution?* an informative, stimulating, and worthwhile experience, and an appropriate reference source for information on the basics of life care.

Overview

Most of us are becoming keenly aware that in the coming decades the world will experience a dramatic increase in the number of older people. Improvements in living conditions, health delivery systems, nutrition, and education have helped to bring about a rapid increase in longevity, particularly impacting the most developed nations. It is expected that the increase in the world's elderly population will peak between the years 2030 and 2050. Before then, nations such as Japan and Sweden are projected to have populations with over 25 percent who are sixty-five years and older.

In the United States alone, it is estimated by the U.S. Bureau of the Census that there will be some 35 million older Americans by the year 2000. This is up from 25 million in 1980, and represents a 40 percent increase in just twenty years. In 2030, this figure is projected to be more than 2.6 times the 1980 number, or some 66 million older citizens. What is most impressive about these changes is that the over-seventy-five age group will be the fastest growing segment of the entire population. The over-eighty-five age group will increase its numbers even more dramatically. To know, in future years, of someone over the age of 100, will not be the rarity it is today.

With this shift in the age of our population, a wide range of demands will be imposed upon housing, health care, and service systems. Preparing to meet the needs of an aging population takes time. Unusual among people of developed nations, the American people seem to be more reactive than proactive in matters pertaining to social and human services. We wait for problems to occur before dealing with them. In fact, as a youth-oriented society, we try hard to evade the reality of growing old. We are not so accepting of disability and have over the years tended to hide or "warehouse" the elderly and the disabled.

On the other hand, the European nations are more proactive and have been developing a variety of housing and health-care options for their increasing elderly populations. Nations such as Denmark, Sweden, Switzerland, and the Netherlands have been developing enlightened public policies that, along with housing and care systems for the elderly and disabled, provide for all rather than a few. This approach has evolved from the belief that in the long run it will be less costly to a nation and its people to provide a rational, comprehensive national health program for all ages and all conditions. As it turns out, our health system, while offering high-quality care, is more costly per capita than all other industrialized nations, with fewer people served, and with greater disparities in the service they receive.

Universal health insurance programs exist in all developed nations except the United States and the Union of South Africa. Although the costs are high, other countries feel the alternatives are unacceptable. Is it possible that if we do not provide for all, the eventual cost will be greater than we can imagine in terms of both the financial and human condition? Should the quality of our health, like the quality of education, be one of our first lines of defense as we work to maintain our position of leadership in the world?

Much work in all areas of our economy is necessary so that we can maintain or rebuild our nation's infrastructure, our cities, our sense of community, our compassion for our fellow human beings. For example, considerable research and development work is needed in our fragmented housing industry. A coordinated effort among manufacturers is being undertaken with the "smart house" program, but more funding and industry commitment is needed. The Japanese, looking into the needs of the next century and beyond regarding the housing and care of their future elderly citizens, have been in the forefront of research and investigation of the benefits of innovative technology. They have for the past decade been intensely involved in researching building systems, manufactured housing, and products to accommodate the elderly and disabled as their needs change due to diminishing physical or mental ability. The goal of this research and development is to create enabling environments so that people can maintain a high quality of life with minimal dependency on a caregiver. When caregivers must be involved, the design goal is to reduce the stress and strain on all concerned. Life care offers one approach toward providing solutions with appropriate housing and support systems for the elderly, and has particularly great potential in the United States, where 75 percent of older people own their own home, giving them a major asset to help solve more than just housing problems.

Fortunately, when we can solve environmental problems in the housing and care of the elderly, we are at the same time creating systems that can be used by all ages. Concepts such as "universal design" serve everyone regardless of age or disability. Our chapter on innovative technology will introduce you to such concepts and products being developed overseas.

Housing and health-care programs as we currently provide in the United States will require rethinking and adjustment if we are to adequately prepare for the needs of our rapidly increasing elderly population. Fortunately, public awareness is developing as "baby boomers" become the "sandwich generation," involved with the housing and health-care needs of parents or elderly relatives. As the population ages, and physical deficits develop, and more care and attention is needed to service older people, the public will become more cognizant that the costs of caregiving, of long-term care, and of dealing with a catastrophic illness can be a devastating drain on the mental, physical, and financial resources of an individual, a spouse, a family, the community, and the nation. And if they are not sufficiently aware, the increasingly vocal, well-organized, and powerful groups representing the elderly will make themselves heard with increasing force.

Going back to Roman times, the notion of care for the elderly had been expressed in the creation of such special purpose structures as "old sailor's rest homes." From time to time throughout history, we learn of the existence of purpose-built shelters for the old, the poor, and the disabled. Private and nonprofit organizations, religious and fraternal groups, communities and public agencies have all developed facilities for the special needs of the aged in the past as well as the present.

In the United States today, with a variety of programs and funding sources, there are a number of options available. The particular option that we cover in this book is the life-care model. To help you see where this model fits in relation to other models that are familiar to us, such as congregate, group, or assisted living, we provide the following definitions list.

Definitions

To define our terms from the general to the specific, we are covering *congregate housing*, and within that broad category, the *continuing-care retirement community* (CCRC) variation. Within the CCRC definition, we are focusing on the insurance-based *life care* model of continuing care.

Congregate housing is sheltered housing for the ambulatory elderly, with accommodations ranging from a room to a full apartment. Shared common areas and services include, at a minimum, a meals program and management assistance. Although often aimed at lower-income levels because of the economies that can be achieved through sharing, there are an increasing number of luxury examples.

Assisted living, catered living, board and care, and personal care are among the descriptive names for forms of congregate housing, where residents require more assistance with activities of daily living, such as bathing and grooming. Many facilities are unlicensed, and as long as their staff provides no specifically medical services, can stay that way. Estimates vary but suggest that there are from 100,000 to 300,000 such homes nationally in a great range of sizes and configurations, serving over one million people. This compares with possibly 20,000 licensed nursing homes with approximately 1.5 million beds.

Continuing-care retirement communities (CCRCs) offer long-term care contracts (at least for one year), to provide residents with a broad range of services, including housing, meals, housekeeping, laundry, transportation, social programs, and access to nursing care. There are probably more than 1,000 CCRCs operating in the United States today, with an approximate maximum population of some 250,000 to 350,000 residents.

Life-care communities are CCRCs that furnish nursing and other health-care services on a prepaid or insurance basis, much like an HMO. If you can afford to take up residence in a life-care community, then it is said, "you can afford to be sick." Residents generally enjoy their remaining years with financial and emotional security.

In the chapters that follow we try to cover all the facets of a complex field, and whether you choose to read straight through or use this book as a reference, we hope it will be clear and informative. We also hope that it will further encourage the much-needed development of additional life-care alternatives for the coming generations of elderly, of which we all hope to be a part.

Robert Dana Chellis, M.P.H. &
Paul John Grayson, M.Arch., AIA
Boston, MA, February 1990

Life Care

1
All About Life Care

Robert D. Chellis, M.P.H.

This introductory chapter presents the insurance-based life care model as a hybrid of congregate housing. Other forms of housing such as continuing care retirement communities, assisted living, board and care, personal care and life care at home are identified as sub-sets of the congregate form. This chapter discusses affordability as a major challenge for the life-care industry and offers options in providing some type of life care for all income levels. It explores such issues as protection against catastrophic illness through various approaches, one being a national long-term care insurance safety net which it is believed will help the life-care movement thrive.

—Editors

Life care is a comprehensive network of interrelated programs. The different elements included in a given life-care community, such as elderly housing, congregate housing, assisted living, home care, respite care, intermediate nursing care, skilled nursing care, rehabilitative care, health and fitness programs, and health education, are all useful taken alone, but enhance one another and become more effective when part of a continuum of mutually supportive services. The typical problems of older people, such as lack of catastrophic health insurance, difficulty maintaining a home, isolation, lack of activity, gradually increasing frailty, poor nutrition, lack of services, and lack of transportation, can nearly all be solved or managed within a good life-care program.

Life-care programs in the United States are inspired by many cultural and historical traditions. Probably the most important is the English tradition of local responsibility for outdoor and indoor relief. From the Middle Ages into the nineteenth century, there was a generally accepted village or town responsibility to furnish basic food and supplies to the poorest families in their own homes (outdoor relief), or to bring paupers, the homeless, or elderly people unable to cope alone into a poorhouse or workhouse setting (indoor relief). The poor farm and the municipal home became normal elements of many nineteenth century American communities. These services were deliberately kept to a minimum to discourage overuse. Increased affluence combined with the energies and available volunteer time of the Victorians to create additional, more attractive alternatives. By the late 1800s, most major towns and quite a few minor towns had their own Home for Aged Women, Odd Fellows Home, or other shelter, many with quite specific objectives of benevolence in mind. With the advent of Social Security in the late 1930s, Medicare and Medicaid in the 1960s, increased pension coverage, and more affluence generally, more retirement and nursing options were both demanded and created.

Widespread home ownership among the elderly (75 percent nationally) of increasingly valuable homes has encouraged increasingly rapid development of entrance-fee-based life-care communities since the 1960s. When resident entrance fees pay for development costs and monthly fees pay for operations, life care gives older people a way to form a self-insuring group, pooling their resources in a type of well-financed, communal, modern utopia. In an era of increasing health costs and decreasing government willingness or ability to create or even facilitate an appropriate, complete range of services for older Americans, the life-care concept is a way for people to secure their own old age—a private sector response to a real need and demand. With less than 1 percent of older people covered by life care so far, this is a field poised for rapid growth if, first, attractive and solid projects are proposed and, second, the public is educated to the desirability of paying for the services, protections, and opportunities of these rather expensive options.

An interesting trend in retirement housing is the creation of more varied and more specialized communities. Traditionally, many have been founded by church-sponsored and other local nonprofit grass roots organizations. Their primary concern was naturally to provide the housing, health care, support services, social life, and financial security unavailable elsewhere. Now groups are looking beyond these universal basics, and we are seeing special-interest facilities, particularly college-based centers for lifelong learning, as well as YMCA-based centers with an emphasis on fitness and cross-generational programs, or programs admitting primarily retired military or other affinity groups. Sponsorship is becoming more varied and may be from hospitals, existing area nursing homes, older retirement facilities that are expanding, housing developers looking for a different market segment, or, often, from nonprofit groups of like-minded citizens developing a life-care center primarily for themselves that is tailored to their tastes. Models now include urban, suburban, and rural communities, low-rise and high-rise apartments, and free-standing cottages. Fee structures are becoming more creative; co-ops, condos, leasehold condos, rentals, membership programs, refundable life-use fees (RLUFs), and even nonrefundable life-use fees, are all available somewhere.

The availability of life-care insurance from commercial carriers has already had a dramatic impact, encouraging a number of continuing-care retirement communities (CCRCs) to adopt a fully insured true life-care program, thus becoming a life-care community (LCC). Even some sponsors who have reviewed the commercial offerings and then decided to self-insure in the traditional way were reassured about the reasonableness of the insurance concept simply by the emergence of commercial products. Life care at home, which in theory makes it possible for those elderly who want to remain at home to do so, may evolve into another successful product, and possibly into major competition for life care. It is more likely, however, that the two programs will complement each other and will eventually be offered by the same sponsor, broadening the overall market. New sponsors should be encouraged to offer both products because, for example, life care at home should work especially well when wrapped around a life-care campus and when the affiliated members can enjoy the hospitality aspects as well as the guaranteed health care of their life-care center's campus, much as one uses a country club. Other hybrids of the concept, including urban scattered-site projects, affiliations of different service providers, or insurance-based nonresidence programs involving preretirees, may emerge over time as strong local programs.

Affordability

A major challenge for the life-care industry will be affordability. The market must be broadened to include not just those with upper and upper-middle incomes, but also those with middle and lower-middle incomes, and even some people with very low incomes, through various scholarship-like subsidy programs. It is especially important to cover people not currently eligible for Medicaid. As yet, no one has the definitive answer or model, but more and more groups are making progress in making specific projects more affordable.

The first major goal for a new sponsor should be to make the basic life-care option available to anyone owning a home in their market area, even a home well below the median area price. This is simply done by offering a broad range of unit sizes, entry fees, and monthly fees. It may also be necessary to lower monthly costs by unbundling some of the less critical services, like laundry or housekeeping. Construction costs might be kept down by using panelized or modular construction for some or all of the housing units. All project costs should be subjected to a value-engineering analysis. This should reduce construction costs. Rapid construction and rapid occupancy will also permit great savings in interest on the construction loan and other costs. Any innovative option deserves consideration.

Some percentage of entry fees, or a portion of development fees or existing charitable funds, may be set aside from a successful development to offer some individual scholarships, grants, discounts, or subsidies.

Possibly, the local housing authority can contract for a small number of units, say for example, 10 percent. This would open up the life-care option for at least a few very needy individuals without putting an unbearable burden on the project. This would also be a highly attractive part of the project when local zoning approvals are required. A nonprofit or community-service posture is often nearly a prerequisite for local approval of a large and highly visible project. Medicaid, possibly on a specially negotiated capitation basis, might take the place of life-care insurance for some lower-income residents, allowing the sponsors extra funds to assist more people.

Reducing the artificially high-income thresholds required by many projects would also broaden the market. Projects that require additional income of only $400 to $500 per month over what is required for the monthly maintenance fee have had no more problems collecting fees over time than projects that restrict their market by demanding income levels of up to twice the monthly fees. For instance, if a monthly fee is $1,000, or $12,000 per year, then $1,400 per month, or an annual income of $16,800, not the often asked for $24,000, should be satisfactory.

Rent skewing is a useful technique for broadening the market. This involves charging less per square foot for the more modest units and more for large or luxurious units. This is an attractive bit of social engineering, but perhaps should not be stressed or described too explicitly in marketing literature so as not to offend those being maneuvered into enforced philanthropy.

The above are just a few ways to open up the life-care option to those with moderate to low incomes, supplementing the usual underfunded efforts of nonprofit organizations and federal organizations, state, and local governments. Each development team should devote time to the creative search for its own most appropriate local solution.

The Government's Role

If government agencies will acknowledge that private sponsors, given some incentives, can carry much of the burden of elderly housing and health care, we must encourage these agencies to help unlock the billions of dollars tied up in the home equity of those over the age of sixty-five. If we want government agencies to make positive moves we must, in most cases, point out the moves. Government initiatives or subsidies might include rapid approval of zoning for life-care proposals, tax breaks, or use of public lands. An attractive sponsor standing ready to carry out an attractive program, and generating popular support for that program, should help the authorities make a decision, particularly if the project provides a needed service and if it involves a net gain in revenue from taxes on the project.

There is a great deal of specific help that can come from local, state, and federal agencies to encourage the life-care concept, decrease risk in the approvals phase, lower project costs, or expand the market. Some help is being offered in scattered instances already:

Zoning: The local approval process might be made less risky, and the zoning process less costly, if the developer offers to provide a percentage of affordable units, as is done in Newton, Massachusetts. There, all multi-family developments of more than forty units must make 10 percent of the approved units affordable, 20 percent if a special permit is required. It has not stifled development interest. There are other towns currently encouraging proposals under which, in return for services to local elders, taxes, and other social benefits promised by the life-care sponsors, the town will donate town land to the project as well as grant zoning approvals.

Certificate of Need: In Massachusetts, to encourage true life care, and so that once a person is in a life-care community the Commonwealth knows they will never be a Medicaid recipient, a life-care community is allowed "sheltered beds," one nursing bed for every five units, regardless of the bed need in the area. This takes so much risk out of the certificate of need (CON) process that, combined with the newly available life-care insurance policies, many developers and sponsors are upgrading their plans to a full life-care program, rather than settling for more modest or limited programs.

Federal Catastrophic Insurance: This option to cover long-term care, while a highly desirable possibility, might have unpredictable effects on life care. On the one hand, it would remove a major reason for people to consider life care—fear of a catastrophically expensive illness. On the other hand, by reducing or eliminating the costs of private life-care insurance, costs could be reduced enough to broaden the market considerably, and life-care centers would then stress other features, such as lifestyle, sociability, culture and education, availability of appropriate services, guaranteed access to appropriate nursing, or health maintenance, rather than the catastrophic insurance factor. Many citizens who do not generally favor expanded government programs might welcome a national long-term care safety net that does not demand prior impoverishment. The life-care movement would survive, and possibly thrive.

Government Regulatory Efforts: Currently, these efforts are directed toward consumer protection, which is reasonable, until they get so restrictive that they actually eliminate potential projects in the name of consumer protection. Maine stifled its only life-care proposal, after 300 cash deposits were in hand, through hastily passed, misguided, overprotection of the consumer. New York, Massachusetts, and many other states are flirting with the same stifling blanket of proposed regulation, although anything would be an improvement over New York's former consumer protection policy of simply forbidding all prepaid life-care insurance programs. Pennsylvania, Florida, California, and current Massachusetts regulations are among those that come closer to the right combination of carrot and stick. This approach has great potential, and few will object to sensible regulation if, at the same time, some of the risk is taken out of the development process.

Self-regulation of course has the most cost-effective potential of all, and the list of facilities approved by the Continuing Care Accreditation Commission is growing rapidly. Other assistance to life-care programs could come from:

Financing Guarantees: Life care is unfamiliar to most lenders and so complex that even with the reassurance of presales, many potential lenders are uncomfortable. It would be a major help to have financial guarantors available. This would be a great specialty area for a knowledgeable passive investor or an investment group wanting to get involved with this type of project with minimum investment of manpower or time. The bonding capacity of state and local agencies has increased in some states and can be tremendously helpful in this area.

Regardless of what government bodies may or may not do, it remains up to individual sponsors and developers to take the initiative, make plans, make proposals, argue for them, and find ways to make these projects zonable, marketable, financable, approvable, and operable.

The Present

What the life-care industry consists of today is a growing universe of over 800 facilities. While over 95 percent of these life-care communities are still sponsored and managed by nonprofit organizations, much of the most visible activity is generated by a variety of for-profit development groups. Of the three typical payment options (nonrefundable entrance fee; refundable entrance fee; or fee for service), it appears that the trend is toward refundable entrance fees, with a strong interest in life-care insurance. Much of the interest in fee-for-service continuing-care programs, and much of the skepticism of life-care insurance, seems to come from for-profit developers who are new to the field and cautious about unfamiliar formats. But we have barely penetrated the potential market, and a wide range of choices for the consumer is eminently desirable. What should be required of every project are sound demographic and market research studies that will help shape a product appropriate to the specific market area.

The Future

There should be a bright future for life-care communities, fueled by:

- Increasing numbers of older people;
- Increased longevity;
- The wish of today's elderly to maximize their later years;
- The desire for more independence, options, choices, services, and friends;
- The desire for and increasing recognition of the need for catastrophic nursing-care insurance coverage;
- The interest some enlightened government agencies show in the concept; and
- The fact that nearly $1 trillion in potential funding, currently locked up in the home equity of thirty million people over age sixty-five, can be unlocked if the right products are made available.

A movement with great potential is the accreditation program offered by the Continuing Care Accreditation Commission (CCAC), sponsored by the American Association of Homes for the Aging (AAHA). The trade organization AAHA, representing nonprofit nursing and retirement homes and service providers, is by far the most useful organization to the planner or operator of a life-care center. The CCAC offers a voluntary self-regulation through accreditation program, which, though rigorous, should strengthen the participating facility and show prospective residents that it is among the most outstanding 20 percent of the industry.

Potential problems for the growth of life-care include: unenlightened, stifling overregulation; possible Wall Street or other financial catastrophe; a collapse of the real estate market (preventing easy home sales); the discrediting of the industry by some ill-conceived projects; increasing difficulties finding staff; and often unmanageable increases in staffing, insurance, or medical costs. However, there should be a major, growing market for life-care to share with continuing care, assisted living, and similar, more limited, alternative programs.

> Life care can satisfy the needs of a vast majority of older adults with its wide array of services. Most interesting is the fact that close to one trillion dollars of equity is available to some thirty million people over sixty-five years which can be unlocked for the potential

funding of their needs through life care. This chapter provides predictions of a bright future for life care as a utopian but viable form of housing for older adults and sets the theme for the comprehensive collection of informative chapters which follow.

—Editors

2 Clinical Geriatrics and Life Care: Ethical and Health Policy Considerations

Jerry Avorn, M.D.

In this provocative chapter, the author reviews the background to many of our current health-care dilemmas, leading up to problems such as those raised by the "under-caring" pressures created by DRG's (Diagnostic Related Groups) and HMO's (Health Maintenance Organizations). It makes a strong case for patient-specific decisions responsive to the wants and needs of the individual patient which cannot be bureaucratically codified.

—Editors

The current status of long-term care for the elderly, and particularly of life care, is the result of important changes in the nature of health care that have set the stage for the sweeping demographic changes we are witnessing. It was the broad-based public health developments of the first half of this century, such as improved nutrition, housing, and sanitation, that made it possible for children to live into early adulthood and thus eventually become elderly. However, it is developments in biomedical science which have played such an important role in making it possible for these adults to live into advanced old age in our time, well beyond the point at which many of them would have died of acute or chronic illnesses in earlier decades.

As a result, we now face a burgeoning population of elderly people, some of whom are in robustly good health uncommon in earlier generations. However, many of today's elderly (and even more of tomorrow's elderly) can be expected to experience a level of disability that would have been fatal in earlier times. Our success in medicine requires that we devise compassionate, effective, and appropriate care for the elderly, whatever their clinical or socioeconomic status. In earlier, simpler times, the questions we faced were not as difficult, since nature tended to run its course, oblivious to the weak ministrations of the medical profession. Now, however, modern medicine is capable of literally restoring the dead to life, as well as restoring good health and vigor to many with chronic illnesses. Unhappily, we have not yet mastered the science or art of restoring wholeness to those afflicted with some of the worst chronic illnesses facing the old, such as Alzheimer's disease, arthritis, diabetes, and cancer. As a result, a national debate has begun over when to use such life-sustaining measures, on which elderly people, and at what cost.

Like acute-care hospitals, life-care communities find themselves at the center of this battleground at both the individual and policy levels. The development of powerful economic forces has upped the ante in this debate considerably, and the difficult questions have only recently begun to be discussed in public. Various factors—some as old as the medical profession itself, others much more recent—have come together to influence the mobilization of therapies and technologies to prolong life in a manner that has never before been possible. On the other hand, equally powerful factors have come into existence in the past decade that, by contrast, encourage the undertreatment of frail elderly patients. Often, it is precisely those geriatric patients, who are least capable of voicing their own position on these matters, whose care brings out the greatest conflict. In this chapter, I will focus on the plight in which the aging patient finds himself or herself as a result of these conflicting forces, the impact this struggle will have on the conception and management of life-care communities, the roles of specific decision makers, and some possible solutions for an increasingly difficult situation.

The Aging Population

The growing concern over economic and humanistic limits to care is a result of the very successes that biomedicine has had since World War II. In 1900, only 4 percent of the U.S. population was over age sixty-five; today, the figure is 12 percent and is projected to increase to 20 percent by the year 2030, when the baby boom generation will be entering retirement. The survival into advanced old age that we have seen since World War II is caused by the unprecedented capacity we now possess to replace failed kidneys, strengthen degenerating hearts, maintain desperately ill people with no capacity for self-care, and perform heroic procedures, both surgical and pharmacological, that were undreamed of in earlier generations.

Those over age eighty-five, the subgroup of the "old-old" that deserves particular attention in this regard, are now the fastest growing segment of the population. Every day, about 4,000 Americans turn sixty-five and every day, 3,000 of those who are already over age sixty-five die. This produces a net increase of about 1,000 people over age sixty-five, each day, every day of the year. Even more important than the fact that there are more and more Americans over age sixty-five is the fact that the *average* age of those over sixty-five is itself increasing. Thus, the cohort of elderly people today is a much older group than the Americans who were over age sixty-five earlier in this century. Because the utilization of health care in general and of long-term care in particular rise with advancing old age, as does the prevalence of most chronic conditions in geriatrics, the impact of this growing population on the health-care system is magnified. At present, those over age sixty-five, at 12 percent of the population, consume nearly 30 percent of all health-care resources, and this number too is rising.

New Technologies, New Possibilities

Thorny decisions about which patients to resuscitate when they suffer a cardiac arrest were irrelevant before the mid-1950s, since the very procedure of cardiopulmonary resuscitation was not well developed until after this time. Similar arguments can be made about deciding on whom to dialyze; as recently as the 1960s, the availability of dialysis centers was so limited as to make this decision uncommon in most medical settings—a situation analogous to liver transplantation today. More modest, low-technology interventions have also had an enormous effect on our capacity to keep frail, disabled elderly alive. For example, careful nursing care may well explain much of the improved longevity of patients who have had cerebrovascular accidents. Many individuals who would have died in the immediate post-stroke period are now pulled through by meticulous attention to their care, supplemented as needed by treatment with antibiotics for transient infections. Very little function may be restored, but once the acute episode is past, the patients may go on to live long, although not normal, lives.

Factors Predisposing to Undertreatment

Foremost among the factors that discourage the delivery of care to frail elderly people is the advent of prospective payment systems, most notably through the implementation of diagnosis related groups (DRGs) in hospital payment, and the increasing penetration of health maintenance organizations (HMOs) into the health-care delivery system. With these developments, we have moved from the problems created by the "more is better" philosophy of health-service utilization, which evolved under fee-for-service reimbursement, to a system in which we face the very real prospect of a "less is better" philosophy. While it is indeed the case that some of the therapeutic interventionism helped along by the older reimbursement system was probably not medically necessary, it is equally true that important sins of omission are being encouraged by the current "less is better" method of reimbursement.

These new trends interact with and aggravate a much older phenomenon, that of *ageism*—the belief that to be old is to be sick, and that little of use can be done in treating many ailments of the elderly. This often results in an attitude of therapeutic nihilism, with justification that is labeled as "clinical judgment": failure to initiate a diagnostic workup or institute a plan of therapy for a particular problem in an aged patient, on the grounds that no useful outcome could be expected.

In the world of clinical decision making, there are also some aspects of ageism that stem directly from the poor job done by medical schools in training students to understand and deal with the medical problems of the elderly. Given the frequent absence of curriculum material in geriatric medicine in most programs of medical education, it is not at all uncommon to find interns, residents, and senior physicians who have all the best intentions in the world and not a trace of prejudice toward the old, yet who fail to provide appropriate care for their elderly patients simply because they do not know any better. The atypical presentation of thyroid disease in the elderly, the reversibility of some forms of cognitive impairment, the "silent" myocardial infarction—all of these represent instances of care that might have been delivered to the elderly but are often omitted, not because of any villainous cost-containment program or because of negative thoughts toward the old, but because of that oldest of human attributes, simple ignorance. It is stupefying to speculate on how many people are confined to nursing homes or to cemeteries because of the inability of medical education to integrate systematic instruction in geriatric medicine into medical school curricula in a more complete and timely fashion.

While ageism is best thought of as a set of preconceptions based on incorrect stereotypes, there is a more malign aspect of ageism, as is often seen with "isms" relating to demographic characteristics—discrimination. The success of the "gray lobby" in the 1960s and 1970s in winning entitlements for the elderly in areas such as Social Security and Medicare has brought with it a powerful generational backlash, with the nonelderly increasingly voicing concern over whether the old have in fact gotten too much. Papers abound on the "disproportionate use of medical resources by the elderly." (The absurdity of this concept is apparent if one considers the concept of "disproportionate use of education by the young.") Different phases of the life cycle demand different kinds of resources from society, and it should surprise no one that those who are old need more medical care than those who are not. Nonetheless, the well-publicized difficulties with the Medicare budget, the tenuous financial viability of Social Security, and a general sense of suspicion about any public entitlement program in the current political climate have all placed even greater pressure on the use of health-care resources for the elderly.

At a time of particular anxiety about how much the public purse can be squeezed, the very successes of the elderly in the past make them prime targets for cutbacks in the future. The strong voting record of those over age sixty has deterred such cutbacks thus far, but in doing so has only intensified the resentment that some in other age groups have begun to voice about this perceived inequity. Rivalry and discrimination among different subgroups within society is never easy to understand or sympathize with. However, it becomes particularly perverse when the subject of discrimination is a cohort that represents one's own parents and grandparents, as well as—most mind-boggling of all—oneself in just a few decades. The apparent incapacity of the young to relate to the problems and needs of the old is an appalling statement about our own sense of family and of our own mortality as individuals.

Feeding on this tension is a new way of looking at health care for the elderly. It purports to objectify quality of life issues, and takes a position that meshes nicely with economically driven inaction and ignorance-driven inaction. Viewed from this perspective, diagnostic or therapeutic nonintervention is often justified by the judgment that the quality of existence of a given patient is so low that attempts to prolong it are ill-advised or simply not cost-effective. While it is certainly true that for some patients with devastating illness this is an appropriate conclusion, it is striking how often such a conclusion is drawn without input from the patient, even when that is possible. When one applies pseudo-quantitative approaches to quality of life (or the even more offensive "human capital" method of analysis), it becomes irrelevant to ask the patient, since one can simply look up the "quality adjustment factor" or other measure of "worth" from a set of tables or published norms, which are as easy to use as they are absurd.

Taken together, these forces—some old, some new—create a climate in which nontreatment of the elderly is an increasingly important force to contend with in decision making at both the bedside level and the policy level. Unfortunately, such forces are generally devoid of either scientific or moral justification. In this, they are similar to a set of opposite forces, equally powerful and equally worrisome, which act to push the individual clinician, patient, and hospital in precisely the opposite direction.

Forces Encouraging Overcare

Oldest among these forces is the ancient stance of the physician as the opponent of death, whose role is to forestall the end of life as long as possible, no matter what. In a sense, this view of the role of the physician is analogous to the view of the lawyer, whose job is to defend the client (or to convict the accused) using all possible legitimate means, without engaging in internal debate about whether a given person should ideally go free or be sent to prison. In a time when the therapeutic armamentarium was less powerful, doing one's best for the longest possible time did not present complex questions of resource allocation or ethics, since apart from a modest number of interventions that were truly effective, nature tended to take its course in the majority of cases more or less as it pleased. Thus, the development of a culture of constant opposition to death became imprinted on the profession of medicine, and has persisted for many years after the development of antibiotics, hemodialysis, organ transplantation, and mechanical respirators. Granted, once we admit the possibility that forestalling death is not always the foremost of a physician's actions, it becomes difficult indeed to tread along the "slippery slope" that develops, but tread it we must.

The *technical imperative* offers another impetus toward overcare in all age groups, particularly the elderly. This term describes the Everest-like presence of medical technology, which often comes to be used in the acute care hospital because it is there. If one is working a stone's throw away from a CAT scanner or a magnetic resonance image machine, or a coronary angioplasty facility or an intensive care unit, these resources tend to influence clinical decision making and therapy by their very presence. An important part of this phenomenon seems to be the need for physicians to feel that we are indeed scientists and healers. This feeling is sometimes hard to sustain if one's practice contains a large proportion of aging patients whose main ailments have evaded scientific conquest thus far and are poorly responsive to anything recognizable as healing.

Often lost sight of in analyses of why physicians do things as we do is a recognition of our genuine desire—powerfully selected for by admissions procedures, and aggressively reinforced during years of training—to help sick people to get better through our use of rational therapeutic interventions. This is who we are, this is why we chose this line of work, this is what all of those hundred-hour weeks and sleepless nights were designed to accomplish. It thus goes against the grain quite painfully when we are asked to do nothing, to *not* treat a particular condition, and to sit passively by as a patient of ours dies, even if by all accounts it is in his or her best interest to do so.

Feeding on these trends, much as a parasite feeds on its host, is the current climate around litigation in medical care. In addition to the numerous cases of innocent patients genuinely harmed by inept physicians, there exists an appallingly large number of cases brought to trial (or to settlement) whose main *raison d'etre* is breathtaking greed on the part of the litigants, rather than any issue of improper clinical practice. There seems to be an assumption out there that if a bad outcome occurs in a patient, a bad doctor somewhere must have been at fault—a view that may be the monster offspring of our scientific hubris that modern medicine can cure everything.

The number and scale of settlements made against physicians and hospitals with no genuine evidence of any wrongdoing is large enough to terrify even the bravest surgeon or administrator. If one adds to this the even more numerous cases, equally content-free, whose only result is hours of needless litigation and preparation, the impact upon the practitioner and the health-care system is even greater. In this climate, such fear of malpractice litigation cannot help but stay the hand of the physician who might otherwise allow a bedridden, comatose, and gradually terminal patient to succumb to pneumonia, "the old man's friend," as was done in earlier decades.

It is not only the bizarre world of tort law that is distorting clinical decision making. Increasingly, we read of criminal cases being brought to bear against physicians who, as in the case involving physicians from California, were caring for a terminal patient whose death came somewhat earlier and with greater dignity and comfort because of the physicians' use of morphine. The "right to life" antiabortion movement has sent its tentacles into this end of the lifespan as well, and it is not at all clear where this will end. I vividly remember the sense of paranoia (not yet dissipated, and it probably will never be) when, during my training in internal medicine in Boston, I heard of the case of the chief resident in obstetrics at the Boston City Hospital who was charged with manslaughter for failing to perform cardiopulmonary resuscitation on a second-trimester fetus *which he was aborting*. The fact that he was exonerated, as was the case with the cancer doctors in California as well, is only somewhat encouraging. One day, one of us will not be as lucky.

What is similar about these often mindless forces encouraging overtreatment is their similarity to the often mindless forces encouraging undertreatment. That is, none of them are patient-specific, but rather they attempt to guide clinical decisions along lines that are determined by forces external to the doctor, the patient, and the family, and often serve to drive that care in a direction that is precisely opposite to the genuine needs and interests of the patient. In a way, they can be seen as adding a considerable amount of noise to the already difficult signal-to-noise ratio that is involved in the care of elderly patients. For very different reasons, the volume of that noise has been steadily increasing in the last decade, creating a din in which the still, small voice of the patient is all but drowned out.

One Possible Solution

The best antidote to the patient-irrelevant forces described above is to find a way to enhance the power of the individual patient in determining the outcome of a given clinical decision. It should go without saying that the conscious, competent patient must in all instances be given the ultimate decision-making power over therapies that are to be given or withheld. This truism, obvious as it may be on the printed page, is often ignored in practice, and this is one of the most straightforward issues to address. (In Massachusetts, mecca of medicine in the known solar system, the official state document declaring a person to be legally incompetent has as one of its categories, along with mental retardation and psychosis, "mental frailty by reason of advanced age.") Physicians and family members sometimes act as if the Bill of Rights expires at age seventy, and old patients often have life and death decisions made for them by family members or health-care providers, even when the patients are perfectly capable of doing so themselves. Having someone willingly defer such a decision with the words, "Whatever you think is best, doctor," is fine as long as those words are in fact felt and spoken. Often they are not.

Where the ice really gets thin is in the instance of the patient with impaired competency, whether by virtue of a dementing illness such as Alzheimer's disease (not "by reason of advanced age"), or a transient loss of mental capacity resulting from an acute illness (such as delirium induced by fever or hypoxia), or outright coma. In these instances, the wise and compassionate physician *should* find himself or herself saying, "I only wish I knew what Mrs. Jones would want me to do about her pneumonia/emergency cardiac surgery/amputation. If only she could tell me!" A variety of solutions have been proposed over the years, some attractive, some not.

One of the most popular concepts has been that of the *living will.* In such a document, the patient, while still of sound mind, states something to the effect that, "If my health deteriorates to the point where a meaningful quality of existence is no longer possible, heroic measures should not be used to prolong my life." While useful as a step in the direction of opening discussion of these issues, in practice this approach often falls apart in the conceptualization and implementation of both its first and second halves. First, what is a clinical situation in which "meaningful quality of existence is no longer possible"? Complete brain death certainly seems to fit this rubric, but the law has already addressed this one easy case. (Its efforts along these lines were helped considerably by a 1968 consensus statement by members of the faculty of Harvard Medical School who set forth guidelines on the matter.) But what about a dementing illness in which a patient can still enjoy food and watch television, but cannot read and does not recognize anyone? Is that a "meaningful quality of existence"? For some, but not for others. Or what about a massive stroke that leaves a patient unable to walk or speak, but preserves intellect and the capacity to understand all that is going on?

Similarly, on the output end of the living-will concept, the question of what is truly a heroic measure becomes more intractable the closer we look at it. Clearly open-heart surgery is, but what about renal dialysis, which is now so routine that many patients do it for themselves at home with no medical supervision whatsoever? Or antibiotics, which are certainly miracle drugs by 1930s standards, but are rather humdrum today, as far as medical interventions go. The question has even been extended to intravenous fluids and nutritional support via nasogastric tube feedings. Are these normal supportive care measures, or are they extraordinary in the sense that they are not part of normal noninstitutional care?

Thus, it becomes very difficult to operationalize the terms of most living wills. A far preferable alternative is the concept of *durable power of attorney.* This is simply the legal delegation of the right to speak on one's behalf to another person, which continues beyond the cessation of one's own competence. The term *durable* refers to the fact that conventional powers of attorney are deemed to cease to exist if the delegator loses competency, whereas such a durable delegation does not. This enables the patient (or patient-to-be) to name a relative, a clergyman, a health-care provider, or anyone else to have all the legal standing that the patient would have when issues of medical decision making are involved. Some states have moved quickly and effectively to establish enabling legislation that ensures such delegation will have the full force of law behind it; in other states, their legal status is less clear.

Durable power of attorney enables the patient to retain power over clinical decision making even beyond the cessation (whether temporary or permanent) of the patient's own capacity to make decisions. It is rooted in the belief that the patient will be able to designate someone who will speak for his or her best interests without the other motivations that may distort the decisions made by clinicians, health-care institutions, insurors, or even non-designated family members. In my view, this is the best way of empowering the patient to continue to play an active role in defending his or her interests when most vulnerable.

The hard part is that such documents need to be executed, and the initiation of the discussions necessary to choose and then inform the person so designated are inherently difficult. Yet it is a discussion that we must all learn to engage in if we are to maximize the right of the individual vulnerable patient. It may be our best weapon to empower the patient to have his or her own preferences about care met in a health-care environment increasingly subjected to external forces in which the patient's needs are not always at the top of the agenda, where they belong. All of us concerned with the care of the elderly—particularly through the approach of life care—must learn to do a better job of empowering the old to make their wishes prevail if we are to provide the humane care that we would like to expect in the latter portions of our own lives.

> This chapter describes a serious problem relating to the over- or undertreatment of the old, and suggests a specific and practical way of empowering patients and future patients to control their lives, even when mentally or physically incapacitated, through the use of a durable power of attorney. This is advice we all should heed—for ourselves, our older family members, our patients, and our friends.
>
> —Editors

3
Demographics and Market Research

Maria B. Dwight, M.S.G.

This practical, informative chapter combines experience and observation as the author freewheels through the life-care field—from the general to the specific and from national trends to significant case studies. This is a full, clear introduction to an often murky and jargon-filled subject.

—Editors

The elderly are the demographic discovery of the late 1980s. After thriving on the creation of "yuppyism," the marketing mavens have now turned to the WOOPs (well-off older persons) and, for the same reason, their numbers and affluence. The demographic imperative that drives the marketplace is well-documented. For example, if we were to gather together all the people in the United States age sixty-five and older in one geographic area and call it a "state," it would be the most populous state in the country. It would have surpassed California's count of 23,667,902 in 1980 by almost 2 million. If we made this elder state a country, it would be the thirty-first most populous country on earth. In 1987, there were 29.9 million people in this country over the age of sixty-five, representing 12 percent of the total population. (See figure 3–1 for some demographic projections on our past and future elderly populations.)

Gerontologists have segmented the older population into three categories. Chronological age is generally used to differentiate markets, which creates more exceptions to the rule, since no two people age alike. A popular description is the *young-old* (65–75), the *old* (75–85), and the *old-old* (85 +). Dr. Herb Shore has described this as the "go-go," "slow-go," and "no-go" segmentation. These are even too general for marketing purposes. However, the old and the old-old constitute the fastest growing segment of this population, with the age seventy-five and older population projected to increase by 116 percent, and the age eighty-five and older group projected to triple between 1980 and 2020. It is this seventy-five to eighty-five and older market that is presently the target market segment for life care and other service-enriched housing options for the elderly.

It has been suggested that the elderly are becoming one of the wealthiest segments of the marketplace. According to the American Association of Re-

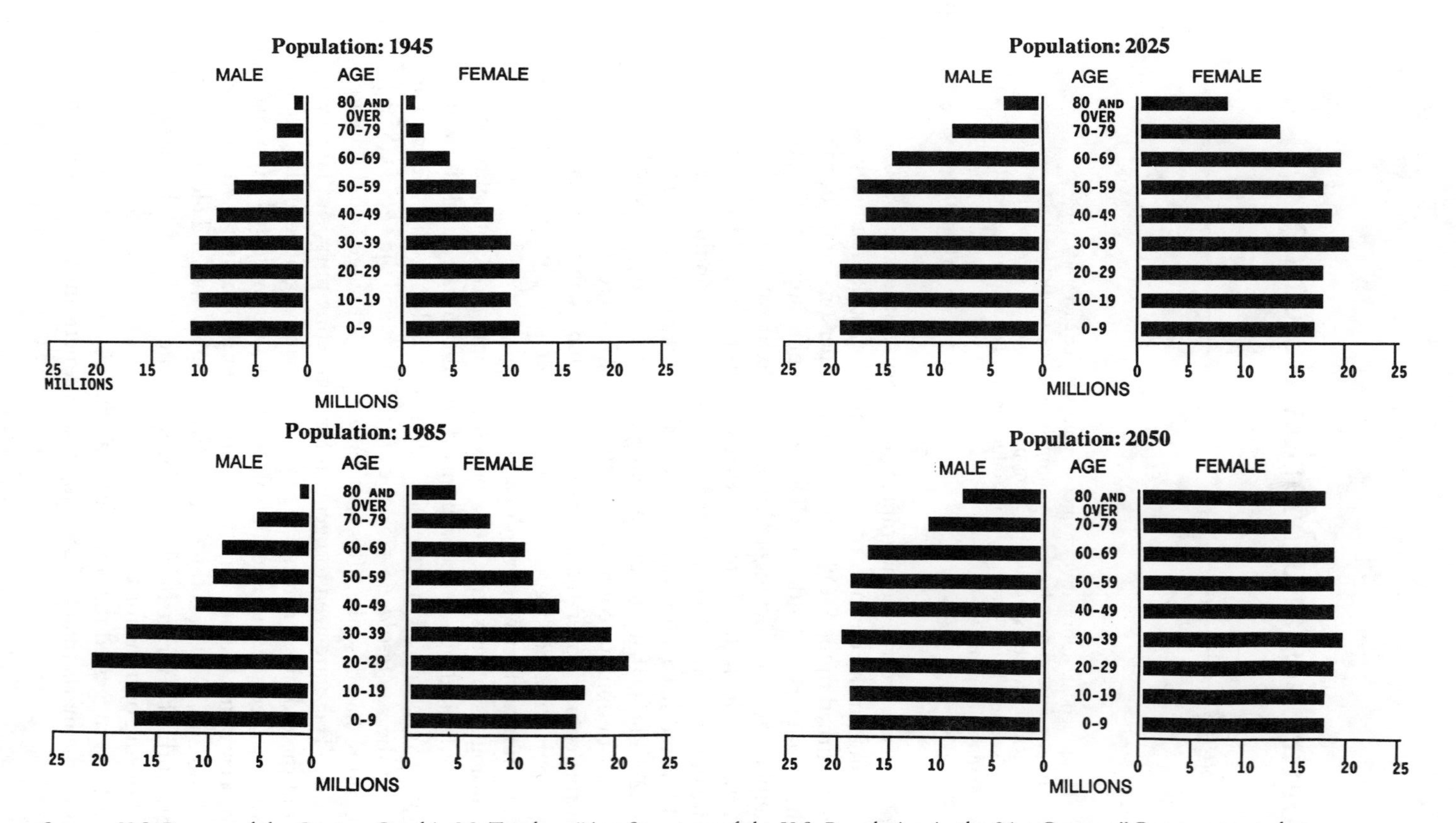

Source: U.S. Bureau of the Census. Cynthia M. Taeuber, "Age Structure of the U.S. Population in the 21st Century." Paper presented at conference, "Tomorrow's Elderly: Planning for the Baby Boom Generation's Retirement." Americans for Generational Equity, Washington, D.C., April 1986. Projections based on Census Bureau's "Middle Series" which assumes neither extreme decrease nor extreme increase in current population trends.

Figure 3–1. Age Structure of the U.S. Population in the 21st Century

tired Persons and the Administration on Aging (AARP/AOA) study of 1986, *A Profile of Older Americans,* 35 percent of households over sixty-five had incomes of over $25,000, and the net worth of elderly households ($60,300) is almost twice that of the general populace ($32,700). In 1980, almost 75 percent of the elderly owned homes, and 80 percent of those homes were mortgage-free. The inflationary trends in real estate over the past two decades have created substantial equity assets for these primarily suburban homeowners. Based on this kind of information, it is easy to see why the population over age sixty-five has received unprecedented attention in recent years. But the trends of today are only fuzzy harbingers of our future. It is confounding for researchers and planners to look to that future because the past has taught us irrelevant lessons in understanding an aging society. We have few individual role models and no societal precedents.

In the absence of clear understanding, a myriad of psycho-babbling experts, marketing wizards, and economic prognosticators have arrived on the scene to increase our current confusion and create chaotic approaches to what should be the most thoughtful and effective planning process in our human history. Within the context of national confusion, collective ageism, and societal bemusement, we must take a realistic approach toward analyzing the potential for one alternative shelter and service option: life care. As this analysis is undertaken, it must constantly bring together a variety of disciplines and fields of knowledge concerning the value systems, life experiences, and future expectations of those we demographically describe by age, income, gender, marital status, health status, location, and living arrangement.

Why Market Research and Feasibility Studies?

Good market feasibility studies are expensive and time-consuming, and therefore many sponsors and developers resist this initial investment in the project. It is, however, probably one of the most important components of the planning process and the keystone for many of the major decisions along the critical path to successful completion.

There has been considerable media attention paid to the financial failures of retirement communities. This has justifiably caused concern in the banking and financial institutions that provide the capital for projects. One of the most compelling reasons for undertaking a market study is that lenders demand it. Lenders are also insistent that the study be performed by a professional firm, unrelated to the developing corporation, to ensure objectivity and unbiased results.

However, the market study will serve a variety of purposes. It assists on the go/no go decision, and it will be the basis for the operational program, schematic design development, and marketing plan. It can assist in zoning applications, and its data are used in applications for certificate of need.

Moreover, the market researcher becomes an integral part of the project development team. The market study should identify the major market-driven issues for the specific project and help the developer quantify the risks involved in reaching success.

Who Does the Market Research?

There has been an amazing growth in the number of experts in this field, within the last two years alone. Many claim a longevity record that is suspect, since the field has been very narrow, and until recently, dominated by the nonprofit sector, which historically did not rely on market research.

The qualifications on each market research firm should be carefully analyzed, and references should be contacted. At minimum, the principals should be professionally trained in the disciplines of research, demographics, gerontology or planning and should be experienced in the type of project under consideration.

Lenders are recognizing that market feasibility studies are different products from financial feasibility studies, and increasingly look for separate reports by independent parties. Many of the national accounting firms provide both services, and their products seem to vary in quality between area offices.

The market research firm is accountable for the information generated by its study and for the professional judgments put forth in the recommendations. If the consultant is based in an academic setting, it is wise to explore the experience and capabilities of the entire research team.

Good business is the art of people working with people toward a common goal. Among the important qualities in the selection of a market research firm are integrity, experience, knowledge, and the ability to work well with other members of the development team.

When Does the Market Research Take Place?

Each project varies in its conception and execution. The earlier the market research takes place, usually the more efficient the process. If the research shows an inadequate market, it is best to abort the project before significant funds are expended. If the project is to be undertaken, the information generated from the research becomes invaluable in the definition of the project and in testing the assumptions of the developer. The financial feasibility study should review all its assumptions in the light of data generated from the market study. The design of living units and communal spaces should be predicted on the market's demands and desires. Location preferences, competitive products, and market niche are all delineated in the market research phase.

All too often a developer gets an option on a site, calls in an architect to design a building with a five-color rendering for zoning purposes, and then, after the footprint has been accepted and a three-column article has appeared in the paper, the developer seeks a market study to satisfy the lender. The results of this research may not match the published dreams. Instead of being well on its way to success, the project has raised expectations in the community that may not be met. The development's costs may be greater than the market can bear. Major demand may be for a different product than the developer planned. The marketing effort will be continually hampered by loss of credibility in the project, which is an extremely damaging image to overcome.

A life-care project is a particularly complex undertaking because it involves multiple shelter and care options, a variety of contractual possibilities that can affect feasibility, licensure requirements and state regulations that impact design, and density and critical mass issues that influence affordability.

The sooner the market's demands are part of the planning process, the clearer becomes the path to sound decisions.

What Is Market Research?

There is a variety of ways to look at any market segment. The approach is usually dictated by the product to be tested and the budget (of both time and money) that is allocated.

Life care offers multiple products under its rubric. Each must be tested individually and then examined as a whole. The effects of one component upon the others must also be considered. The symbiosis within the continuum is the key that will make the project mature successfully.

There has been an inordinate amount of public discussion about demand- or need-driven products. It seems to be based on the idea that the needs of more frail and sickly persons, rather than their desires, dictate their selection of retirement milieux. It is difficult to support this assumption based on research among middle-income and upper-middle-income older people who have environmental options. If one is a private paying client, one may select the hospital, nursing home, assisted living, congregate living, or independent living option of one's choice, or stay home if preferred. Our research suggests that as retirement options proliferate in the marketplace, all levels of care shall increasingly be demand-driven.

It is difficult to measure demand, however, for institutional care. When the nursing unit is within the continuum of care, as in a closed-loop model like life care, one can only rely on actuarial data, which may be misleading for future utilization rates.

Market research can be divided into two broad categories: secondary data research and primary data research.

Secondary Data Research

Secondary data are gathered from published existing or public sources. They include demographics, competition, and economic evaluation. Their sources include local planning and regulatory agencies, county, state, and national agencies and departments, the U.S. Census Bureau, commercial data companies, real estate boards, licensing boards, health and welfare departments, zoning records, certificate-of-need records, and informed personal observation of competitive projects.

The reliability of secondary data analysis is predicted on the definition of the primary, secondary, and tertiary market areas. A too-optimistic assumption of the geographic size of the marketplace can obviously affect the outcomes of the penetration rates on age and income eligible households. Seldom do market areas fall in concentric five- and ten-mile radii from a site, and there are usually intervening psychosociological or physical barriers that define a market area. It is important to recognize these nuances and incorporate them into the analysis design.

There is an old rule of thumb that says that 80 percent of the residents of a life-care community will come from within twenty-five miles of the site.[1] There is compelling evidence that older people do not want to move away from their community ties; therefore, in most suburban and urban markets, the twenty-five mile rule is too generous. Conversely, some sponsors have geographically scattered constituents (e.g., universities, colleges, religious institutions) that may in fact draw a significant portion of their market from outside a traditional market area. The only way to define the parameters of the market area is to test them through the generation of primary data.

The secondary data analysis should, at a minimum, contain: demographic data and trends of age- and income-eligible households, economic conditions and trends, competitive analysis and proposed competition, comparable products, political environment, and demand analysis.

Research indicates that realistic age eligibility for life-care is seventy-five years and older; however, younger cohorts should be studied to ensure long-range viability of the project. Income criteria will vary, depending on the cost of the development; however, a rule of thumb for the affordability of the lifestyle is a minimum of $25,000 a year income, and preferably a minimum of $30,000. The developer and lender should decide the level of risk they will accept by lowering standards to broaden the market.

The data are developed on households (rather than on population) because people relocate as a household, and single-person households are accounted for in the data. People living in group quarters (facilities without kitchens in the individual apartments) need not be removed from the market pool in demand analyses because they are not accounted for in the original 1980 census data.

Because life-care includes a variety of products, the competition is not limited to comparable projects. Any development that is targeted toward the upper-income, older retirement market will compete for some part of the available pool. The degree of competition can only be measured through primary data collection.

Developing the demand analysis based on secondary data is difficult, particularly for a continuum of care. Penetration rates will vary by age, geographic distribution, and by-product segmentation.

Assuming that the project will initially be open for admission at all levels of care, a demand analysis for independent, age-segregated living, congregate living, assisted living, and nursing care must be undertaken. The nursing-unit analysis is often predicated on the prevailing certificate of need (CON) formula, which may or may not be rational. Some states have CON exemptions for life-care products, but the criteria should be carefully considered in advance. Penetration rates for congregate and assisted living are variable, to say the least. By developing a formula based on the National Center of Health Statistics study[2] on Activities of Daily Living (ADLs)[a] in congregate living, and Instrumental Activities of Daily Living (IADLs)[b] in assisted living, some realistic measures can be applied to local data to determine the potential universe. However, there are not enough historic data upon which to build a credible body of knowledge for penetration rates, so a conservative approach is highly recommended.

Primary Data Research

Primary data are generated for the specific project. They are collected from the target market through several methodologies. The primary data are synthesized with the secondary data to give a more accurate demand analysis.

Experience indicates that the most reliable, consistent, and cost-effective method of collecting primary data is a mailed survey. Developing good mailing lists is a key factor in the process, and often the most time-consuming and frustrating phase of the survey research. The survey sample should be representative of geographic distributions of the age- and income-eligible households. Fortunately, upper-income, more highly educated people tend to respond more readily to survey instruments and, depending on the reputation of the developer, the time of year, and the disposition of the marketplace, we generally receive a 12 to 24 percent return rate to our surveys. The surveys

---

[a]ADL need describes those who require assistance in walking, going outside, bathing, dressing, toileting, getting in or out of bed or chair, and eating.

[b]IADL need describes those who require assistance with managing money, making telephone calls, grocery shopping, preparing meals, or doing routine household chores.

are totally anonymous, but a separate postcard is enclosed, which can be returned with a request for additional information on the proposed project. We realize a 2 to 11 percent return from these cards, which become the initial market pool for the leasing personnel.

The survey instrument is carefully worded, the questions thoughtfully laid out in a meaningful sequence, and the length controlled to obtain higher response rates and more reliable data. The questions are pretested and scrutinized inhouse to avoid collecting fascinating but useless data. The questionnaire must be easy to understand and to complete and is typeset in print large enough to read but not so large as to be demeaning. We recently received a survey instrument design for measuring demand for retirement housing in the Midwest. It was nineteen pages long and rivaled the Graduate Record Exams in complexity. We would not be optimistic about its success.

We do not believe in using cash or other incentives to increase the response rate.[3] Incentives may bias the data and result in an untrue measure of demand. They may also create a negative image of the developer as a spendthrift in a very economy-minded market segment and may suggest that the ideas of the potential respondent have a value only equivalent to the dollar value of the incentive.

A mailed survey allows the recipients to complete the questionnaire at their own pace. It is not unusual to have the open-ended responses include comments like, "Thank you for making me think about the future. This has been difficult to complete because I have not thought about this before."

Figure 3–2. You Can Torture the Numbers Until They Confess

The mail piece is also a major marketing strategy, which identifies the sponsor or developer as a sensitive, interested person (or corporation) who wants to know what older people want, and what they are willing to pay for.

Our experience shows that the next best methodology is face-to-face interviews. Results are accurate, complete, and fairly rapid to finish, but the expense of developing the sample, training older interviewers, and administering the interviews is usually high.

Telephone interviews have a variety of problems associated with them, the greatest being the obvious and prudent reluctance of older people to divulge important demographic data (income, living status, etc.) to the anonymous interviewer. It is also difficult to control the length of the interview, and valuable data may be lost in the name of efficiency.

Focus groups are of value to the planning process, but not in the market feasibility phase. Focus groups can complement market research and provide indepth discussions and data on detail: symbols associated with architectural design, advertising copy, words and images, and so forth.

Information generated from the market research survey is analyzed in a variety of ways. Obviously, the demand factor for life care is an important issue and may be articulated through several cross-tabs. Estimates of demand are derived from a synthesis of the survey data with the secondary data to show the depth of interest in each age- and income-eligible market segment.

We run a number of formulas to arrive at our final recommendations. By using the specific market-penetration rates generated from the survey, we can develop best-case and worst-case scenarios by primary, secondary, and tertiary age groups, income groups, and geographic markets.

The impact of vacant units, future projects, and real estate turn-around intervals are examined. The open-ended comments are carefully reviewed for qualifiable information and perceptions. Response rates are studied by subareas for both survey and inquiry cards.

We reference each data set back to our national database of similar demographic profiles to study deviations or idiosyncratic responses. If the project is feasible, recommendations will include definition of the type of contract (refundable, nonrefundable, entry-fee, or life-lease), the extent of prepaid health-care coverage, the service package (both alone and those services included in the monthly fee), designated use of public spaces (library, health club, etc.), unit sizes, mix of unit types, size of the total project, and size of each level of care.

The profile of the target market will be described, including its demographics and its motivating factors. The market research document will have a wide audience, from lenders and investors, zoning planning commissions, architectural landscapers, and interior designers. It should be concise, straightforward, and should try to avoid jargon and gobbledy-gook.

Case Study of a Successful Project

In anticipation of service diversification, Baptist Hospital and Health Systems (BHHS) in 1980 purchased twelve acres of land several blocks from its Phoenix Baptist Hospital. Located in an older, stable residential neighborhood, the site was well-served by public transportation, a major shopping mall, and health and recreational facilities.

Discussions with various consultants and a review of available literature led BHHS to conclude that a life-care community represented the most appropriate use of the site. A typical life-care community was envisioned—one with an entry fee and monthly payment contract that included a guarantee of lifetime occupancy in the housing unit and some degree of prepaid health care in a nursing facility.

However, before proceeding with development, BHHS retained the services of our company to undertake a market study in mid-1983. Secondary data analysis included a demographic study of the primary, secondary, and tertiary market areas, as well as a review of current and impending contenders in a highly competitive marketplace. Primary research consisted of a mail survey to a sample of 3,000 people, which was developed from a computer model that ranked and rated census blocks based on the market's characteristics, the geographic boundaries of Phoenix Baptist Hospital's primary service area, and proximity to the site.

The survey identified the sponsor and was designed to address a variety of health and support-service issues and to gauge the demand for housing with services on the specified site. Included was a separate postcard by which survey recipients could request additional information. Its use retained anonymity of responses to the survey itself and provided BHHS with a valuable mailing list for future use.

Choice of a mail survey as the instrument reflected the marketing company's experience. If it was correctly structured and anonymity was ensured, this method would provide the most effective way to reach the older consumer. The resulting 17 percent response rate bore this out. The primary market segment, those age sixty-five or older with an annual income of $20,000 or more, and living within five miles of the site, responded positively. Some 48 percent indicated that they would move into the community at the site and price noted.

The surprises? The market was significantly older (75+) and more demanding of services than the sponsor suspected. It was also one that had aged in place in the neighborhood, as opposed to a population that had migrated from the Snowbelt.

The primary market area contained several continuing-care retirement communities, some of which offered life-care contracts. So the concept was widely understood. Nonetheless, the life-care contract concept had little ap-

Table 3–1
Services Demanded by "In-Movers"*

	Phoenix	*Tucson*
Nurse on call	84%	55%
Home health care	47	28
Medical examination room	68	48
Nursing home	65	32

* *In-movers* are defined as those respondents who indicated on the survey that they would or might consider moving into the specific project at the price indicated.

peal. Respondents overwhelmingly preferred a straight rental agreement (48 percent) versus life lease (11 percent) or condominium ownership (28 percent). The other most significant finding concerned the strong demand for support services, including a nursing home.

The latter contrasts with data from a similar study, completed shortly beforehand by the same company, in Tucson, Arizona. The demographic characteristics of both samples were alike. Yet the requirements noted by each of the primary market segments were different, as shown in table 3–1.

Demand analysis indicated a strong market for a congregate living facility with support services, a wellness component, and a skilled nursing facility. The continuum of care became a program with an unbundled fee-for-service package and rental agreements rather than life-care contracts with prepaid health insurance. Thereafter, development of the project, named Chris Ridge Village, relied heavily on market demand data and on the community-need assessment.

The first component that was slated for completion is a 150-bed skilled nursing facility. Sixty beds are designed for postacute, rehabilitative care; another sixty for the chronically physically impaired with multiple degenerative disorders. The remaining thirty constitute a special unit for the diagnosis, care, and treatment of the chronic and acute mentally impaired patient.

Positioned as a physical link between the housing facility and the nursing home is a wellness center, which houses the care assessment and management teams, an ambulatory clinic, adult day care, therapies, and a home-care agency.

The residential complex features 245 one- and two-bedroom apartment units, each with its own kitchen. Among the amenities are a sheltered recreational swimming pool, whirlpool, an exercise center, and an informal as well as a formal dining room. Services include a general store, a post office, beauty and barber shops, craft and meeting rooms, a woodworking shop, and a library.

Staying within the price constraints identified by the market data was a chief design concern. In the process of bringing development costs into line with the market's ability and desire to pay, BHHS constantly referred back to the priorities set by the survey respondents. What could be tailored without adversely affecting the product and lowering market receptivity?

Plans called for a preconstruction rent-up of 70 percent, which was achieved and maintained despite a major fire on the construction site and a six-month delay in completion. BHHS maintained continuous contact with over 665 prime prospects, which included individuals who returned the survey postcard and those attracted by subsequent publicity and site signage. In addition to telephone calls, letters, and a monthly newsletter, an important communication channel was the grapevine established by many of the prospective tenants.

Chris Ridge Village opened in September of 1987 and was 70 percent occupied by January of 1988. This achievement has occurred in one of the most competitive marketplaces in the country. Though marketing research is certainly key in Chris Ridge Village's development, other factors should not be overlooked in contributing to the project's steady course. Among them are:

- A high level of interest by BHHS' CEO, with direct access to top management and decision makers by the development team.
- A board not afraid to challenge its concept of a life-care community and to adapt to a variation on the theme.
- The generation of a great deal of community support.
- Commitment to fast action. Neither costs nor markets stay constant.
- A high-powered development team led by the executive vice president for long-term care, an individual who was involved in every facet of the project, from meeting neighbors before rezoning hearings to working out financial models.
- Input and involvement by the whole organization, including the medical advisory committee, in the operational and design process.

Conclusion

The elderly are an extremely diverse group, spanning a thirty- to thirty-five-year age range. If we were to treat such a large age group together, earlier in the life cycle, people twenty to fifty-five years of age, for example, no one would assume that the motivations, expectations, and behaviors of a college-age person are enough like those of a middle-age person to justify the use of such a broad age category. Nor would anyone suggest that the demands of such a heterogeneous group could be met by a limited product line.

Each generation experiences a variety of historic, social, and economic events that have a significant impact on its values, preferences, demands, and needs in the later years. These events include, but are not limited to, World War I, the Prohibition Era, the Depression, the New Deal, World War II, the advent of mass automobiles and commercial air travel, the dawn of the Information Era, and increased medical technology, which results in decreased debilitating ailments. There is also a lifetime of investing in Social Security and the increased number of pension plans. Societal changes include accessibility of higher education for both men and women, increased divorce rates, a majority of women in the work force, and the mobility of the World War II veteran and his family. Perhaps the most important change is in the role expectation of who and what an older person is. Vanishing rapidly are the stereotypes of Grandma rocking on the porch and Grandpa snoozing on the couch, to be replaced by a silver-haired, race-car-driving Paul Newman, or a wisecracking, cigar-smoking George Burns.

At the risk of falling into our self-described trap of generalizations, there are trends that bear future discussion in relationship to life care:

- The primary market for life care will continue to be older (81+) women (75%)[4] who are more affluent ($30,000+), as long as the perceived value of the life-care model remains within the health-care component. When individual long-term care insurance becomes a marketable entity, the value of the life-care community may have to shift in order to compete with other models of shelter and care.
- The graying of the post World War II suburbs will increase significantly between now and the year 2000, when there will be more than nine million veterans over age sixty-five (twice the number as in 1984). The ability to acquire and develop suburban sites will become even more difficult than it is at present. Antigrowth sentiments that involve density, traffic, sewage, and waste issues will become prevalent as land availability diminishes. Scattered site developments made up of multiple in-fill housing components with a central health facility may be one solution. Experimental models of life care at home are also being tested now.
- In order to afford premium sites, developers may have to design multiuse facilities that incorporate compatible, income-producing components. These may include commercial, professional, educational, and health-providing services.
- Residents of continuum-of-care communities will continue to resist relocation within the CCRC, particularly within the intermediate levels of care. Home-delivered services will be utilized by the residents until financial resources are exhausted or a traumatic incident requires hospital or nursing-home care. This management accommodation to the very frail

will continue the trend toward occupancy by the old-old and limit the market segment of life care.

- Life care appeals to the more affluent, better-educated population. This group will expect, if not demand, an active role in the management of the community, particularly as women with business experience reach later life. Management will take on a different role from what we have experienced in the past.
- Many of the older care communities will not survive the increased competition of the 1990s intact. Small dwelling units will attract only the very frail who cannot appropriately use the expansive, nonrevenue producing public spaces. These facilities, often in changing neighborhoods, may be recycled into other types of supportive living environments for different market segments, or may be abandoned or replaced by the owners.
- The demand for larger living units will continue to grow regardless of income criteria or location. This includes the personal-care component as well as congregate and independent living. There is high value placed on privacy, and the smallest private nursing-home room is preferable to the largest semiprivate room.
- Older people will continue to take an increasing interest in preventive health and healthy aging. The shift in the life-care product may well be from the health center to the health club. This should impact physical design as well as marketing strategies and program development.
- Prepaid health care, managed care, long-term care insurance, and other new forms of delivery systems will impact the marketability of life care.
- Multidisciplinary case assessment and management will become a formal and critical component of CCRC membership.
- State and federal regulations may continue to inhibit the growth of traditional life-care communities and may limit development capabilities to large, tax-paying proprietary companies or health providers, such as hospitals or insurance systems.

The definition and configuration of life care will continue to change as it reacts to new generations of older people and to their increased life expectancy.

Older people, just like younger people, want to maintain their individuality, dignity, and independence. They also want to maintain input and decision-making authority over those policies that directly affect their lives. Older consumers are discerning, selective, and prudent, even more so than longer consumers, due to the greater length of time over which they have accumulated experience. They will demand to have a say in selecting the programs, services, and facilities designed to serve them. The desires and demands of future markets of older people are being formed now in the young-old generation.

Because of demographic changes and variations from generation to generation, the older population is constantly being renewed, expanded, and transformed. The new entrants into the older population have quite different life experiences and socioeconomic and health characteristics than those who are already sixty-five years of age and older. The older population is diverse now, but future older markets will have even more varied expectations.

The life-care industry is faced with a large and growing market—people who have become aware that choices exist and who have the means, understanding, and experience to access those alternatives. These trends and lifestyles may well be our maps to future development.

> A glance at this concluding forecast of trends emphasizes the increasing need for the kind of critical market research described above, as well as the need to create life-care communities that have flexibility, and that can grow, alter, and continue to serve the evolving needs of a constantly changing clientele.
>
> —Editors

Notes

1. Laventhol & Horwath. *The Senior Living Industry.* Philadelphia: Laventhol & Horwath, 1986, pp. 33, 56.

2. Feller, B. A. "Americans needing help to function at home." Advance data from *Vital and Health Statistics,* No. 92. Hyattsville, MD: National Center for Health Statistics, DHHS Publication No. (PHS) 83–1250, Public Health Service, September 1983.

3. Dwight, Maria B. and Urman, Harold N. "Affluent elderly is a unique segment." *Marketing News, 19(17)* August 16, 1985, pp. 1.

4. American Association of Homes for the Aging and Ernest & Whinney. *An Industry in Action.* Washington, D.C.: American Association of Homes for the Aging, 1987.

4
Marketing Life Care

Ann Hambrook

This chapter presents a clear summary of the lessons learned from the author's career as head of the oldest full-service marketing company serving the life-care industry. The author has watched life care evolve and has helped effect many of the changes, both in the product and in how it is sold. This chapter should be required for anyone with an involvement or interest in life-care marketing.

—Editors

It is almost impossible to "sell" life care. A sales effort, even with advertising support, will rarely achieve the developer's occupancy goals on its own. The way to achieve those goals is through an all-out strategic marketing campaign.

"Marketing" is a generally misunderstood term. Contrary to popular belief, marketing is *not* sales, it is *not* advertising, and it is *not* research. Rather, marketing is the sum of all of these parts and more. Marketing is actually the overall strategy that launches all these parts into motion, and then monitors and adjusts them as the project succeeds on time and on budget.

People say that business is war. A good military strategist knows that it takes more than foot soldiers or cavalry to win a war. A bold raid must be backed by reserves and supply lines, by a thorough knowledge of the terrain, and by an accurate assessment of the enemy. No one in their right mind would expect to wage a winning war without strategy and military strategists at the helm.

This chapter will discuss each component of marketing strategy for the life care industry: Sales—the foot soldiers on the front line; Advertising and Promotion—the support functions that supply prospects to the foot soldiers; and Research—the critical assessment of the battleground, obstacles, and targets. Throughout this discussion I will share the state-of-the-art concepts on marketing life care that I and the other "battle-scarred generals" have evolved over the course of the industry's twenty-plus-year history. The chapter will conclude with my thoughts on the future of life care from a marketer's perspective.

Sales

Many factors contribute to a successful sale. These factors can easily be grouped into the physical elements—the sales office, systems and procedures, and goals; and into the people—staffing, recruiting, compensation, and motivation. Separately, telemarketing is a key sales technique that can turn an average sales program into a dynamically successful one.

The Psychology of the Sales Office

Since the marketing objective is to create an environment in which sales occur most easily, everything in the sales office should contribute to the sales and not distract from it. Decorative items should complement a soothing decor. Nonthreatening colors, framing, fabrics, and literally everything including people in a sales office should exude warmth, friendliness, and optimism.

While creating this nice and welcoming atmosphere, the work must be done as inconspicuously as possible. The sales office manager (discussed later under Staffing), who usually acts as a receptionist and telephone operator, must be very adept at slight of hand because he or she has a very busy job that when necessary, must disappear like magic.

The display area should contain mood-setting graphics, renderings of the proposed project, and available options in the form of display boards and floor plans. Years ago, I adamantly said that model apartments should never be used in this industry because life care is an insurance sale, not a real estate sale. However, at that time, the industry largely employed nonprofessional salespeople, people who typically used a model as a sales crutch. I now offer an amendment, you may use model apartments with a professional salesperson. A good salesperson will know how to use a model as a sales tool in a way to affirm the buyer's decision.

In the sales office the client reception area should include a small work station with little visible work, seating for at least five in sturdy arm chairs (sofas are difficult for the elderly to get up from), a conference area to seat at least five, coffee service, and bathroom facilities.

Preferably, the salesperson's area should contain a table rather than a desk because a table is more friendly and conveys equality among the people seated around it. There should be no clutter or obvious work, and no knickknacks because these items can distract the attention of the prospect.

The traffic flow should be designed to create the best possible impression on the visitor and to maximize the selling opportunity. (See figure 4–1.) *Never* create an office where prospects pass the front door after you have shown them the models and are returning to your office to close the sale.

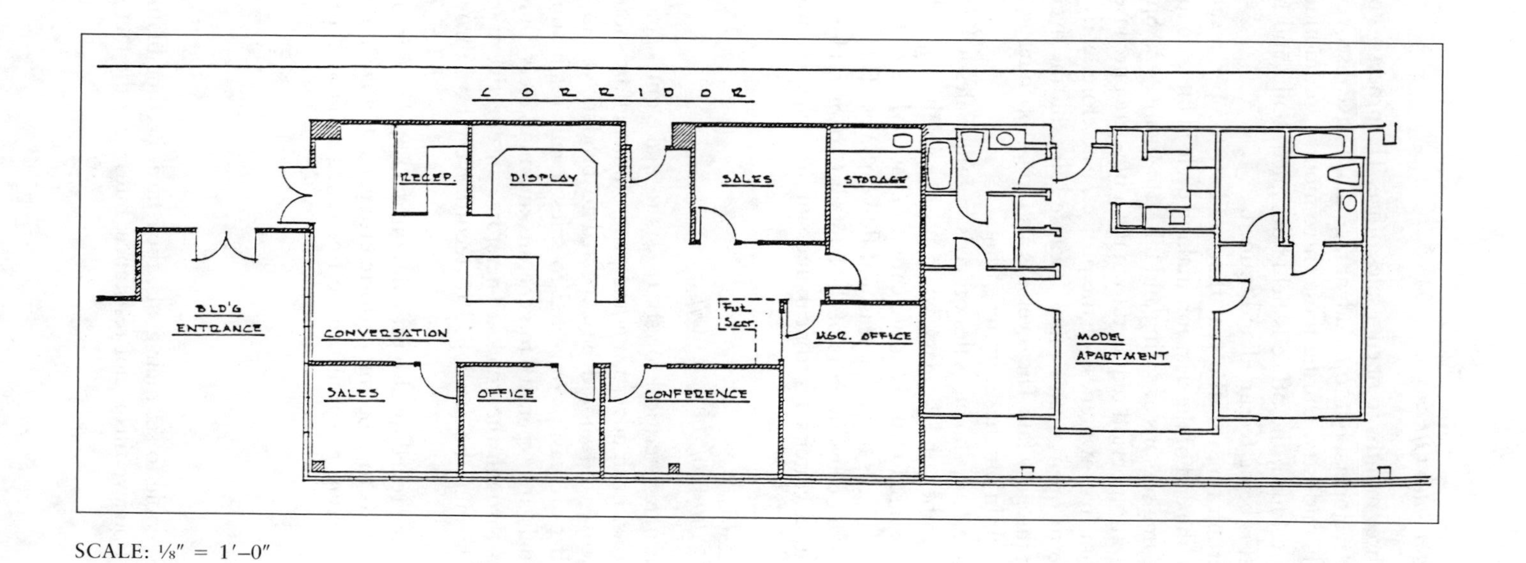

SCALE: ⅛″ = 1′–0″

Figure 4–1. Revised Floor Plan: Sales Office

Timing: Opening a Sales Office

It usually takes three months to open a sales office. The process is often hurried by anxious developers, but to no advantage that I have discovered in my fifteen years in the industry. During these three months, promotional materials are being developed, the office is being designed, built, and furnished, and the sales staff is being recruited and trained.

There are certain times of the year that are best to open a sales office. These times force the end of the decision-making cycle in life care to coincide with the prime selling seasons of spring and fall. (See figure 4–2.) Specifically, the average maturation period required to make a life-care purchase decision is six months from first awareness of the project. Therefore, early spring is an excellent time to open a sales office because sales, on the average, will start to mature in the early fall. The reverse is also true—opening a sales office in the fall will result in purchases in the spring.

The worst time to open your sales office is in June. Sales will then begin to mature in December and January when no one in the cold climates is psychologically prepared to make a life-care purchase. Most of the Western United States experiences a similar seasonal flow to sales. The exception to this seasonal pattern occurs in parts of the Sunbelt (Arizona, Florida) where snowbirds can cause winter sales to peak and summer sales to flatten out.

Systems and Procedures of the Sales Office

Accurate, current data is critical for strategists to make quick and effective marketing decisions. Each advertising and promotional effort should have a measurable objective and should be expected to produce results—namely, qualified leads that are easily converted to sales. Leads (or inquiries) from qualified individuals are expensive to generate, and marketers cannot afford to let them drop through the cracks. Therefore, an effective tracking and monitoring system must be developed to record every lead throughout its lifespan.

The monitoring procedure also provides the data by which results can be analyzed against goals to spot any performance gaps. If goals are not being achieved, the marketing program can be fine-tuned as needed to optimize marketing efforts.

Sales Goals

When I ask salespeople to set their goals, their faces become blank and uncommunicative. I believe this is not resistance, but rather the fact that most

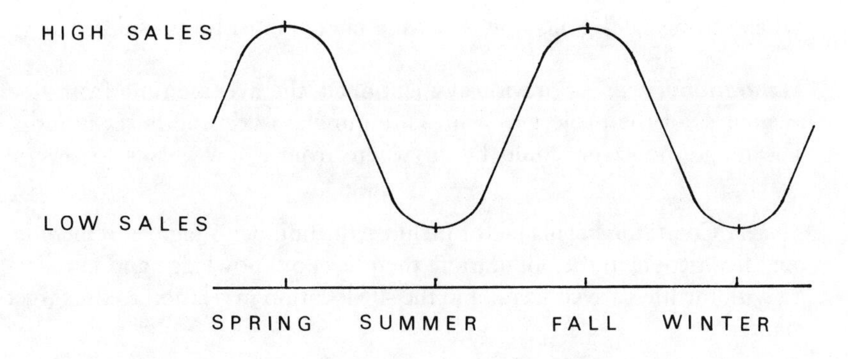

Figure 4–2a. Seasonal Sales Variations

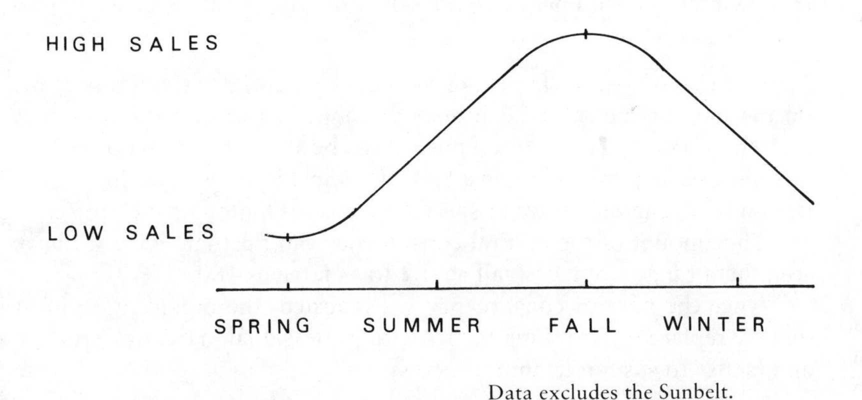

Figure 4–2b. Spring Opening: Decision Making

people do not develop concrete goals in their own lives. Since they do not know how to set goals, they have no idea how to achieve them.

Most sales goals have been established by management, usually with no firm base in reality. At one life-care project I am familiar with, the sales group achieved thirteen sales during their first half month of being open. The next month they sold twenty-five units. Based on this track record, the administrator, who had no previous selling experience, set the sales goal for *each* of the following months at twenty-five, a highly unrealistic expectation and an unaccessible goal.

When setting sales goals, the following factors must be considered:

Maturation Time: As previously mentioned, the average time from first awareness of the project to a life-care purchase decision is six months. The range, however, could be anywhere from a few weeks to several years.

Market Conditions: This factor includes the number of age- and income-qualified people in the population, their level of knowledge and familiarity with the life-care concept, and the site location in relation to the target market.

Competition: This consists of area life-care and rental retirement communities that offer what may appear to be similar benefits to your target audience, their advantages and disadvantages, and their occupancy rates.

Seasonal Variations: The best-selling seasons are spring and fall. By contrast, winter and summer often see sales dropping by as much as 90 percent in some areas.

Natural Constituency: These are the sales that come without any effort on the part of the sales force once the news is out that the project is underway. This built-in natural market can be attributed to many factors, including early public relations, lack of competition resulting in pent-up demand, or religious or other special interest affiliation of the project.

The amount of the natural constituency can fluctuate widely. I have seen them range from as small as five to as large as 180.

Once the natural constituency is exhausted, the organization must quickly replace order-taking tactics with professional marketing strategy and tactics to sustain its initial success.

Level of Marketing Effort: Marketing becomes increasingly effective with prolonged effort. Therefore, slower sales should be expected in the beginning (but after the natural constituency has been depleted), with mounting momentum over time.

Staffing

My experience with salespeople demonstrates that if given responsibilities in addition to selling, they will regularly perform their other duties first. As a result, salespeople should be hired only to sell. The other duties of a sales office should be filled by support staff. The staffing and responsibility and organization I prefer are detailed in figure 4–3.

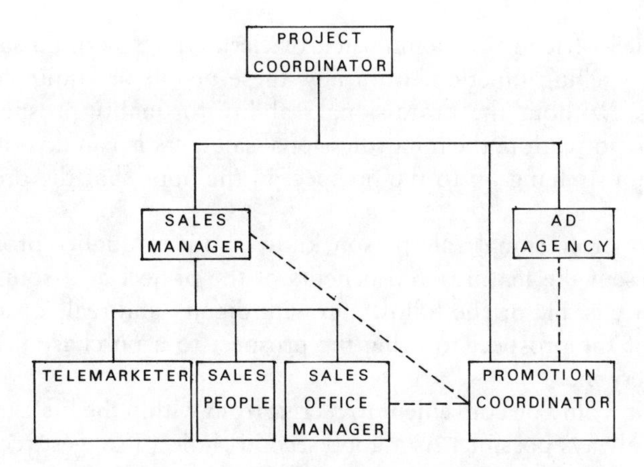

Figure 4–3. Organizational Chart

Sales Manager: Responsible for achieving goals, selling prospects, and managing the other salespeople. Hires, trains, and motivates sales staff, closing for staff as necessary, and is responsible for accuracy of records of the activities of the sales staff.

Salesperson: Sole responsibility is to sell.

Sales Office Manager: Responsible for data control, move-in coordination, clerical support, and generally managing the office and the paper flow.

Telemarketer: Sole responsibility is to generate leads and appointments through telemarketing.

Promotions Coordinator: Responsible for generating public awareness and increasing traffic flow through special events coordination and networking. Although located in the sales office because of the need for clerical support, the promotions coordinator does not report to the sales manager, but to the home office or the project's marketing director, project manager, or executive.

Recruiting

My philosophy is to look for the very best salespeople in an area—those who have good records as "closers." By contrast, the nonprofit sector of the life-care industry, because of its historical concern over hard-sell, will often hire "nice people"—friends of the minister, or clerk typists with no sales experience for the selling function. Ironically, these people are quite consistently hard-sellers. Without the professional's ability to qualify prospects and to understand motivation, the nonprofessional salesperson can do nothing more than tenaciously hang on to the prospect in the hope that the prospect will eventually give up.

A good professional salesperson knows how to qualify prospects and how to present the features and benefits of the project as a solution to the prospects needs. He or she follows up with dignity and real concern for the problems of the prospect to bring the prospect to a purchase decision that satisfies everyone.

While it would be convenient to recruit from within the life-care industry, that is not always possible. As a good second choice, I suggest recruiting the best salespeople in your geographical area, preferably from a consumer-oriented industry. Local salespeople will understand local customs, speak with a local accent, and already have a built-up networking system to draw on. By recruiting the very best talent in the area, your marketing program will progress faster, therefore saving money in the long-run.

Compensation

Two types of compensation exist in the industry: straight salary and commission. Because the life-care industry has been historically dominated by nonprofit groups, the traditional compensation has been a straight, often minimal, salary for nonprofessional salespeople. Although the actual salary expense is small for these nonprofessionals, their lack of experience can result in an expensive and severe cash drain on the project as the time-line for sales completion repeatedly slips.

The best professional salespeople are typically paid a small salary plus commissions or a draw against commissions. The amount of compensation varies widely by geographic area and is largely dependent on what other good salespeople in the area, regardless of their industry, can expect to earn. Although this may appear to be the more expensive course than employing nonprofessionals, professional salespeople need only be trained in product knowledge and provided with an understanding of the market to be quickly productive. They need not be trained in sales technique, a process that can only be absorbed by the nonprofessional over the long-run.

Motivation

Even the best salespeople need regular motivation to perform at a high level. Motivation techniques include performance bonuses (small or large depending on the goal), continual training, and incentive programs. Beyond that, a general upbeat feeling of "go team go" that is generated from the top down will go far toward maintaining the sales team's day-to-day enthusiasm.

Telemarketing

Telemarketing is a highly specialized sales technique. Its objective is to bring people to the site or to make an appointment for a presentation. Failing that, the telemarketer's goal should minimally be to make an appointment for the next telephone call.

Telemarketing is done with a script that specifies exactly what the telemarketer should say. I have heard pros and cons about using a script. *Hamlet* is a script. If it is poorly presented, it is awful. If it is well-presented, everyone stands up and cheers. The lesson: the quality of the actor is critical.

Telemarketing is a numbers game that generates a 15 percent success rate in making appointments. We usually set quotas for salespeople of thirty phone calls a day. Minimally, they should be able to make one phone call every fifteen minutes. One salesman I have heard of who came from the securities industry was not told the quota was only thirty, so he made upwards of two hundred calls a day.

Telemarketers, who work exclusively on the phone, usually work in short shifts of about four hours. As a result, we usually recruit part-timers: homemakers, students, actors, and the physically handicapped. Motivation is maintained through praise and small incentives for particular accomplishments.

Advertising and Promotion

Advertising is the area in which everyone *thinks* they are an expert. Picture the developer who scowls at the advertising account executive, "I showed this ad to the cleaning lady and she hated it!" Fortunately, nearly everyone does understand the need for attractive collateral materials—the corporate brochure, the corporate letterhead, floorplans, all materials reflecting the corporate image.

Beyond the collateral materials, however, additional sophistication among developers shows itself by the desire to advertise in the yellow pages, in the major metropolitan newspaper, on television, and with direct mail. The less sophisticated use radio and small local newspapers because of their perceived lower costs. Industry wisdom, however, proves the cost high because they yield poor sales results.

It is important to remember that life care is a direct-response industry. Our advertising objective is to get immediate responses from qualified pros-

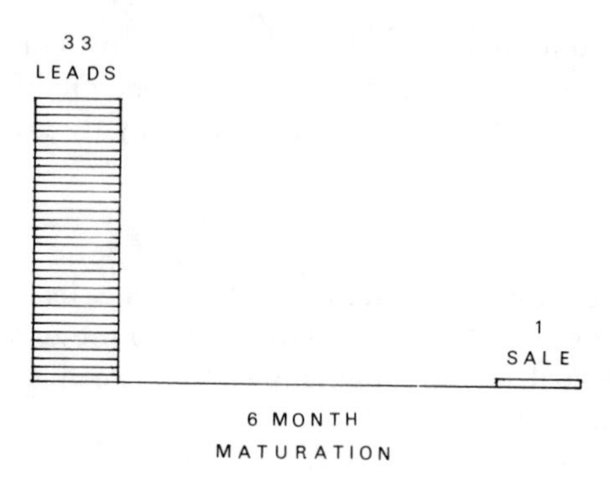

Example: 50 Sales objective
×33 Leads
1650 Leads needed 6 months prior to goal

Figure 4–4. Lead Scheduling

pects. We are only secondarily interested in image building for our project, or in education, when the project is being introduced to an uninitiated market.

Promotion is used to generate a sufficient number of qualified leads for the salespeople to convert to purchases on schedule. National averages indicate that three to five sales are made for every one hundred leads generated. (See figure 4–4.) Given that the average buying decision takes six months and that it takes one hundred leads to make five sales, we can plot the seasonal and annual lead goals the same way that we can plot sales goals. This information provides important benchmarks by which to judge whether performance is measuring up to the requirements.

The problem I most frequently encounter these days is a lack of positioning. Positioning is a somewhat sophisticated concept. It is the unique definition to the market of who you are and what you are compared with your competitors. A clearly defined and consistent positioning should be projected to the market through each and every element of your marketing materials.

Our company has meticulously tracked promotion results over the past ten years, and I will share some of our general findings with you. There are four major sources of leads for most life-care projects throughout the country: major metropolitan newspapers, television, direct mail, and networking.

Major Metropolitan Newspapers

Advertising in the major metropolitan newspaper in the area almost always produces high-quality leads with a strong sales conversion rate. It is, however, a high-cost item in the marketing budget and, to be effective, must be monitored carefully as to the cost per lead and cost per sale. In some geographic areas, the major metropolitan newspaper is not affordable because its coverage is much too broad for the project's more narrowly defined target audience. The days on which to advertise, the section to be in, and the size and positioning of the ad layout are further considerations.

As a rule of thumb, local small newspapers as well as radio and billboards do not produce for this industry. Every advertising agency I have ever worked with has told me that small local newspaper advertising in support of direct mail is inexpensive and should produce well. It *never* has. Small local newspapers may be cheap to advertise in, but they are not cheap at all if you get no response.

Television

Television advertising produces fewer leads than a major metropolitan newspaper, but a higher quality lead that converts to sales quickly. Television is, however, very expensive because you pay a substantial amount not only for media time, but also for producing the commercial. As such, it is only affordable within a relatively large marketing budget.

Direct Mail

Direct mail is probably the most cost-efficient and effective medium for the retirement industry to generate qualified leads. It is much more selective than newspaper or television because it is inexpensive to buy age- and income qualified mailing lists targeted directly to your geographic market area.

On the average, a good direct mail response rate is 1 to 2 percent. Keeping the following points in mind when evaluating a direct mail letter will help generate a strong response:

Length: There is no such thing as a letter that is too long. A two-page letter works better than a one-page, a three-page letter works better than a two-page. Recently we experimented with a seven-page letter (largely because the copy was so engrossing that we hated to cut it), and it achieved an outstanding 10 percent response rate.

Personalization: The response rates rise measurably if the letter is personalized (for example, "Dear Mr. Jones," rather than "Dear Friend").

Author: The letter is more effective if it is signed by a person of easily recognizable importance (for example, the administrator, the president, or a well-known spokesperson).

Process of reading a letter: People read a letter in the same order almost every time. First they look at the letterhead, then the salutation. Next they flip to the signature on the last page, read the postscript (P.S.), and then go back to the beginning of the body of the letter. Therefore, if you want a key message highlighted, the postscript is a good place to reinforce it.

Incentive: Direct mail programs that offer something for nothing usually bring in a better response than a simple direct mail letter (for example, the invitation to come for lunch can generate as much as a 20 percent response). This is, however, more of a traffic generator than a qualified lead generator. People responding for a free meal will not be as motivated to buy as those who respond without a free incentive offer.

Networking

Another key component of promotion is the networking system. Networking means getting out into the community, reaching churches, civic organizations, and professionals whose awareness of the project might have a positive impact on lead generation.

We usually hire a local person who is well-connected in the community to coordinate these events. We have had good success with people who were active in cultural and charitable activities (for example, past presidents of the Junior League who are looking for ways to establish a new career). They are able to put on events that are efficient, cost-effective, and reach the right target market.

Holding special events such as teas, card parties, and seminars effectively generates new leads. By also inviting applicants to these special events, they serve to reinforce the buyer's decision and commitment to move to the project. This is especially important in life care, where the time from application to move-in can be as long as three years.

Special events provide the added bonus of putting residents in touch with your best prospects in a situation in which the fun of the event and the camaraderie that is established support your sales effort.

Research

No general would launch a campaign without having a firm understanding of the terrain on which the battle was going to be held and an assessment of the obstacles standing between the army and victory. Market research provides this informational foundation for the life-care industry.

In addition to measuring the size of a potential market, marketing research should also test the depth and breadth of that market. Many issues can be clarified, such as the market's understanding of what you plan to offer, what people are willing to buy, how much they are willing to pay for it, and when they would be ready to purchase it.

Armed with this understanding of the target audience, an assessment of what competitors are doing, and an understanding of the developer's mission, hopes, and goals, long-range strategic marketing plans can be developed.

The strategic marketing plan is where the marketing generals map out the campaign, where they anticipate unforeseen contingencies, and where they develop benchmarks by which to measure progress toward victory. If good planning and strong execution are combined, your life-care project should achieve its goals on time and on budget.

Life Care: Its Future

Life care is still the easiest product to sell to the retirement market and, in my opinion, will likely continue to be so. It has a strong appeal to the "rational planners," a select group within the affluent elderly market, because it protects the buyer from the catastrophic costs of long-term nursing care.

It is only the rational planners who are willing to uproot themselves from the homes where they have lived comfortably and happily for many years in order to secure the peace of mind that comes from having the insurance life-care offers.

Despite this strong desire for a guarantee, however, rational planners have changed dramatically in their willingness to spend on lifestyle rather than on just insurance. Where twenty years ago, life-care residents would have shared a room or lived in a studio, many now request two- to three-bedroom apartments with two and a half bathrooms. Now they are demanding more personal and environmental satisfaction in their quest for insurance and security.

The newest frontier in the retirement industry today, one becoming increasing attractive, is the idea of keeping the body and mind well and active into the very advanced years of life. Americans today universally reject the idea of ever having to be cared for in a nursing home. Rather, the "optimum" death seems to be dying quickly on the tennis court, on the golf course, or digging in the garden.

As a result, I believe that an increasing emphasis on wellness—on maintaining health and vigor until death—rather than on providing a continuum of care will be what the marketplace looks for in the near future. For the rational planner, however, that will *always* be coupled with the need for a life-care insurance safety net.

> The practical advice offered in the preceding chapter is realistic and wise. The final paragraphs summarize the feelings that motivated this book, namely, that along with a rewarding lifestyle and the increasing emphasis on health and fitness, life-care insurance is the key to the best retirement programs and should no longer be left out of any first class package.
>
> —Editors

5
Life-Care Resident Preferences: A Survey of the Decision-Making Process to Enter a CCRC

Jeffrey M. Kichen, M.S.
and Joseph L. Roche, M.S.

"Ask The Man Who Owns One" recommended the old Packard auto ad. This chapter describes that approach to market research, and analyzes a "user" survey of life-care and continuing-care residents, asking those who've made the choice why they did so and what they like most and least about their new retirement life.

—Editors

Planners and developers of life-care and continuing-care retirement communities (CCRCs) have become increasingly sophisticated in the use of market research techniques that are commonly employed in real estate feasibility studies.[1] This new sophistication is a result of a variety of forces, including the obvious need to determine demand for life care in a given area; what services and amenities should be included; and the need to assess the probable effectiveness of alternative marketing, sales, and promotional strategies. The demands of potential lenders for information has also contributed to the increase in sophisticated market research.

In general, market research strategies include demographic and competitor analyses and consumer research. Life care consumer research has usually focused on the preferences and intentions of potential and prospective residents. Data is usually collected from consumers through surveys (including mail, telephone, and personal interviews) and focus groups. Although these data are of vital importance in determining the viability of any specific project, as well as in adding to our general knowledge of the CCRC industry, an important source of consumer information has been curiously neglected, namely current residents of life-care centers and CCRCs.

Information from these current residents is usually only collected by management of an existing facility to measure satisfaction, to evaluate staff, or to assess current services. In an effort to further expand the CCRC industry knowledge base, we sponsored and carried out a national survey of current CCRC residents to explore their decision-making process regarding entrance to their CCRC, to ascertain the most sought-after services and amenities, to further illuminate the demographics of residents, and to measure overall satisfaction with specific elements of their community.

Methodology

A list of CCRCs across the country was developed from a variety of directories, through our experience as consultants to the industry, and through our personal contacts. From this list we drew a sample of forty-five facilities. Next we developed a listing of residents at these facilities, and then drew a sample of 1,280 residents who were to receive our questionnaire through the mail. The survey instrument used in this research was an expanded version of an instrument that we used for a similar survey we had piloted in New England in 1986. Results of that survey have been reported elsewhere.[2,3] The survey for this national study was mailed out in the spring of 1988 by first class mail with a first class return mailer. A cover letter explained the purpose of the survey and assured potential respondents that we would not now or in the future attempt to sell them or interest them in any goods or services, nor would we give their names to any organization for solicitation purposes. People were requested to complete the survey and return it to us within ten days.

Return Rate

Of the 1,280 surveys mailed out, 422 completed questionnaires were returned, and 103 surveys came back as undeliverable. This yielded an unadjusted return rate of 33 percent and an adjusted return rate of 35.9 percent. This return rate is significantly higher than is usually expected from a mail survey. This is a result, we believe, of people having the leisure time to complete the instrument, and perhaps more importantly, of the subject being of vital interest to the respondents. Our pilot study in New England during the previous year also yielded a high return rate (41.2 percent, adjusted for undeliverables). No premium or other inducement was offered as part of either survey.

Demographics

Age and Sex

The majority of respondents, as expected, were female (65.4 percent). The median age of those who completed our survey was eighty-one years. More importantly, the median age of entry was seventy-four years. This is somewhat lower than other studies, including our own previous studies. For example, we have completed historical resident profiles of individual facilities that included the examination of *all* residents past and present and found that the median age of entry was around seventy-seven years. We attribute the lower median age found in our national study to the fact that it is based on existing residents. People entering at an older age would have lower survival rates. Also, older people may have been less likely to fill out the survey.

A further analysis of age of entry indicated that 24.4 percent of the residents were younger than age seventy when they entered their retirement community. Although this percentage is subject to the cautions noted above for median age, this finding is still important for those carrying out a feasibility study, which includes a demographic analysis for a specific market area. There has been considerable controversy regarding the lower age limit to be set when conducting a demographic analysis. Many today are maintaining that age seventy should be the lower limit and many financing sources that review the demographic studies support the age seventy floor. However, as our results indicate, a significant number of residents enter a CCRC below age seventy. With the type of data we are collecting on age of entry, the validity of demographic studies designed to assist in forecasting demand can be increased through adjusting for the historical record of age at entry.

Marital Status on Entry

Table 5–1 presents the results of the question: What was your marital status when you moved into this retirement community?

The high percentage of married couples entering CCRCs is a relatively new phenomenon. For example, 40 percent of those who entered their CCRC before 1981 entered as a married couple, while 54 percent of those who entered in 1981 and later were married. The increase in the proportion of married residents may have a profound effect on how both future as well as existing facilities approach marketing and forecast turnovers. Planners and developers of new facilities will have to provide more larger units since married couples tend to demand units with more square footage. In addition,

Table 5–1
Marital Status on Entry

Marital Status	*Percentage*
Married	49.5
Single	13.5
Widowed	34.1
Divorced	2.9

more services and amenities may be needed to attract men. Finally, as married couples become the norm for entrants, it may become increasingly difficult to promote prices that include an added monthly maintenance cost for the second person in the unit. This is not to say that the added person fee should be eliminated, but rather that thought needs to be directed as to how this added fee can be integrated into pricing schedules without standing out as a "marriage penalty."

Distance from Previous Residence to the CCRC

A crucial question in marketing CCRCs is the determination of market area, that is, the area from which one can anticipate attracting the majority, or a critical proportion, of residents. Establishing the market area is more than just a simple task of drawing a ten-, fifteen-, or twenty-mile radius around a project site.[4] Although the industry is becoming more sophisticated in setting a market area, the question still remains to be answered for any given project of how far away people will come in any high proportion to that facility. Given geographic and social boundaries, often an elaborate polygon rather than a circle defines the best target area.

The results of our survey provide some assistance in defining a target market by offering some parameters from respondents from across the country. Table 5–2 shows that nearly 48 percent of these life-care residents came from beyond fifteen miles, while almost 30 percent relocated from fifty miles away or more. What we see then is that the typical CCRC can potentially draw well outside what is usually considered a feasible market area. Our prior research with residents indicates the draw from many miles away is often related to the presence of children or other relatives in the area; some prior experience by residents with the life-care or CCRC host community; or the unavailability of similar services near their present residence. It is our belief that as CCRCs proliferate and geographic access increases, this latter reason for migration may diminish in importance and hence, lesser numbers will come from greater distances. But until CCRCs are widely available, it appears that they will continue to draw across wide areas, beyond the typical area of market feasibility.

Table 5–2
Distance From Previous Residence

Miles From Previous Residence	*Percentage*
15 or less	52.1
more than 15 but less than 50	18.3
50 or more	29.6

Previous Living Arrangements

The large majority (78.7 percent) of residents formerly lived in a house or a condominium that they owned. The rest either lived in rental housing (20 percent) or in another retirement facility (1.2 percent).

Income at Entry

Of all respondents, 61.7 percent had yearly incomes at entry of $25,000 or more, and 22.2 percent reported yearly incomes at or above $50,000. For those who entered in 1981 or later, 69.5 percent indicated that their income was $25,000 and over, while over 29 percent had incomes at or above $50,000. However, what is particularly important is that a high percentage of people entered a CCRC with yearly incomes below $25,000. Surprisingly, 42.4 percent of those who entered in 1986 or later reported incomes below $25,000. Again, these results provide cause for review of the accepted demographic parameters that are used for determining feasibility.

The Decision to Enter a Life-Care Community

Understanding how people make the decision to enter a CCRC is critical to effective marketing. This understanding can be approached from two directions that are by no means mutually exclusive. The actual activities and steps that individuals take regarding entry, and the psychographics of those who enter, are both fruitful lines of inquiry. For this survey we were concerned with the former. Elsewhere we have addressed psychographic issues related to the adoption and diffusion of an innovation such as life care.[5]

The Time It Takes to Make the Decision

For many people (62.2 percent), entry into a life-care community occurs two years or less from the time they first consider making a move or begin their search for a retirement community. However, nearly 20 percent indicated a period of five years or more passed from initial consideration to entry into their retirement community. If we agree with the assumption that CCRC entrants may be more likely to engage in long-range planning than others of their age group,[6] then a sales staff is faced with many strong prospects investigating a facility long before they actually expect to enter.

Number of Retirement Communities Visited

The decision to enter a CCRC, like the purchase of a home, is one of the most important and largest purchases that an individual or couple will make. Sur-

Table 5–3
Number of Communities Visited Before a Decision Was Made

Number of Communities Visited	*Percentage*
One	45.3
Two	18.5
Three	15.9
Four	7.6
Five	6.8
Six	2.5
More than Six	3.3

prisingly, then, a high proportion of people (45.3 percent) only visit one facility before they make their decision to enter. Table 5–3 shows that it is rather rare for people to visit more than six facilities.

For the sales staff it is important to understand that not a great deal of comparison shopping takes place among those who eventually seek entry into a CCRC. The low number of visits to multiple facilities is also obviously a function of the low number of facilities available that meet certain prospective resident criteria, such as geographic location.

The First Source of Information About Their Retirement Choice

Consumer behavior research indicates that there are three primary sources of information available to consumers concerning a product or service: (1) personal sources, such as family and friends; (2) professional sources, including experts, consumer groups, and government agencies; and (3) marketing sources, such as sales personnel and advertising.[7] Although it is difficult to weigh the relative importance of the three sources, it is important to note that the third, marketing sources, can have significant influence over the first two sources. Therefore, marketers of CCRCs should have an understanding of the major sources of information so they can develop strategies to influence those sources. Table 5–4 presents the results of our question on how people first learned about the retirement residence where they are now living. The "other" category included a variety of sources such as "saw them building it," "helped plan it," and some were duplicative of the sources presented above. As is presented in table 5–4, personal sources apparently are the most important regarding first knowledge of the facility.

In addition to examining first sources of information, we also explored exactly how personal sources influenced the resident's decision to enter a

CCRC. We examined the influence of children and friends and other associates as we describe next.

The Influence of Children

Of those who had children, slightly over 36 percent indicated that their children were involved in some way in the decision-making process. Table 5–5 shows to what degree children were involved across a number of factors.

Table 5–4
How First Learned About Retirement Residence

Source of Information	*Percentage of Respondents*
Friends	37.7
Newspaper advertisement or article	11.5
Other	11.2
Other relatives	10.0
Religious organizations	9.8
Brochure or materials mailed directly from retirement community	7.6
Children	6.8
Presentation by staff from the retirement community	2.4
Magazine advertisement or article	1.2
Senior citizen's group	0.7
Television	0.7
Radio	0.2

Table 5–5
Involvement of Children in Entry Decision

Involved in What Way	*Percentage Reporting Children Very Involved/Involved*
Discussing retirement living concept	72.6
Providing emotional support during selection process	60.2
Discussing financial options	42.9
Participating in final closing or signing of lease	32.8
Collecting information about retirement communities	30.9
Visiting various communities	21.9
Contacting communities	20.8
Providing financial support	6.6

Children were mostly involved in passive activities, such as discussing the concept and providing emotional support. Although we did not ask directly, it appears that children generally do not take the lead role in seeking out a facility for their parents. In fact, we have learned through our qualitative research with residents that children very often have to be convinced by their parents that the parents are making the right decision regarding entry into a CCRC.

The Importance of Other People in the Decision

The most important people according to the residents in their decision to enter a CCRC (other than a spouse) were their friends, and friends living already in a retirement community. The next most influential category was physicians. (See table 5–6.)

It is important to consider the relatively high proportion of people who cited friends living in a retirement community as important influences. Many managers and operators of existing facilities have long recognized that their residents are potentially the most effective marketers of a facility. Here we find a strong reliance by our respondents on people who previously made a decision to enter a retirement community.

Important Factors in the Decision to Enter a CCRC

Beyond the influence of family, friends, and others, we also examined the factors that people recognized as being important in their decision to enter a

Table 5–6
Importance of Other People in Entry Decision

Other People	*Percentage Reporting Other People as Very Important/Important*
Friends	39.8
Friends living in a retirement community	37.6
Physicians	16.8
Relatives other than children	13.5
Clergy	12.2
Financial advisors	10.7
Comembers of religious groups	10.3
Lawyers	8.6
Comembers of clubs	4.9
Work or business colleagues	3.2

CCRC. Understanding these factors can have direct application to marketing a facility, since they can provide the substantive issues around which a promotional campaign can be developed. (See table 5–7.)

Availability of a nursing home or other long-term care services was most often cited as a very important factor in respondents' decisions to enter a CCRC. In our experience, many marketers believed the availability of a nursing home should not be a main focus of sales and promotion because there was a tacit belief that older people did not want to face the reality of thinking about a nursing home. That may or may not be true among the general population, but it is our belief, which appears to be confirmed by this finding, that people who seek entry into a CCRC are more likely to have a history of planning ahead and recognize that this includes planning for the possibility of future health problems. Hence, marketing and promotional literature should perhaps focus on the presence of long-term care services and, ideally, prepaid nursing care, just as it has focused on how the CCRC or life-care program contributes to maintaining people's independence.

Table 5–7
Factors in the Decision to Enter a CCRC

Factor	*Percentage Reporting Factor as Very Important*
The availability of nursing home or other long-term care services	77.6
Desire to maintain independence	76.3
The availability of health maintenance services	71.8
The availability of many services and amenities	63.9
Financial factors such as entry and monthly fees	43.5
Difficulty of upkeep of former residence	41.9
Desire to be part of a community with people whose background and interests are like mine	26.7
The availability of planned outings and social activities	25.2
Recommendations of friends and relatives	23.8
Ownership, sponsorship, or management by a religious organization	21.4
Concerns about safety and security where I formerly lived	17.8
Desire to be part of a community with people about my own age	17.6
Desire to live closer to children or other relatives	17.0
Concerns about loneliness	9.6

Resident Satisfaction

Services and Amenities

A full understanding of residents' likes and dislikes is critical to the successful operation of any CCRC. But, as with much of the information we have presented previously, this area of inquiry has direct relevance to the development and marketing of new facilities. New facilities should stand on the shoulders of those developed before them if they intend to be strong competitive market forces.

In our survey we presented a listing of forty-one services and amenities (excluding food services) and asked respondents who had the service or amenity to state whether it was important to them. For those who did not have a particular service or amenity, they were asked to state whether they wished their community had it or whether it was not important to them. Based on an analysis of the response to the forty-one items, we were able to develop a ranking of the twenty most important or desired services and amenities. (See table 5–8.)

The listing in table 5–8 provides, in our view, the minimum menu of services that a CCRC should offer as well as what should strongly be promoted by its sales staff. Security issues and long-term care were the leading services that people found important. But interestingly, individual thermostats received the highest ranking. This is something most people were certainly accustomed to having in their previous living circumstances and should be included in any new development.

Food Services

Over 96 percent of respondents indicated that they had some type of meal plan at their community. In general they were satisfied with their food services along the following dimensions: (1) quality of food (93.9 percent); (2) variety of food (93.7 percent); (3) flexibility of serving times (88.8 percent); and number of available meal-plan options (90.4 percent). We were somewhat surprised by this finding since we assumed, based on anecdotal evidence, that the level of satisfaction with food services would be somewhat lower. We found similar high levels of satisfaction with health services, management, and other employees.

Health Services

Over 96 percent of respondents were satisfied with the quality of health care at their communities. Ninety-five percent were satisfied with the range and

Table 5–8
Rank Order of Top Twenty Services and Amenities

Service/Amenity	*Ranking*
Individually controlled thermostat in apartment	1
Emergency call system	2
Nursing or convalescent home on site	3
24-hour emergency system	4
Housekeeping or maid service	5
Library	6
Air conditioning	7
Fully equipped kitchens in unit	8
Linen service	9
Transportation such as a community van	10
On-site cultural events such as concerts and lectures	11
Barber and beauty shops	12
Assisted living units	13
Washer and dryer in apartment	14
On-site laundry or dry cleaners	15
Activities, scheduled outings	16
Exercise facilities	17
Religious services and facilities	18
Educational programs	19
Woodworking and creative arts	20

variety of health-care services that were provided. There was also a high level of satisfaction with the personnel who provide health-care services (95.9 percent) and with the hours and time of services (95.4 percent).

Management, Other Employees, and Overall Satisfaction

In terms of satisfaction, management (89.9 percent) did not fare quite as well as other employees (97 percent). Ninety-eight percent of the respondents indicated that they were satisfied with the physical appearance of their communities. Nearly 92 percent indicated that their living accommodations were about the right size. Finally, we asked, “Knowing what you know now, would you make the same decision to live in a retirement community?” Only about 84 percent said “yes.” This gives us some indication that the existing facilities still must continue to strive to keep their residents satisfied.

Conclusion

Planners and developers of new facilities, to ensure a marketable facility, should not only assiduously complete research and feasibility studies on their target market area, but also should consider the rich and valuable data that can be collected from those who have already made the decision to live in a CCRC or life-care community. This data can be used for product definition, the training of sales staff, and the development of promotional strategies and literature. Finally, we feel that the survey that we have presented and those that both and others may do in the future will significantly increase the useful knowledge base of the life-care industry.

> Some of the above findings are surprising, others reinforce "common knowledge." In either case, this survey gives us an interesting benchmark against which to contrast the more typical prospective, the project specific survey, and is another useful planning tool to give a project its earliest direction.
>
> —Editors

Notes

1. Barrett, G. Vincent and Blair, John P. *Real Estate Market & Feasibility Studies,* 2nd ed. New York: Van Nostrand Reinhold Company, 1988.

2. American Hospital Association. *Hospitals.* Chicago: American Hospital Association, November 1986.

3. Meister, Steven W. "The residents' viewpoint." *Retirement Housing Report,* March 1987, pp. 8–10.

4. Laventhol & Horwath. *The Senior Living Industry 1987,* Philadelphia: Laventhol, Horwath, 1987.

5. Kichen, Jeffrey M. "Adoption and diffusion of innovation: Implications for marketing CCRCs." *Retirement Housing Report,* January 1988, pp. 10–12.

6. Kichen, p. 11.

7. Hawkins, Del I., Coney, Kenneth A., and Best, Roger J. *Consumer Behavior: Implications for Marketing Strategy.* Dallas: Business Publications, Inc., 1980, pp. 330–358.

6
Two Perspectives on Life-Care Communities: A Researcher's and a Trustee's

Laurence G. Branch, Ph.D.

The various professional and volunteer roles of the author give him an unusual interest in, and unique access to, information on how the health programs of life-care centers really work. His ability to determine, as well as study, policy at the largest life-care center in Massachusetts lends this chapter a special flavor. This should be required reading for anyone interested in or involved with the health or health insurance programs of a life-care center. The author identifies key questions and makes a strong case for the true (insured) life-care community as the most effective health-care provider system for older people.

—Editors

This chapter will consider three issues in life care. One is the nursing-home utilization rates in life-care communities. This is an important factor that each of us involved in the development and operation of life-care communities needs to understand. This chapter will consider some data on this topic; this will be my academic perspective. Second, I will review accounting in the life-care field, including the ever-developing skirmishes between accountants and actuaries, which I think reflect a very important issue. And third, I will discuss future regulation in the context of life care.

Nursing Home Utilization

First, let me review the nursing home utilization rates from some life-care communities, including one I have been involved with for many years. That facility is North Hill, a life-care community located in Needham, Massachusetts. I have been a member of North Hill's board of trustees since its inception in 1979 and have served as the president of the board for the last three years. North Hill is situated on fifty-nine acres of land leased from Babson College. It has 341 independent-living units and sixty nursing home beds: forty skilled beds and twenty intermediate-care beds. There are approximately 425 to 450 residents in the 341 apartments; their average age at move-in was seventy-nine years; and, typically, 70 to 75 percent are women. North Hill residents enjoy a higher socioeconomic status than typical eighty-year-olds in Massachusetts. The first resident moved in during September of 1984, and we completed construction and completed initial occupancy in August of 1985. North Hill had a relatively rapid planned move-in of eleven months, largely because the board thought it would be a good idea to start the cash flow as quickly as possible. Consequently, when the first apartment wing and the common areas of the facility were completed, the first residents moved in while construction continued for eleven more months. The last resident moved in as construction was completed.

We also were trying to finance the construction of North Hill at a time when the interest rates were extremely high (in the 17 to 18 percent range). The board thought long and hard about the cost of long-term loans in that environment. We ended up developing an alternative financing system in which we asked our residents to provide fairly substantial endowments to obtain their lifetime use of their residence. At the same time, we guaranteed to them by contract at least 90 percent return of that endowment, a strategy that has subsequently been used by many other facilities. (Actually, several facilities were moving in the direction of higher endowments with guaranteed return of capital at the same time; as often happens, multiple entities are on the verge of innovation at approximately the same time.) In effect, the higher endowments, with 90 percent guaranteed return to the individual or the estate, became a vehicle for residents to obviate the need for a long-term debt service. At the time of original occupancy, the endowments ranged from nearly $90,000 to approximately $250,000, depending on whether the person was in a convertible one-bedroom or three-bedroom apartment. With an average endowment of approximately $150,000, 341 endowments precluded the need for long-term loans and the expensive debt service of that time.

In addition to their endowment fees, residents contracted to pay monthly service fees that originally were between $550 and $870 for the first person, depending on the size of the unit. Service fees fund the ongoing services, including apartment-based assistance in living and institutional long-term care, specified by contract for the residents of North Hill.

I will next outline the mechanisms by which nursing-home care is typically paid for in this country at present. The United States basically has a long-term care system that can be characterized as fee-for-service with minimal insurance.

Why is there so little insurance for long-term care (less than 1 percent of all nursing-home payments in 1986)? There are many reasons, but I will discuss the one which in my opinion has the least merit. The reason simply is that insurers and policy people have talked themselves into fearing the possibility that some people who do not really need nursing-home care will nevertheless take advantage of the system if the care is prepaid. Now I ask you, have you ever seen or heard of anyone who has snuck into a nursing home when they really were not appropriately placed in that nursing home? However, when health policy people get together and talk about the possibility of insuring nursing-home care, we always talk about the possibility of moral hazzard. Moral hazzard in this context is the problem that would occur if people who really do not need a nursing home were to sneak in just because it is a covered expense. The problem of unnecessary use of health service because it does not cost the individual any money out-of-pocket may exist in some segments of the health sector. It may be a real worry for home care. However, I do not share the opinion that it exists, or will exist, in institutional long-term care.

In the current context of fee-for-service, uninsured coverage of nursing homes, we find that Medicare payed for less then 2 percent of nursing-home care in this country during 1986. Why is that? Medicare, as you know, was established in 1965 as the insurance mechanism for the hospital care of older people, and still remains as insurance for hospital care for older people. The use of nursing homes as an appropriate adjunct to hospital care occurs quite rarely, according to the definitions of appropriate nursing-home use of the Health Care Financing Administration, that agency of the federal government charged with implementing the Medicare program. So the very few people who are in nursing homes and have their care paid for by Medicare are usually those people who are experiencing brief rehabilitation following an acute-care event, such as a hip fracture or a stroke. They are undergoing rehabilitation in the nursing home, and in that very specific context, Medicare reimburses the cost of nursing-home care to the amount of about 1 to 2 percent of the total bills per year.[a]

More than 50 percent of the costs of nursing-home care was borne directly by individuals themselves in 1986. This private payment mechanism is just what happens when you have a fee-for-service, uninsured program of nursing-home care. People need it and they pay for it. This considerable amount of self-financing of institutional long-term care can lead to dire economic consequences for many older Americans.

Most people enter nursing homes paying for care out of their own pockets, spend down their income and assets over time, and become impoverished according to the definitions of their individual state. Then that state, with federal assistance, assumes financial responsibility for their nursing-home care as well as their other medical care under the state's Medicaid program of health care for poor people. Medicaid is administered differently in each

---

[a]Editorial note: Any expansion of Medicare coverage for long-term care may affect a significant increase in this number.

state, but in all states, Medicaid will cover nursing-home care once the person is both economically eligible for Medicaid, meaning they have become poor, and medically needy of nursing-home care. Medicaid paid about 45 percent of the nursing-home bills in this country during 1986.

In the Massachusetts Health Care Panel Study, we asked a series of questions to determine how long it would take typical older people in Massachusetts to spend down their income and lifetime assets to the state's Medicaid poverty level if they needed long-term care.[1] Individuals aged seventy-five years and older (which corresponds very closely to the life-care market), living alone, and going into a nursing home in Massachusetts, will in nearly half the cases (46 percent) spend their lifetime assets and their income down to the Massachusetts level of impoverishment within thirteen weeks (three months) and thereby become eligible for the state Medicaid program to pick up their nursing-home costs. Within six months, 59 percent of the population seventy-five years and older living alone would have spent down to poverty level by paying their nursing-home bills out-of-pocket; at the end of one year the rate is 72 percent. Those are staggering rates for that spend-down process.

We also calculated the hypothetical rates of spend-down for married couples, one of whom is seventy-five years of age or older. If one spouse goes into a nursing home, 25 percent of these households would spend their joint lifetime assets down to the Medicaid poverty level within thirteen weeks (three months)—that is one out of four. By the end of the year, the rate would be 57 percent.

Think of the implications of those spend-down rates—that most individuals who need to enter a nursing home in our current financing context of fee-for-service with minimal insurance or government support, will, in most cases, spend their lifetime income and assets down to poverty level within one year. For substantial minorities (46 percent of individuals and 25 percent of spousal households), this will happen within three months.

These spend-down rates are why we were reminded earlier in this book that the older people who plan ahead are the people who look at life-care communities. They are the ones who understand the financial implications if they had to pay for all nursing-home costs out of their own pockets.

As a developer of a life-care community, what is the sponsor's financial liability for the cost of the nursing-home service? To begin to answer that question, let me remind you of some terminological distinctions offered by the American Association of Homes for the Aging. They define three kinds of life-care communities: Type A, Type B, and Type C. Type A life-care community accepts full responsibility for the provision and payment of nursing-home care to their residents in return for the contracted initial and monthly fees. Full financial liability rests with the sponsor. In Type B life care, the sponsor has limited liability, and the resident shares the financial liability. The range of liability is extremely broad. Sometimes the life-care sponsor will

Table 6–1
Risk of Entering a Nursing Home for Elderly: The General Population and CCRC Residents

	General Population		*CCRC Residents*
Age Group	*Estimated Lifetime Risk*	*Sex-Adjusted Lifetime Risk*	*Estimated Lifetime Risk*
65–69	35.6%	38.6%	55.0%
70–74	36.9	41.9	59.1
75–79	40.1	44.5	65.1
80–84	41.6	43.4	67.0
85 and older	38.8	39.5	82.7

Source: Cohen, M.A., Tell, E.J., Bishop, C.E., Wallack, S.S. and Branch, L.G. "Patterns of nursing home use in a prepaid managed care system: The continuing care retirement community." *The Gerontologist*, 1989, 29(1), 74–80.

accept financial liability for up to two years, other times the sponsor's liability will be as minimal as ten days. But the common element among Type B life care is that there is shared liability for the costs of nursing-home care. Type C is the life care, or, actually, "continuing-care" community in which the sponsor accepts no financial liability for the nursing-home care; any care that is needed is paid fee-for-service by the user.

Why would anyone in their right mind want to sponsor a Type A life-care community? (By the way, North Hill is currently (1988–89) the only Type A life-care community operating in Massachusetts.) I am not sure I have an answer to this question that would satisfy a skeptic or the traditional real estate developer, but I can tell you that I am proud North Hill accepts the responsibilities of a Type A life-care community. Table 6–1 reveals some of the implications of Type A life-care residents' use of their nursing-home beds; the data come from a study by M. A. Cohen and colleagues.[2] The issue this table clarifies is how much more nursing-home care is used by life-care residents compared with the national average. The lifetime risk of nursing-home admission for the general population as reported by others is presented in the first and second columns. The third column presents the estimated lifetime risk of over 3,000 residents from six different life-care communities. The lifetime risk of nursing-home use in life-care communities is about 50 percent greater than the risk for the general population. What does this tell us about planning for nursing-home use in life-care communities? Do not use national data unless you like underestimating your admission rates by about one-third. It is important to recognize that the life-care resident is going to be admitted for nursing-home care more than the general population of the same age.

Table 6–2 presents additional information on the parameters of nursing-home stays in both the general population and for life-care residents. Life-

Table 6–2
Length of Stay for an Admissions Cohort of Elderly and CCRC Nursing-Home Entrants by Age Group

	Entry Age-65–74		*Entry Age-75–84*		*Entry Age-85 +*	
Length of Stay	*General*	*CCRC*	*General*	*CCRC*	*General*	*CCRC*
< 1 month	28.6%	65.8%	26.7%	52.7%	23.5%	42.8%
2–3 months	19.6	14.7	15.2	18.1	18.8	15.8
4–6 months	10.8	5.3	12.3	8.8	11.7	11.0
7–12 months	10.0	4.7	11.8	7.9	11.4	11.0
1–2 years	10.4	4.7	10.5	6.6	13.8	10.0
2–3 years	6.3	1.6	6.2	2.6	7.1	6.3
3–5 years	5.3	2.6	9.6	2.1	9.6	2.3
> 5 years	9.0	0.5	8.1	1.1	4.2	1.3
Average number of days	419	129	497	159	425	231
Median number of days	56	13	66	25	123	48
Weighted average	General: 462 days		CCRC: 179 days			
Weighted median	General: 71 days		CCRC: 28 days			

Source: Cohen, M.A., Tell, E.J., Bishop, C.E., Wallack, S.S. and Branch, L.G. "Patterns of nursing home use in a prepaid managed care system: The continuing care retirement community." *The Gerontologist*, 1989, 29(1), 74–80.

care residents in each of the three age groups have nearly double the rate of nursing-home stays of one month or less; that is, they have short stays in the nursing home compared with the general population of the same age. Not surprisingly then, with the exception of one pair of numbers (15.2 versus 18.1 for those aged seventy-five to eighty-four with lengths of stays between two and three months) every other pair of numbers in table 6–2 indicates that fewer life-care residents had the longer stays than the general population.

In table 6–1 we saw that life-care residents have greater lifetime risk for nursing-home entry than the general population, while table 6–2 indicates that their length of stay is shorter. Taken together, the data suggest that the increased rate of admissions to nursing homes by life-care residents is coupled with shorter stays. Why is this pattern occurring? Consider this interpretation: If you are a person in the outside community and you suddenly need nursing-home care, the bed is not likely to be available immediately due to an over 90 percent average occupancy rate. Conventional wisdom suggests that private paying patients will get a bed more quickly than Medicaid or Medicare patients because they pay more than the reimbursement rates of Medicaid and Medicare. Nevertheless, the bed would still not be immediately available in most cases. If the stay you needed was truly a short stay, you might not get off the waiting list during the short interval, regardless of who is paying for the care. A resident of a Type A life-care community, on the other hand, generally has a contract that guarantees the resident a nursing-home bed as medically necessary—and immediately. Life-care residents who need a short-term stay are more likely to get one than the general population, who have to contend with waiting lists. If the contract guarantees nursing-home access, one would expect to find Type A life-care residents using the nursing home more frequently.

Additional data in table 6–3 support this line of reasoning. Sixty-five percent of the admissions during the first two years of operation at North Hill were for lengths of stays of thirty days or less—the short-stay people. This is approximately double the national rates that might have been expected (columns two and three). In addition to the shorter lengths of stay, we found that individual Type A life-care residents have much more frequent admissions than the national population. Again, this pattern is easily explained. If you are from the general community without guaranteed access to a nursing home, given the waiting lists that exist, the practice of going in and out of a nursing home, particularly for short stays, is not feasible. If you are a resident in a Type A life-care community, this practice can work. Let me illustrate this with an example. One of my colleagues, an original board member of North Hill, subsequently became a resident. Several months after she became a resident, she developed a brain tumor that ultimately caused her death and some physical and cognitive demise prior to that. While her med-

Table 6–3
Comparison of Lengths of Stays

	North Hill	*Liu and Manton*[a]	*Lewis, et al.*[b]
1–30 days	65%	34%	28%
31–60 days			15%
31–90 days	19%	18%	
61–365 days			17%
91–360 days		22%	
91–365 days	10%		
> 360 days		26%	
> 365 days	6%		40%

[a]Source: Liu, K. and Manton, K.G. "The length-of-stay patterns of nursing home admissions." *Medical Care, 21,* 1983, pp. 1211–1222. Synthetic sample; all ages; based on life table analytic principles.

[b]Source: Lewis, M.A., Cretin, S. and Kane, R.L. "The national history of nursing home patients." *The Gerontologist, 25,* 1985, pp. 382–388. Stratified random sample of 563 discharges; lengths of stays for first admission only (n = 228; median = 116 days).

ical team was trying to come to grips with the implications of her disease process, she ended up having seven stays in the North Hill nursing home, most quite short. She used the nursing home in a very appropriate way. When her level of function was sufficient to enable her to live independently in her apartment, she went to her apartment. As soon as she was unable to care for herself in the apartment even with apartment-based support, she came back to the nursing home. This pattern in my opinion is exactly how a long-term care system should operate. This pattern is what you can expect to find in the nursing home of a Type A life-care community.

What will the frequency of admission and the length of stay patterns be in the Type B life-care in which the individual resident makes some form of copayment? I do not know. No one has developed an appropriate data base to make the comparison, but I will offer an opinion. The nursing-home utilization patterns of Type B residents will not be the same as one finds for the national cohorts. I think their utilization patterns will be closer to the utilization rates that you find for Type A residents. In both cases, the resident need not *resist* entering the nursing facility since they know that discharge will come as soon as possible and that their apartment will be kept available for them, in almost all cases, as long as there is hope of returning to it.

Accountants Versus Actuaries

Next, I would like to discuss the minor skirmishes between the accountants and the actuaries concerning financial audits of life-care communities. First, I think we need to understand the basic issue of contention. A layman's definition of *auditing* is basically a periodic (usually annual) financial review or assessment of the financial health of a corporation. The traditional way of trying to assess the financial health of corporations usually has been based on what are called the generally accepted accounting principles (GAAPs), which provide both a balance sheet as of a particular day and a cash-flow analysis of the interval. The problem is that the GAAP approach does not make use of *actuarial* principles to measure both the assets and liabilities associated with *future* obligations stemming from the contract that the sponsor has with residents. What does this mean? If you are only looking at the assets and liabilities of a current year, which is the traditional interval for a GAAP annual audit, you only see the assets and liabilities that occurred during that year. But as part of the definition of life-care, the individual has a contract for the lifetime use of certain services. If I want to assess the financial health of a life-care community, I have to know how well that life-care community is organized financially to meet its future obligations. It is necessary to take into account the present value of assets, the present value of expected income, and the present value of expected liabilities for future services to those people under contract. How does one do that? It is not done by the GAAPs. Some actuaries have developed methods for dealing with the future obligations and have adapted for life-care some of the actuarial accounting principles used in the insurance industry. The logic is to weigh the present value of the life-care community's assets, both present and future, against the present value of its future obligations: what the life-care community has to pay out. We must develop an accounting system in the life-care industry that takes into account the present value of future assets and the future liabilities of the whole life-care community.

Suppose your college roommate called you tomorrow and said, "My mother is considering going into a life-care community. You are in the business. Tell me how I go about selecting one." How would you tell that individual to go about selecting a life-care community for his mother? I know what I would want to know: is the life-care community's financial posture based on actuarial financial accounting, not on the generally accepted accounting principles.

Jarvis Farley, the original president of the board of trustees of North Hill (my predecessor) helped the North Hill board to think through the specific components of an actuarial-based financial accounting system.[b] As of 1987, North Hill has actuarial-based financial statements that assess the present value of our assets against the present value of our future liabilities.

Regulation

What are the different approaches that can be taken to regulate life-care communities? In the traditional (i.e., free-standing) nursing-home industry, we have basically a life-safety code approach for the conditions of participation. Certain aspects of the physical plant must be in compliance with the standards, criteria, and conditions of the safety code. Life-safety regulation has occurred when the facility is in compliance with the code. Is that what we want for the life-care field? I do not think so. In my personal opinion, I would rather have a different approach, based more on the model of the Securities and Exchange Commission. You set up some expectations. If you violate them, you are prosecuted. Now what are the basic expectations of practice and ethics in this industry that we would want to have? The fundamental expectation must be to disclose accurate information in a public manner to potential consumers. The information has to be easily available, it has to be

[b]See the appendix for the discussion from the panel on financing long-term care. Mr. Farley had some additional comments on actuarial-based financial accounting in that panel of which he was a member.

comprehensive, and it has to be accurate. From my perspective, if the information is not publically available or does not cover all the necessary points, you should not be able to develop a life-care facility, and if the information is intentionally inaccurate, you should go to jail. In my opinion, this kind of approach is better than the life-safety code approach that says current nursing homes have to be in compliance with 24 conditions of participation, 294 standards, and 655 criteria. For example, I am not sure I agree with a life-care regulatory standard that requires the sponsor to put all deposits into escrow. That may seem like a good idea right now, but it might not always be the best approach. I think we have to allow flexibility for developers to make improvements in an evolving industry, without locking the industry into the status quo. In order to allow creative flexibility (as North Hill demonstrated during the era of mid-teen prime rates), I think we cannot tie our hands by regulation, but we must still protect consumer interests.

> The preceding statistics and conclusions, rounded out by direct observation, are strong endorsements of the life-care approach. The advantages of easy nursing admission and discharge policies within a life-care community are important and the warnings, such as the importance of a sound actuarial base and the desirability of full financial disclosure, are well taken.
>
> —Editors

Notes

1. Branch, L.G., Friedman, D.J., Cohen, M.A., Smith, N., and Socholitzky, E. "Impoverishing the elderly: A case study of the financial risk of spend-down among Massachusetts elderly." *The Gerontologist,* 1988, *28* (5), 648–652.

2. Cohen, M.A., Tell, E.J., Bishop, C.E., Wallack, S.S., and Branch, L.G. "Patterns of nursing home use in a prepaid managed care system: The continuing care retirement community." *The Gerontologist,* 1989, *29* (1), 74–80.

7
The Life-Care Development Process

Gardner W. Van Scoyoc

This chapter combines a complete checklist of development tasks with some surprising anecdotes and many insightful comments drawn from the author's broad experience

—Editors

There has been a rapid increase in the number of life-care retirement communities since 1980. During the same period, a series of creative variations have been added to the basic life-care concept. Refundable contracts, pay-as-you-go plans, group long-term insurance, "life care without walls" concepts, and new financing options are all influencing the nature of the life-care offering for the future. In this climate of growth, planning the development of a life-care facility may tend to resemble a chicken trying to lay an egg on an escalator.

Each life-care facility has its own unique characteristics. While reasonable standards have been established in such areas as market analysis, actuarial evaluations, and operations, many other facets of life care are ready for new ideas and techniques. Add to this the differing lifestyles, expectations, and financial abilities of the potential residents in each market area, and you begin to understand the uniqueness of the planning process for each new facility.

To illustrate, over twenty years ago I served as the CEO during the development and early operations of Goodwin House, a 225-unit life-care facility in Alexandria, Virginia. It has been home for many residents of the Washington D.C. area, and for others who have come some distance to live near their children and grandchildren. The residents have included college professors, business men and women, clergy, and military and foreign service personnel. there are also a number of the first female career civil servants employed by the federal government.

This past year, the Goodwin House corporation completed a new life-care facility about a mile away. Called Goodwin House West, it has a capacity for 322 residential and 120 health unit beds. The new building reflects many of the recent trends in life care. The resident apartments are larger overall, and there are many more one- and two-bedroom units. The activity and service components are larger and better-organized. The facility will operate more efficiently than the original Goodwin House, although the original remains very functional compared with many other later facilities.

One administrative staff manages both facilities. The policies, procedures, and overall operations of both are virtually identical. The residents of Goodwin House West have backgrounds similar to those of Goodwin House residents, although, as you might expect, they average several years younger in age.

So how was the new facility received? Goodwin House West was built in part because of a waiting list for more than 400 units at Goodwin House. However, less than 20 units were filled from that list! Further, all current residents of Goodwin House were given the opportunity to move to larger accommodations at Goodwin House West, but only three accepted. Most of the Goodwin House residents attended the opening ceremonies of the new facility. The word came back that while the new building and accommodations were very nice at Goodwin House West, theirs was still "Goodwin House Best"! Clearly, the elderly do not change directions quickly and do not often move for frivolous reasons.

Sponsorship

In practical terms, the organizational structure of the sponsor greatly influences the characteristics of a life-care facility. Furthermore, realistic goals and objectives are important indicators of future marketing and operational success. Historically, most life-care facilities have been developed by religious groups or other benevolent organizations. The purposes of such organizations have usually led to laudable projects; however, sponsors who have traditionally served the sick and poor elderly may find it difficult to adjust to the demands of the healthy and independent residents of a life-care facility. Careful review of the sponsor's goals may prevent the development of a product this new market does not want.

A sponsoring committee or organization will usually be established before the development process begins. The majority of life-care projects have been developed as nonprofit, tax-exempt corporations. Religious and other constituent organizations can tap their existing pools of talent for board members and other leadership positions, potential donors, and future residents. The latter gives them a great advantage over nonconstituent organizations. On the other hand, a number of membership organizations have not had effective leadership for life-care development and management. The reason may be that the sponsor has selected board and committee members as potential donors or as representatives of their congregations or districts, rather than for their development or management skills.

Hospitals and other nonconstituent organizations are becoming major players in the elderly housing field, developing facilities and services through a variety of subsidiary organizations. They are usually well-organized and experienced in the development process. Many hospitals fear the future health-care liabilities imbedded in a true life-care program. Therefore, they have developed more limited programs and have an interest in the growing group long-term nursing-care insurance program.

Nursing-home chains, hospitality corporations, real estate developers, builders, and other entrepreneurial groups have also entered the continuing-care field. Most also avoid a full life-care program. For the most part, their facilities are targeted more to the young, more affluent segments of the senior housing market. They often feel most comfortable with rental programs. These for-profit organizations have excellent access to initial development funds and capital markets. They have well-crafted management systems for development and operations and a strong understanding of effective marketing techniques.

An increasing number of life-care facilities are being formed as joint ventures or other cooperative endeavors between the various types of sponsoring organizations. Often a joint venture between a for-profit entity with money and development skills and a nonprofit with "image" and health-care delivery skills can come up with a workable and marketable product. The chapter on financing covers these possibilities in more detail. The kind of organization and its reasons for developing life care will shape the structure, the development process, and ultimately the character of the retirement community itself.

Initial Steps

Successful development of a life-care facility is the result of careful planning and scheduling of the key tasks to be accomplished. My purpose is to describe the major steps, the relationships of the tasks, and typical time frames required to complete a life-care facility, and to show their relationships to each other. My example is that of a life-care facility being developed by a 501(c)(3) tax-exempt sponsor.

The life-care development process is comprehensive and systematic in scope. As you can see from the accompanying sample project schedule (figure 7–1), there may be more than fifty major activities undertaken during the four- to six-year development period. A systems approach is required if the sponsor is to cope with the avalanche of tasks within the same time frames. The sponsor also will need to be flexible in decision making. Many major decisions will have to be made with inadequate information, insufficient time, and no guarantee of favorable results.

Figure 7–1
Typical Development Schedule of a Continuing-Care Retirement Community: Organizing Tasks

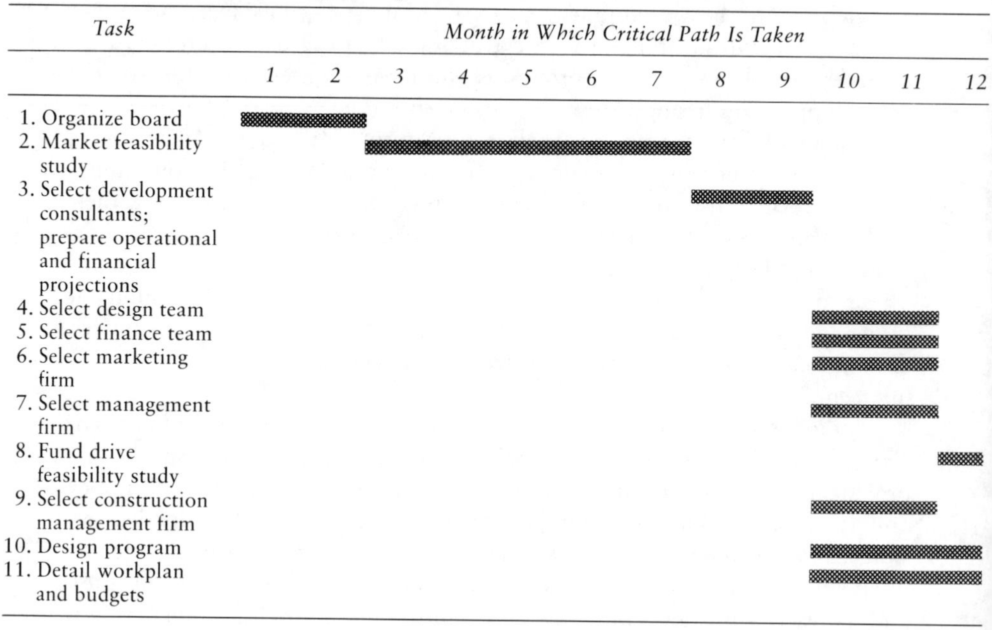

Task	*Month in Which Critical Path Is Taken*											
	1	*2*	*3*	*4*	*5*	*6*	*7*	*8*	*9*	*10*	*11*	*12*
1. Organize board	■	■										
2. Market feasibility study			■	■	■	■	■					
3. Select development consultants; prepare operational and financial projections								■	■			
4. Select design team										■	■	
5. Select finance team										■	■	
6. Select marketing firm										■	■	
7. Select management firm										■	■	
8. Fund drive feasibility study												■
9. Select construction management firm										■	■	
10. Design program										■	■	■
11. Detail workplan and budgets										■	■	■

Organization of the Sponsor Board

Selection of the life-care facility board of trustees should take into account the wide-ranging talents needed for facility development. The board of trustees is responsible for establishing the goals and objectives of the life-care corporation and for making sure that the development activities it authorizes are properly executed. Professionals in accounting, finance, insurance, real estate development, construction, and architecture could all be suitable candidates. Attorneys, social workers, nurses, and clergy can also prove to be excellent choices. Physicians may be better utilized on committees of the board, since most have severe scheduling difficulties.

The size of the board of trustees is important. Large boards of twenty or more members will require more time to reach consensus. Timely decision making is vital for an efficient, effective, and economical development. When boards delay or reverse themselves, they run the risk of increasing costs or even jeopardizing the project. Just the cost of inflation for one month's delay on a large life-care project can exceed $100,000. Potential board members should be informed of the time commitments the development process will require of them. Continuity of the board during this period is very important to the success of the development.

A number of sponsors delay incorporation until completion of a market analysis and economic feasibility study. However, to avoid potential delay in IRS and state approvals, an earlier incorporation is recommended.

Market Analysis and Economic Feasibility Study

A full market analysis and economic feasibility study is necessary to establish the size and economic parameters of the proposed facility. In addition, information from potential residents themselves is highly recommended. Their input will be invaluable in shaping programs and services to better meet their preferences and expectations.

Consultant Team Selections

A sponsor planning a new life-care facility without advice from outside experts is asking for trouble. The experienced multifacility corporations that have developed at least one life-care facility since 1983 may be the one exception. Our most recent recession ended that year; since then construction costs and methods have been fairly stable. However, development now has almost nothing in common with development of the 1960s and 1970s. Goodwin House West, referred to earlier, had a square foot construction cost quadruple that of Goodwin House twenty-two years before. This means new facilities have to be very carefully planned and constructed to be able to compete with facilities built at lower costs more than five years ago.

Consultants involved in the development of life-care projects on a continuing basis can provide the up-to-date information and support the sponsor needs for the new facility to be attractive, marketable, and cost-effective. Consultants may be disliked by some, tolerated by others, praised by few, but are nonetheless vital for success in this specialized life-care field. Because of the comprehensive nature of a life-care facility, consultants from more than one discipline are needed. The development will require specialists in life-care development and operations, in legal matters, design, marketing, and management. The sponsor will need a fund-raising feasibility and capital development firm if a fund-raising campaign is contemplated. Obviously the sponsor will need to engage architectural and financing teams, and if a negotiated construction contract is desired, a construction management firm as well.

The sponsor will require professional advice from time to time on such things as zoning approvals, insurance coverage, interior design, food service, and telephone systems. Usually the major consultants can recommend specialists in these and other areas as required.

There are several schools of thought about working with consulting teams. One maintains that the sponsor should select the needed consultant team, receive all of their recommendations, decide the best course of action, and then coordinate the implementation by the consultant. The advantage to this method is that the sponsor receives the widest range of advice possible and is able to deal effectively with the complexities of the development.

The weakness is that the sponsor may not have the background to coordinate the varying and sometimes conflicting recommendations of different consultants. Further, if the sponsor considers all recommendations as of equal value, some proposed actions may not be recognized as having negative impacts on other areas of the development.

A second school of thought recommends that one development consulting firm act as the primary consultant of record. They, rather than the sponsor, would review the input of the other consultants and coordinate the schedules and flow of events. The lead consultant would advise the sponsor of all consultant recommendations, and all coordination activities would be conducted with the continuing knowledge and approval of the sponsor. The advantage of this approach is that the sponsor does not have to weigh conflicting recommendations without fully understanding their implications. The lead consultant firm typically has professional employees from the fields important to the life-care process, such as architecture and design, health care, management, marketing, financing, and construction. The firm can more easily handle coordination issues for the sponsor. The down side of this approach is that a consulting firm is no stronger than its weakest specialty.

Yet a third approach is the use of a development firm experienced in life-care facilities. There are several corporations with successful track records in this field over a number of years. Some firms serve as developer through the construction period for a development fee paid in installments related to project progress. Others act as an equity partner, relieving the nonprofit sponsor of most or all financial risk and looking for longer-term involvement under varying types of financial arrangements.

There have also been a number of new development firms entering from other fields. These include multifamily, office, and hotel developers, and construction of health-related industries. However, the majority of these developers leave the field after completing one project. They discover how complex and difficult life-care is to develop and market compared with "bread and butter" projects in other fields.

One advantage of using a development firm may be their willingness to front a portion of the high-risk preconstruction costs for a cash-short nonprofit sponsor. The down sides of the use of a development corporation are loss of control and that they may not be sensitive to the philosophy and program objectives of the nonprofit. There can be turf battles over the control of the decision-making process. The developer with a significant cash investment in the project will resist losing money because of the action or inaction of the nonprofit. Development fees may also seem quite high. Nonprofits, particularly membership organizations, may find their reputation damaged by an expensive developer contract and the resulting high fees.

Wherever the sponsor turns for professional assistance, the trustees must conduct a thorough examination of the reputation and experience of the firm under consideration. It takes time and effort to verify past performances and corporate and individual references, yet it is a small price to pay when a multimillion dollar project and thousands of man-hours are at stake.

Selection of Legal Counsel

The sponsor will require adequate legal counsel for the development of a life-care facility. It is recommended that the sponsor not appoint attorneys as trustees for the purpose of serving as legal counsel to the board. The legal work required is too heavy and specialized to request a board member and his or her firm to perform the work as a charitable act. Also, the attorney may have to defer completing the work of the sponsor in order to meet the needs of paying clients. However, attorneys serving as trustees can perform several valuable functions. They can be very helpful in the selection of outside legal counsel. They may also be able to help the board gain consensus and improve the decision-making process. They can help the trustees recognize potential conflicts of interest or other acts that may not be in the best interest of the facility.

The development of retirement communities involves a number of legal actions and decisions. It may be prudent to choose a firm with legal specialists in areas required by the development process. The major specialty areas may include real estate and zoning, federal, state, and local taxation, finance, state and local health-care regulations, resident contracts, licensure, and landlord-tenant relationships. Often a separate, local attorney is retained to manage zoning approvals.

Design Team Selection

The largest development dollar outlays for a life-care facility are those for the actual construction of the buildings. The design process of a life-care community also requires a substantial up-front dollar commitment. The design team selection becomes even more important when you consider how significantly the marketability of the life-care facility is affected by its architecture. Operational efficiency is also of critical future importance. The sponsor should therefore search for an architectural firm with significant experience in the life-care field. I recognize that any firms wishing to practice in this field must have had at least one life-care commission. However, there are now a fair number of highly qualified firms with ten to twenty years experience in life care to their credit.

The sponsor needs to conduct an initial screening of firms to reduce the list of architectural firms to a manageable number of six to eight for interviews. The firms under consideration should be large enough to ensure that they can perform the assigned tasks within the sponsor's time frame. The sponsor will also want to know how major engineering services will be provided. If an independent engineering firm is proposed, it is important to know about their prior record of collaboration with the architectural firm, how they propose to coordinate the assignment, and what are their current workloads, to be sure there will be adequate staffing and timely response.

The sponsor should check the client references of the architectural firms in the life-care field as well as those in similar fields, such as condominium development, multifamily housing, and hospital construction. Construction firms, subcontractors, and even building officials with whom they have worked can provide helpful information.

A visit to several life-care facilities designed by competing teams can also be very revealing. A firm's work can best be evaluated by comparing a sponsor's design goals with the finished product. No development can possibly meet all the objectives of a sponsor, nor does any project operate exactly as intended. Yet feedback from previously designed life-care facilities can be helpful in gauging the sensitivity and flexibility of firms with the sponsor's programs and budgets.

The most important question is one of chemistry. Will the sponsor be comfortable with the architectural firm? Does the firm show sufficient creativity to meet budgets while keeping the overall design aesthetically pleasing and usable by older residents?

Architectural firms can and often do propose special consultants to assist with land use and landscaping, environmental design, interior design, kitchen design, and cost estimating. Any such consultants proposed by the architectural firm should also be carefully evaluated. The sponsor may choose to directly negotiate with a special consultant other than one proposed by the architectural firm. However, architectural firms may respond negatively to proposed substitutions. Sponsor-mandated marriages of architectural with engineering firms or special consultants can be very difficult arrangements in practice. If the sponsor does choose to use outside consultants, they should be retained shortly after the architectural team has been selected so that the project can evolve collaboratively with support of the lead consultant.

Some sponsors have approached the selection of architects by searching for the lowest fee arrangement. If so, as in many other areas of life, you get exactly what you pay for! The better way to go is to select the architectural firm first, and then negotiate the fee. If the sponsor cannot reach an agreement with the first firm, another finalist may be invited to submit a proposed agreement for services.

A life-care facility lends itself better to a fixed-fee arrangement than a percentage contract. Under the latter circumstance, the fees of the architectural firm are reduced if the size or cost of the project has to be reduced, which can be somewhat of a disincentive to obtaining the best in cost-efficiency.

Because the life-care community involves design and construction that is quite complex, the sponsor should contract for full architectural inspection services. In addition, the sponsor will also desire to maintain a full-time project representative on the site during most of the phases of construction (a clerk of the works, project inspector, or similar title). The sponsor will more than save the dollars assigned for these added fees and services. Sometimes this person is retained later as the permanent director of plant and property.

Selection of the Financing Team

The sponsor will need to select financial institutions and make preliminary assessments of financing requirements, terms, rates of interest, and other applicable provisions before moving too far into initial development activities. However, the financing options need to be kept open. Many indicators will undoubtedly change as long as the financial markets continue to be volatile. By making early and continuing contact, the sponsor can monitor the impact financing costs will have on financial structure and life-care resident fees. Also, if one source of financing dries up, the sponsor has the lead time to find an alternative lender without slowing or stopping other development activities.

Marketing Firm

Another member of the consulting team will be the marketing firm. As most financial institutions and several states require that 50 percent or more of the residential units of the life-care facility be reserved prior to construction, it is important to have a marketing plan early on. Deposits of 5 to 10 percent of the entry fee on the selected unit are normally required for a reservation. The marketing firm may act as marketing consultant or may be engaged to assume full responsibility for the management of all marketing activities.

Management Firm

In recent years there has been a trend toward the use of professional management firms by the sponsors of life-care facilities. Sometimes the use of professional firms has been mandated by financial institutions. Also, nonmembership sponsor organizations are inclined to use management firms unless they are managers of other life-care communities or facilities for older people. There are a number of management firms specializing in life-care facilities. Several are national corporations that manage from twenty to fifty life-care facilities. If the sponsor needs or desires a management firm, one with strong life-care experience and well-defined operating systems should be sought. There is usually no need to sign a contract with a management firm early in the development process. However, the management firm might be retained to review development decisions that may impact on future operations and to confirm estimates of operating costs and fees prior to marketing. final firm selection could be deferred until the time of construction financing.

Fund Feasibility Consultants

Many nonprofit sponsors experience difficulty obtaining funds for preconstruction development expenses. Construction financing typically takes place when 50 percent or more of the residential units have been successfully marketed. Expenses until then are usually for control of the land, consultants, attorneys, architects, and marketing. These up-front costs could total more than $2 million for a large project. One way to help constituent-related sponsors cover these costs is to conduct a capital funds campaign. The case for raising capital funds for a life-care community is a very narrow one. It is difficult to raise funds for construction of a life-care community because potential donors see the proposed fees as beyond the means of many older people, and the project will serve few, if any, needy, in the traditional sense.

Nonprofit sponsors, however, have been able to raise capital funds by pledging the proceeds to support worthy people unable to afford the stated rates. The funds, when received, are first used to cover a portion if not all of the preconstruction costs. By establishing resident rates that ignore the contributed funds in the financial structure, the original contributions are freed up for use. Then discounts can be given on the resident fees to people who meet all requirements except the ability to pay the full cost of their care. Further, a portion of these benevolent funds can be used in the future to support residents who outlive the purchasing power of their assets.

Sponsors with benevolent programs have conducted campaigns for annual giving and for assignment of bequests. A number of life-care facilities have been very successful in receiving very large gifts for their fellowship programs over the years. Gifts may also be received for specific purposes, such as a chapel, auditorium, swimming pool, or landscaping.

It should also be noted that the IRS is now scrutinizing the 501(c)(3) status of retirement homes in greater detail. My personal belief is that they will sooner or later ask all 501(c)(3) life-care communities to demonstrate their charitable nature. You may recall several years ago the government made a similar request of the Hill-Burton grant hospitals. I would think that the case against tax-exempt retirement communities without reasonable benevolent programs will have more serious results.

The sponsor should consider conducting a capital fund campaign before the beginning of construction and preferably before the marketing activities. If a campaign is contemplated, the use of fund-raising professionals with experience in the life-care field is necessary. The fund professionals would conduct a feasibility study once the case for the campaign has been developed. They would also require an outline of the facility's program to determine potential donor interest. In a typical capital fund-raising effort, 80 percent of the contributed funds come from 20 percent of the donors. The fund professionals and sponsor representatives develop a list of potential donors and then conduct personal interviews in order to estimate the fund campaign potential. On the basis of their responses, the campaign schedule and plans for organization can be established.

A limited campaign targeted toward major donors, rather than whole congregations or other constituent groupings, is usually the most successful. While pledges are typically for a three- or four-year period, often one-third of the campaign goal will be received in initial contributions.

A further advantage of the capital fund campaign is the stimulation it provides to the marketing activities of the facility. Many potential residents will require six to eight months to decide whether to reserve a unit. An initial campaign can help spread the word among the constituency that the facility is being planned, allowing interest to build up in advance of the actual marketing.

A capital fund campaign can place a heavy burden on board members. The sponsor may decide to form a separate fund campaign organization, with several board members acting as liaison between the fund campaign committee and the board. It is also helpful if the sponsor can request the commitment of the fund campaign committee for a limited time. The most effective people serving on capital campaigns are usually very busy people who are much more willing to work on a campaign if it has a four- to six-month shelf life.

Construction Management Firm Selection

A number of sponsors have engaged a construction management firm to negotiate the construction contract for a guaranteed maximum price (GMP) in lieu of seeking bids. There are several advantages to this approach. One is that as an equal partner in preconstruction planning, the construction management firm can provide constantly updated estimates of material and labor costs. The sponsor and architect can then determine if the proposed construction will be within the parameters established by the economic feasibility study. Further, the construction management firm may be able to suggest more efficient construction methods or lower-cost materials. A review team of architects, development consultants, and the construction management firm should examine the plans during each phase of design to confirm that the financial targets and program goals are being met. If the GMP approach is utilized, a further advantage is that the rate structure for the residential units can be adjusted early in the marketing process if the construction cost estimates show the need for change. Some states and financial institutions require the sponsor to execute a negotiated construction contract. Surprisingly, others require that the project be put out to bid.

If the sponsor selects a construction management firm, the construction contract will typically be negotiated at this time. The firm will usually propose a construction fee that includes overhead, profit, and contingency. It is important to evaluate these items and to know which trades the construction management firm will subcontract and which it will handle internally. We recommend that the major subcontractors (plumbing, electrical, HVAC) be included on the construction management team. While the GMP approach allows for early projections of cost from the construction management firm, the architectural team should also provide their own estimates of cost to the sponsor. The sponsor may also utilize a professional estimating firm to be sure that all estimates are reasonable.

The sponsor should insist on the right to put the project out to bid if the GMP seems unreasonably high or if there is a changing construction climate. Under these circumstances the construction firm would be entitled to a retroactive estimating fee. They still might be allowed to bid. With their knowledge of the project they could well become the low bidder.

Design Program and Guidelines

The lead consultants typically develop the design program and guidelines before the architectural team begins the master planning and schematic designs. The purpose of the design guidelines is to provide the architectural team with a "recipe book" of the sponsor's physical and operational programs for the life-care facility. The design guidelines describe the program outlined in the feasibility study, modified by events and information received before its completion.

In addition, the design guidelines should describe other required elements, such as food service, health programs, and residential living arrangements. The guidelines should also consider the special environmental design needs of older people. Each proposed space is then described in detail in a space program, including dimensions of each space or area calculation, intended use, and relationship to other spaces. The design guidelines are then reviewed and approved by the sponsor.

Site Selection

To the traditional three most important principles for selection of real estate, the site selection for a life-care community needs to add three more—again: location, location, and location! Heightened competition both within the field and from indirectly competitive housing and living arrangements outside the field—condominium and leisure communities—has underlined the importance of appropriate site selection. The site will have to be carefully located, preferably close to the residential neighborhoods where the bulk of the future residents are expected to come from and close to shopping and the other amenities of the community. The safety and security of the neighborhood will be of concern, as will access from the facility to the amenities of the community by automobile as well as public transportation. Accessibility to the social, recreational, worship, and business centers of the community is very important for the residents to maintain continuity with the identifying and supportive elements of their lives. Access to physicians' offices and the local hospitals is also important, though a location immediately adjoining a hospital is often not attractive for the retirement community.

When speaking on this topic once, I titled one subsection "Gifts of Land and Other Terrible Problems." Nonprofit organizations are often offered sites of land for development of life-care communities. Like some other gifts, they should be evaluated very carefully for their suitability for development. For this reason, the architectural team and the lead consultant should assist the sponsor in evaluating the site. A gift of land may seem to be a bargain, but in our experience it may cost many times its appraised value for lack of utility lines and hookups, site and grading problems, rezoning issues, and other environmental issues.

It is sometimes hard for organizations to realize that the nature of a life-care community, providing there is an adequate market, means that this type of utilization of a site will represent the highest and best use of the property for any type of residential purpose. Therefore, the nonprofit organization can budget an amount per acre higher than what might otherwise be expected in the community for the right piece of land.

The value of the land is related to zoning; that is, to the number of residential and nursing units that can be developed on the site. The size of the site should be neither too large, so as to increase the land cost per unit beyond 8 to 10 percent of the total construction cost, nor so small as to preclude the possibility of expansion at some future date.

The size of the site should be more than adequate for the number of residential, nursing, public, and support elements described in the feasibility study. A number of successful life-care facilities have constructed large additions within 5 to 10 years after opening. Most life-care facilities are now being constructed in phases to lower their financial exposure. This means that a site allowing for significant future expansion is even more desirable.

The sponsor may defer site selection until a market analysis and feasibility study has been completed. If so, the study can pinpoint the sectors of the community most attractive for the location of the new facility. With that information in hand, the sponsor can retain land acquisition specialists or other real estate professionals to locate and negotiate for a specific site that meets the sponsor's requirements.

The architectural team and the lead consultants should evaluate the suitability of any proposed site prior to purchase. Of special concern are accessibility, potential for construction, zoning concerns, financial impacts, and marketability.

Because the life-care community will require 50 percent or more presale reservations, the time between property acquisition and construction will be lengthy. This fact complicates any potential deferment of payment for the land until construction financing is in place. An option may be able tie up the property until it is rezoned, but marketing and architectural activities will take much more time. If the property must be purchased at the end of a three- to six-month option period, the seller may be willing to finance the purchase for the sponsor until the construction loan is negotiated.

The legal arrangements with the seller of the property should be carefully tailored to the life-care model. Negotiations should work for potential cancellation of the option or sales agreement under certain conditions, including denial of zoning approvals or of the certificates of need for nursing beds. With acquisition of site control, the initial development activities can be undertaken. (See figure 7–2).

Project Director Selection

A project director or manager should be retained for the project when the site is secured. This position might also be described as the facility adminis-

Figure 7–2
Typical Development Schedule of a Continuing-Care Retirement Community: Initial Development Activities

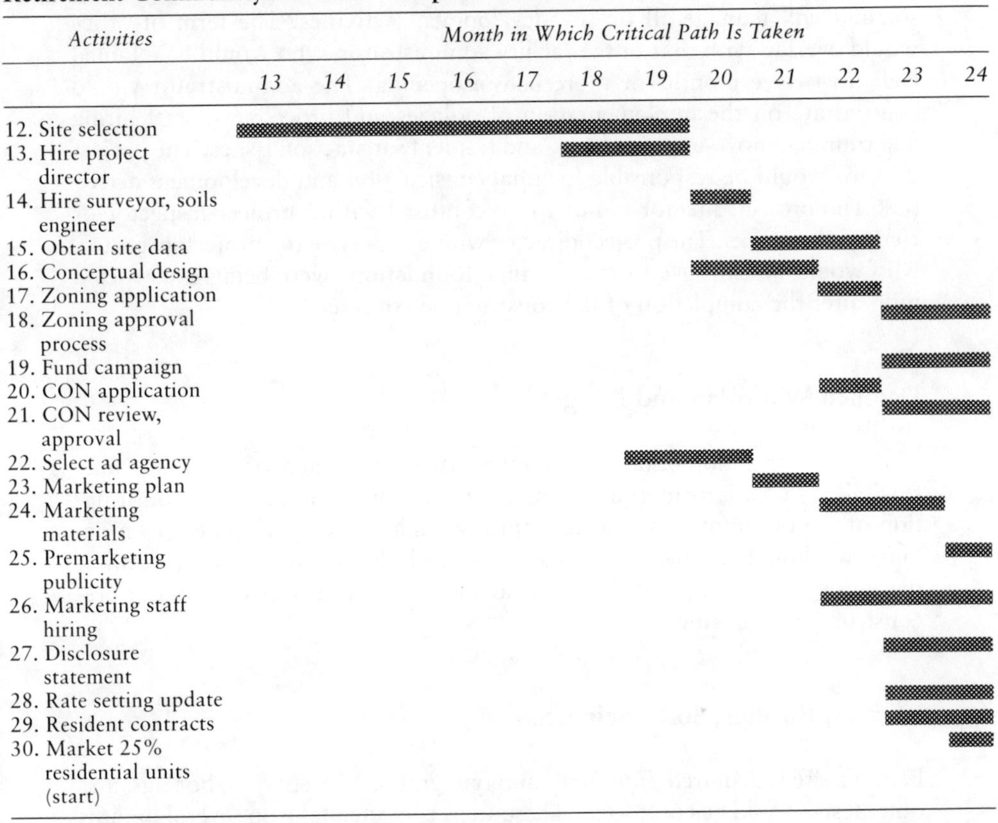

Activities	*Month in Which Critical Path Is Taken*											
	13	*14*	*15*	*16*	*17*	*18*	*19*	*20*	*21*	*22*	*23*	*24*
12. Site selection												
13. Hire project director												
14. Hire surveyor, soils engineer												
15. Obtain site data												
16. Conceptual design												
17. Zoning application												
18. Zoning approval process												
19. Fund campaign												
20. CON application												
21. CON review, approval												
22. Select ad agency												
23. Marketing plan												
24. Marketing materials												
25. Premarketing publicity												
26. Marketing staff hiring												
27. Disclosure statement												
28. Rate setting update												
29. Resident contracts												
30. Market 25% residential units (start)												

trator for the development period. Traditionally, many sponsors have chosen experienced life-care facility administrators to fill this role. While some have performed admirably, others with outstanding management backgrounds have had difficulty with the development environment.

Administrators of life-care facilities are hired to be effective leaders of staff and residents and deliberate and thoughtful conservators of the resources of the sponsor. However, the quick, often intuitive, and even risky decision making required in development can be almost the antithesis of the average administrator's training and experience. The conservator-manager can find development exasperating and exhausting; the developer-manager often finds administration frustrating and boring.

To obtain the best of both worlds, we typically propose that the lead consultant hire and supervise the project director through the entire development period. He or she will be the professional representative of the sponsor and will manage all on-site development activities. The term of office would overlap with that of the facility administrator, who would be retained eight to twelve months or more before opening. The administrator would concentrate on the implementation of policies and procedures, staff hiring and training, move-in procedures, and resident satisfaction issues. The project director would be responsible for final construction and development activities. The project director is not to be confused with a project inspector or clerk of the works. The project director would supervise the project inspector, who would be employed from the time foundations were being constructed until after the completion of the construction contract.

Detailed Workplan and Budgets

With the information obtained from the initial market analysis and economic feasibility study, information on estimates of acquisition of a site, confirmation of the program fees, and unit turnover allow the development of a detailed workplan and budgets. This should include the projection in detail of the initial cash flows and the needs as mentioned previously to secure preconstruction financing sources.

Surveys, Borings, Soil Engineers

Before a site is acquired, boundary and typographic site surveys, borings, and other tests should be completed. These steps can often take up several months early in the planning process. High priority should be given to obtaining complete information and to satisfying environmental requirements.

Conceptual Design

When a specific site has been selected for consideration, the architects will develop a conceptual design reflecting the design guidelines. The design concept will show how the footprints of future buildings can fit on the site, allowing for natural features and environmental considerations.

This design stage does not have the degree of detail that the later stages will require. However, it does set the course for subsequent phases and should be reviewed by the sponsor and consultants carefully. Alternative concepts should be sketched out in consideration of the site, and the architectural team may need to develop conceptual designs for several sites before one is actually acquired. The contractural arrangements with the architectural firm should take this possibility into account.

Zoning Applications and the Approval Process

Conceptual designs must be complete to meet the requirements of most zoning applications. The sponsor and legal counsel should review the zoning process with local officials well in advance of site acquisition. Many jurisdictions do not have zoning ordinances in place that apply to a life-care facility. In some instances it may be necessary for the sponsor's representatives to propose changes to the zoning ordinances or bylaws to allow for a specific definition and zoning classification of a life-care facility. Nonprofit organizations sometimes overestimate their ability to obtain zoning approvals in spite of serious opposition from community leaders and neighboring property owners. Potentially negative neighbors and officials need to be fully apprised of the plans and given the opportunity to express their objections well before any public hearing.

In recent years, sponsors have often had to agree to pay property taxes or a service charge instead of taxes, despite their tax-exempt and charitable nature, in order to obtain zoning. Initial feasibility studies and all subsequent financial projections need to reflect these potential taxes or fees.

Certificate of Need Application and Approval

The typical life-care facility needs to develop a nursing unit at the same time as its residential units and common areas. Although some sponsors wish to defer the nursing unit's construction to reduce initial costs, most find the lack of an on-campus nursing unit impedes successful marketing. Further, even though all initial residents will have been admitted in reasonable good health, a number will require either short-term or long-term nursing care within the first year of residency.

Construction and operation of the nursing unit will require a certificate of need (CON) under most circumstances. In most states, applications are now handled at the state government level. The application will require financial projections for overall facility construction and operations and for the nursing unit as well. The application will require conceptual architectural plans of the unit, and in most states the sponsor will have to justify the need for new nursing beds in the health district. Often control of a site, with zoning approvals, must be demonstrated.

The life-care concept has not always been fully understood by health planning officials. The construction costs projected for the average life-care nursing bed usually are much higher than those of free-standing nursing facilities. Obtaining a CON usually requires a state staff review to determine whether the application is complete. Public hearings are then held, and if the application is believed to meet the criteria for determining bed need, the CON is granted by the appropriate state agency board and commissioner.

A number of states are attempting to control nursing-care costs of Medicaid programs by limiting the supply of nursing beds. The numbers of beds actually needed in some jurisdictions are much more than the need projected by the state. Because of these difficulties, some sponsors have acquired older nursing homes where, in some states, those beds can be legally transferred to the operations of the new owner. In still other situations, the sponsor has had to arrange with nearby nursing-home owners for coverage until a bed allocation is available for the life-care facility. Still others have developed their home health-care services to provide a high level of nursing care to residents in independent living units. Others have used personal care or assisted living units to provide nursing care where a state has allowed bedfast care in these units.

A number of states allow life-care facilities to develop nursing beds without having to meet the CON requirements. However, the sponsor may not use the beds authorized under this provision for direct admissions of nursing patients from the community. Some states make provision for direct admissions for the first several years of operations. The sponsor will need to project nursing bed utilization by residents and the financial impact of a closed nursing unit before constructing beds under this provision.

Marketing Activities[a]

The schedule of major marketing tasks should be developed so that the activities will begin shortly after successful zoning of the property. (See figure 7–3). The major activities of marketing include the selection of the ad agency, development of the marketing plan, development of the major marketing and collateral materials, premarketing publicity, hiring of the marketing staff, and the marketing office opening. Once the property is rezoned, marketing will be critical to keeping the project on schedule.

The sponsor will need three other tasks completed before marketing can begin. First, a number of states require that a sponsor file a disclosure statement. Typically they require a full description of the sponsor, the facility, the plan of operations, and financial statements. In addition, some states review all promotional materials and resident contract forms as well.

Second, as mentioned previously, the sponsor, consultants, and legal

---

[a]Refer to the chapters in this book on marketing for more detail.

Figure 7–3
Typical Development Schedule of a Continuing-Care Retirement Community: Preparing for Construction

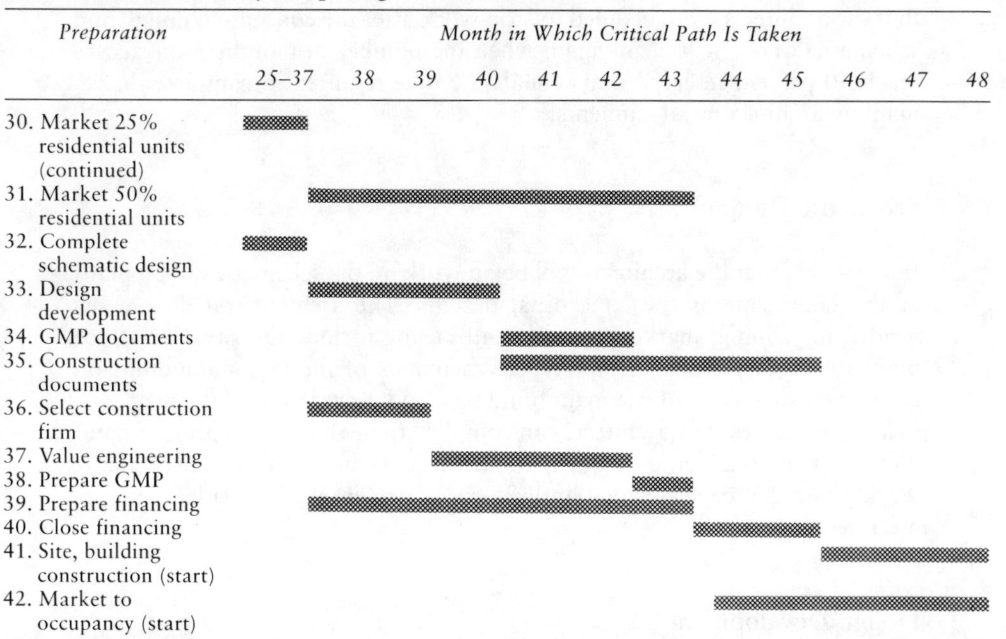

counsel will need to complete the resident contract. The contracts should cover the major contigencies in life-care living arrangements and allow the sponsor to make reasonable changes to the facility program without revising contracts.

Third, the financial prospectus needs to be reviewed and updated to be sure that the rate structures to be marketed are sufficient to meet all costs of operations, health-care liabilities, and debt service. The rates in a life-care facility need to be actuarial-based, and projections based on the experiences of other facilities will have to be used initially for validation. An actuarial study for a new life-care facility should be conducted upon completion, or earlier if the age characteristics of the new residents vary markedly from the projections.

Schedules

Schedules for the development of a facility change almost daily. The project director must factor-in zoning, CON submissions, hearing dates, and construction cost estimates in order to project the timing of the next steps. Sponsors are often surprised that the marketing pace is on the critical path rather than the architectural design activities. The schedule will also usually show that the architects are scheduled to stop work after the conceptual design and schematics. They will begin again when the number of months projected to reach 50 percent reserved units equals the time required to complete the remaining architectural documents.

Schematic Design

It is possible that the architects will begin work on the schematic design plans at the same time as the conceptual designs. The architectural documents needed for zoning, marketing, and fund-raising include the site plan, floor plans of major residential unit type, schematics of the major buildings on each level, elevations of the main buildings, and a rendering of the proposed facility structures. The architects can complete these documents prior to completion of the schematic designs. Conceivably, completion of the schematic work phase can be suspended until 25 to 30 percent of the residential units are reserved.

Design Development

The level of detail in the facility design is increased at the design development stage. At its completion, the consultants and sponsor should have a very good idea of the final architectural and engineering designs. The architectural firm will proceed immediately into the final construction drawings and specifications.

GMP Documents

The architectural firm will develop the contract documents to permit preparation of a guaranteed maximum price (GMP) by the construction management firm if engaged or by a selected contractor. As stated previously, the GMP approach provides early projection of construction costs.

Construction Documents

If the sponsor is going to receive bids, the architect must go further with the work, the construction plans and specifications will need to be completed, and a bid package will need to be developed. It is not recommended that the sponsor choose what is known as fast-track construction. The complexity of a life-care facility and the more stringent building codes that generally apply, as well as the length of time required for premarketing, will most often negate the advantages of beginning construction before all plans are complete and approved.

Selection of the Construction Firm

In order to bid the project, a screening of construction firms will be necessary. The same steps will apply to the selection of a construction management firm. The sponsor will require a firm qualified to handle multimillion-dollar projects. The architects usually handle the bid selection process and make recommendations to the sponsor whether to accept the lowest bid.

Preparation of Financing Documents

Lenders require financial feasibility and market demand studies, usually conducted by a major accounting firm and recognized market research firm, prior to the financing of the project. The sponsor needs to schedule this work far enough in advance so that it is completed in the same time frame as the awarding of the construction contract.

Financial Closing

Final financial closing on the construction loan can occur when all major elements are in place. These usually include architectural plans and specifications, the financial feasibility and market demand study, the construction contract, and the major financing documents. The construction phase can now begin.

Site and Building Construction

In some circumstances the sponsor needs to begin construction to satisfy land purchase, obtain zoning, or obtain CON approvals before the financial closing. Some sponsors have signed a separate agreement with the construction firm for clearing and grading to meet the pertinent requirements. The construction period can run from fifteen to twenty-seven months for the typical life-care community, depending on the size, type of construction, weather

Figure 7–4
Typical Development Schedule of a Continuing-Care Retirement Community: Preparing for Operations

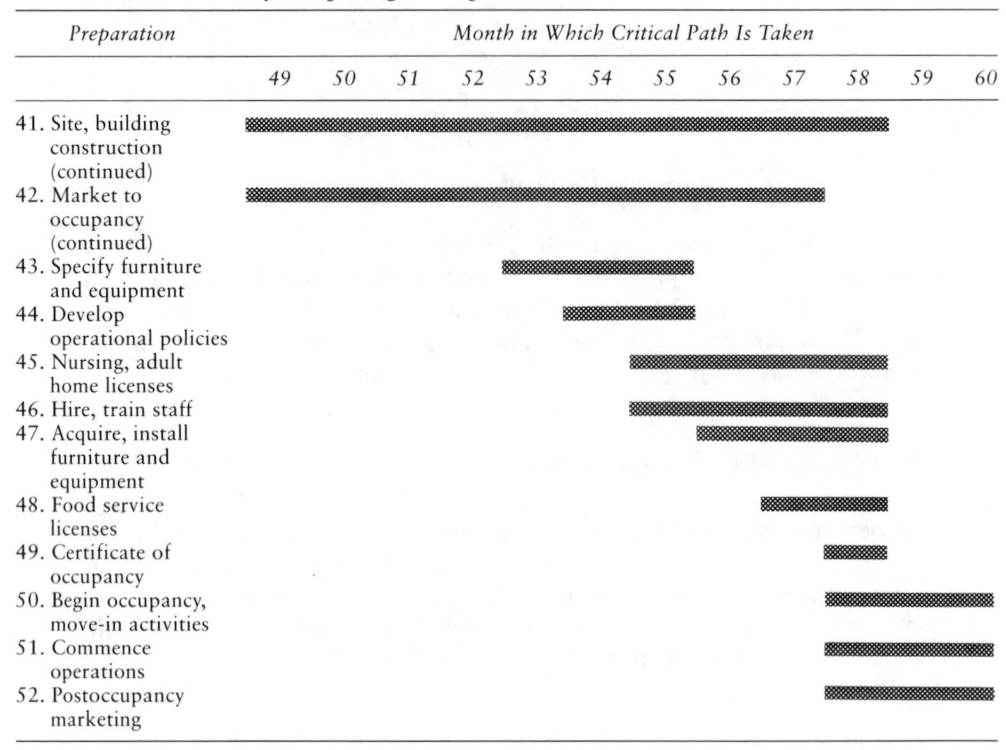

conditions, and labor disputes. (See figure 7–4). The clerk of the works will monitor all construction activities, alerting the project director, architects, and sponsor to poor workmanship or deviations from the plans and specifications. Clearly defined communication channels between all parties will help avoid serious construction difficulties.

Tasks During the Construction Period

Marketing activities continue unabated during the construction period. The sponsor may authorize the construction firm to complete some sample units and other spaces for marketing purposes prior to the facility opening.

Once the contract plans and specifications are complete, the consultants can develop the final furnishings and movable equipment lists for bid. Because styles and models of many types of furnishings change annually, it makes little sense to make selections more than a year before opening. Some consideration should be given to custom design when large orders of specific items such as carpet or dining room seating are required. Commercial grade furnishings and equipment should be specified where possible for longer wear, providing the choices are noninstitutional in design and comfort.

Preparation of operating policies by the sponsor, development consultants, management firm, or future CEO takes place at the beginning of the marketing period to be sure resident contracts accurately reflect the intentions of the sponsor. Finalization of all major policies should be completed during the construction period so that the administrator and key staff members can develop the operating procedures well in advance of opening.

The sponsor will hire and bring on site the key management staff, beginning with the administrator, at least eight months and preferably twelve months or more before opening. Adequate lead time should be projected for advertising, screening, interviewing, and hiring of new personnel.

The schedule will also allow for the time it will take to obtain the necessary inspections and licenses. State and local regulations will normally require final building inspections for the construction and licensure of retirement housing, personal care, and food service components in the facility. Building, fire, and safety inspections are a dreaded but necessary part of the process. The more information provided and interpretations asked of the various officials ahead of time may (only may!) help the inspections go a little smoother.

Occupancy and the Beginning of Operations

Residents are usually allowed to move in and operations begin once the certificate of occupancy is obtained. Final construction items, such as punch lists, warranties, and operating manuals should be completed or put in the hands of the sponsor if still outstanding.

The marketing of uncommitted residential units may still continue after opening. If so, some adjustments in locations and schedules for the marketing staff may be required. Once all units have been committed, the marketing staff can be reduced, often to a single person who can also function as the admissions officer. But, of course, marketing never stops.

The opening months of a life-care facility usually involve a difficult shakedown period. The residents and staff are discovering the advantages and limitations of the new accommodations—and perhaps of each other as well! The value of thoughtful planning and scheduling should be readily apparent throughout this period. It is always hoped that good planning for development will shorten the shakedown period and that everyone will be pleased with the final results.

> One should keep in mind that although the novice may find the preceding task lists mind boggling, the complexities will sort themselves out after living through even one project and agonizing over individual items for weeks or months at a time. Each piece of the puzzle becomes identifiable and distinct, if not always wholly understandable. The more times one works through the process, the more ingrained each step becomes, at the same time becoming endowed with a rich complexity of variations since each project will have deviated from the norm in a number of ways. Further, each project will evolve through the process in its own unique sequence of tasks, surprises, set-backs and shortcuts, varying from the sequence outlined above. This is not necessarily a negative. In fact, many of us will say "Viva la difference"!
>
> —Editors

8
Financing Life Care and Increasing Its Affordability

Robert B. Haldeman, M.S.S.W., J.D.

This chapter provides clear definitions and explanations of complex financial terms and concepts. It should help even an experienced developer or sponsor to identify and clarify issues relating to development, construction financing, permanent financing, investor conditions, how to make a project attractive to investors or lenders, life care insurance (see also Chapter 18), various types of resident contracts, and risks at various phases of a project. Affordability, too rarely addressed in connection with life care, is addressed here.

—Editors

Life care is assumed in this chapter to refer to a program of residential living services, including housekeeping, home maintenance, transportation, and food service; and health care, including ambulatory care, home care, assisted living, nursing care, case management of hospital care, physician visits, other medical specialists, surgical treatment, and pharmaceutical services. The long-term assisted living and nursing care is assumed to be funded on a risk-pool basis initially by people capable of independent living and later, as the group ages, by those living independently and those receiving long-term care. Funding of the risk pool may be through lump-sum prepayments and periodic charges only, but it is assumed to involve the accumulation of reserves through a portion of the initial charges to offset increased utilization by group members as the group ages.

The financing of life care involves locating capital to: (1) construct physical facilities, purchase equipment, and fund start-up working capital; and (2) fund the future cost of long-term care at home, in assisted-living or personal-care units, and in nursing-care facilities.[1] The first funding category is referred to in this chapter as *capital funding;* the second as *operation funding*. Capital funding consists of: (a) equity investments (i.e., money invested in exchange for a share of the increase in value of the enterprise); and (b) debt investment (i.e., money invested in exchange for a specified and limited return from the enterprise for a specified term). The second category, operation funding, is typically derived from revenues generated by the enterprise in the form of user charges, investment earnings, and receipts from third-party government and private insurers. An understanding of the financing of life care and efforts to increase its affordability requires analysis of capital funding and operation funding.

Capital Funding

Special Risk Factors

The funding of capital for life-care facilities is affected by several special characteristics that are currently viewed by capital sources as creating a higher than normal investment risk. These characteristics include:

Special or dedicated use. Life-care facilities include physical improvements that make an adaptation or change in use of the project uneconomical or unlikely. Hotel financings faced this problem as recently as the early 1960s. A broad acquisition market does not exist for life-care projects. As a result, the fair market value upon resale for this specific purpose is not predictable.

Retail consumer market-dependent. In comparison to a single tenant office building developed for a specific client (i.e., bank building), a life-care project requires marketing to a significant number of individuals. Since in many states deposits made by future residents are fully refundable until occupancy,[2] deposits at the start of construction do not bind the consumer to pay his or her fee to the enterprise when the project is completed. This dependence on a fluctuating retail market substantially increases the risk to the investor.

Development issue complexity. In addition to the government approvals typically required for single-use, general-category projects (e.g., office buildings, market-rate apartments, and shopping centers), life-care facilities involve governmental approvals certifying need for health-care facility construction, licensing of the facilities when constructed, and registration for the sale of life-care contracts.

Integration of several complex operating businesses. Life care involves the business of residential services, food service, health-care administration, and insurance. Not only do each of these businesses require special management skills, they also cut across the traditional divisions of capital investor underwriting staff. Consequently, no single contact point exists for orienting lender representatives; instead, representatives from several lender departments must be involved to obtain approval for capital commitments.

Tax law implications. Life-care investments involve analysis of real-estate–related tax laws for treatment of depreciation, preconstruction costs, and start-up losses. They also are affected by resident health-care deductions, gift loan and imputed interest restraints, rules governing losses and repurchase options between taxable and nontaxable entities, and taxation of insurance and self-insurance entities.

Securities laws, land sales acts, and laws governing condominium and cooperative forms of ownership. Elsewhere in this paper, we describe alternate forms of ownership for interests in life-care facilities. Use of such ownership forms may require compliance with consumer protection laws for residents and disclosure laws designed to protect investors.

The Phases of Capital Funding

Capital funding is usually divided into three distinct phases: the preconstruction period; the construction period; and the operation period. In a typical life-care project, activities in each period involve the following:

1. Preconstruction period (twelve months to eighty-four months):
   a. Definition of sponsorship and program design;
   b. Site selection and control;
   c. Public approvals (zoning, certification of need, water and sewer allocation, etc.);
   d. Market analysis testing and presales; and
   e. Design, engineering, and permitting.
2. Construction (twelve to twenty-four months):
   a. Building construction and equipment purchase;
   b. Marketing; and
   c. Preopening activities (staff inspections for occupancy licensing and certification by third-party reimbursement sources.
3. Operation (continuous—minimum 20-year estimate for the life-care services for the initial resident population):
   a. Completed marketing;
   b. Full staffing; and
   c. Programs, financial, and asset management.

The Impact of Alternate Ownership Forms

Ownership forms directly affect the capitalization alternatives available for life-care facilities. Ownership forms currently being utilized include the following:

Nonprofit sponsor ownership. A corporation qualified as exempt from federal income taxation under Section 501(c)(3) of the Internal Revenue Code of 1986 (the "Code"), owns and operates the project. Preconstruction funds may be advanced by a coventure developer to be repaid at construction loan closing or completion of construction out of entrance fees, or such funds may be available through donations.[3]

For-profit ownership/lease to not-for-profit sponsor. The partnership or corporation acquires and develops the real estate for lease to the not-for-profit entity, which operates the life-care program and may have a right to acquire the project on a leveraged buy-out basis at the end of a reasonable holding period.[4]

Condominium ownership. The sponsor develops the project and sells individual units to the residents, typically retaining ownership in the special common areas (such as the assisted-living, nursing-care, and food-service areas) and a sufficient number of units to maintain control of the condominium.[5]

Cooperative ownership. The sponsor develops the project and either sells shares in the cooperative to each resident or sells the project to the cooperative as a whole, with individuals acquiring shares in the cooperative. Retention of property interests in the special common areas may be effected by (a) defining certain property interests as separate from the cooperative through use of a ground lease or (b) the construction of health facilities in a separate structure owned by the sponsor.[6]

General Principles Governing Capital Investment in Life-Care Projects

Several general principles apply to all three phases of capital investment.

1. The cost to the life-care sponsor for investment capital is reduced as investor risk is reduced (i.e., the investor is willing to accept a lower yield where the risk is lower). The inverse principle is true, except that a level of risk can be reached for each investor at which no potential yield is worth the risk. The inability to comprehend or quantify a risk will usually result in this latter conclusion.
2. In a properly designed project, the risk of investment decreases as the project progresses through each phase.
3. The cost of financing also is determined by:
   a. The available capital in all investment markets;
   b. The availability of capital specifically for life care;

c. The cost of capital to the investor; the source of that capital; the terms under which the investor has obtained it; and the tax paid by the investor on the investment yield;[7]
d. The risk and return associated with the specific life-care project as compared with other life-care projects being evaluated by the investor;
e. The availability of non-life-care investments compared on yield, risk, complexity, and term;
f. The aggressiveness with which other investors are pursuing the project or life-care projects in general;
g. The investor expectation of future interest or yield over the project investment period;
h. The investor reinvestment risk at the end of the investment term; and
i. The certainty of the investment term.

4. Risk is perceived by the investor to be reduced as investor control is increased.
5. Secondary rewards to the investor such as new accounts and other product placement opportunities can affect the investor's decision.
6. Risk is reduced by the availability of collateral with readily determined fair market value and an immediate resale market; risk is increased to the extent the value of collateral and its resale market are uncertain.[8]
7. Risk can be reduced through the use of third-party guarantees that may cost less than the difference in investment yield without such a guarantee.[9]

Yield

The calculation of return to the capital investor should include all of the following:

1. Annual interest,[10] whether fixed or variable[11];
2. Amounts paid initially (points) treated as interest rate equivalents and deductions from the principal amount of the loan (original issue discount) as a similar expense;
3. Annual administrative costs of the lender paid by the borrower;
4. All consultant reports (appraisals, market studies, financial feasibility studies, inspection fees, special audits, etc.) required by the lender;
5. Negative arbitrage[12]; and
6. Credit guarantee fees.[13]

Risks, Conditions, Capital Market Segments, and Pricing Applicable to Each Phase of Capital Funding

Each of the phases of capital funding entails special risks and rewards that attract segments of the capital funding market and repel others. The risks are controlled and limited by the imposition of conditions and compensated for in the pricing. An overview of these factors by phase follows below.

1. The Preconstruction Phase.
   a. Special Risks:
      i. The denial of required public approvals—any one of which may be fatal to development effort and beyond the control of the project;
      ii. Failure to obtain a favorable market response—this can be affected by inadequate market analysis, inadequate administration of marketing, and competition;
      iii. Undercapitalization which results in project failure even though the project might otherwise be successful;
      iv. Changes in the regulatory environment;
      v. Community opposition engendered in opposition to public approvals and litigation over unforeseen environmental issues;
      vi. Design constraints from governmental units or market conditions that make construction of the facility impractical within economic feasibility constraints; and
      vii. Inability to obtain construction or permanent financing because of project design, general economic conditions, inadequate market, etc.[14]
   b. Typical Investor Conditions: Preconstruction capital will be conditioned upon the capital source being convinced that the development entity is knowledgeable, well-managed, and experienced. It will be invested only where preliminary data indicates that the risk factors can be addressed with a likelihood of success. Those contributing capital as passive investors[15] will require:
      i. Capital investment by the development entity or capital risk by it in the form of guarantees and deferred fees;
      ii. Rights to substitute the developer entity if the project does not achieve results in a timely fashion;
      iii. Preliminary assurances of market, public approvals, and site control; and
      iv. The right to discontinue further advances if development targets are not achieved.
   c. Capital Market Participants: As previously noted, the principal investors at this stage are:

i. Sophisticated individual investors with substantial resources;
ii. Institutional investors, including:
  (a) Insurance companies;
  (b) Manufacturing and retail sales companies desiring to diversify into real estate equity holdings; and
  (c) Savings and loan associations[16].
iii. Development firms using stock equity to fund preconstruction expenses;
iv. Equity-oriented real estate investment trusts (REITs)[17]; and
v. Master limited partnerships (MLPs)[18].

It should be noted that many lifetime care facilities were initiated through the use of special bequests of endowments. To the extent that such resources can be located, substantial savings can be obtained for the project.[19]

d. Pricing: An equity interest is designed to permit the investor to participate in the appreciation in value of the project. The substantially higher risk associated with the initial development equity investment requires a minimum expected return materially in excess of a return on debt. In addition, since the initial return on development equity is likely to be deferred for several years, a higher cash-on-cash yield in the years a return is received will be required to produce an equivalent present value[20] return. In an interest rate climate of long-term rates at 10 to 12 percent, the range of after-tax returns on equity will be 10 to 18.5 percent for domestic investors, assuming that most of the development issues are resolved when the investment is made. Earlier returns on investments are likely to be in the 20 to 25 percent range. Each of these returns is typically projected over a minimum of five years from the year in which the initial return is paid.

2. The Construction Phase.
  a. Special Risks:
    i. Unforeseen construction problems (e.g., strikes, weather, casualties such as fire or collapse, soil problems, poor construction management, cost over-runs, faulty work);
    ii. Market changes (e.g., failure to complete marketing, the emergence of new competition);
    iii. Regulatory changes; and
    iv. Failure to obtain permanent financing.
  b. Typical Investor Conditions:
    i. Contracts for design and construction in place with acceptable design drawings, fixed or guaranteed construction cost and reasonable contingency funds within the economic constraints of the market;

ii. Market demonstration through primary and secondary market studies, substantial life-care contract deposits, and continued market achievement;
iii. Adequate credit assurance through presales, contractor guarantees, surety payment, and performance bonds and possibly developer/sponsor guarantees;
iv. Evidence of the adequacy and availability of zoning, building permits, water and sewer, environmental permits, and health-care facility permits;
v. A sound operating plan, including actuarial projections for funding of the life-care obligations or commitments for commercial insurance covering this liability;
vi. Source of permanent financing[21]; and
vii. Continuous inspection by the lender of construction progress and approval of all periodic loan draws.

c. Capital Market Participants: The principal sources of construction loan financing are:
   i. Commercial banks in the local area or national-international banks participating with a local lender[22];
   ii. Savings and loan associations;
   iii. Trustee-held funds produced through the sale of retail tax-exempt or taxable notes or bonds[23];
   iv. Specialized credit companies, typically subsidiaries of manufacturing or retail sales companies used to diversify risk;
   v. Insurance companies[24]; and
   vi. Pension funds.[25]

d. Pricing: Construction loans are short-term debt instruments typically priced on the basis of: the lender's cost of capital; the cost of loan administration; and a profit margin based on the estimated project risk. A typical mark-up for the cost of loan administration and the profit margin will be in the range of 2 to 3.5 percent. Because the lenders' borrowing rate may fluctuate with the interest rate offered to their best customers (the prime rate), construction loans are often pegged to some percentage rate above prime. Where retail bonds are used to fund construction and permanent financing, the sponsor may be able to obtain a fixed interest rate for both construction and permanent financing in a single borrowing. Initial fees for planning, committing to, and making a conventional construction loan range from 1 to 4 percent. A few lenders charge a review fee only and take the loan at par. The sale of retail bonds or notes without credit guarantees will require payment of points in the range of 2.5 to 8 percent, depending on market conditions, project strength, and investment banker leverage.[26]

3. The Permanent Funding Phase.
   a. Special Risks:
      i. Market: Failure to obtain full occupancy of the project after completion;
      ii. Management: Failure to establish required operating systems and failure to efficiently and effectively handle daily operations;
      iii. Financial instability: Inability to maintain fees and charges at levels that will maintain debt service payments and properly fund all operating liabilities, including the obligation for lifetime care.[27] This risk is directly affected by the emergence of competitive projects, unusual costs of facility maintenance and replacement; economic trends and events affecting the costs of goods and services; the value of income and assets of existing and future residents; the character of the area surrounding the specific project; and the value of income generated from the project based on changes in federal, state, and local taxes; and
      iv. Regulatory changes: Governmental intervention that makes continued operation uneconomical or impractical.
   b. Typical Investor Conditions:
      i. Market: In addition to satisfactory market studies, most permanent lenders will require a significant level of presales and occupancy before permanent funding.
      ii. Management: Lenders will require approval of the management arrangement and the key executive, particularly where the sponsor is a start-up nonprofit entity; and
      iii. Financial reporting and covenants: The desire of the permanent lender is to avoid operating trends that are likely to result in financial defaults or impairment in the resale value of the project. Typically, these covenants will require maintenance of a surplus of operating revenues over operating expenses; cash receipts producing net revenues in excess of debt service by 10 to 40 percent of debt service by the third or fourth year of project operations and maintenance of reserves as required by actuarial-based financial projection.
   c. Capital Market Participants:
      i. Commercial banks: The maximum loan term for domestic or international commercial banks will typically be seven to ten years. Such loans will be made on a very selective basis and often matched with a borrowing by the bank from another capital source. This approach will often limit the right of the sponsor to prepay or require substantial prepayment penalties;
      ii. Savings and loans associations: The terms of loans from such entities are similar to those for commercial banks, although they

previously were substantially longer when passbook savings were thought to be a stable source of capital;

iii. Insurance companies: Because premium reserves are maintained for an extended period of time, insurance companies are a major source of permanent financing;

iv. Mortgage REITs: REITs obtain funds through the sale of stock on a retail basis and can offer terms of ten years or longer; and

v. Pension funds: Like insurance companies, many of the obligations of a pension fund are deferred to future years with real estate mortgage investments constituting a significant portion of the investment portfolios of large pension funds.

d. Pricing: Permanent lenders commit to a long-term investment of capital. They may provide a fixed interest rate for the full term or provide for resetting the interest rate on a periodic basis throughout the term. As in construction lending; the rate required is tied in part to the cost of funds to the lender. In permanent loans, however, the rate is also significantly affected by the expected yields in the marketplace over the term of the loan. Interest rate volatility has substantially increased in the last twenty years, making permanent lenders much more cautious about fixed rate loans. Typically, the longer the loan term, the higher the investment yield risk to the lenders because of the increased likelihood of general changes in economic conditions, circumstances affecting the project, and possibility that the fixed rate will become unattractive in the future interest rate market. Initial points for permanent loans range from 0 to 4.5 percent, depending on project risk, the interest rate, and current market conditions (particularly lender appetite).

Operation Funding

The special issues for operation funding in life-care facilities relate to funding of the future health-care liabilities of the sponsor.[28] The following is a discussion of the major alternatives emerging for the funding of health-care liabilities.

Self-Insurance

Under this scenario, the sponsor assumes the risk of funding the long-term care liabilities out of entrance fee receipts and periodic charges. Emerging state laws are beginning to require actuarial reviews[29] demonstrating that, on the basis of reasonable assumptions, the sponsor will have adequate resources to fund the future liabilities for residents currently under contract and for future residents. Major elements affecting the adequacy of such self-insurance arrangements are:

1. Clearly established eligibility criteria and criteria governing transfer to personal care and nursing care to match probable care needs to the estimated utilization experience incorporated in the projections.
2. Contractual provisions that provide economic disincentives for inappropriate utilization of self-insurance risks.
3. Policies that match investment liquidity and yields to the self-insurance payment obligations.
4. Institution of procedures providing for regular re-evaluation of the adequacy for funding based on changes in cost, investment rates, utilization, and covered services (if applicable).
5. Contractual provisions that permit adjustments in the periodic charges to reflect utilization experience, expense inflation, and changes in investment performance of reserve funds.
6. Changes in tax law or governmental regulations that can adversely affect the sponsor's capacity to fund the self-insurance obligations.

Commercial Insurance

All or a portion of the life-care liabilities can be transferred to a commercial insurer through either group insurance[30] or individual indemnity policies in which the individual assigns the benefits paid to the sponsor. In order for the insurer's liability to match that assumed by the sponsor under a full life-care contract, such policies must contain the following provisions:

1. Guaranteed renewability: An agreement that as long as the premiums are paid, the insurance remains in force. Under such a contract, premiums are subject to change, depending on cost, inflation, investment yields, administrative costs, and utilization.
2. Eligibility criteria and transfer criteria that match those of the sponsor.
3. Financial strength and claims-paying capacity of the insurer satisfactory to ensure the sponsor of timely payment under the policy.
4. Benefit provisions that fit the assumptions of the sponsor in its financial projections.

Commercial insurance can be structured to offset only a portion of the liability of the sponsor. In this instance, the residual sponsor liabilities will be affected by the issues described under the self-insurance system.

Government Insurance

At the current time, the only government program applicable to long-term care is Medicaid, a program for which income and asset qualification applies (i.e., individuals above a specified income and asset level are ineligible). Life care was originally structured to help people with high and moderate incomes avoid the Medicaid spend-down of assets by spreading the catastrophic cost among the community of insureds. A substantial number of continuing-care facilities operating on an *a la carte* basis provide nursing care funded through Medicaid.

A limited amount of rehabilitative nursing care is provided through Medicare. Additional proposals have been made to provide a government long-term care insurance policy for older people by expanding Medicare. The beginning emergence of commercial long-term care insurance policies has generated a significant policy debate regarding the appropriateness of a competitive government program. The market appeal of life-care facilities could be substantially affected by the existence of such a government program.

Increasing the Affordability of Lifetime Care

Strategic Issues

The strategic issues to be solved in expanding the affordability of life care are:

1. Reduce the capital costs associated with the construction of continuing-care facilities;
2. Reduce the cost of capital funding for life-care facilities;
3. Increase the volume of insureds who constitute the insurance pool to reduce the risk of utilization volatility and associated administrative costs; and
4. Control utilization of higher-cost care by more effective incentives to use lower-cost care, including the exclusion of extraordinary life saving techniques from the insurance program.

Program Concepts

The following are program concepts currently under development or appropriate for consideration to address portions of the strategic issues associated with affordability.

1. Reducing Capital Costs.
   a. Reduce Capital Facilities:
      i. Provide life care for individuals remaining in their homes during the period residential services are provided. The Jeanes/Foulkeways model of life care at home (LCAH), discussed elsewhere in this book, is designed to implement this concept. Critical issues are the marketability of such a service package for older people where the initial lump sum payment is not associated with acquiring the right to live in an independent living unit; the establishment of economic and program screens to protect against overutilization and underpricing; future drop-out by healthy people and adverse selection; and generating a large enough population to support centralized health-care facilities; and
      ii. Reduce the luxury elements of life-care centers and increase project phasing techniques to reduce capital costs and associated fees to residents in the early years of project operation.
   b. Reduce the Price of Capital:
      i. The systematic creation of preconstruction risk pools through governmental and foundation resources would enable less expensive development start-up and more consistent control of development;
      ii. Modification of the HUD insurance programs to include entrance fee communities offering life care would reduce the cost of permanent financing and increase its availability;
      iii. Obtaining funding through HUD direct loan programs such as Section 202 projects and low-income cooperatives for projects that incorporate mixed use activities such as independent living and health care and provide long-term care funding;
      iv. Development of commercial credit enhancement sources to enable ready access to the secondary retail market for permanent financing; and
      v. Continued development of accreditation sources that incorporate appropriate standards of actuarial pricing and standardize evaluation standards for life-care communities.
2. Maximize Insurance Vehicles:
   a. Develop sponsor reinsurance techniques to increase the strength of self-insurance funding; and
   b. Continue to press the competitive advantage of self-insurance in ways that will encourage the development of more competitive commercial insurance.
3. Contractual Liabilities: Focus on the careful selection of the minimum services necessary to provide security against nonelective catastrophic

loss associated with long-term care, and unbundle most other residential care services.

> While this chapter enumerates the financing complexities of life care in great detail, it should not discourage potential sponsors, but instead may give them a checklist and manual on how to achieve their goals. It also presents affordability as a realistic goal. Affordability, indeed, deserves the attention of the whole industry—to come up with a more broadly affordable product. Even more effective will be government encouragement of internally generated subsidies, encouraged by tax laws, approval processes, and possibly donation of public lands.
>
> —Editors

Notes

1. While a few life-care facilities have assumed contractual liability for the cost of hospitalization, surgical, physician, and pharmaceutical services, all such communities have assumed the continued existence of public insurance and commercial supplemental medicare policies to reinsure contractual liability. Since such communities are unlikely to withstand the costs associated with substantial retraction in the public and private insurance markets, capital sources view this structure as unacceptable.

2. Most of the current statutes regulating life care require escrow of deposits during the preconstruction period and the right of residents during this period to obtain a refund without penalty in the event of death or illness, and typically at least 96 percent of the entrance fee for any other reason. After occupancy, entrance fee refund arrangements typically are not mandated unless the community discharges a resident.

3. This ownership structure is unusual for lenders because those controlling the ownership entity have no direct economic interest in project success. This concern typically is addressed by focusing on the special market position that the nonprofit sponsor may offer and establishing operating covenants designed to produce reserves that are nondistributable because of the constraints on tax-exempt entities under Section 501(c)(3) of the Code.

4. This structure may provide the best mix of centralized ownership control with economic risk in a for-profit entity and the long-term operating responsibility and favorable market position generated by the nonprofit sponsor. Special issues involve proper financial covenants to avoid enforceability problems under the lease in the bankruptcy context and tax compliance issues to assure ownership treatment by the partnership for tax purposes. These issues relate primarily to the risk exposure of partnership equity investors. The comfort of the debt sources will depend on the strength of the partnership, the project, and the contractor providing a fixed construction price for the project.

5. This structure reduces the amount of equity required for the project because traditional contract rules apply to the sale of the condominium units. Pricing must be sufficient to pay all unit construction costs plus developer profit upon completion.

Reserves for health care will need to be funded through periodic charges, more typically through a commercial insurance product because of the restrictions applicable to the condominium association tax exemption and the limitations imposed under Section 501(c)(3) of the Code. Long-term debt financing for the project will apply only to the special common areas and units owned by the sponsor. Debt service on the health center typically will be covered through per diem charges. Construction financing will be required for all facilities, but unit sales contracts can be used to collateralize the loan for the units.

6. The financing structure for the cooperative is similar to that described in note 5 for condominiums except that (a) lenders are less familiar with cooperative forms, and (b) the statutory framework for cooperatives is less definitive in many jurisdictions and may require more extensive legal work to structure the cooperative.

7. The yield on obligations issued by certain governmental units and loaned to life-care organizations exempt from tax under Section 501(c)(3) are not included in the taxable income of certain investors. This means that a lower yield will produce the same after-tax return to such an investor. From 1965 to 1985, tax-exempt unrated retail obligations constituted the major source of funding for life-care projects. This provision of the tax law has been restricted in various ways by Congress from 1969 through 1986. It is likely that this restrictive trend will continue, making this source of funds limited or unavailable.

8. Collateral refers to property of value that can be transferred or seized and liquidated by a capital investor if the promised yield or principal is not paid. The following collateral is listed in general order by certainty of value: cash, cash equivalents, rated securities, real estate, equipment, accounts receivable, contract rights, contribution pledges. This order may vary by particular asset and by changing market conditions. The value of collateral to a capital investor will also be affected by such liquidity considerations as market size, cost of liquidation, difficulties of seizing control, tax effects of liquidation, and potential liabilities associated with liquidation. Life-care facilities pose unusual problems in the evaluation of collateral because of possible statutory provisions applicable to the disposition of life-care projects; the interests of residents; and the negative publicity associated with liquidation of interests in the life-care project, its reserve accounts, equipment, etc. Because the number of life-care facilities is very small and the valuation of future care liabilities is complex, establishing market value for such facilities is currently very difficult. As the volume of life-care projects grows and the disposition of such projects occurs more frequently, valuation techniques will become more standardized and decrease the difficulty of liquidation and the determination of fair market value.

9. Third-party guarantees in life-care projects take the form of bank letters of credit, insurance company financial guarantees, contractor guarantees of the maximum construction contract price, and corporate developer guarantees. As in the case of collateral, such guarantees are more valuable to the extent that their market value is readily determinable. Credit worthiness of letter-of-credit issuers and insurance company guarantees are evaluated by several credit rating agencies, including Standard & Poor's Corporation and Moody's Investor Rating Service. To date, neither rating agency will evaluate the credit of free-standing nursing-care projects or life-care facilities. In addition, under rating agency covenants, insurance guarantors may not

currently guarantee life-care facilities unless additional credit from a bank or corporate guarantor is available to support the project credit.

10. The frequency of interest payments will affect the actual cost to the life-care sponsor, since less frequent payments permit long investment periods for monies to be paid.

11. The cost of a variable interest rate is calculated on an estimated basis and should be evaluated under several alternative scenarios.

12. Reserve requirements of the capital investor may have a cost equal to the difference between the project borrowing rate (assuming application of the reserves to debt repayment) and the yield at which the reserves can be invested.

13. See note 9. Credit guarantee fees are typically calculated as a percentage of the interest rate savings generated by the guarantee. Where the project could otherwise not be financed, of course, such a calculation is not applicable, and the guarantee fee will probably be priced on the capacity of the project to carry the fee and produce an acceptable debt service coverage.

14. This factor can only be addressed by assessing such requirements early in the project so that the project and program are designed and developed to conform to construction-permanent financing requirements.

15. There are a variety of state and federal securities laws to protect passive investors. In general terms, even with extensive disclosure of the risks, the early period of development is inappropriate for small investors not sophisticated in selecting development investments. In addition, the cost of preparing the required disclosure statements at this early investment period is probably prohibitive.

16. Changes in the regulations applicable to federally insured savings and loan associations in 1987 have substantially limited the freedom of such associations to invest in real estate equity. Proposals to require sizing of bank reserves to fit the risks associated with each investment will further constrict this market.

17. Real estate investment trusts (REITs) benefit from favored tax treatment. Negative experiences with REITs in the late 1970s resulted in more conservative investment patterns, with most preconstruction conditions resolved before acquisition of an equity interest by the REIT.

18. Master limited partnerships (MLPs) permit small investors to benefit from equity investments. Most MLPs require satisfaction of preconstruction conditions before the MLP will invest and require guaranteed cash-on-cash returns in the early years. The tax status of MLPs may be less favorable than REITS.

19. Experience indicates that entities providing endowment resources or loans from related nonprofits for development are likely to impose minimum conditions.

20. Present value calculations establish the value today of a sum to be received in the future, assuming the capacity to invest today's dollar at a given interest rate. When applied to the future receipt, this interest rate factor is referred to as a discount rate. A simple interest rate of 10 percent on $100 is $10 if paid in the first year. To generate an equivalent return, assuming a 10 percent compounding (or a discount rate of 10 percent), a payment five years later producing the equivalent of the first year's interest would need to be $16.00 (or 16 percent of 100 in year five).

21. Construction loan sources often will provide medium-term financing in the form of mini-permanent loans extending through the project start-up period (three to

five years after completion of construction.) In the absence of such an arrangement, either a stand-by commitment for the permanent loan is required or a capital partner of sufficient strength to assure the ability to obtain permanent financing. Certain mini-permanent loans carry postconstruction-period interest rates designed to force replacement of the mini-perm as quickly a possible after completion.

22. The nature of the construction loan process involves careful monitoring of work in place for which loan draws are made. Typically, a local lender will participate with responsibility for supervising construction loan draws.

23. See note 7 as to tax-exempt bonds. Notes and bonds are securities in which the sponsor directly or indirectly (in the case of tax-exempt obligations) promises to pay specified amounts of principal at designated interest rates. Notes refer to short-term obligations of one to five years; bonds to longer-term obligations. In tight capital markets, the sale of retail obligations may require the delivery of recognized credit guarantees. See note 9. Commercial banks often make such guarantees available only in exchange for construction loan administration and customer accounts. Life-care project reserves offer a major attraction for such lenders. The largest source of construction and permanent financing for multifacility residential projects, nursing homes, and assisted living units are loans insured through the United States Department of Housing and Urban Development (HUD) funded through the sale of bonds issued by the Government National Mortgage Association (GNMA). Life-care facilities and continuing-care facilities are excluded from such programs if they include entrance fees or a mixed use of independent-living and health-care facilities.

24. Insurance companies frequently use their construction loan division primarily to originate permanent loans.

25. Pension funds frequently invest through a participation in loans structured by insurance companies and commercial banks that have staff more experienced in loan origination and monitoring.

26. When a government issuer is required to participate, it may require that a specific investment banking firm be used. In this circumstance, the tax-exempt bond issuer and investment banker may enjoy a monopoly position and exact the major portion of savings from the tax-exempt issue as the price of sale.

27. Most permanent lenders in this field will require actuarial funding reports. Actuaries providing such reports will be required to comply with the standards published by the Academy of Actuaries. *See* Interim Actuarial Standards Board: Actuarial Standards of Practice Relating to Continuing Care Retirement Communities, American Academy of Actuaries, July 1987.

28. See note 1 for a discussion of certain unacceptable health-care liabilities.

29. See note 27 for reference to newly established standards for actuaries applicable to continuing-care retirement communities.

30. In such insurance the sponsor acts as an employer equivalent, arranging the group policy and collecting premiums. The residents are analogous to employees receiving the benefit of the insurance to cover all or a portion of the cost of nursing care and assisted living care.

9
Designing for the Elderly and the Disabled: The Canadian Approach

Pamela J. Cluff, FRAIC, FRIBA

The following chapter is an excellent starting point for planning specialized facilities. The author uses Maslow's Hierarchy of Basic Needs as a reference point in setting forth the specific and general needs of the elderly in order to provide for a full "compendium of needs." For the benefit of designers and programmers, principles of design to meet the environmental needs of the elderly are provided along with a series of design guideline matrixes identifying the design issues and the human needs issues in the physical, service, and program components of a project.

—Editors

While most elderly people in the Western world enjoy favorable physical and mental health and continue to live independent lives in the community at large, there are also those who are less fortunate, such as dependent, frail, elderly or disabled people, whose health and care needs are significant. This dependent group may also include elderly people with various physical or psychiatric disorders who have very specific care, shelter, or service needs. There is a further and distinct group who are neither fully independent nor yet totally dependent on others—these might be identified as semi-independent seniors who may require some services delivered to them in their own homes.

During the latter half of the twentieth century, there has been a profound improvement in the economic well-being and health status of seniors and disabled people in the developed countries of the world. In addition, and almost universally, the expectations and lifestyle preferences of these individuals have changed significantly. Today, the majority of seniors and disabled people clearly express their wish to live autonomously, in their own home or community, or in supportive environments of their own choice for as long as possible.

While specific delivery mechanisms of providing shelter care and services vary throughout Canada, the underlying principle of supporting autonomy for these seniors is now shared by the majority of policy makers. However, in practice this principle is proving harder to achieve, largely due to the need to increase significantly both human and fiscal resources to ensure appropriate community service delivery, to much higher levels than in the past. In addition, the territorial and coordination problems that exist between service and housing agencies have proven a major limitation for both the government and the private sector. Society also has a substantial investment in existing facilities and more traditional models of service, and it is both reluctant and slow to change.

The major problem facing Canada today, therefore, is to achieve an effective transition from traditional solutions for services and shelter to cope with the expanding population of seniors as well as increasing vocal groups of disabled people—to ensure that the major support services they require are available to them in their own homes and also to ensure that where specialized health and personal-care services are required, these services are made available in appropriate settings on a short- or long-term admissions basis.

With the increasing number of seniors who are living beyond seventy-five and on into old-old age, (eighty-five and older) or for people who require more than three major services on an ongoing basis, there still remains a need to provide a variety of solutions offering shelter with services. There is also a need to ensure that the increasing number of frail elderly or multiply handicapped people who need totally supportive environments are accommodated in appropriate settings, with a full range of personal-care and health-care services.

Physical solutions that address this "continuum of care" approach for seniors can be broadly grouped under three generic living-arrangement categories: independent living; semi-independent living; and dependent living.

The specific needs of seniors, using these three distinct categories, have recently been examined by an interdisciplinary working group of Canadian experts under the auspices of the Federal Department of Health and Welfare. As a result, national guidelines have been developed for sponsors considering the development of solutions for seniors, whether through community-based or facility-based service delivery mechanisms or through living arrangements sponsored by the government or the private and nonprofit sectors.

To ensure that these guidelines represented an appropriate framework for decision making, the basic needs of seniors or disabled people in these various living arrangements were analyzed and organized into a "compendium of needs," which groups the basic needs of seniors under four major headings: physiological needs; psychological needs; social needs; and environmental needs.

These basic needs (discussed further in the next section) permit the development of principles for the design of typical living arrangements in the aging continuum. They also provide a systematic framework for isolating those care and support services required by individuals as their personal-care or health-care needs change over time or as their level of physical or mental competence declines.

The final national guideline documents[a] developed by the Federal Department of Health and Welfare utilize the three basic types of living arrangements as their titles and are the first in Canada to present a comprehensive framework for decision making not only for physical design, but also for the design of the complementary care services or programs needed to assist seniors in living autonomous lives in these diverse settings. These guideline documents include performance criteria suitable for designers, planners, sociologists, policy makers, or care personnel within a systematic framework. Information in the three documents has been organized utilizing the four needs identified previously as the vertical components of a matrix. The horizontal components of the matrix are presented under the following three major headings:

- Physical Design Considerations (Utilizing the sequence of decisions typically encountered in the design/decision process) (See table 9–1);
- Program and Service Design Considerations (Based on the major personal-care and health-care services typically provided to seniors with special needs) (See table 9–2); and
- Other Considerations (Based on the contextual framework in which decisions are typically made, such as legislation, funding, etc.) (See table 9–3).

Compendium of Needs

While the physiological, psychological, and social needs of elderly or disabled people are generally the same as those of the average population, age-related changes and various disabling conditions may make it more difficult for service providers to meet those needs. (See figure 9–1). It is therefore important that designers, program managers, and service providers have a broad understanding of the needs common to most people, as well as those specific to seniors.

Psychologist Abraham Maslow generated a hierarchy of basic needs, (see figure 9–2), which serves as a useful organizational model for determining a broad spectrum of needs that can also apply to seniors. Maslow also postulates that individuals, regardless of the physical environment in which they

---

[a]Canada's national guideline documents, which include the 'Compendium of Needs', were published in the spring of 1989 by the Federal Department of Health and Welfare, Facilities Design Division, Ottawa, Canada, in both English and French.

Table 9–1
Framework for Independent, Semi-Dependent, and Dependent Living Arrangements: Physical Components

Human Needs / *Design Issue*	*Location & Site Planning*	*Design Factors*	*Functional Relationships*	*Space Requirements*	*Accessibility Factors*	*Mechanical Services*	*Electrical Services*	*Special Services*	*Communication Services*	*Signage*	*Interior Design and Finishes*	*Furniture and Fittings*	*Equipment*	*Landscape Design*
Physiological	P–1	P–2	P–3	P–4	P–5	P–6	P–7	P–8	P–9	P–10	P–11	P–12	P–13	P–14
1. Health			◆			◆		◆	◆		◆		◆	
2. Nutrition													◆	
3. Hygiene				◆		◆		◆			◆		◆	
4. Mobility	◆	◆		◆	◆		◆	◆	◆	◆	◆	◆	◆	◆

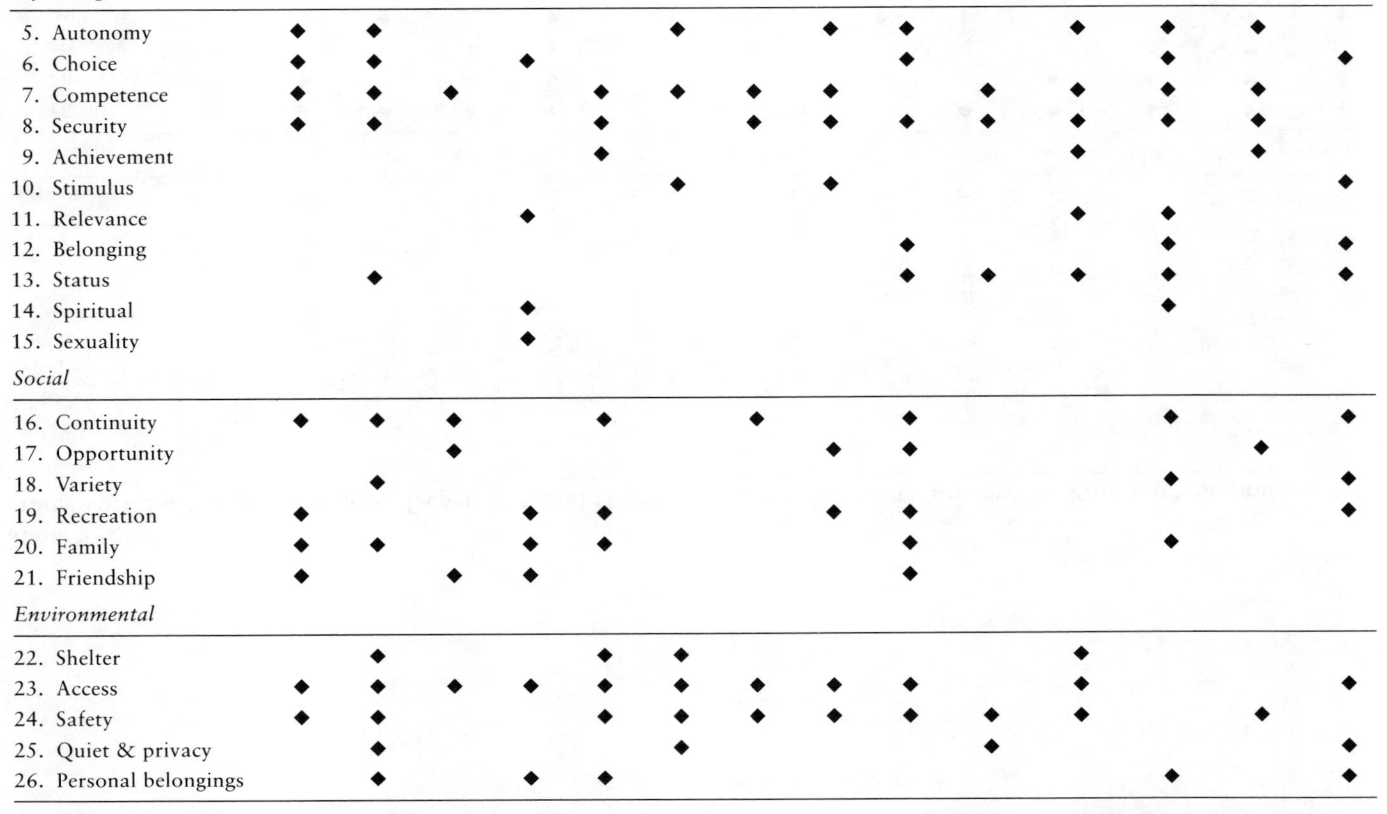

Psychological														
5. Autonomy	◆	◆				◆		◆	◆		◆	◆	◆	
6. Choice	◆	◆		◆					◆			◆		◆
7. Competence	◆	◆	◆		◆	◆	◆	◆		◆	◆	◆	◆	
8. Security	◆	◆			◆		◆	◆	◆	◆	◆	◆	◆	
9. Achievement					◆						◆		◆	
10. Stimulus						◆		◆						◆
11. Relevance				◆							◆	◆		
12. Belonging									◆			◆		◆
13. Status		◆							◆	◆	◆	◆		◆
14. Spiritual				◆								◆		
15. Sexuality				◆										
Social														
16. Continuity	◆	◆	◆		◆		◆		◆			◆		◆
17. Opportunity			◆					◆	◆				◆	
18. Variety		◆										◆		◆
19. Recreation	◆			◆	◆			◆	◆					◆
20. Family	◆	◆		◆	◆				◆			◆		
21. Friendship	◆		◆	◆					◆					
Environmental														
22. Shelter		◆			◆	◆					◆			
23. Access	◆	◆	◆	◆	◆	◆	◆	◆	◆		◆			◆
24. Safety	◆	◆			◆	◆	◆	◆	◆	◆	◆		◆	
25. Quiet & privacy		◆				◆				◆				◆
26. Personal belongings		◆		◆	◆							◆		◆

Note: ◆ indicates the intersection of a need with a decision required by the designer or sponsors of a project to ensure that a physical or service solution is created or that a contextual issue is appropriately identified and resolved. In the wealth and welfare documents described, criteria for each of these issues have been addressed.

Table 9–2
Framework for Independent, Semi-Dependent, and Dependent Living Arrangements: Service Program Components

Human Needs	*Design Issue*	*Assessment Services*	*Health-Care Services*	*Therapeutic Services*	*Personal-Care Services*	*Social Services*	*Counseling Services*	*Psychological Services*	*Recreational Services*	*Transportation Services*	*Information Services*	*Education Services*	*Financial Services*	*Special Services*
Physiological		S–1	S–2	S–3	S–4	S–5	S–6	S–7	S–8	S–9	S–10	S–11	S–12	S–13
1. Health		◆	◆	◆	◆		◆	◆		◆	◆	◆	◆	◆
2. Nutrition		◆		◆	◆						◆	◆	◆	◆
3. Hygiene				◆	◆							◆		
4. Mobility		◆	◆	◆	◆				◆	◆			◆	◆

Psychological													
5. Autonomy	◆	◆	◆			◆	◆		◆			◆	
6. Choice			◆	◆	◆	◆	◆		◆	◆		◆	
7. Competence	◆	◆	◆	◆					◆		◆		◆
8. Security		◆	◆		◆		◆			◆		◆	◆
9. Achievement	◆	◆		◆		◆			◆		◆		
10. Stimulus		◆		◆					◆	◆	◆		
11. Relevance			◆		◆		◆			◆			◆
12. Belonging				◆			◆			◆			
13. Status				◆	◆		◆				◆	◆	
14. Spiritual						◆	◆						
15. Sexuality		◆		◆		◆	◆						
Social													
16. Continuity	◆				◆			◆	◆	◆			
17. Opportunity		◆		◆	◆	◆		◆	◆	◆	◆	◆	◆
18. Variety								◆					
19. Recreation				◆				◆	◆	◆			
20. Family						◆	◆		◆				
21. Friendship						◆	◆	◆	◆		◆		
Environmental													
22. Shelter					◆							◆	
23. Access	◆	◆						◆					
24. Safety		◆	◆	◆						◆		◆	◆
25. Quiet & privacy	◆	◆	◆	◆		◆						◆	
26. Personal belongings				◆								◆	

Note: ◆ indicates the intersection of a need with a decision required by the designer or sponsors of a project to ensure that a physical or service solution is created or that a contextual issue is appropriately identified and resolved. In the health and welfare documents described, criteria for each of these issues have been addressed.

Table 9–3
Framework for Independent, Semi-Dependent, and Dependent Living Arrangements: Other Considerations

Human Needs / *Design Issue*	*Policies & Guidelines*	*Legislation & Regulations*	*Funding & Costs*	*Special User Groups*	*Regionalism*	*Time*	*Family Involvement*	*Staffing*	*Agency Involvement*	*Volunteer Involvement*	*Professional Involvement*	*Management & Administration*
Physiological	O–1	O–2	O–3	O–4	O–5	O–6	O–7	O–8	O–9	O–10	O–11	O–12
1. Health	◆	◆	◆		◆	◆		◆			◆	◆
2. Nutrition	◆	◆	◆		◆		◆	◆	◆	◆	◆	◆
3. Hygiene		◆	◆				◆	◆		◆	◆	◆
4. Mobility	◆		◆	◆	◆	◆	◆	◆	◆	◆	◆	◆

Psychological												
5. Autonomy	◆			◆	◆							
6. Choice			◆		◆	◆			◆			◆
7. Competence				◆							◆	
8. Security	◆	◆		◆		◆	◆	◆		◆	◆	◆
9. Achievement											◆	
10. Stimulus						◆	◆	◆	◆	◆		◆
11. Relevance	◆		◆		◆	◆	◆	◆	◆		◆	◆
12. Belonging					◆		◆					
13. Status	◆			◆	◆		◆				◆	◆
14. Spiritual	◆					◆		◆	◆	◆	◆	
15. Sexuality	◆					◆		◆			◆	
Social												
16. Continuity	◆				◆	◆	◆					◆
17. Opportunity	◆			◆		◆		◆		◆		◆
18. Variety								◆	◆	◆		
19. Recreation	◆		◆	◆	◆	◆		◆	◆	◆	◆	◆
20. Family	◆	◆	◆		◆		◆		◆			
21. Friendship					◆		◆		◆	◆		
Environmental												
22. Shelter	◆	◆	◆	◆	◆						◆	
23. Acceses	◆	◆	◆	◆	◆	◆	◆	◆	◆	◆	◆	◆
24. Safety	◆	◆	◆	◆		◆		◆			◆	◆
25. Quiet & privacy	◆	◆						◆			◆	◆
26. Personal belongings	◆	◆		◆			◆			◆		◆

Note: ◆ indicates the intersection of a need with a decision required by the designer or sponsors of a project to ensure that a physical or service solution is created or that a contextual issue is appropriately identified and resolved. In the health and welfare documents described, criteria for each of these issues have been addressed.

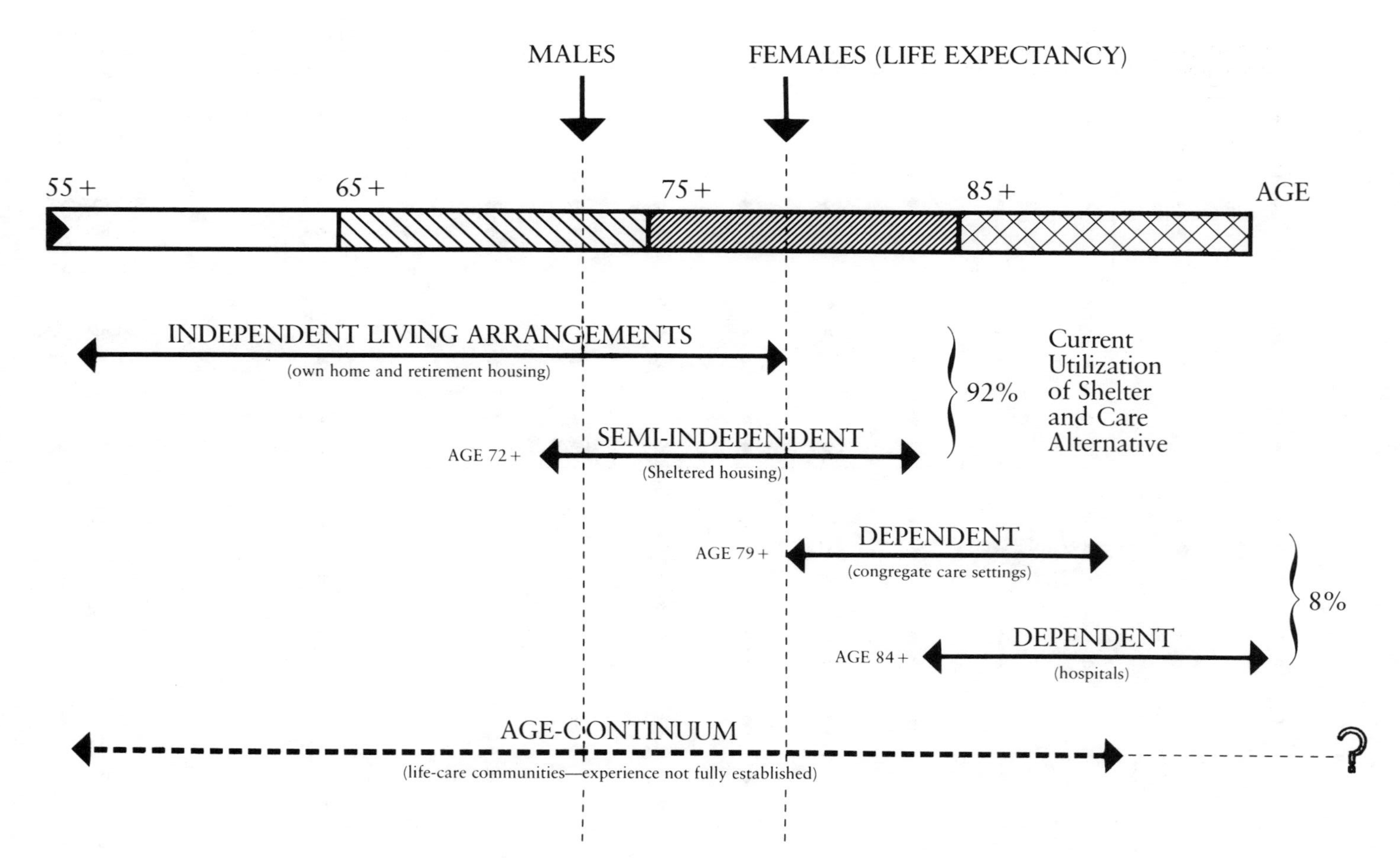

Figure 9–1. Shelter and Services: The Canadian Experience

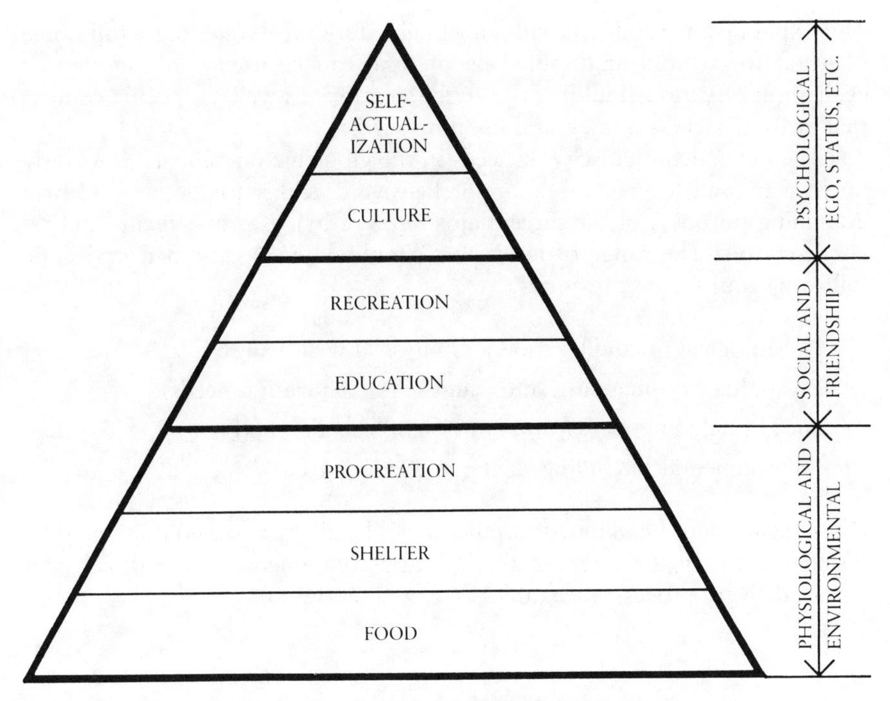

Figure 9–2. Maslow's Hierarchy of Needs

live, tend to aspire to higher levels in the hierarchy only after the lower levels of need have been met. Thus, a person whose basic physiological needs have not been met would concentrate on those before striving to meet the higher needs of safety, social interaction, or ego.

For the purposes of relating these human needs to the creation of appropriate solutions for shelter or services, Maslow's hierarchy could be expanded as follows:

1. *Physiological needs* such as food, water, sex and shelter;
2. *Safety needs,* relating to protection against external danger or threat; deprivation, or personal security;
3. *Social needs,* such as the giving and receiving of love, friendship, affection, belonging, association, and acceptance;
4. *Ego needs* of two types—the need for autonomy and independence as well as the need for self-esteem and self-worth, derived from status, recognition, appreciation, and prestige; and
5. *Self-actualization needs,* including the need to achieve one's potential or the need for ongoing self-development.

This expanded hierarchy provides a valuable tool for developing a full range of needs for seniors or disabled people and can be used in the design or evaluation of various building or service solutions as well as specific contextual factors, such as human and fiscal resources.

The expanded hierarchy of needs in the guideline documents previously noted was used to generate a comprehensive checklist for design and programming purposes of the three major types of living arrangements and related services. The range of needs was simplified and regrouped under the following four major categories:

- Physiological (including food and physical well-being);
- Psychological (including status and self-actualization needs);
- Social (including recreation, family, and friends); and
- Environmental (including shelter and safety needs).

Using these major headings, a number of subheadings emerged that could be systematically cross-referenced to the other components of the design and service delivery process. (See tables 9–1, 9–2, and 9–3).

Principles of Design to Meet the Environmental Needs of Seniors and Disabled People

Bearing in mind the hierarchy of needs previously identified, and respecting the special differences that age or disability can create, the first and underlying principle that emerges is:

1. **The designer must accept a level of social responsibility by becoming familiar with the specific needs of the intended users of the buildings or services under consideration.**

From this one principle a number of questions arise:

- Who is to be served (by age, sex, marital status, socio economic, health, or disability status)?
- Why is the project being developed (to meet the perceived needs of the users or to meet other philosophical, political, or financial objectives)?
- What are the underlying objectives for the project, both in the short-term and long-term?
- What is to be provided in terms of shelter and services?
- What changes can be expected over time?

- Where is the facility to be located and how large is the area to be served?
- Which other guidelines, criteria, or contextual issues should be considered in developing the solution?
- When is the project required?
- How will the needed information about the users be established and how will that information affect the resulting solutions?

The second most important principle is:

2. **The designer must fully understand both the specific disabilities and related limitations that elderly or disabled people may experience.**

Typical functional limitations affecting elderly or disabled people and requiring design responsive solutions may include any or all of the following:

- *Physical changes,* resulting from the aging process, an accident, or progressive disabling condition, involving mobility, strength, endurance, or coordination;
- *Health status changes* as a result of illness, a traumatic incident, or increasing immobility;
- *Acuity or perceptual changes* as a result of aging, including loss of sight or hearing, the onset of illness, or a neurological disorder such as Alzheimer's disease;
- *Social status changes* as a result of the loss of a partner, parent, or friends; and
- *Financial status changes* as a result of retirement or loss of job, pension, or assets.

These changes or losses in function or status generally affect the coping skills of the individual, particularly in the physical environment. For design purposes, such losses can best be described as *functional limitations,* which affect their use of or encounter with the physical world, and may generally be defined as follows:

- Mobility impairments;
- Sensory impairments;
- Comprehension impairments;
- Strength or endurance impairments;
- Coordination impairments; and
- *Situational impairments* (such as difficulties arising out of particular conditions involving language or culture).

As a result of understanding the impact of these functional limitations, both the third and fourth principles emerge as follows:

3. **Buildings, sites, and services should be accessible to and usable by people with various functional impairments.**
4. **Physical solutions should be designed as enabling and supportive of people with various functional limitations.**

Enabling or supportive solutions are sometimes referred to as *enhanced environments,* that is, settings in which people with reduced perceptual skills involving sight or hearing can function more easily, for example, by the inclusion of brighter colors, higher levels of lighting, use of supplementary hearing equipment, specific signage, or other "supportive cues" in the environment.[1] Solutions for people with mobility impairments or reduced strength typically include the installation of grab bars beside toilets or tubs, handrails in corridor areas, special baths or toilets, and wheelchair ramps so that people in wheelchairs can remain independent.

The number and type of creative, supportive solutions and technologies for people with various functional limitations is increasing. However, some of the frequently missed environmental opportunities include the need for enhanced or appropriate building systems that are particularly appropriate for those elderly who suffer from limitations involving the senses or who have problems with breathing.

Such solutions might include:

- *Heating systems* that can be individually controlled over a broad range of temperatures to compensate for reduced body fat and poor blood circulation.
- *Cooling and ventilation systems* that can be individually controlled and do not create drafts, high velocity air currents, or too much background noise, and that contain sufficient oxygen and humidity at all times as an aid to breathing and skin care.
- *Lighting systems* that can be easily adjusted to provide bright, even lighting without direct or reflected glare for those whose vision is reduced or have yellowing of the eye lens.
- *Acoustic design* that controls or modifies background noise generated by building systems, people, or equipment through the appropriate selection of floor, wall, and ceiling finishes, as well as the use of insulation between spaces and in building systems.
- *Alarm systems* that can alert seniors with sight or hearing problems through both audible and visible signals.

The fifth principle that emerges is also supportive of autonomous action by seniors as well as ensuring diversity of solutions:

5. **Options and diversity should be built into facilities or services, to ensure that the intended users can exercise autonomy and choice.**

Choice is a necessary expression of individuality and may involve a range of issues, including:

- Choice in the design of the unit or suite, the number of rooms, the interior layout, the design of the bathroom or kitchen, the choice of color scheme or furnishings, and the choice of balcony, patio, or garden access.
- Choice in the location of the unit, for example, whether it is in a busy or quiet location, urban or rural setting, overlooking a garden, activity area, or the main entrance, and with a sunny or shady exposure.
- Choice of neighbors, companions, or roommates.
- Choice of tenure, for example, whether it is an accommodation that can be owned, leased, or rented, as well as the amount, style, and frequency of payments.
- Choice of what, when, and how services should be provided, such as meals, laundry, housekeeping, health or personal care, and security, and the times of day and locations in which such services may be provided.
- Choice of activities, planned or unplanned, in which the user might take part, such as social or therapeutic activities and group or individual pursuits.
- Choice in terms of privacy, both in a physical and territorial sense as well as in terms of information sharing or social interaction.

The sixth principle that arises out of this latter consideration and affects both the designer and the service provider is:

6. **Privacy for the user should be ensured.**

In a physical setting this may mean the provision of a private sleeping area, room, or suite especially for such activities as dressing, bathing, toileting, health examinations, and so on, or through the use of specific design strategies, including the appropriate placement of walls, doors, and windows. In operational terms this principle would include privacy of information, privacy from unwarranted intrusion by staff or regulatory authorities, or the use of various controlling strategies or devices.

The seventh principle is one learned through experience, but it is particularly important with respect to seniors over the aging continuum:

7. **Every solution (facility or service) should be able to accommodate change over time.**

One of the most prevalent factors of change in settings for seniors is that the residents will age in place and become less physically able and more dependent as time passes. However, change may occur not only as a result of changes in the health or physical or mental capability of the individual users themselves, but may include changes in social expectations, changes in technology, changes in operational terms (whether in management policies, practices, or staffing), as well as changes in legislation, financing, or sponsorship. Inevitably, these changes affect the buildings, programs, or services that are designed for special users. Therefore, the buildings or settings themselves must be flexible and able to accommodate such changes over time. This may include changes in how spaces are allocated or used as well as changes in decor, maintenance, or operation.

Bearing in mind such aging-in-place realities and the ongoing reduction in user functional abilities, the eighth principle for designers and operators is:

8. **Physical environments and other solutions should provide a safe environment for the intended users.**

For seniors and disabled people, safety in environmental terms means not only safety from fire and smoke, but also personal safety from accidents. It is therefore important to ensure that hazards in the setting are eliminated or minimized as well to provide protection from traumatic incidents involving intruders, or basic safety in terms of adequate protection from the elements. In operational terms, personal safety of residents can also include security issues in terms of the management of personal affairs, money, and belongings, as well as safety from pressure or abuse by staff, family members, or others. Solutions to these problems are frequently a matter of clearly established policies and philosophy-of-care, adequate staff training, and monitoring.

The best sites offer both choice and security, and give rise to a ninth principle:

9. **Sites and facilities should be located in active residential neighborhoods where social interaction with the community can be encouraged and enhanced.**

With this in mind, isolated sites that are remote from settled communities or that have poor public transportation may pose security or staffing problems and generally should not be selected, no matter how beautiful or economically desirable the setting. In addition, it should be remembered that seniors or disabled people are particularly vulnerable in a social sense and may already have little contact with others. In addition, those with mobility or perceptual problems usually cannot manage to independently negotiate distances over three blocks or a quarter of a mile. They may therefore be constrained to the building or site itself, thereby reducing their opportunities for social interaction with others. As a result, they will become more and more dependent on the community coming to them.

Notwithstanding the limited functional abilities of many elderly and disabled people in care settings, the next issue is one that is frequently missed by designers and building owners. Having acknowledged the need to provide supportive, enabling environments, we run the risk of providing environments that are too passive, encourage dependency, and represent a denial of the human condition by limiting self-actualization. In fact, society is in danger of considering that seniors or disabled people have little potential worth developing and that their role in retirement and care settings should be one of passivity and dependency as well as one in which owners, staff, and families will become overprotective. It is therefore becoming increasingly important that the physical and social world in which these individuals live continue to offer diversity, choice, and challenge to personal growth regardless of any physical, health, or status changes.

The final principle therefore, is:

10. Challenge should be a component of all solutions.

Challenge can take many forms in physical settings and can include solutions that encourage walking, mobility, or social interaction in a diversity of spaces and activities. Challenge in terms of service solutions may include the need to "dress up" for specific meals or events, to take part in group as well as individual activities, or to take on responsibilities for oneself or others. Challenge can also exist in the simplest of things, from modest changes in routine, shopping trips, the creation of a garden, or further education and skills development. Challenge is the "stuff of life" and can encourage and optimize the remaining capabilities of seniors, even those with limited physical resources.

Conclusion

Today, in this period of rapid and incremental change, there is a great need to respond appropriately to the burgeoning number of seniors and disabled adults in our society who wish to live autonomous and meaningful lives, which can be in a life care center or in the greater community. Those of us involved in the design and health care professions must become fully aware of these needs and be prepared to exercise our skills and responsibilities in providing appropriate solutions. One way to achieve this objective is to increase our understanding of these special needs and to develop the necessary sensitivity, analytical, design, and management skills to ensure that we create appropriate shelter and service solutions that optimize the remaining abilities of such users and ensure them of a quality of life that addresses their unique needs as well as their expectations. Only in this way can we be assured that the solutions we generate today will continue to be effective and responsive into the twenty-first century.

> This explanation of the functional needs of the elderly and disabled is particularly clear. Without an awareness and understanding of the effects of the aging process on the frail or disabled elderly, no designer, developer, or sponsor could effectively produce appropriate housing environments that are supportive and that encourage self-help and independence. The above focus and succinct presentation on the benefits of providing housing in attractive neighborhood settings, that are barrier-free, safe, and supportive environments, with the option for flexibility and privacy, can serve well as a guide for successful development.
>
> —Editors

Note

1. Pastalan, L.A. "Privacy as an expression of human territoriality." In Pastalan, L.A. and Carson, D.H. (eds.) *Spacial Behavior of Older People*. Ann Arbor: University of Michigan Press, 1970.

10
Applying Innovative Technology to Create Enabling Environments: Trends in Other Countries

Paul John Grayson, M.Arch., A.I.A.

This chapter will bring you face to face with the "cutting edge" of high tech as it can help us care for the elderly. It describes and illustrates how countries as diverse as Sweden, Japan, and Switzerland allow for aging in place, energy efficiency, and humane, helpful, "enabling" environments. Robotics, the "intelligent house," and the potentials of manufactured housing are discussed with clarity and concern.

—Editors

Happiness is the meaning
and the purpose of life,
the whole aim
and end of human existence
—Aristotle

Experience in other industrialized nations has resulted in a shift in public policy away from the building of large-scale, stand-alone, institutional-type facilities for the elderly and disabled. The trend is toward keeping the elderly and disabled in the community, in their own home or apartment, or in smaller-scale community-based residential settings, such as congregate housing or assisted-living units.[1] Also provided are more sophisticated residential settings that offer a wide range of on-premise services similar to what in the United States is called a life-care center or a continuing-care retirement community. In whatever the setting, be it a private home or a congregate facility, the focus is to make it possible for older people, including the frail and old-old, to age in place.[2]

In other countries in the past decade, joint partnerships have developed

The data and illustrations presented in this chapter were developed by the author in researching "How Other Countries Care For and House the Elderly." This study program was made possible through the Arthur W. Wheelwright Traveling Fellowship in Architecture (1986–87) from the Harvard University Graduate School of Design.

among private companies, public agencies, and nonprofit agencies to develop improved housing and construction systems, new architectural building products, innovative appliances, and all types of "tools for living." Such public–private efforts have made considerable gain in improving the quality of the environment for the elderly and disabled.[3] This approach in designing to satisfy the user's wants and needs has translated into more creatively designed residential unit layouts and in products and appliances that assist and encourage those with certain deficits in the activities of daily living to remain as independent as possible for as long as possible.

Innovative electronic technology now being developed permits kitchen appliances to communicate with one another, infrared sensing and control devices to signal a mechanism to open or lock a door or window, and home automation systems that can be set to turn on or off the lights or automatically turn off a stove if a pot is overheating.[4] The application of interactive robotic technology as an optional means of serving the elderly and disabled is being extensively researched and examined worldwide.[5] Such applications, along with current improvements in basic products of the home, such as an accessible shower/bathing area, an adjustable-height washbasin, a paperless toilet machine, or lifting devices to move an immobile person from bed to bath without straining the caregiver, will help reduce the overall health-care cost burden, help manage more effectively the critical shortages of qualified and well-trained staff, and more importantly, with the appropriate community-based support systems in place, will further the notion of aging in place.

This chapter will provide general information on public policy in other nations, on current research, and on the application of innovative technology in creating enabling environments. These concepts, design options, and the development of new products can be adapted to our particular needs here and be used in any type of residential situation—not just for the special needs of the elderly or disabled.

Public Policy in Other Countries

Over the years, many countries have developed a variety of different housing models for the elderly, from sophisticated equivalents, to our own life-care centers and continuing-care retirement communities, to other forms of congregate living, such as group facilities, shared or sheltered housing.

Besides providing nursing homes, which are equivalent to our skilled and intermediate levels of care, an array of institutional facilities exists for the chronically ill, for the developmentally and severely disabled, and for those with Alzheimer's or other debilitating illness.

Among most citizens in other developed nations, there appears to be more common concern, compassion, and respect for the elderly and disabled than one is generally aware of in the United States. The strength of the family unit, the support of the community for its citizens, and the strong sense of social responsibility results in public policy that by our standards is very generous. Although many refer to these countries as *welfare states*, the varied programs that are provided in so many areas beyond just health, homecare, and housing for the elderly are voted upon by the citizens in a democratic process. It is considered that by paying now, up-front, for such services through taxation, the individual and the community burden later on will be much less. All citizens will therefore be covered. People in other developed nations also plan more carefully for their retirement than we seem to do here. They save more and prepare for their future long-term needs.

In other developed countries one senses that the elderly can live their golden years with dignity, pride, and self-esteem, and that they will be secure if financial need arises, that they will be cared for when unable to care for themselves, and most importantly, that there will be a place to live, whatever their financial or physical condition. Relieved of the fear of becoming destitute or of losing their assets, home, or possessions due to the financial drain of a catastrophic illness, on the whole, the elderly in other developed nations seem at peace. One does not easily find old people hollow-eyed or sleeping in doorways, picking food from garbage cans, or walking aimlessly about.

From the aggressively entrepreneurial countries like Japan or Switzerland to very socially conscious nations such as the Netherlands and the Scandinavian countries, public policy protects the elderly so that they may live a decent and reasonable existence and be provided with whatever health-care services may be needed. In this manner then, it could be said that "life care" is guaranteed through public policy. The elderly are not put out of mind and sight, discarded, or sent away. The elderly are encouraged to remain active members of society, regardless of their frailties or disabilities. Aging is not denied; it is accepted as part of life.

Because the cost of health care, housing, and services are rising and straining national and regional budgets, much in the way they are here, serious financing problems are developing that will have an impact on programs and public policy. In Great Britain, the National Health Service is experiencing a major crisis in that the costs of providing "free" services for all are much too high and are becoming more difficult to access. In countries like Sweden, Denmark, and the Netherlands, budgets are being cut back or are held at current levels. Retired people who have a reasonable amount of assets are being asked to cover part of the cost for their services.

These financial strains have forced an evaluation of public policy. But it is interesting to note that changes will not come about due only to budget deficits. Many of these countries which initially, in the 1960s and 1970s, invested heavily in large-scale retirement housing and institutional facilities learned that the elderly living in such facilities generally deteriorated faster than their cohorts living in their own homes or in smaller-scale congregate housing. It became apparent that the quality of life for an elderly person, even though frail and disabled, was less than desirable when institutionalized or isolated away from the community and familiar surroundings.

Further, it has been determined that the overriding wish of the elderly is to continue to live independently.[6] With the cost of nursing care, construction of specialized facilities, and skilled staff so high, other approaches have been addressed. And the predominant direction appears to be centered on aging in place, or more clearly stated, life care at home, with community-based health-care and home-help services.

By keeping the elderly out of institutions, we see a return to traditional values of the community as the source of support, as the provider of care and services, as the marketplace and center of social interaction. With this comes reaffirmation of the benefit and importance of maintaining intergenerational ties: that all members of the community remain together, and by being together, a healthier and stronger society will result.

It is estimated that in the United States some 90 percent of the elderly population will age in place.[7] Recognition that their special needs for appropriate housing and tools for living have not been fully addressed presents considerable retrofit and new construction opportunities for builders and developers, product manufacturers, and service providers.

To meet the needs of the rapidly rising numbers of older people, a considerable amount of private and public funds in other nations are being invested in research and development of housing systems and products. In the development of new forms of housing and products, the direction is to find solutions that will serve all people, regardless of age or ability, not just the elderly or disabled. This approach helps to eliminate institutional-looking products and helps to diminish the dislike by the elderly of special "handicapped" aids. The look of these products and the attitude that they are just for old or sick or disabled people helps to further the stigma of growing old. The challenge before us therefore is to create environments of a universal design that are ageless, capable of supporting the needs of everyone, can encourage human interaction, and can enhance the joy and the quality of life.

Environments Encouraging Independent Living

In order to develop enabling environments we need to take into account the wants and needs of the user, the service provider, and those who will be involved with maintenance and repair. We also must understand the wants and needs of the owner, developer and builder, the financier, the designer, the community, and so forth. If after all the time and money spent in creating an environment, the user is not satisfied, then the development team has failed. In reviewing solutions being researched and developed in other countries, we can learn what makes an enabling environment, what are its special features, and indeed, how many varied options can be made available to meet individual wants and needs.

An enabling environment is one that has been designed with the prime objective being to satisfy the user's needs. It supports the independence of the occupant and enhances the quality of life. It provides for flexibility as needs change. It is secure, safe, convenient, barrier-free, affordable, comfortable, and durable, and sustains one's feeling of well-being.

Often we hear criticism that there is a tendency for those in the development and design professions to develop projects based upon perceptions and feelings about what the user or service provider considers desirable or necessary, rather than to develop solutions based on what are the actual needs or wishes of the user. We hear complaints quite frequently about developers and designers who have skimped on materials and finishes, on space arrangements, and on quality in appliances and building systems.

If a design has not been developed appropriately, if adequate time in programming and planning a project and in establishing long-range goals and objectives has not been allowed, then it seems inevitable that difficulties will develop. The downstream cost to correct problems is quite likely to end up higher than it would have had the work been done properly in the first instance. Such an additional cost burden cannot adequately take into account the inconvenience, frustration, and loss of time to the user and to those who manage or maintain the environment.

Designers of housing for the elderly, or for any other age group for that matter, must develop a clear understanding of how people want to live. Owners, developers, builders, and service providers need to become more sensitive to such issues. The goal should be to increase sensitivity to user needs, to develop more understanding of aging, and to encourage participation of all parties, including the user, in the design process. New approaches and new methods need to be tested with adequate time for research, experimentation, and observation. We need to be more innovative and to be open to suggestions from others. We need to be less image-oriented and more function-oriented.

To build right and to build to last seem to be the bases of any construction undertaking in other countries. In Switzerland or Sweden, for example, building codes are very strict, and the cost of construction is very high by our standards. In either new or old construction of, say, a multi-family apartment project, you will rarely hear through the demising walls, your next door neighbor playing the hi-fi or flushing the toilet. One does not hear footfalls from the floor above or from a corridor. Street noises are kept out when windows are closed. Light switches are easy to operate, and dimmers keep functioning for years. Hot water heaters heat the water as it is being used and do not waste energy by keeping a large supply hot all day long.

Window units are either double or triple glazed, they are easy to operate, and they do not get stuck. The same window unit can operate both as a hopper or a casement, and the exterior can easily be cleaned from a standing position inside. Bathroom and kitchen floors are really waterproof. Heating and ventilation systems are developed with air-to-air exchangers, and therefore buildings can be designed to be air tight. Insulation factors for the building envelope are almost twice ours, and heating costs are a third of average heating costs in the United States. The notion to build to last is based on the long-term view that quality construction is a good investment that will require less in operating costs, maintenance, and repair.

In dwelling units designed for the elderly, adequate room is provided in an entry for wheelchair passage, as well as for storage of the wheelchair or a walker, and there is room to put packages, and floor space for more than one person. Kitchens and bathrooms are generally larger than ours and more accessible. Sometimes we find the kitchen, the dining area, and living space all in one to allow more economy, convenience, flexibility, and a sense of spaciousness. Bathrooms are more flexible too. Some provide a completely waterproof room, and thereby eliminate the need for a separate shower stall with a curb that hinders access for a wheelchair and that may present a safety hazard for a frail elder wishing to shower.[8] If a bathtub is provided, the room is adequate in size for wheelchair or walker access and for an attendant, a lift, or a transfer seating area at the tub.

One Approach: Japan

Since 1980, the Japanese Ministry of International Trade and Industry (MITI) has funded a research and development program at Tokyo's Metropolitan Institute of Gerontology. The goal was to develop housing with functional flexibility that could change as the occupants' needs changed, through partial remodeling, by replacing components, by installing self-help equipment, or by constructing additional space.

As one reads on, it should be kept in mind that the concepts presented here are adaptable to all levels of housing—private, congregate, group, lifecare, or continuum-of-care—and that the concepts presented not only provide barrier-free and safe environments for the elderly and disabled, but can be beneficial to people of all ages and abilities.

The MITI House principal researcher, Ms. Tamako Hayashi, coordinated the development of a prototype for an innovative house for the elderly and handicapped, in collaboration with a prefabricated housing manufacturer, Sekisui House, Ltd. The prototype was designed to accommodate four stages of change: self-care, partial ambulatory care, personal care with a full-time wheelchair user, and nursing and medical care with a bedridden elderly or disabled younger occupant. It was assumed that the residents were family members and that one or two elder parents or a disabled child or relative would be cared for by the family or with assistance from outside when needed. The overall goal was to minimize caregiving and maximize self-help and independence. The goal in stage four was to reduce stress on the caregiver in sustaining a bedridden elder or disabled person, to discourage institutionalization, and to encourage life care at home.

Along with the prefabricated housing manufacturer, the product manufacturers of the various housing components, such as sanitary equipment, windows, electrical fixtures, kitchen equipment, and the companies involved in self-help equipment, such as electric lifters and environmental and automated control systems, were included as part of the design team. Also included in all aspects of the project were gerontologists, social workers, representatives from community agencies, and the user.

Level I House (figure 10–1) is a house with average or above average architectural standards. Because the standard traditional house design imposes various limitations on disabled persons, the research goal was to determine what type of phased alterations would permit an elderly person to remain as independent as possible as disabilities develop. In other words, how could the house be adapted to permit aging in place.

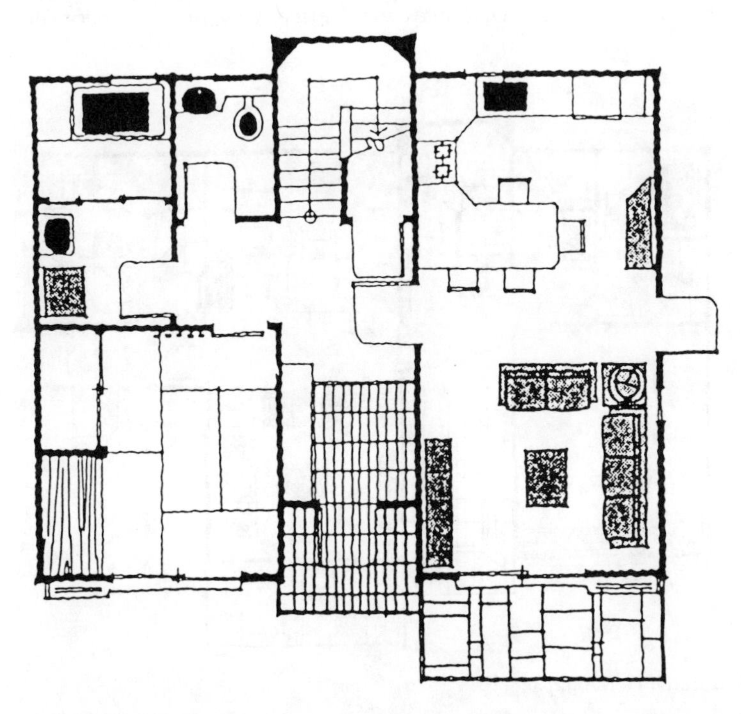

MITI Research House, Japan

Figure 10–1. Plan View: Level I

Level II House (figure 10–2) has been adapted to permit a wheelchair user to have a first-floor bedroom by converting the traditional Japanese Tatami room into a bedroom. The kitchen, living room area, and toilet-bathing areas are in this example designed for *universal use,* that is, they are adaptable to the needs of all, regardless of age or ability.

Level III House (figure 10–3) provides for the installation of a lift to the second floor (the Japanese feel such an investment is cost-effective) and revision of the washbasin area adjacent to the bathing area into a handicapped-accessible toilet with sliding accordian door. In this example, the traditional Japanese Tatami room has been retained and an existing second floor bedroom, accessible by means of the lift, is adapted for the disabled person.

Level IV House (figure 10–4) has been expanded by the addition of a new room adjacent to the kitchen-dining-living room area. The goal in designing this room for a severely disabled person was to provide all services as close to the person as possible, and therefore the toileting and bathing functions were brought to the room for the convenience of the occupant and for maximizing independence and minimizing caregiving. It was further desired that the new room be as close to the main activity spaces in the home so that the disabled person could have convenient and efficient contact with other members of the family. Distances were effectively reduced between social,

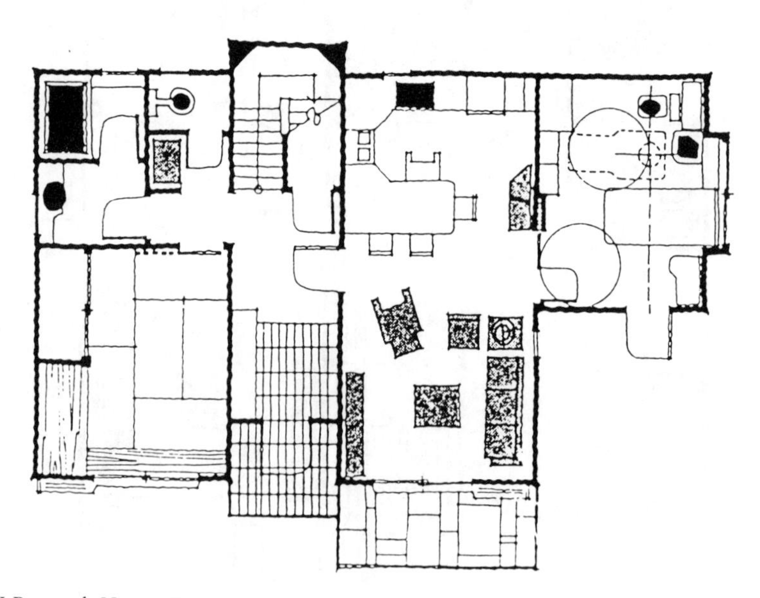

MITI Research House, Japan

Figure 10–2. Plan View: Level II

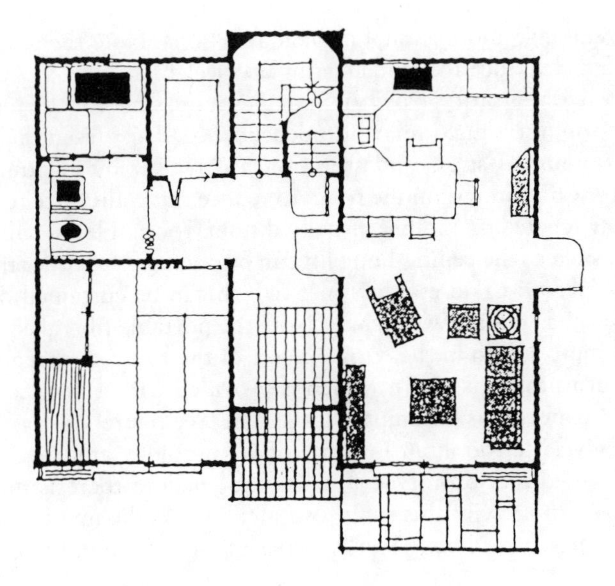

MITI Research House, Japan

Figure 10–3. Plan View: Level III

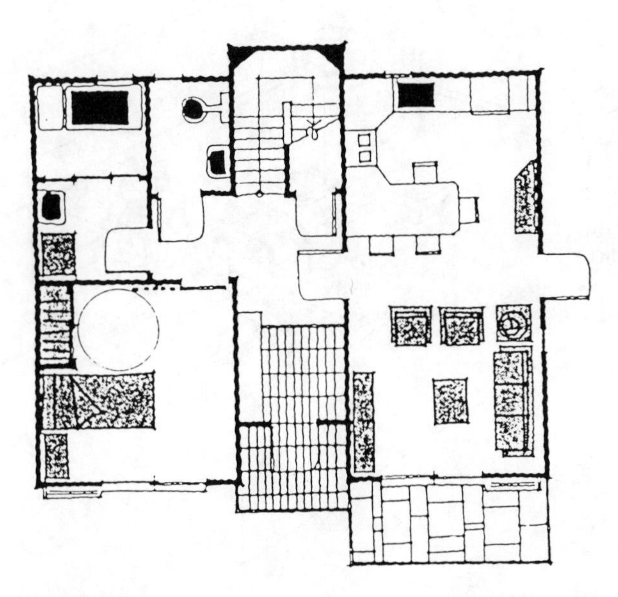

MITI Research House, Japan

Figure 10–4. Plan View: Level IV

eating, caretaking, and personal hygiene functions. Note the circles, indicating adequate clearance for maneuvering a wheelchair.

The Level IV prototype bedroom makes it possible for the most severely disabled to obtain a maximum of independence. This design helps to minimize the amount of stress and strain on a caregiver by locating the water closet and washbasin within the room to reduce travel distance to these items traditionally located in another, usually distant, room. Electrically motorized equipment such as the ceiling-hung lift can be operated by either the caregiver or disabled person to access the toilet (which can be curtained or screened-off), the washbasin, or a wheelchair. Note the portable fiberglass bathtub on a wheeled stand stored in the corner closet of the room. A caregiver can roll this unit out to the washbasin, which is provided with a hose to fill the tub and a drain connection for emptying the tub. (See figure 10–5.)

The Tokyo Metropolitan Institute of Gerontology and the MITI design team established this prototype because they believe there is an increasing need for a bedroom with this range of functions. As the number of disabled, and particularly bedridden, elderly increases, and the number of caregivers

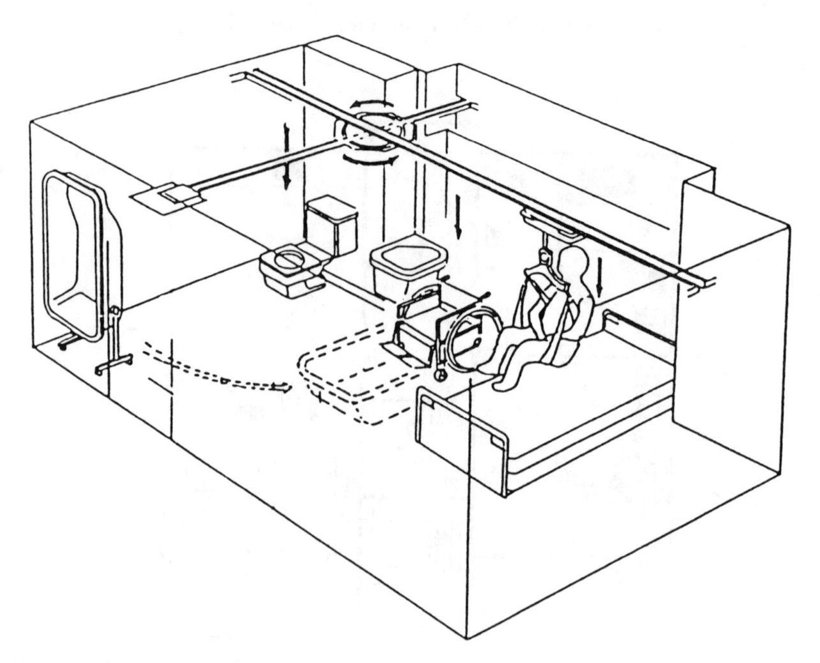

MITI Research House, Japan

Figure 10–5. Isometric View: Prototype Room for Severely Disabled

decreases, modifications are required in the form of the living unit to meet changing conditions. This approach also has application in other housing models, such as assisted-living and nursing-care facilities, where already in the United States, the shortage of caregivers is critical.

Figures 10–6 and 10–7 indicate the Japanese approach to design of an

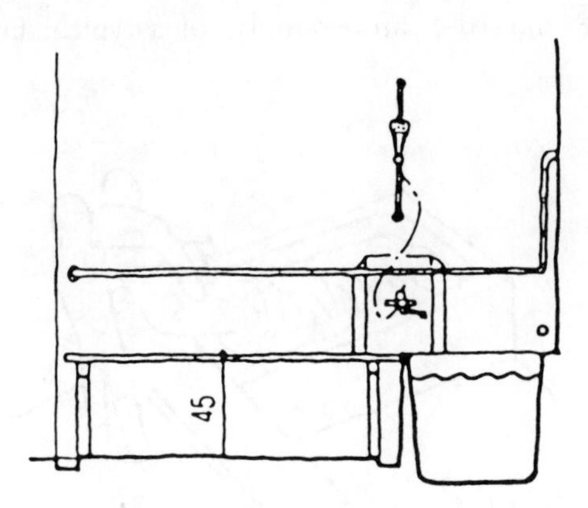

MITI Research House, Japan, Self-Help Bathing Study

Figure 10–6. Elevation View: Prototype Bathroom

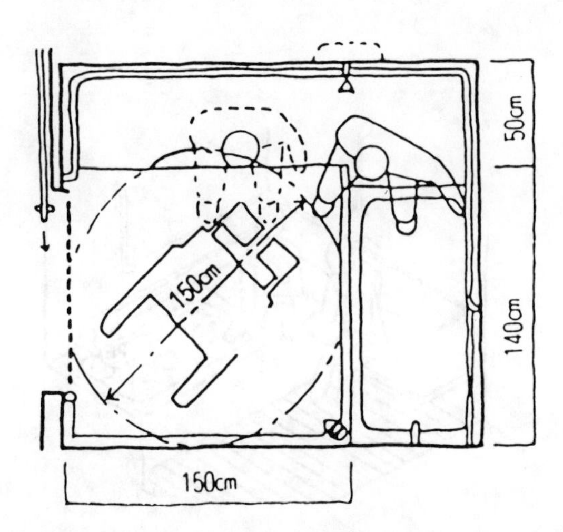

MITI Research House, Japan, Self-Help Bathing Study

Figure 10–7. Plan View: Prototype Bathroom

accessible bathing space to permit a disabled person with upper-arm mobility the opportunity for independent bathing. Observe the wide transfer shelf at tub-lip height, the handrail running along the wall, and the flexible shower hose, mounted on the wall over the shelf, which permits showering while seated on the shelf and in the tub. Note the sliding door to bathroom, the clear turning radius for the wheelchair and the floor drain in a waterproofed floor.

Figures 10–8 and 10–9 are examples of a typical Japanese tub room

MITI Research House, Japan, Self-Help Attendent-Help Bathing Study

Figure 10–8. Isometric View I: Prototype Bathroom

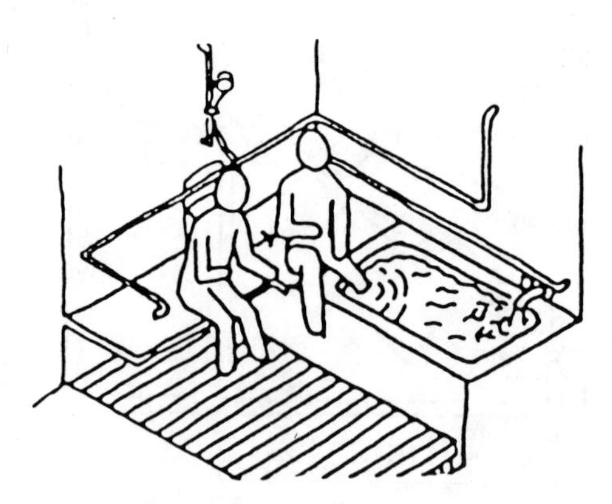

MITI Research House, Japan, Self-Help and Attendent-Help Bathing Study

Figure 10–9. Isometric View II: Prototype Bathroom

modified with a shelf-type transfer bench permitting self-help or attendant-help for elderly or disabled people.

Figures 10–10 and 10–11 illustrate a do-it-yourself removable tub seat and a box seat adjacent to the tub, with a convenient and functional handrail (grab bar) combination towel bar running along the wall to permit more accessible bathing with minimal physical room change.

The next area of industrial leadership in which the Japanese are expected to excel, with their extraordinary technology, is the housing industry.[9] Differ-

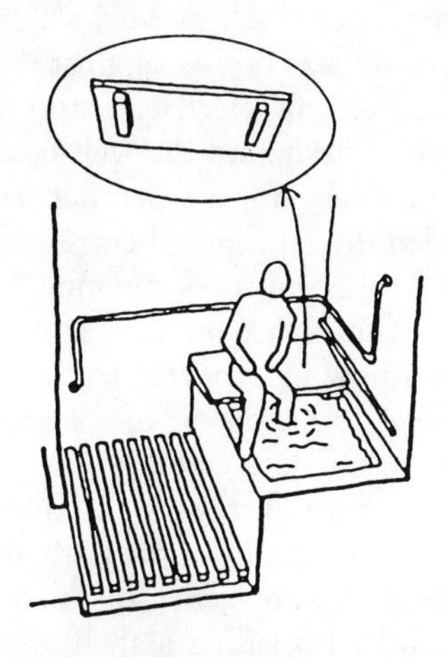

MITI Research House, Japan, Self-Help Bathing Study

Figure 10–10. Isometric View III: Prototype Bathroom

MITI Research House, Japan, Self-Help Bathing Study

Figure 10–11. Isometric View IV: Prototype Bathroom

ences between the Japanese environment and that of the United States are that in today's Japan there is a more stable financing system, the political and regulatory process is more streamlined and, in particular, there is great emphasis on innovation in building technique, in materials used, and in the products that must be effectively integrated to form an efficient structural and operational building. They place great emphasis on research and development in the manufacturing process and in understanding the functional living requirements of a home. Firms such as Sekisui, which participated in the MITI prototype adjustable house for the elderly and disabled, and other manufactured housing producers such as Misawa and Daiwa all have laboratories in which they test full-size houses against the elements. They study a resident's circulation, mechanical, electrical, and environmental patterns. They analyze the impact of a design on the well-being of a user.

The Japanese work in a very holistic manner. For example, the Misawa Homes Laboratory has identified through their research some twenty possible medical links between a house and its occupants. They believe the environment for living has a strong influence on character and health. New housing produced by most builders now incorporate features such as those described above for the MITI house. Another aspect of research by these firms looks at how to maximize efficiency and safety and how to minimize movement and potential accident. Even the path of travel of an occupant who has just done some shopping is studied in moving from the parked car to kitchen pantry to determine the best location and adjacency of functional spaces. Consideration, for example, is given by providing a shelf at the entry door to permit setting down packages until the key is found and the door is opened. A light with a motion sensor at the entry door will automatically provide a safe level of nighttime lighting so one can have security and find the keyhole.

The example shown in figure 10–12 is also from the MITI prototype. It shows an efficient kitchen-dining layout adaptable for the able and disabled. Further efficiency and economy is achieved by elimination of separate rooms for kitchen, dining, and living. Such consolidation of kitchen, eating, and living spaces reduces the amount of construction volume and can help bring construction costs down to more affordable levels.

Additional research is under way in the areas of home automation, lighting, safety and security systems, heating, ventilating and air conditioning, waterproofing, and structural integrity against flooding, earthquake, and temperature extremes. Development of new materials, production, and erection techniques are also an important part of research and development.

Some European Examples

Swedish factory-crafted housing has had over the past decade perhaps the world's highest standard in energy efficiency and cost-effectiveness. The superior performance of the Swedish House™ is due, in no small measure, to

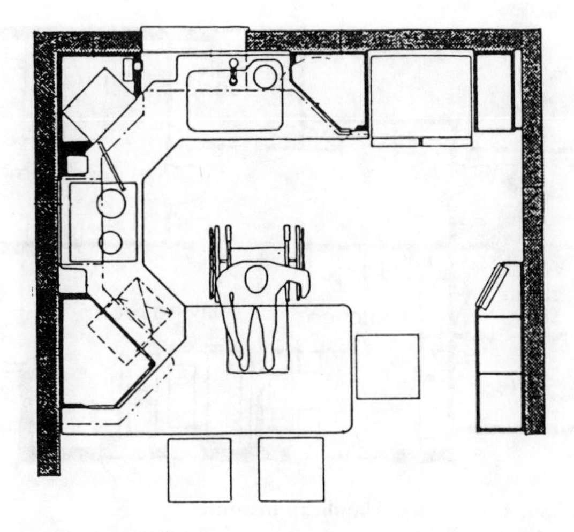

MITI Research House, Japan, Self-Help Food Preparation Study

Figure 10–12. Plan View: Prototype Kitchen

the technical sophistication of the product. The approach is holistic. Factory-crafting of the Swedish House™ involves an integrated manufacturing program. It is a single-team process from harvesting of trees to the sale of a turnkey home. This technique minimizes on-site labor, the middleman, and independent subcontractors. A typical house can be erected in a matter of hours by a crew of four handling all operations. Although produced in a factory with sophisticated manufacturing procedures, the Swedish House™ is not mass-produced. The process allows custom production and tailoring to suit many individual tastes and regional markets.[10]

In urban settings where multifamily housing dominates, typical masonry, concrete, steel, and prefabricated construction prevails over the wood frame of the single-family unit mentioned above. Nevertheless, the design approach still recognizes the need for flexibility and layouts that accommodate all situations. In figure 10–13, a unit designed to accommodate a family with a disabled person, there is consideration given to wheelchair storage and battery charging, convenient access to the bathroom through provision of a sliding door, a corner shower space without a stall or curb, and modular storage in the bedroom and entry hall, which can be added to or modified as needed. Note the generous entrance area that is adequate for functional uses, such as for temporary wheelchair or walker storage, storing or putting down packages, or putting on outer garments.

In Switzerland, as in other countries, the trend has been toward smaller households. More Swiss men and women over sixty-five years of age are living alone or in group housing. Some 10 percent of the elderly population

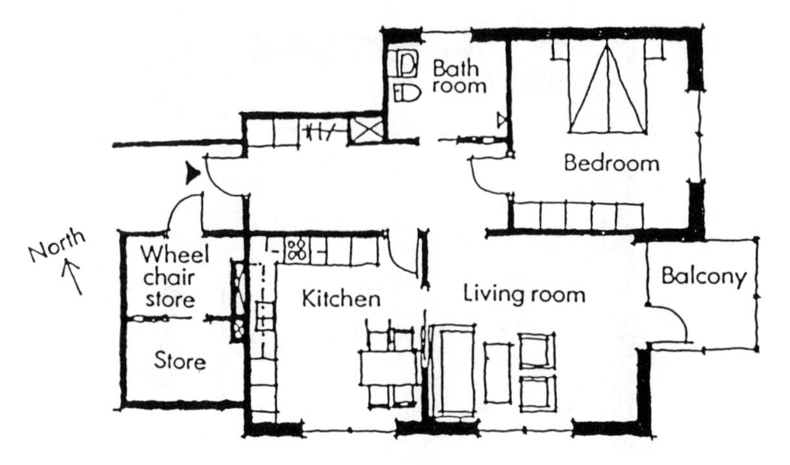

Parkmöllan in Malmö, The Swedish Handicap Institute
Architect: Sven-Iver Ekstrand

Figure 10–13. Plan View: Apartment for the Severely Disabled and Aged

live in purpose-built housing such as old people's homes or skilled nursing facilities. The public policy is to discourage new construction of old people's homes or nursing facilities and to promote an increase in group housing with community-based support services.[11] However, newer policies are to encourage aging in place. This is made possible by government financing of a residential retrofit, so the elderly can remain in their own home. By remaining in familiar surroundings they can keep up their social contacts and be close to familiar shopping, transportation, and support services for as long as possible. The government policy of keeping people at home requires the availability of efficient, mobile support services, including nursing, homemaking, and housekeeping, and equipping each living unit with an emergency call system linked to a central community support station. The government feels that this approach is far less costly to the taxpayer than establishing stand-alone institutional facilities.

The Swiss plan in figure 10–14 illustrates a unit layout for an elderly person living alone. In this example, the living, eating, and sleeping functions are contained in one flexible open space. The bath and kitchen are enclosed. Sliding doors to the kitchen and bath can be retrofitted, if needed. This unit can be arranged by the occupant in any desired form. The entrance is defined by movable storage units to provide some privacy in the sleeping area. A comfortably sized balcony can accommodate a breakfast table, a wheelchair, and space for guests.

As flexibility and choice of layout is an important feature for a resident, the example from Denmark (figure 10–15) shows a single room and bath in a housing cluster for group living and central dining, with a mix of activity spaces. This minimal-size room permits variety in the furniture arrangement.

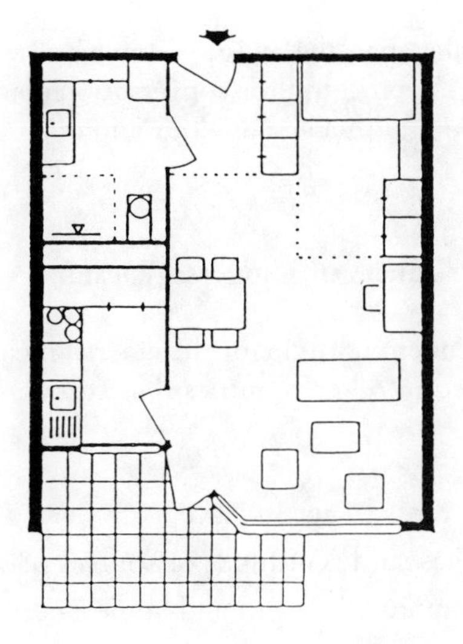

Gerlinger, RFA, Switzerland, Architects: Aichele, Fiedler, Weinmann

Figure 10–14. Plan View: Apartment for an Elderly Person Living Alone

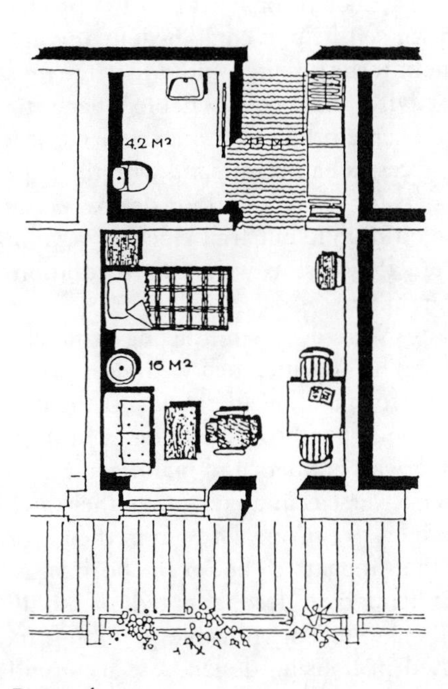

Plejecentret Møllestien, Denmark

Figure 10–15. Plan View: Assisted Living Room for an Elderly Person

Although much smaller than the Swiss example and with no kitchen, it still allows flexibility for sleeping and for conversational and recreational grouping. Note the bathroom with a sliding door and open shower area.

Tools for Living: Products of Universal Design

To achieve an independent lifestyle for the elderly, including the frail elderly, it has been established in other countries that certain conditions need to be met, including:[12]

1. The participant wants to age in place.
2. The participant has sufficient funds or sources of support.
3. Availability of community health and home care.
4. There is an enabling environment.

We find in such countries as Switzerland and those of the Scandinavian tier that a great deal of research goes into the development of "tools for living." As these nations progressed in the development of specially designed products for the elderly, they recognized that if a product or space was well-designed to provide for self-help, it could benefit anyone. In other words, any occupant could benefit if the design could satisfy the most extreme condition. For example, if an environment could enable a person in a wheelchair to be independent, it could serve others without the need of wheelchair as well. If a wheelchair could access a bathroom, and with the appropriate shower temperature controls, transfer seats, and floor drains, permit the disabled occupant to shower, then a mobile but frail elder, or a young child, would have the means to shower safely just as well, and in addition, there could be adequate room for a caretaker.

If all our buildings were designed utilizing principles that would achieve barrier-free and safe environments, then we indeed would not require special purpose-built housing for just the elderly or just the disabled.[13] Principles of universal design can be applied to a building, a product, or an appliance. I am hopeful that American builders and manufacturers will evaluate the success of manufacturers overseas and encourage their architects and designers to incorporate principles of universal design in their work.

Another trend that appears to be on the horizon is the development of products capable of being converted, adapted, or modified in a simple fashion. The notion of "plug-in" or movable plumbing fixtures, for example, needs to be addressed in housing design. We accommodate changes in the office environment with movable partitions, under-floor wire raceways, and modular ceilings and light fixtures. If our housing could be manufactured so that it could be modified to meet the varying needs of an occupant or a family through the different cycles of life, that is, with occupants changing from a dependent child to an independent single person, to a couple with one child, to two or more children, to a family with an elder relative, to "empty nesters," to an aging couple, to a widower or widow living alone, then indeed, we would be truly achieving the notion of universal design. Recognizing the benefits of adaptable living environments, Japanese housing manufacturers are at work studying techniques applied to office buildings to creating modular, interchangeable components for residential settings.

Regulatory Considerations

Building codes in the United States have traditionally been under the jurisdiction of the individual states and towns. Inconsistent interpretation of codes and regulations can hinder positive improvements and appropriate, consistent nationwide development. Performance codes and zoning regulations sensitive to all of society's needs should be emphasized. In some communities there is an abundant supply of housing stock that is underutilized. In many suburban towns large single-family houses are being occupied by a single elderly person. If an attractive alternative were available, such as a nearby life-care center, which could provide a variety of support services, then an elderly "empty nester" might decide to relocate to the life-care center and permit his or her home to be recycled in a more efficient way. But if the elderly resident did not want to move, then there should be some way for the zoning regulation to permit the resident to invite other elderly people or even younger people to share the home. Some zoning boards are beginning to modify their regulations to permit such use.

As zoning and building regulations in the United States become more sensitive to user needs, we must encourage innovative development of new products for an American market. Although improvement in American product design is known to be needed, and many products that encourage independent living can be found in foreign countries, there seem to be very few products of the type shown on these pages available in the United States.

One reason that manufacturers here are slow in developing innovative products is fear of liability suits. Also, a number of foreign manufacturers have hesitated in exporting their products to the United States out of fear of excessive and frivolous litigation. Even though there has not been an obsession with product liability litigation in other countries, manufacturers are careful to produce products of quality design and fabrication that reduce the exposure to litigation.

Another concern of manufacturers is the cost of producing new products that will require a careful research and development effort. Most American manufacturers are in a financial stance that gives priority to short-term profits, whereas in other developed countries, the emphasis is on long-term profit.

Innovative technology applied to products for the elderly will be beneficial in the long run not only for the elderly user but also for the caregiver or nonhandicapped user. Its application will be a means of keeping costs down. Above all, products that enable the elderly to live independently result in the elderly feeling good about themselves, maintaining their self-esteem, and being generally happier in a home setting than in an institutional environment, where so many deteriorate so rapidly.

Innovative Products

In our living units of the future there is no doubt that electronics will continue to play an even greater part. Intelligent-house technology programs in this country and in others are moving rapidly ahead with major developments for residential and special needs applications. In the future, most, if not all, of our appliances will have micro chips and be capable of functioning on a remote-control basis.

The various products discussed next indicate directions in the development of more sophisticated and flexible devices for the living unit. Even automobile manufacturers in Europe are developing automobiles adapted to elderly or disabled needs as part of their standard line. In Japan, housing manufacturers include in their sales brochures housing packages that are changeable for special needs as individual needs change.

When an American developer is shown new unit layout schemes and innovative products, the first question is, "How much does it cost?" The answer is: it costs more initially, but less in the long run. Besides, these products provide something of greater value when they can help provide a better quality of life.

Adjustable-Height Kitchen Units. Those elderly and disabled who find difficulty in reaching or in standing for long periods, or who may be wheelchair bound, and yet have the ability to prepare a meal, will find adjustable-height kitchen counters and cabinets an innovative approach to serve their needs. These units are electrically operated from a control panel on the face of the counter. (See figure 10–16.)

Solutions that enable the elderly and the disabled to maintain more independence have benefit for others as well. An adjustable-height counter will provide more comfort to other members of the family who may be tall or short. (See figure 10–17.) Designing products for all, which do not carry with them the stigma of institutional use or appear to be designed for the infirm, is a goal we all need to strive for.

The ADR Reduced Swing Door for Wheelchair-Bound People. To open a standard hinged door in a seated position is quite difficult. A reduced swing door can be opened without displacement. The ADR door is an innovative two-panel articulated door, which requires one-third or less the square feet taken by a conventional swing door. (See figure 10–18.)

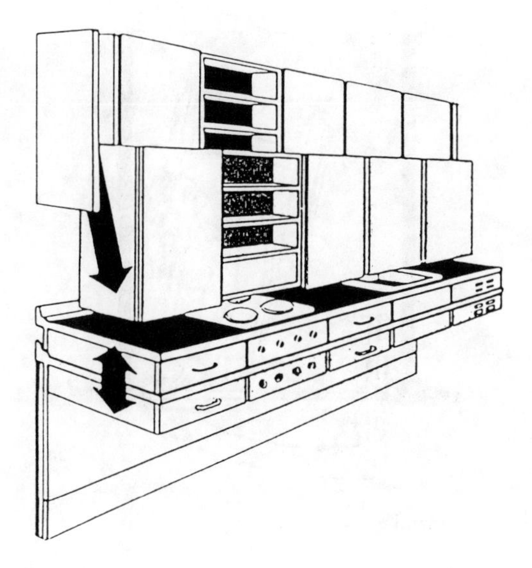

System Apfelbaum, West Germany

Figure 10–16. Adjustable-Height Kitchen Unit

NESA A/S, Help-Aids Centers, Denmark

Figure 10–17. Prototype Kitchen for the Handicapped

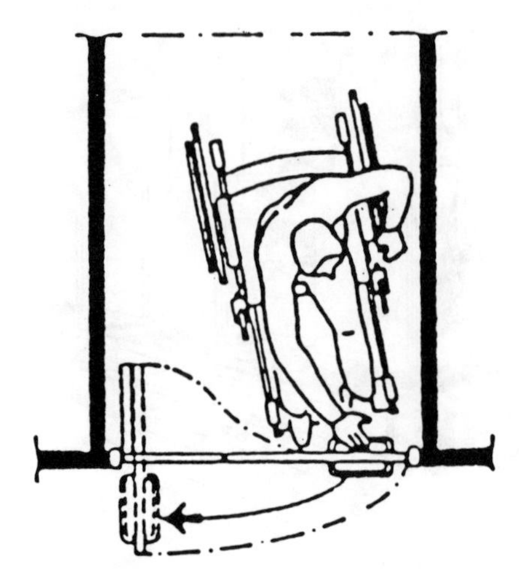

Reduced Swing Doors, England

Figure 10–18. ADR Two-Panel Articulated Door for Wheelchairs

Home-Automation Technology

The Japanese approach to the intelligent automated house utilizes available electronic technology to permit remote control of various mechanical, electrical, and communication systems. It is the same type of technology as used in a remote-control system for a television set or for a garage door opener. One system may use infrared beam, the other a radio frequency. (See figure 10–19.)

In the example provided in figure 10–20 showing a disabled elder, bedridden or wheelchair-bound, a remote control system is set up to provide environmental, communication, and security control. This system helps provide more independence and reduces the amount of time required of a caregiver. As shown in figures 10–19 through 10–21, the bedridden person can from the control device manage such activities as:

- Adjust bed height;
- Operate heating, ventilating, and air conditioning;
- Open or close window and blinds;
- Turn on or off room lights;
- Receive annunciator panel signals such as "the stove had been left on";
- Contact control center panel through signal voice or video;
- Hear or see fire or smoke or security alarm; and
- Lock or unlock doors and windows.

MITI Research House, Japan

Figure 10–19. Home Automation: View I

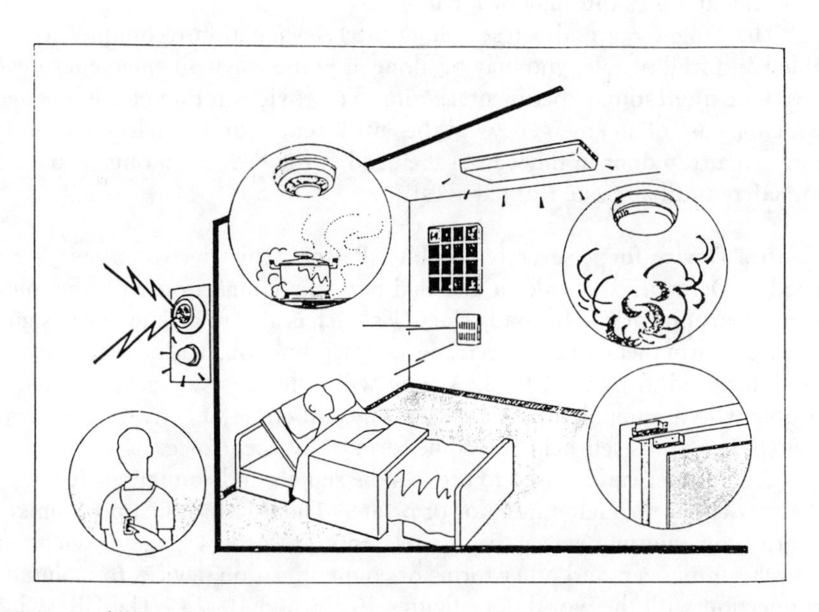

MITI Research House, Japan

Figure 10–20. Home Automation: View II

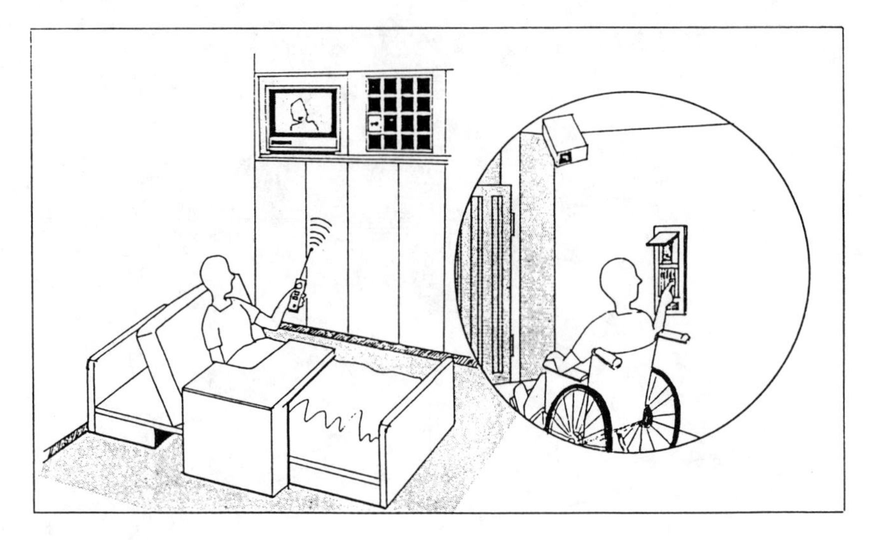

MITI Research House, Japan

Figure 10–21. Home Automation: View III

Home automation systems similar to these are on display and for sale in department stores throughout Japan.

The Japanese are also researching safety evacuation techniques for disabled and frail people who may be alone at home when an emergency develops. One interesting experimental prototype provides for an ejection system, which in case of an emergency has the entire bed, with the bedridden, ejected through a trap door in the wall at the head of the bed, to an outside balcony for safety until a rescue team arrives!

Control Device for a Severely Disabled Person. This electronic unit, developed in Denmark, provides a disabled person a connection with the immediate environment and beyond. The CIF switch is able to pick up weak signals and transform them into an electronic contact function. The activator options are illustrated in figure 10–22. As you will note, this switch is suitable for people who are unable to produce the physical effort of activating a normal switch. It permits self-help and some form of independence.

A computer can be used to process the signals and communicate back to the user either through a monitor or printer. The user has the opportunity to control the environment, activate a television, recorders, page or telephone, speech synthesizer, and other forms of communication devices to maintain a connection with the world. (See figures 10–23 and 10–24.) The CIF switch, when connected with an Apple II and a MAC-APPLE program, has given

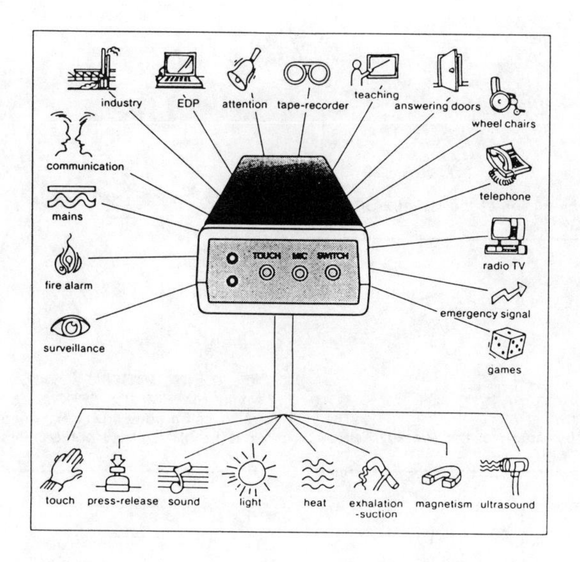

Synaps Electronic ApS, Denmark

Figure 10–22. Home Automation: CIF Electronic Switch Base Unit

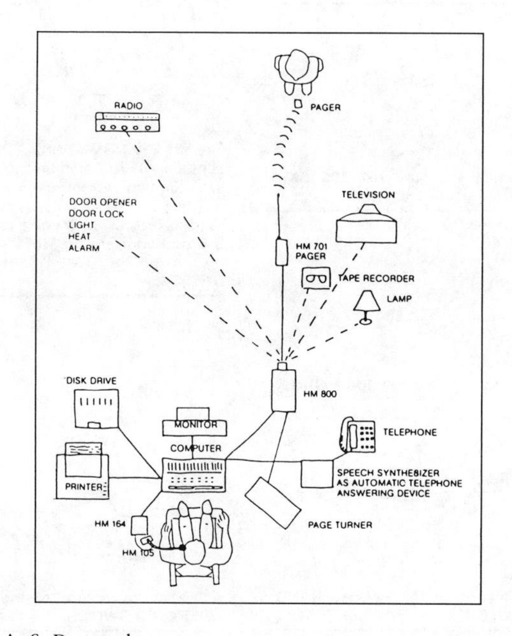

Synaps Electronic ApS, Denmark

Figure 10–23. Home Automation: Communication Options

Activation by means of the **HM 102 SPECIAL MICROPHONE.**

Activation by means of the **HM 103 THROAT MICROPHONE.**

Activation by means of the **HM 112 BENDING SWITCH.**

Activation by means of the **HM 105 SKIN CONTACT.**

Activation by means of the **HM 104 EXHALATION SWITCH.**

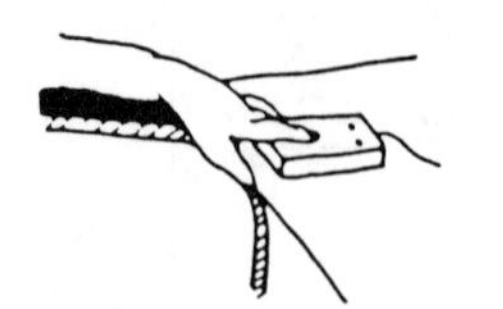

Activation by means of the **HM 110 HAND-OPERATED SWITCH.**

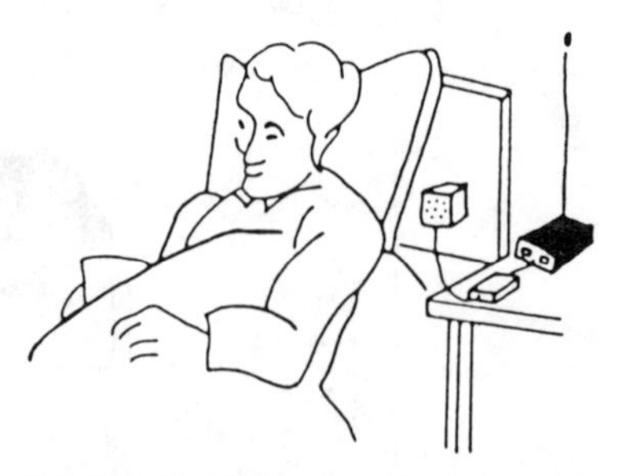

The **HM 701 PAGER** transmits an alarm call, when the **HM 102 SPECIAL MICROPHONE** receives an open vowel. Between the HM 102 and the HM 701 the HM 160 CIF-switch is to be used.

The **HM 230 COMMUNICATOR** is used by persons unable to communicate normally and is used for training from yes/no communication to pointing out up to 100 words or symbols. Can be used as preliminary training before a computer is procured. Here the HM 230 is activated by means of the **HM 110 HAND-OPERATED SWITCH.**

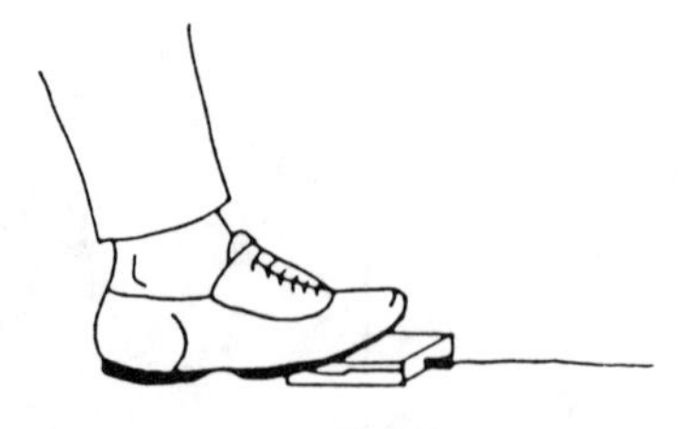

Activation by means of the **HM 111 FOOT-OPERATED SWITCH.**

Synaps Electronic ApS, Denmark

Figure 10–24. Home Automation: Activation Options

even totally paralyzed people the opportunity to communicate with the world around them. Severely disabled people unable to speak or move can now have new possibilities of communicating with their environment. (See figure 10–25.)

An Adjustable-Height Washbasin and Toilet Unit. A result of research and development from the MITI House, this wall panel contains a hidden motor. With the press of a button, the unit will raise or lower the washbasin or water closet to a desired comfortable height. The water closet is provided with a

The activating of electric toys. Above a train is being operated by the CIF-switch **HM 162**, which is being activated by means of the **HM 127 TOUCH PLATE.**

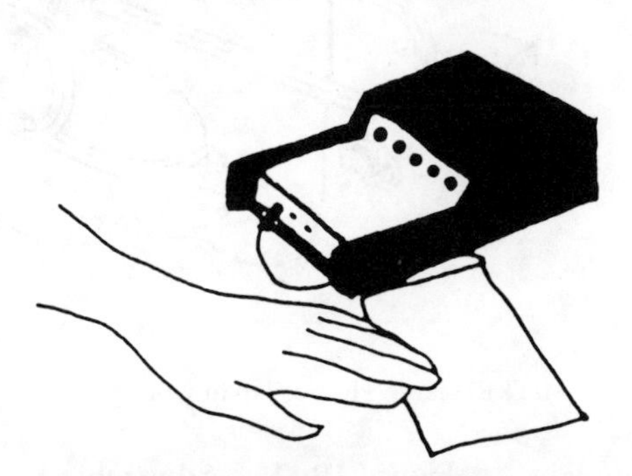

The **HM 405 5-STEERING UNIT.** By activation the moving light is stopped at the desired function. The corresponding electric device is being activated.

By means of the **HM 164** a computer is being operated. The activation aid is here a **HM 103 THROAT MICROPHONE.** The normal function of the computer can be used. Furthermore the **HM 800 COM STEERING UNIT** can be connected to the computer. When connected so the system can be used for controlling the environment and control up to 8 different electric devices and an alarm call.

Synaps Electronic ApS, Denmark

Figure 10–25. Home Automation: Communicator Unit

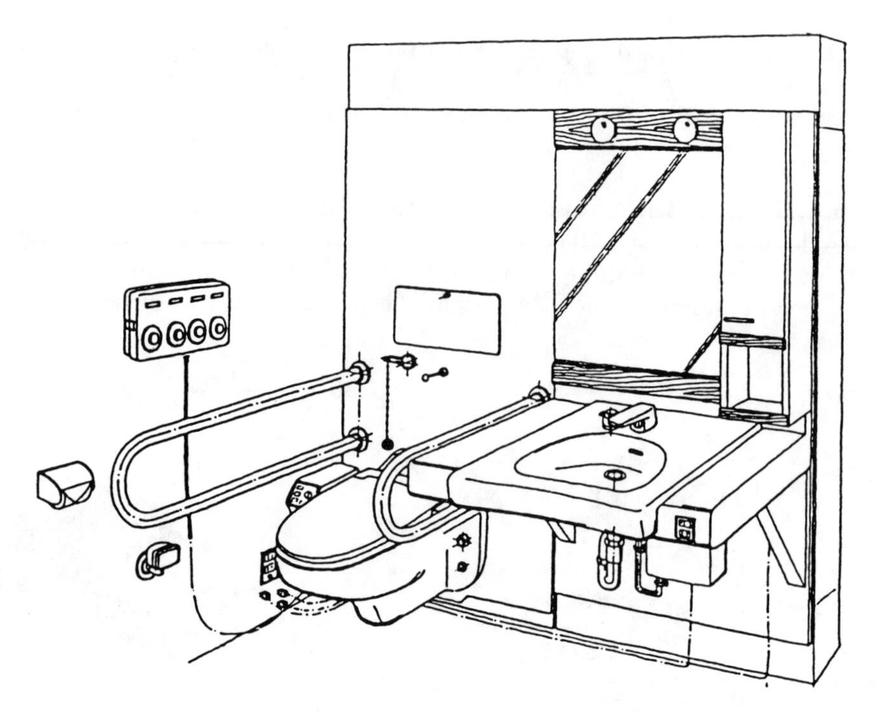

MITI Research House, Japan

Figure 10–26. Adjustable-Height Washbasin and Toilet Unit

special toilet seat that assists those with special needs with their personal hygiene. The unit, developed from a system created in Switzerland more than thirty years ago, will wash and dry the bottom at the press of a button, a floor pedal, or even through voice activation. (See figure 10–26.)

Handytub: A Walk-in Tub for the Elderly and Disabled. Many accidents occur in the bathroom, particularly in entering and leaving a bathtub. This West German product, of fiberglass-reinforced polyester, permits the elderly and disabled who would like to bathe without the help of others the means to be independent. For those who need assistance, this design helps reduce the strain of caregiving. The lateral door enables direct access from a wheelchair to the nonslip tub seat. An integral run-around handrail provides support while entering and leaving the tub. While seated one may comfortably lock the door so that it is tightly sealed. As an accessory, a hair-washing bowl is available, which is integrated in the tub at the top of the seat back. The hood-cover swings back when access to the bowl is desired. (See figure 10–27.)

An Adjustable-Height Shower Seat With Arm Rest. Similar to the MITI bathroom panel, this unit can be mounted directly to the wall surface with four bolts. It contains a hidden 24-volt electric motor that can operate from a control cord or a remote hand-held infrared device. The shower seat/arm rest unit can be raised or lowered and tilted-up, to be out of the way. For those elderly or disabled wishing to shower themselves seated, this unit will enhance their independence. This adjustable-height motorized wall panel unit can be used to mount a washbasin, a shower plank bed, or a shower seat. The backboard comes in a white laminate and has a postformed round edge and an adjustable height range of sixteen inches. (See figure 10–28.)

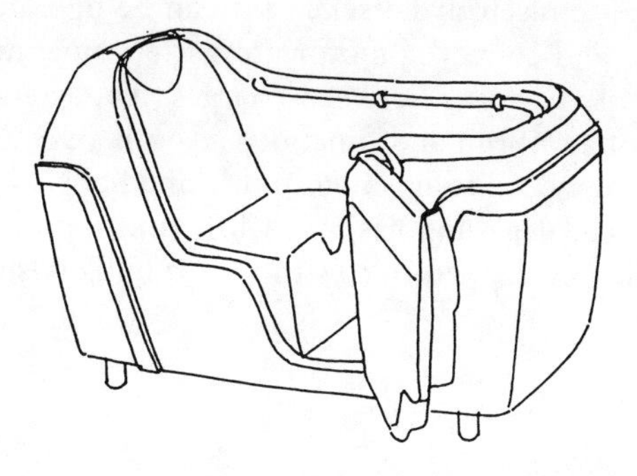

Blanco, West Germany

Figure 10–27. Walk-in Bathtub with Hair-Washing Headrest and Bowl

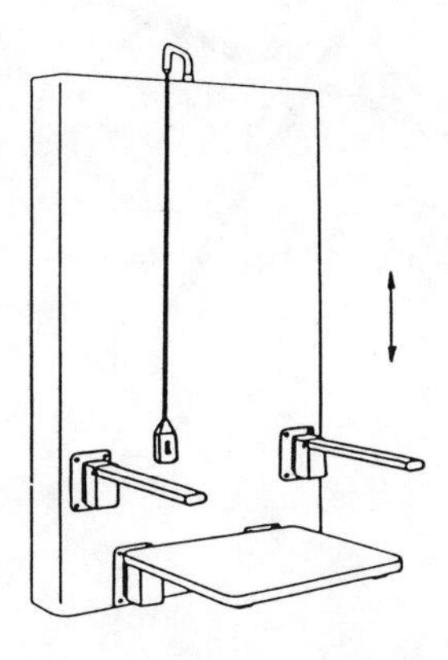

Ropox, Denmark

Figure 10–28. Adjustable-Height Tilt-up Shower Seat and Arm Rest

A Ceiling-Mounted Lift for the Disabled. To reduce stress and strain on the caregiver of a severely disabled person, or for a disabled person who can manage the transfer from a bed to wheelchair, or to a bathroom, this device will ensure user-safe mobility from room to room, independent of electric cables. Created and manufactured in Denmark, Dan-Hoist was developed to provide maximum reliability and easy operation from a hand switch with a discrete and unobtrusive design of the housing and support system and of the rails, brackets, and switch points. Minimum space is needed for rail-mounting from the ceiling. (See figure 10–29.) The lifting motor is compact and glides along the aluminum rails with minimum effort from an assistant. The conveyor motor is an additional feature that can be used by a disabled person who wants to help himself or herself, or it can be operated by an assistant. The lifting motor and conveyor motor are battery operated with a capacity of twenty to twenty-five lifts between charges. The charging set can be located at the end of a rail run and functions as both an end-stop and charging socket. A wide variety of lifting slings and lifting hangers are available, with divided or undivided leg supports, with low and high backs, from bed or floor, from wheelchair, for return to sitting or a lying position, for amputees, and for toileting.

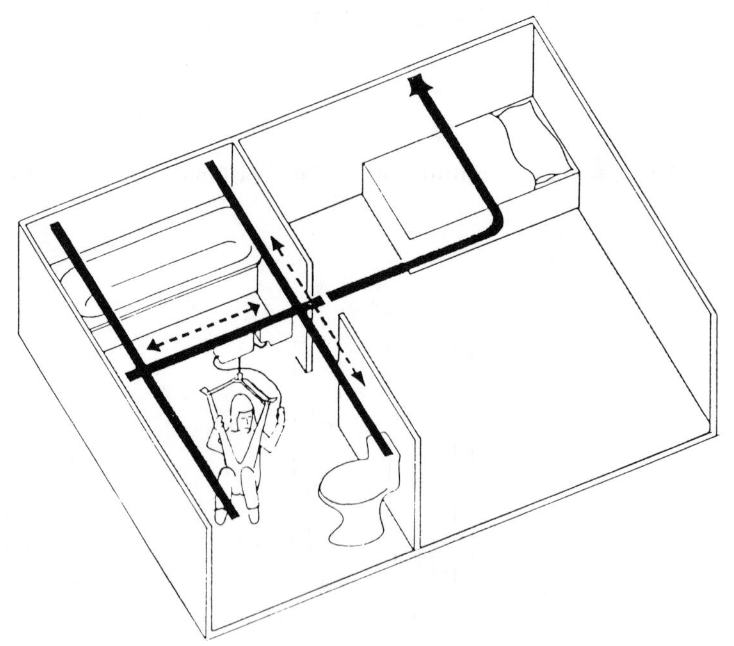

V. Guldmann A/S, Denmark

Figure 10–29. Ceiling-Mounted Lift for the Disabled

A Retrofitted Toilet Seat Lifting Mechanism for Frail Elders. The "Electro" toilet seat lift, manufactured in Denmark, is used for people who have weak lower limbs but who have balance and upper-limb strength and do not require arm rests. The unit can be placed where the existing toilet seat is removed. (See figure 10–30). Another system, the "Hydro," features arm rests that move with the seat as it rises and provide stability and balance. Both units are applicable for use in private homes as well as in congregate housing.

A Water Closet That Does It All. This Swiss product has been on the market for over thirty years, and it is used extensively in many private and public facilities in Europe. It combines the European douche and toilet in one unit, with the added feature of warm air drying. (See figure 10–31.) Another Swiss

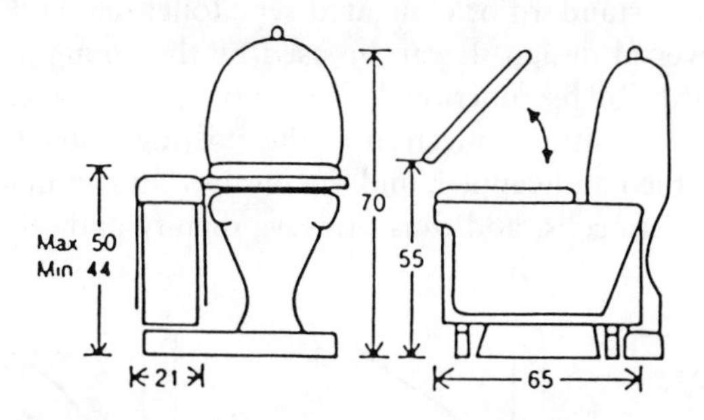

V. Guldmann A/S, Denmark

Figure 10–30. "Electro" Toilet Seat Lift

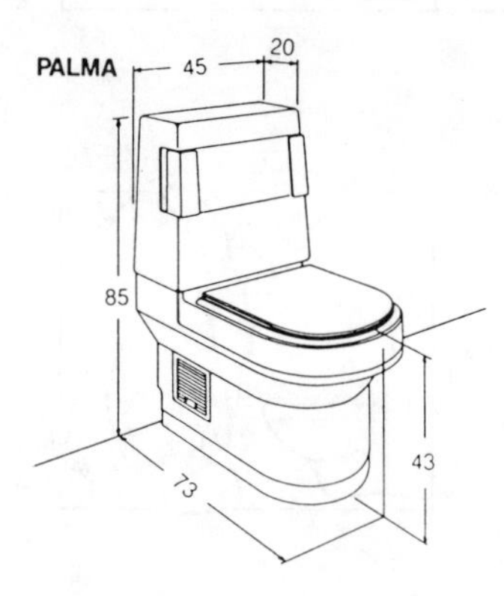

Closomat AG, Switzerland

Figure 10–31. Closomat® Paperless Toilet Machine: View I

manufacturer has recently introduced a similar product with an adjustable-height feature, resulting in a universal-design product, usable by young, short, tall, elderly, and disabled. The unit is a one-piece ceramic glazed porcelain body with a phenolic plastic seat; both body and seat are available in a range of decorator colors. An electric connection is required for the hot water heater, the exhaust, and warm air fan. Odors are drawn directly from the bowl, the douche arm cleans the perineal or anal area with preset water temperature controlled by pressing a switch corner of the water tank with the elbow. The warm air fan continues to perform as long as one remains seated. (See figure 10–32.)

A Microcomputerized Wash/Dry Toilet Seat. This innovative product, a state-of-the-art aid for personal hygiene, retrofits over an existing water closet, replacing a standard or elongated-type toilet seat and cover. This is a product of universal design. It can be used by the young and old, the able and handicapped. To be functional, it simply requires a grounded electric convenience outlet and a connection to the existing water tank supply line. For the elderly, the handicapped, and the disabled, it can make it possible to care for one's own needs, and thus preserve dignity and self-esteem. For an

Closomat AG, Switzerland

Figure 10–32. Closomat® Paperless Toilet Machine: View II

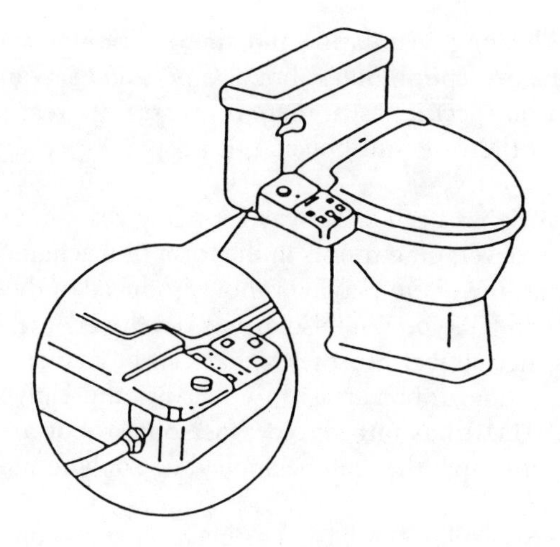

TOTO, Japan

Figure 10–33. "Washlett SIII": A Paperless Toilet Machine

attendant it can help reduce the stress and strain of caregiving. (See figure 10–33.) This microcomputerized wash/dry toilet seat manufactured in Japan, is a practical alternative to conventional bathroom procedures and brings us toward the concept of the paperless toilet. With the touch of a button, the microcomputer sends a gentle spray of warm water, followed by warm air for drying. The temperature of the water and air and the water pressure rate, are adjustable by the user from the attached control panel. Alternative control systems are available, such as foot operation, hand-held remote, and voice.

Robotics as Assistive Tools for Living

Are robotics really in our future? If so, when? They are definitely in our future, and to some degree they are here now. Depending on how and what you perceive a robot to be, robots, or mechanical tools for living, are being used in our everyday life without much notice.

Our perception of a robot may be that of a mechanical person on wheels, rolling about as a house servant, but any mechanical device that makes life easier, such as a microwave, is in a way a very simple form of a robot. It can be programmed to act on our behalf with preset instructions. There are many devices or mechanisms in our homes or offices today that are robotic in that they are guided by automatic controls: thermostats, timers, microwaves,

VCRs, security, heating, ventilating and air conditioning systems, and so on. And between the perception of a robot as a personal servant and the devices used today that do specific tasks, there is an area of great potential application of robots in the care and housing of people, especially the elderly and disabled.

Research work has been underway for many years in technologically advanced countries developing robots in the form of mechanical human beings. There is Wasubot, the piano playing robot, produced in the Kato Lab at Waseda University in Tokyo. But also being developed are bionic arms and hands, such as mechanical prostheses that can be activated by electrocutaneous stimulation and robot arms. In Great Britain, Universal Machine Intelligence, Ltd. (UMI) has introduced a personal robot arm, representing a cost/utility breakthrough that can be applied not only to industry, but also to health care.

Until now, particular emphasis has been on the application of robotics to serve the severely disabled. According to UMI, there are in the United States alone, some 8 million people using special mobility aids, and some 33 million suffering from some major activity limitation. Attention is now being directed toward the use of interactive robots as an aid for independent living among the frail elderly. It is recognized that problems facing the elderly are significant in the area of mental capacity and function, involving degrees of memory loss, cognitive dysfunction, and disorientation. As suggested by Geoff Fernie of the University of Toronto in his article, *Can Robots Help People Help People?*, "metaphorically speaking, the robot should give the elderly user a green light, when everything is in order, and a red light if an inappropriate or dangerous action is being taken or something has been forgotten."[14] In this example, a robot could have two important functions: monitoring and reminding. Examples could be the problem of older people using stoves and the high incidence of fires caused by forgetfulness of confused elders. "Falls are a common cause of accidental death amongst the elderly, and frequently lead to injury that needs medical assistance."[15] A robot that could monitor this situation and call for assistance through the telephone, or in the instance of the stove, serve as a reminder, could certainly assist in encouraging independent living. Another area of loss of independence, according to Fernie, is in the area of lower-limb function. One of the most difficult tasks for a frail older person is to stand up and sit down, or get on or off a chair or transfer to a toilet. A robot that would emphasize assistance for mobility would therefore be of great potential value to the elderly.

Other applications are as described in Arthur Clarke's science fiction novel, *The Songs of Distant Earth,* where a robot as a house servant/caretaker brings food or drink from the kitchen and serves them in the living room.[16] Or, as the robot Arthur did, in Arthur Clarke's short story, *House Arrest,* robots could provide the resident with complete environmental and security monitoring besides performing its usual housekeeping and homemaking chores. Arthur even managed finances, investments, and paid the bills.[17]

According to Gari Lesnoff-Caravaglia, executive director of the University of Massachusetts Center on Aging—National Clearinghouse on Technology and Aging: "The home of the future will be built on technology. We must harness technology to enhance independence. We must integrate its products with the environment and with user needs. Our process should be to develop interactive robotics with the user as a participant in the design. Our goals should be to better understand human systems interaction and apply technology to assist mankind."[18]

What areas in current research and development are being looked at for robotic application? In many of the industrialized nations, work is progressing in a number of areas, including:

- Activities of Daily Living: bathing, toileting, meal preparation and eating, mobility, and communication aids;
- Therapeutic Applications: bodily condition monitors and response equipment;
- Vocational Applications: automated workstations; and
- Recreational Applications: mental and physical game activity participation devices.

In the area of long-term care, robotic applications are being developed to provide a variety of support both for the patient and for the caregiver. These include such items as:[19]

- Transfer lifts from bed to chair;
- Ambulation walkers or Helping Hands;
- Fetch and carry nurses aides as a Helpmate (figure 10–34);
- Physical therapy exercisers, such as a range-of-motion exerciser;
- Depuddler as a urine vacuum;
- Wheelchair Robo-mobile voice or optical pointer activation; and
- Robotic shower bath.

Helpmate

Helpmate is a robotic nurses' aide, designed specifically to carry out mundane fetch and carry tasks, now performed by nurses' aides, and other support personnel. By assuming time-consuming tasks, Helpmate relieves highly

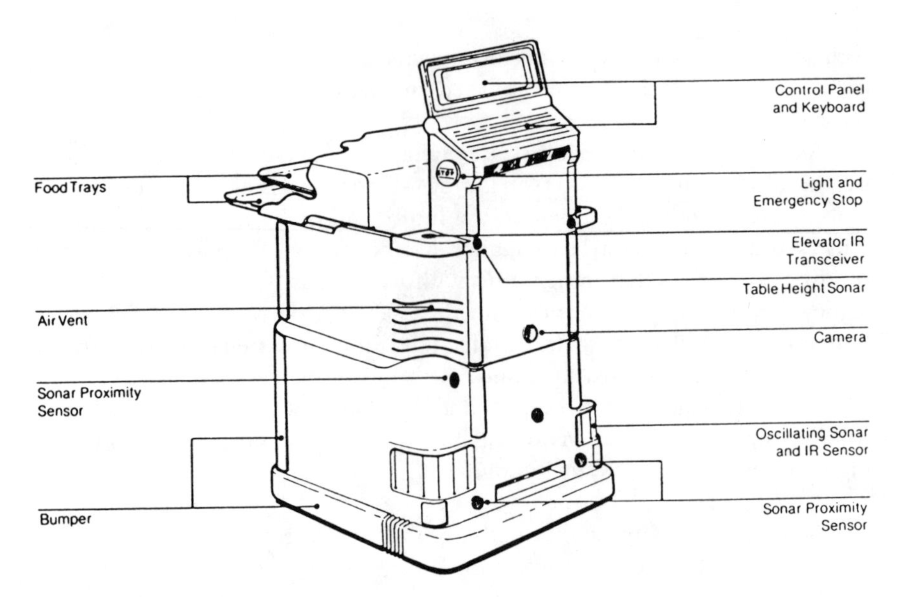

Transitions Research Corporation, Danbury, CT

Figure 10–34. "Helpmate": A Fetch-and-Carry Robot

trained personnel to carry out more critical duties. Such tasks could include transport of:

- Special meal trays;
- Central supply material;
- Pharmacy medications;
- Patient medical records;
- Lab samples; and
- Contagious waste.

Helpmate uses vision, proximity sensors, and dead reckoning to navigate through cluttered hallways, ride elevators, and avoid people and obstacles encountered along its route.

Recently, the Japan Industrial Robot Association took aim at nursing and developed concepts of care, with the Kurasowa Research & Development Center. They are researching the uses of robots in intensive care that are designed to supplement human services. The researchers recognize an increasing awareness in Japan about the rapid growth of its elderly population and the need for adaptations affecting the well and frail elderly. Their goals are to:

- Increase the independence of the bedfast and others severely disabled; and
- Reduce physical and mental stress among caregivers.

The Japanese, in a collaboration between government and industry, are developing products to serve those goals. They have brought to the market or are in developmental stages on such items as:

- A transfer chair lift that can be operated by the user or with an assistant between bed and toilet, between bed and bath or dining room, to parking area, and so on;
- An automatic body temperature control device for the handicapped and elderly as wearable clothing; and
- A multifunctional bed, permitting the bedridden to toilet or to take a shower bath without moving from the bed.

A concept for a Japanese "roboticized" home, described by Masako Osako, Ph.D, permits the bedridden to control the environment of the room; observe through a television monitor who is at the front door, and admit the person or communicate a message; and call up reading material on another monitor.[20] Diagnostic equipment is linked to the doctor's office, and the doctor and bedridden can communicate with each other through telescreens. A robot transports meals, a personal robot arm assists with feeding, and the bed itself helps position the person to prevent bed sores. A bath can be summoned, and a robot can help deliver medications and move or transfer the bedridden.

The Japanese are even working on a guide dog robot. Here in the United States, at the Carnegie-Mellon University, K.G. Englehardt, director, Center for Human Service Robots, is working on:[21]

> *Respite Robots:* If a robot can provide a caregiver with just two hours respite and independence to the user through means of informal monitoring and alerting systems, then the result is a reduction in stress on the caregiver.
>
> *Incontinence Retraining:* Robots have infinite patience and therefore can be put to good use in retraining individuals in bladder and bowel control.
>
> *Home Automation:* Robotic devices for use in the home, such as memory aids, assistive tools for living, and automated kitchens.

For those who believe that the elderly would not be comfortable relating to robots, it was reported that a ninety-one-year-old volunteer at the Robotics

Institute, when introduced to a robot to assist him with activities of daily living, proclaimed, "I don't care what you call it, as long as it helps."

Will other elderly accept these new tools for living, and will the caregiver find relief? Kaji Yonemoto, executive director of the Japan Robot Association, believes that robotization has many benefits for both industry as well as for care services.[22] Besides reducing stress among caregivers, robots can help relieve the problem of skilled worker shortages. The future role for robots will include, besides assistance with the activities of daily living, a contribution toward increasing employment opportunities for the physically handicapped and encouraging the notion of productive aging, that is, helping to keep older people active and productive.

Robotic technology is one option available to us. As technology further develops, we will see more and more applications of robotics in the life-care industry, which will have great impact on improving opportunities for the elderly and disabled to live more independent and productive lives.

Alexandra Enders, who had been with the Electronics Industries Foundation, and who has done much work in development of the notion of tools for living, believes there is no turning back as self-help initiatives gain momentum.[23] This is so, she believes, especially when the issues being addressed are such an integral part of the long-term care dilemma we are facing as a nation.

With the dramatic shifts occurring in the rapidly growing elderly population, new approaches are needed. There is no question that applications of innovative technology, including various forms and types of robotic aids, will be an integral part of our long-term care service delivery and independent-living systems. As well, these special purpose devices will be adapted as tools for living for people of all ages.

Adapting to Changing Needs

How can we in the United States cope with our aging society? How can we put to use the best technology and systems available today to achieve the most advanced and supportive congregate life-care facilities and independent-living units? In my view we need to rethink our values and attitudes. We need to rethink our design and development process and goals.

Ours is a society of great resource, of great wealth, of great promise. In emergencies we pull together. We have fought our enemies and won. There is an enemy out there. It is called *indifference*. We see problems and assume others will care for them. We focus on *me for me*. We seek the pleasures of today and forget that we must pay for them tomorrow. We tend to look at the surface, at images, rather than at the heart of things. In the world of the built environment, we accept what is given, what is done for us. We live in it, we pass our lives in it. We believe that things will get better—but they won't if we don't work together to make them better.

We must now start to question our environment and put our house in order. We must work together. We must communicate at all levels. We need to change *me for me* to *me for we*.

In my study, "How Other Countries Care For and House the Elderly," I realized that much could be learned from others to benefit our nation's approach to the particular needs of our older population. In those nations, there appears to be more caring attitudes and more compassion toward elders, which has been translated into public policy. People prepare for old age, they understand the process of aging. Their children are taught about growing old and how to plan for retirement. They accept this reality of life and show respect and concern and provide a helping hand for those who have reached their golden years.

Can we stop for a moment from our fast-moving pace to think about our purpose in life? What is our aim, what is the value of surviving into old age if we fear it, are unprepared for it? Can we afford to look the other way when there are those in our society needing our help?

My hope is that we will begin to look at the issues of aging more completely, that we ask questions, invest our time and our energy in more research and exploration of innovative concepts, that we work with the user and become more involved with the decisions that involve our built environment. How we deal with our environment and our society will not only prepare us for our future, but will be a measure of us as a people and as a nation.

> It is hoped that the philosophical base and concern represented in this chapter will inspire the utilization and development of even more effective ways of helping us house and care for the next generation of elderly with dignity and success. We should examine all these alternative approaches for ideas that can be utilized, in whole or in part or in modified form, to enhance resident lifestyles and care in our own projects.
>
> —Editors

Notes

1. Ministry of Housing Paper. *Institutions and Housing for the Elderly and the Handicapped in Denmark*. Municipality of Copenhagen, Denmark, 1981.

2. Niemans, W.A.P. *Demographic Development Versus Overall Government Expenditure on the Policy for the Elderly in The Netherlands*. Paper presented at the International Conference on Housing and Services for the Aging, Jerusalem, Israel. February 8–12, 1987.

3. Hayashi, Tamako. *Project of New Housing Development: Japan's Ministry of*

of International Trade and Industry. Research Paper for the Tokyo Metropolitan Institute of Gerontology, Tokyo, Japan, 1982.

4. Smith, Ralph L. *Smart House: The Coming Revolution in Housing.* Columbia, MD: GP Publishing, Inc., 1988.

5. Yonemoto, Kanji. *Robotization in Japan.* Paper prepared for the Japan Industrial Robot Association, Tokyo, Japan: JIRA, April 1987.

6. The Swedish Handicap Institute. *Housing With Day and Night Service for the Severely Disabled.* Stockholm, Sweden: Strängnäs Tryckeri AB, 1982.

7. Hancock, Judith. *Housing the Elderly.* New Brunswick, NJ: Center for Urban Policy Research, 1987.

8. Chancellerie de la Confédération Suisse. *Personnes âgées et logements.* Berne, Switzerland: Office central fédéral des imprimés et du material, 1982.

9. Miller, Norman G. and Kautz, Judith A.: "Automated Homebuilding in Japan: Exportable to the United States?" *Urban Land,* Vol. 46, No. 6. Washington, D.C., July, 1987, pp. 11–15.

10. Schipper, Lee, Meyer, Stephen and Kelly, Henry. *Coming in from the Cold: Energy-Wise Housing in Sweden.* Cabin John, MD: Seven Locks Press, 1985.

11. Swiss National Committee for the 1982 UNO-World Assembly on Aging. *Swiss National Report for the UNO-World Assembly on Aging.* Zürich, Switzerland: Swiss Foundation Pro Senectute, 1982.

12. Steering Committee for Social Affairs. *Proceedings of the Colloquy on the Social Protection of the Very Old: Alternatives to Hospitalization.* Strasbourg: Council of Europe, 1986.

13. Wrightson, Bill and Pope, Campbell. *From Barrier-Free to Safe Environments: The New Zealand Experience.* New York: World Rehabilitation Fund, WRF:IEEIR Monograph #44, 1989.

14. Fernie, Geoff. "Robotics: A Commentary from the Perspective of Applications in Geriatrics (or 'Can Robotics Help People Help People')". *Interactive Robotic Aids—One Option for Independent Living: An International Perspective.* Monograph #37, New York: World Rehabilitation Fund. 1986, pp. 34.

15. Ibid., pp. 34.

16. Clarke, Arthur, C. *The Songs of Distant Earth.* New York: Ballantine, 1986.

17. Clarke, Arthur, C. "House Arrest." *Omni,* 8 (12), September 1986, pp. 43–46, 94–96.

18. Lesnoff-Caravaglia, G. *Environmental Frameworks for Aging: The Spectrum from Home to Institution.* Presentation at 40th Annual Scientific Meeting, The Gerontological Society of America, Washington, DC: November 18–22, 1987.

19. Englehardt, K.G. "Exploring the Potential of Robotic Technology for Use in Longterm Care." *Technology and Aging.* East Hanover, NJ: Sandoz, 1986, pp. 41–54.

20. Osako, Masako. "Robots meet patients: Japan Industrial Robotics Association takes aim at nursing." *Productive Aging News,* New York: 4, June 1986, pp. 5–6.

21. Englehardt, K.G. *Smart Technology for Creating a Caregiving Environment for Aging Individuals: Interactive Evaluation and Innovations.* Presentation at 40th

Annual Scientific Meeting of the Gerontological Society of America, Washington, DC., November 18–22, 1987.

22. Yonemoto, Kanji. *Ibid.*

23. Enders, Alexandra. *Lessons to be Learned from Technologies for Disabled People.* Presentation at the Technology and Aging Conference, Washington, DC., November 17–18, 1987.

11
Preopening Development Steps and Guidelines

Gail L. Kohn

> The following chapter recaps all the basic development steps a proposed life-care center should go through and describes a somewhat unusual and very attractive development approach. The approach described below should be of great interest to any sponsor or developer with the desire to do a superior job that will be uniquely their own, as long as they can access enough up-front funding so that a development firm's risk capital is not required.
>
> —Editors

The management of a life-care community in the period before the doors are open may be the most important and challenging phase in the life of the organization. Management decisions and action through this period can well determine whether the operational stage is ever reached. Perhaps more importantly, the thoughtfulness and comprehensiveness of preopening planning and the execution of the activities envisioned have an impact on every phase of life in the community after opening. This chapter presents preopening activities in chronological order and touches in many cases on information covered more comprehensively in other chapters. The materials included result from my experiences in assisting others to develop and operate life-care communities and in the development of Collington Episcopal Life Care Community, Inc. (Collington), located in Mitchellville, Maryland, where I am Executive Director. Examples are utilized throughout to illustrate the issue being discussed. Many are Collington stories, since I have participated, either peripherally or centrally, in the development of this life-care community from very close to its beginning. Collington began greeting the first residents in April 1988, and was fully operational in November 1988.

Some Background on Collington

Since Collington will be referred to throughout this chapter, some basic information about the community will provide a context for later remarks. (See figure 11–1 for a site diagram of Collington.) In 1982, a gift of 128 acres in Maryland near Washington, D.C. was offered to Episcopalians by a local developer and philanthropist, Homer Gudelsky, who wanted to see a life-care community constructed there. Located just outside the Capital Beltway, sixteen miles from the White House, and roughly the same distance from Annapolis, the site, known in the eighteenth century as Heart's Delight, was partially in use as farm land. The Diocese of Washington, long interested in developing a life-care community, established a core group from nearby Episcopal parishes and supplemented it with a few others from elsewhere in the Diocese to explore feasibility. When an initial sponsor can provide staff assistance, publicity, and an established constituency, as the Diocese of Washington did for Collington in the early days, feasibility studies are aided immeasurably. Analyses were positive and development proceeded. Using a loan of $50,000 from Mr. Gudelsky, a Diocesan grant of $250,000 and nearly $2 million in loans from the Diocese and several of its parishes, Collington followed the steps described in this paper.

The Diocesan grant of $250,000 was used for seed money, but Collington agreed to obtain sufficient financing to replace the quarter of a million dollars in a Fellowship Fund and to use the earnings to help achieve economic diversity among residents. Collington also pledged to the Diocese that efforts to augment their Fellowship Fund would begin immediately. Thanks to the generosity of many, including Collington's future residents, the Fund had grown to $450,000 by October 1988, when Collington was dedicated.

The mission statement was written by a board composed of thirty-three interested and determined men and women who had visited other life-care communities. It included several key elements: the campus-style life-care community would serve an economically diverse, multiracial, nondenominational group of older people, with relationships among board members, residents, and staff characterized by mutual respect, consideration, trust, and honesty.

When ready for a phased occupancy, all 300 independent living units were reserved, and there were two waiting lists, one for the first year and another for future years. Thanks to the grant from the Diocese, Collington offered financial assistance to people moving into ten units. The profile of residents was consistent with the projections made by Howell Associates following a market study. Average age seventy-four and mostly retired but active, they came from Washington, D.C. and the nearby metropolitan areas for the most part; although almost a third came from twenty-one states, and a few from England. Over one-third are couples and, while they are racially, economically, and religiously diverse, an unplanned, unexpected common characteristic among them is awareness and participation in activities at the Smithsonian museums. Sharing an interest in reading as well as outdoor di-

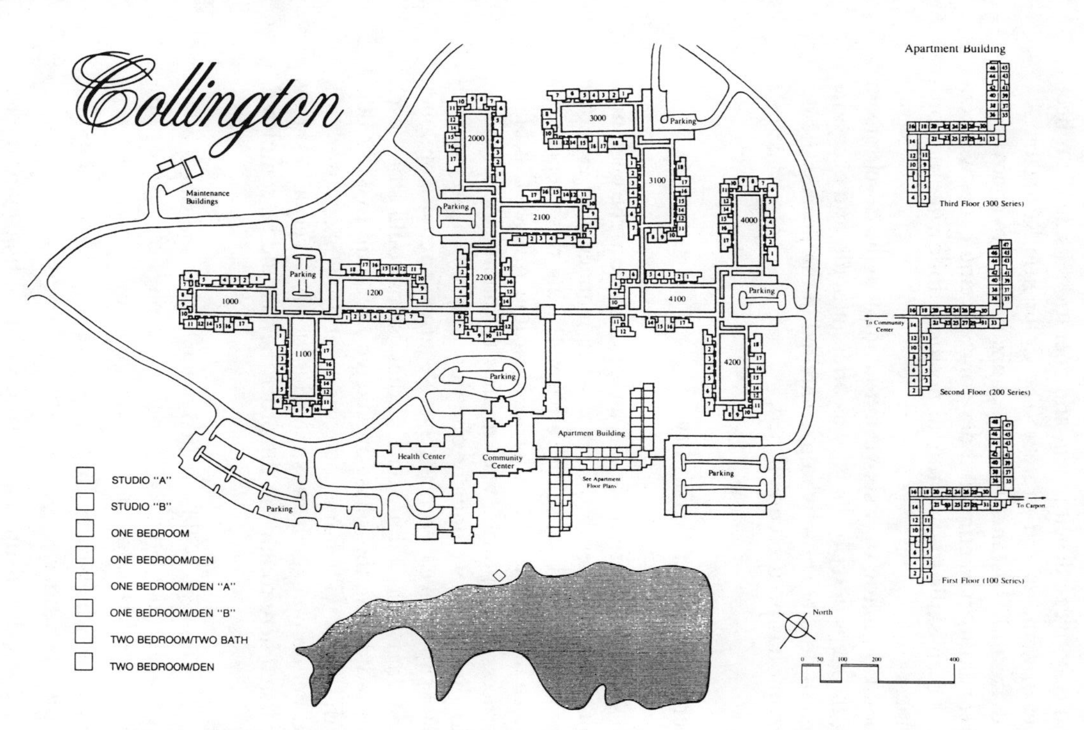

Covering 128 acres, Collington has 180 cottages grouped in 11 clusters and linked by a covered walkway system. In addition, there are 120 apartments, many with lake views, connected by an enclosed corridor to the Community Center. The Health Center, with a clinic, wellness and rehabilitation wing, 30 comprehensive and 40 domiciliary care beds, is an integral part of the public space shared by all residents. Outside the two mile walking trail which rings the campus there is a woodland buffer screening Collington from anticipated future residential development.

Figure 11–1. Collington Site Plan

versions, the majority are retired educators or people who worked for the government.

Collington intends to be a teaching and research-oriented community where opportunities to grow and share will be available to all residents and employees. Continuity between development and operational stages has been an important aspect of management strategy. The Collington Residents' Association offered advice and assistance to the organization for over two years before opening. Preopening marketing and development employees were encouraged to redirect their skills to operational positions following the completion of development.

However, it took Collington over six years to complete the development process. Following the steps described next was often difficult, and occasionally survival seemed in doubt. Those who participated in the process are deservedly proud of what has been accomplished.

Activities to Determine Project Feasibility

It is likely to take a substantial period of time, a year or more at the beginning of the development process, to reach the point when management expertise is necessary, except on a limited consultative basis. During this premanagement phase, a determination will be reached regarding project feasibility. Throughout the process, the sponsor will attempt to minimize expense by seeking answers to the next development question only when previous responses are generally supportive of proceeding. Negative outcomes obtained from the analysis of data collected at some of these steps could stop development. Costs incurred during this phase are likely to total up to $100,000. Other chapters in this book will address activities that prudent sponsors will have accomplished before management is introduced. However, as a means of review, they are listed here roughly in the order they should be completed.

1. Other life-care communities will be visited to enable the sponsor to identify alternatives and initial preferences regarding physical layout, program components, preferred locations, and people to be served.
2. Mission statement will be written by the sponsor to guide development and, if successful, operations.
3. Source list of technical and financial resources, including management expertise, will be devised.
4. Sources of political support will be identified, and explanations of the project's value to representatives of the jurisdiction will begin.
5. List of people possibly interested in residence will be started and regularly

updated. Periodic letters to people on this list will be necessary to reassure them that the project is still a possibility.

6. Initial feasibility study or studies will examine the need for and potential to develop a life-care community in the preferred location. The analysis should review the financial and demographic characteristics of people residing in the area, competitive retirement options, including existing and proposed life-care communities nearby, possible sources of staff, and state and local regulations with which the life-care communities must comply. If the need for a life-care community is demonstrable, a model of its physical and financial parameters will be established.
7. Ability of the sponsor to obtain prefinancing-phase funds will be examined. Possibly as much as $3 million may be needed before construction and permanent financing can be secured.
8. Market survey will indicate whether the plans of the sponsor are compatible with the preferences of older people in the area. A positive analysis will provide the sponsor with confidence regarding project viability, help to refine services and amenities, and establish a foundation of people to contact when marketing begins.
9. Legal status of the sponsor will be established.
10. Control of the proposed site will be obtained, but purchase should be contingent on positive financial feasibility, the availability of regulatory approvals (including any necessary zoning changes), as well as construction and permanent financing.
11. Financial feasibility analysis should be completed using market survey preferences to establish, or in some respects refine, program components, amenities, unit types, and mix. Five-year financial projections, built on project development, construction, operating and financing costs using comparable life-care communities will in turn permit computation of entrance and monthly fees. Market comparisons will produce the most recent in a series of go/no-go recommendations.

Selecting Management

If the project has successfully passed the feasibility tests, the organization can proceed to the prefinancing phase. At this time a professional on-site manager will be needed. It will not yet be clear that development should be completed. Relevant questions in this phase are:

- Can a marketable product be designed within the assumptions utilized in the financial feasibility study?

- Will potential residents, who are financially and medically qualified, find the development preferable to other alternatives?
- Will construction and permanent financing be available within the assumptions utilized in the financial feasibility study?
- Can all needed regulatory approvals be obtained?

Organizing and coordinating the activities necessary to answer these questions requires the availability of time and a specialized knowledge of the field generally not within the purview of sponsors.

- Will a management firm or an individual be selected?

Management firms specializing in the development and operation of life-care communities can offer advantages to projects. A growing number of firms offer full and partial development services that eliminate some or all sponsor responsibility for completing the determination of feasibility and prefinancing phases, including, with some firms, funding concerns. Some management firms will provide capital to cover expenses during these phases, but will precondition a loan by limiting or modifying the decision-making role of the sponsor. Sponsors will vary in their tolerance for changes in their roles but in many cases compromise will be necessary to ensure continuation of development exploration. These approaches are likely to be more expensive in addition to reducing sponsor control, but easier and safer than the sponsors seeking and hiring their own unattached director.

A management firm that can point to many other successful communities may prove useful in obtaining construction and permanent financing and perhaps when marketing the community. Furthermore, if the director departs, such firms might provide a substitute more readily than a project sponsor.

Management firms can also have disadvantages. Centralization of certain work activities in an off-site headquarters should reduce expenses and allow expert support staff to be utilized in project direction. However, distance can create delays and insensitivity to the subtleties of local issues. Furthermore, the application of previously successful approaches for the sake of systematizing operations can adversely limit project alternatives. Life-care communities must change with market preferences, regulatory shifts, new gerontological insights, and sponsor creativity. The local perception of the management firm and how it affects the image of a nonprofit sponsor is also a consideration.

The decision to hire a management firm or an individual will be based on the interest and expertise of the sponsor, combined with the ability of the sponsor to generate sources of funds.

- Will the director continue to manage the life-care community after opening?

It is often said that development and operational management require different skills and interest different professionals. It can be argued, however, that continuity between development and operations strengthens the accountability of a director. This accountability has an impact on the director's scrutiny of architectural, engineering, and interior design, then later, construction; the methods and statements utilized with future residents of the life-care community; the care with which operational contracts are written; the tolerance of operational limitations agreed upon in permanent financing documents; and the statements about the future shared with regulators.

Furthermore, future residents appreciate the knowledge that they will have the same staff, including the director, after opening. Commitments during development seem more likely to be honored if the people who made them on behalf of the organization are present to ensure their occurrence.

- Are the management philosophies of the sponsor and the director compatible?

The preopening approach of management can affect the operational decision-making role of the sponsor, the participation of future residents in the community's design, character, and style, and recruiting and retaining staff.

Sponsors must examine propensities toward hierarchical versus participative management philosophies. Evidence of preferences for one philosophical direction or the other can be obtained from the sponsor's mission statement and organizational decision-making methods. Directors will have examples from their previous experiences which will facilitate the determination of philosophical compatibility.

The sponsor and director must also examine the role of the sponsor versus the role of the director so that the responsibility and authority of each is clear to the other. Variation, based on personalities, will exist but certain responsibilities are certainly the purview of the sponsor such as adopting and modifying policy, assuring that the resources of the organization are prudently utilized and properly accounted for, and selecting and deciding to retain the director. If the sponsor is organized as a corporation, board responsibilities should be delineated in by-laws including the organizational approach to deliberation and decision making. This process is particularly important for the director to understand and accept.

Pre-financing Management Issues

Whether the sponsor has decided to utilize the services of a development firm or has hired an individual professional to manage the activities of the pre-financing phase, an office, full time director and other personnel will be needed soon. During the months ahead, the organization will need to translate the proposed life-care program into an architectural design as well as to develop literature and documents to market the community. These activities will lead to necessary regulatory approvals, followed by construction and permanent financing, which will allow construction and final development to begin. Depending upon regulatory constraints and financing requirements, this phase may consume up to two years. The following activities should be completed, often simultaneously, but roughly in the order they are listed.

1. An operational management plan should be written by the director and approved by the sponsor. To preserve continuity and fiscal control, the plan must be based on the sponsor's mission statement, information acquired from the market survey, and subsequent assumptions regarding the services to be provided that were utilized in the financial feasibility study. It will also incorporate the imprint of the director's management style. This paper will be useful as the architectural program is written and financing is sought.
2. Selecting a firm skilled in writing architectural programs for older people and life-care communities is an essential step at this stage. The community can then be designed from the inside, where most services and activities will take place. Properly written, this voluminous document becomes the design bible, providing architect, engineers, and interior and other design consultants with guidance on the characteristics of every needed space.
3. Selection of the development team should now be completed including legal counsel, financial advisor, builder, interior designer, architect and engineers, all of whom should have had previous experience with life-care communities. It is beneficial to share relevant financial feasibility information with the top contenders before final selections are made. As part of the final interview process, each firm should be asked to comment on its ability to accomplish the project with the resources for their work allocated in the feasibility study. Documentation of the replies may prove useful not only in the selection process but also later in development, as an oversight or control device. Some contenders may be willing to accept deferred financial arrangements contingent upon completion of construction or permanent financing, which may for some projects become an

important reason to select one firm over another. Contractual relationships with team members should allow for termination of agreements if necessary.

4. Necessary regulatory approvals should be obtained. The critical nature of required state and local certificates and licenses, combined with a competitive situation or political necessity, can precipitate the need to seek critical approvals prematurely. When such needs force the production of financial and design materials before relevant information is available, it is desirable, and in some cases essential, to correct prematurely produced information rather than utilize unsatisfactory guidelines in the project. Attempting to obtain these approvals will reveal the importance of political and regulatory contacts having been kept informed about the project throughout development.
5. The architectural team should prepare schematic design drawings based on the architectural program. Pricing by the builder should follow conferences with the architect, interior designer, and director to ensure that the builder understands the envisioned finishes. If necessary, design revisions should be completed to control costs. Elevations, typical floor plans, and independent living unit layouts can then be drawn, labeled "preliminary, subject to change," and utilized in marketing.
6. Examine and select a marketing philosophy, taking into account the mission statement and management philosophy already in place. Prepare a marketing plan that delineates the flow of contacts needed to assist interested individuals with their decision to become future residents and establishes reservation targets. The plan should use information acquired during the determination of feasibility to select productive advertising and presentation locations. This activity will necessitate the participation of people skilled in marketing techniques. The decision making regarding marketing philosophy will be primary in the selection of professional assistance, since some marketing firms advocate a more counseling-oriented approach, while others recommend application of sales tactics.

After the marketing plan was developed, Collington decided to pursue marketing without the consultant who had assisted in development of the plan. As director, I supervised the marketing counselors. An advantage of having the director in close contact with the staff and future residents is identification of the marketing issues that may have design and financial implications. Particularly visible examples of this at Collington were changes in the mix of units during different phases of architectural design to accommodate the preferences of interested people for larger cottages and apartments.

7. If state regulation or lack thereof allows, premarketing can begin as early as the completion of the financial feasibility study. Other papers focusing on marketing will no doubt discuss this important method of establishing a new plateau of interest with possible future residents.
8. An application form for residence must be written that facilitates collection of information for a preliminary evaluation of the applicant's financial and health status.
9. A description of the program and services offered by the life-care community, which also specifies the financial and other commitments undertaken by residents, must be written in contract form (avoiding legal jargon as much as possible), then made available for review by interested people, and later signed by management and the resident. Interested people should be encouraged to have the document reviewed by their attorneys and financial advisors. In the interest of facilitating management after opening, interested people should be informed that the terms of the agreement cannot be individually modified, except as anticipated in the document, to describe variations among individual reservations and overall policy changes that affect all future residents.
10. While sponsor meetings and staff activities can occur in space not identified with the life-care community, an office is necessary where interested people can become future residents by signing the residence and care agreements. This location should be selected with marketing as the primary purpose; therefore, the space, furnishings, and finishes should convey the sponsor's vision of offices in the life-care community. The space should be near the site, easy to find, barrier-free for handicapped people, expandable when necessary, and include ample parking and a nearby place to dine. The office need not be on the site and, wherever it is located, should *not* have a walk-in model of an independent-living unit because the life-care concept is communally oriented, multifaceted, and psychologically difficult to consider. Interested people should be permitted to study the sponsor's vision of a life-care community without the distraction of personal space issues. There are visual aids that can assist with explaining the life-care concept initially, including a scale model of the entire community and a large site plan on which reserved living units can be identified.
11. In addition to the full-time director, staffing at this time should include a receptionist/typist and a financial assistant/data processor, an office manager/secretary, and sufficient marketing counselors to achieve the desired level of market penetration to carry out the marketing plan. Part-time employees should be considered. Everyone in the office will need to understand and be able to explain the basic concept and follow the office

procedure that moves interested people to the next step in the marketing plan.

12. As future residents are identified, a profile of interests and service preferences can emerge if appropriate information is sought. This information has multiple uses.

    Collington publishes a monthly newsletter that is distributed to interested people. An ongoing column has descriptions of people who have reserved units. An impression of how interesting Collington will be, based on the backgrounds and current activities of future residents, has been beneficial in the marketing effort. Furthermore, some future residents have saved the columns to facilitate socializing after their move to the community.

    In addition, the insights obtained from analyzing these data have been used to modify architectural plans. Using the information to change design can impact the costs of the project and will draw future residents closer to their new community. Collington does not have a large rose garden because there is little resident interest in raising these hard to care for plants. However, the swimming pool is longer and narrower than originally planned because there are numerous lap swimmers among the residents. Many other changes resulted from opinions solicited about the envisioned program and preliminary design.

13. If regulatory approvals and marketing targets are meeting expectations, architects and engineers can be directed to proceed with design development drawings. Later, when it is evident that regulatory approvals and marketing are successful, working drawings should be authorized, and building permits sought.

Following Financing

Obtaining financing, both construction and permanent, represents the end of the beginning of development. While many activities remain to be done and issues resolved, the major obstacles to project development have been overcome. Construction time estimates are notoriously difficult, and this activity, along with obtaining final permits and licenses, will dictate the period remaining before opening. Construction time can vary widely, but it will certainly extend well over a year and perhaps closer to two years. During this time the activities that must be accomplished include: marketing; communicating with future residents to involve them in the community and to encourage them to refer others who may be interested in residence; overseeing construction; controlling development expenses; studying the role of the sponsor after opening and preparing a transition plan; reexamining projected operating expenses; planning the move to the community; hiring staff as necessary; and developing operational policies and procedures. These activities, which require professional leadership, are reviewed next roughly in the order to be accomplished during this final preopening phase.

Groundbreaking

During development, all who have a stake in the success of the project need to have periodic and meaningful celebrations. Furthermore, the project's progress must be demonstrated to the public, creating as many situations as possible in which interested people talk about the life-care community.

Groundbreaking is an obvious opportunity to further publicize the purpose and value of the organization as well as to recognize various contributions, including those of government officials. It also serves to validate the sponsor's serious intentions to proceed with development. As with all large events generated by the organization, inferences regarding the ability of the organization to operate a life-care community are drawn from the quality and smoothness of these events.

While it is certainly desirable to hold the event coincidental with directing the builder to proceed with construction, it may be necessary to forego this preference in favor of ensuring that key individuals to be honored can be present, requiring the setting of the date well in advance of the event.

There are a variety of ways to organize the ceremony. The highlight of turning over dirt is usually expected to be remembered more than any other by the audience. However, the most memorable moment in Collington's groundbreaking occurred prior to placing spade to soil. At the end of a presentation by the board president who introduced present and former board members, project consultants, and staff and acknowledged their contributions throughout development, the last group asked to rise were the future residents, who represented a significant block of people scattered throughout an audience of five hundred. The moment validated for many the future existence of a community.

Marketing and Ongoing Contacts with Future Residents

The life-care community will have had to experience some degree of marketing success to reach this stage of development. However, here are some activities to consider that will minimize attrition and reduce long-term marketing costs.

Analyze sources of people interested in learning more about the life-care community to identify those that are most likely to produce future residents. Collington had many inquiries as a result of some club presentations and advertisements from which a small number became future residents, while others produced fewer contacts but many more future residents.

Referrals from future residents are the best source for additional people to contact. The decision to move to a life-care community is difficult, since it requires acknowledgment of advancing age, the possibility of infirmity, and ultimately death. Furthermore, the choice requires moving, which involves learning new territory and making new friends. Finally, interested people must consider how to use accumulated financial resources. Future residents who are willing to discuss their decision with friends are more likely to have accepted their own choice. Indeed, discussions with people who question the decision will often strengthen the future resident's resolve to proceed. Furthermore, committed future residents often want to share the good news, and in doing so persuade their friends to join them. Developing life-care communities that recognize the value of this resource, and use it, will achieve and maintain full occupancy more readily.

In addition, some future residents will enjoy helping to counsel others who are interested. These individuals needn't know one another for the future resident to be influential. The presence of future residents at presentations for interested people can provide the uncommitted with models as well as sources of information who have thought through the reasons for and against residing in the life-care community.

Visits to similar life-care communities also offer effective communication about the concept. Collington accepted an invitation from a nearby life-care community, Broadmead, to provide orientation and tours to groups and individuals. No doubt the residents and staff of Collington will feel similarly disposed to share their homes and their entire campus with interested people from another developing life-care community that embodies a similar philosophy.

Financial incentives, such as periodic increases in the entrance fee, encourage interested people to reserve units. Many will accelerate their decision making about the life-care community in order to save a small amount of entrance fee. Reconsiderations of such decisions, if they are going to occur, are usually soon after the commitment is made. On balance, however, the small amount of immediate attrition is worth the gain in future residents.

Furthermore, Collington, like many other developing life-care communities, does not pay interest to future residents on their refundable entrance fee deposits. Thus, increases in the entrance fees have enabled future residents to appreciate early reservation of units as beneficial financially, rather than viewing it as a lost opportunity to earn interest on the deposit.

With regard to attrition, namely the loss of future residents before they move to the community, some key activities to minimize losses resulting from changes in plans include: utilizing a counseling approach to marketing, keeping in contact with future residents; communicating additional information about the community as it becomes available; and getting the future residents involved in the success of their new home.

Collington's marketing counselors view every interested person as someone who is studying the alternatives for retirement living. A decision requires consideration of other possibilities, including living at home, moving to retirement communities that provide housing only, or moving to other life-care communities. Discussing these choices and helping the interested person to develop a personal list of pros and cons that assists in making an informed decision diminishes the number of people who later change their minds.

Collington has held receptions for future residents nearly monthly since early in the marketing effort when only a small percentage of units were reserved. These events offer an opportunity to share development progress, to encourage assistance from future residents in marketing, to convey an impression about the services to be offered by the community, including meals (through refreshments), to enable future residents to get to know one another and share their dreams and apprehensions about moving to the community, and to enable future residents to meet staff and board members, which increases rapport and trust. Because of the number of future residents who wanted to attend, Collington held two identical receptions on the same day, one in the morning and the other in the afternoon. The staff was alert to identifying future residents who did not attend the receptions. Marketing counselors employed individualized approaches to keep in contact with them as well.

As mentioned previously, Collington has a monthly newsletter that is mailed to all interested people. The *Letter* has a number of regular features: an update describing recent events and progress, particularly construction and marketing; photos of future residents and construction; a wellness column, with topics selected by the readers; area events, especially those near the campus; a calendar of presentations about Collington; a biographical section describing the future residents who will move to Collington. Resident volunteers edit the publication and perform the necessary clerical tasks to get each edition in the mail.

In addition, there is a monthly mailing to future residents. This mailing includes a detailed summary of the most recent future residents' reception presentation. It extends an invitation to attend upcoming activities reserved for future residents and provides a reminder of events open to anyone. Future residents often attend presentations for interested people with their friends. The letter may also include a survey from the staff or one of several Collington Residents' Association committees (discussed later), the results of which are tabulated, reported to residents in future publications, and used to shape services provided to the residents. For example, a recent questionnaire, asking about the types of financial services the residents will use in the Collington branch bank, helped the bank to refine furniture, fixture, equipment, and staffing plans. In summary, monthly mailings keep all future residents informed and invite them to participate in shaping their community regardless of the frequency with which they visit the office.

Encouraging the Establishment of the Residents' Association

Collington's Residents' Association was organized before opening to formalize the means to seek advice on the design, character, and style of the community. All future residents became members of the Residents' Association. There are officers and an appointed governing council with representation from all areas of the future campus. Nine committees formed; they have spun off subcommittees as needed. Bimonthly Residents' Council meetings are attended by the chairpersons of committees who report on their activities and recommendations. The committees, along with their purposes, are as follows:

Interiors. This committee reviewed and commented on the finishes and furnishings in the Community/Health Center. They also traveled to the homes of future residents who offered to contribute furnishings to Collington. The photographs, measurements, and determinations of wood types and colors collected on these visits were sent to the interior designer, who then placed selected items in the plans for furnishing the Community/Health Center. Over one-third of the furnishings in public spaces have been contributed by future residents. They will continue to enjoy cherished pieces, often too large for their Collington cottages or apartments, and the overall cost of furnishing the Community/Health Center has been greatly diminished. Further, when the sponsor is a nonprofit corporation like Collington, donors can claim a tax deduction for the gift.

Landscape. This committee reduced the cost of landscaping Collington by closely examining the site plans and eliminating unneeded and undesired trees and shrubs. Members visited an operating life-care community to compare notes with residents and staff. They returned with invaluable advice on spacing plantings for proper growth and maintenance. This, in addition to their abundance of personal experience, enabled them to advise on landscape plan modifications. This committee also completed a brochure that explains planting policies for residents around their own units.

Activities. The goal of having interesting things to do when the Community/Health Center opened was the main preoccupation of this committee. They even arranged trips for future residents prior to opening. Since the scope of this committee is so great, there are a growing number of subcommittees that focus on music, travel, library, gallery, woodworking, and the gift shop. Other subcommittees will be added as interests emerge.

Dining. Surveys of other life-care communities have provided information on several topics, including meal hours, alcoholic beverages policy, and dress codes. This committee looks forward to assessing resident attitudes toward meals and service through surveys and correspondence.

Health. The committee has become particularly knowledgeable about the continuum of health services Collington offers, from wellness programs to 24-hour professional supervision in the Health Center. It has advised on the selection of the Medical Advisor and has participated in the search for a donation source for dental equipment used in the clinic.

Hospitality. This committee, along with the Residents' Council, participated in planning for the groundbreaking, cornerstone laying, and dedication events. They continue to advise and assist with monthly future resident receptions. They have written a Residents' Handbook, which will be presented to newly arrived people to assist with orientation to the campus and to services throughout the area.

House. Aware that preventive maintenance and early detection of maintenance, housekeeping, and grounds problems by staff and residents will keep Collington running safely and securely, this committee has reviewed and commented on plans for operation.

Pet Care. A pamphlet written by the pet care subcommittee includes rules developed to ensure that people who are not pet owners, pet owners, and pets all enjoy Collington. The group has studied local laws affecting pets and has identified veterinarians and kennels in the area to be listed in the Residents' Handbook.

Finance. This committee reviewed and commented on the way Collington balanced its financing resources and expenditures during development; it continued this work after opening. Members advised on the selection of the Collington bank. Preparation for the first six months' budget of the Residents' Association was coordinated by the group.

Each committee reports to the Residents' Council, and periodically the committees and the Council report to the Residents' Association at one of the monthly future residents' receptions.

The resident committees are expected to remain an important channel for communication among staff and residents. Also, resident committee minutes and staff responses will be presented to relevant quality control and

Board committees. Even before opening, the Association became a significant source of advice and help at Collington.

Overseeing Construction

Oversight of construction is a critical and time-consuming activity. Because of the magnitude of expenses involved, the potential for creating long-term maintenance problems with attendant resource consumption, and the ever-present and costly threat of delayed opening, this is an area that deserves close attention.

Having an owner's representative or clerk of the works who understands the services to be offered by the life-care community, and who is experienced in construction, has saved Collington time and expense. Architects and engineers do not necessarily produce perfect drawings, and builders do not always obtain the anticipated performance from subcontractors. The on-site presence of an owner's representative who has detected and explored issues and then brought together the appropriate decision-making groups to resolve matters has been a good investment for the organization. If possible, the community should retain this employee after opening to oversee the plan and property.

Collington has permitted customization of resident units, and the oversight of proper installation also has been accomplished primarily by the owner's representative. The customizing process began over a year before construction was underway, with future residents envisioning the changes they wanted to make that would improve their cottages and apartments. The process was facilitated by providing quarter-scale drawings of the units, along with furniture templates. Future residents were encouraged to "live in their units" and then lay out their possessions using the templates. The consideration of preferred arrangements produced "dream sheets," lists of ideas for unit design changes. Some of these ideas were incorporated into the standard design. Others were offered in a list of twenty-five standard options, priced to include design, construction, and administration costs. The custom options contract signed by the many future residents who chose to install screened porches, skylights, extra windows, attic storage access, and many other items states that the fee for customizing is not refundable and the future resident or the person's estate must pay for removal of the change if the next resident to occupy the unit does not want it. In addition, periodic maintenance charges will be assessed for prevention and repair of the option as needed. In spite of the restrictions, this activity has been very popular, and over half of the future residents chose to modify their units. Participation is interpreted as a sure sign that the future resident intends to move to Collington. The owner's representative has monitored the proper installation of custom options with staff support and computer assistance, without which the myriad details would be overwhelming.

Furthermore, the owner's representative is providing documentation of construction, which is expected to facilitate maintenance work in future years. Collington has decided not to rely on drawings alone, and documents describing equipment, narratives, photographs, and videotapes will augment the drawings. All of this will reduce uncertainty when repairs are undertaken or modifications to the structures occur in the years ahead.

Finally, comments of the owner's representatives at meetings of future residents have been reassuring and interesting. Most people are not familiar with construction activities. Seeing photographs and hearing explanations of installations has helped to explain why the time consumed during construction is necessary. In addition, carefully monitored on-site individual tours and group events have been exciting for participants, who share their enthusiasm with others. This activity has reduced anxiety and created excitement about development progress, not only among interested people and future residents, but also among board members.

Selecting Furniture, Fixtures, and Equipment

Decisions regarding the variety of furniture, fixtures, and equipment (FF&E) needed for a life-care community will necessitate advice from a variety of specialists. While assembling the necessary specialists can be left to the architect, the director and sponsor must feel confident that FF&E selections will be both functional and affordable.

The interior designer should have a knowledge of gerontology as well as an ability to beautify the interior of the community. The firm selected needs to review architectural design options beginning with the schematic phase, to ensure that furniture and equipment will fit in assigned spaces and can be functionally used. Collington's interior designer had a more complicated furniture selection process because of the emphasis on incorporating suitable resident contributions. About one-third of furnishings to be located in the Community/Health Center were gifts from residents, resulting in a substantial reduction in anticipated expense.

Equipment and fixtures must accomplish assigned tasks during their useful lives with a minimum of operating and maintenance expense. Collington found selection of computer, telephone, and security (fire, health emergency, and intrusive) systems particularly challenging because of the highly technical nature of the topics and the expense involved in purchase and maintenance.

Finally, signage is very important and deserves careful scrutiny to ensure that residents and guests easily can find their way in, around, and out of the community. Collington wanted unobtrusive, residential, yet easily read signs inside the Community/Health Center and throughout the campus. The architect and the interior designer consulted with the signage designer in order to ensure compatibility.

Examining the Operational Role of the Sponsor

During construction, the governing body must be prepared to make an organizational transition from one that has overseen development to one that ensures that the life-care community opens and operates smoothly. This requires examining and revising the organizational structure of the sponsor's deliberation and decision-making process. This discussion is particularly directed to nonprofit facilities run by volunteer boards. However, in organizations with different legal status, the role of the sponsor must undergo a similar process.

At Collington, a board task force was established to work with the executive director to study and make recommendations about organization, decision making, and information flow as Collington moved toward opening. Among the issues considered were the respective roles of the board and staff, advisory participation of the Residents' Association, and the structure and functions of board committees.

The functions of the governing body evolve logically from those carried on throughout development. Planning the overall direction of the organization, ensuring that the financial resources to accomplish the work are available and monitored, developing policy, evaluating the performance of the organization, and recruiting and training board members were and should remain board responsibilities.

Collington's board wants to be as well-informed about the operations of Collington as they were during development. While they do not want to interfere with the management of operations, they want to be certain that the Residents' Association continues to have a meaningful advisory role.

The board will continue to use annual goals to focus activities and controls for board and staff. The goals become the work plan for the year. At the conclusion of the year, as they have in the past, the board and staff will evaluate whether or not the goals have been achieved. The board will then consider and adopt goals for the year ahead. An annual report by the board president summarizes the activities of the year. This, along with the director's report, which details events and accomplishments, provides a corporate history that is useful in orienting new board members.

In addition, the board has been developing a long-range plan, with the mission statement in mind, which anticipates the direction of the organization over the next five years. Until the year before opening, the plan focused solely on development.

The Collington board's decision-making process is organized around committees that evaluate issues related to their particular assignments. The list of committees and their purposes were reviewed and revised to serve operational rather than development issues. Each operational department at Collington has a board committee to which department financial and quality control data are reported. As Collington became fully operational, the appropriate department head joined the executive director to report at board committee meetings. Residents' Association committees will continue to have assigned board committees to which minutes and relevant comments from the Residents' Council will be among the reports regularly presented. This information will be accompanied by staff responses and recommendations. (The relationship among board, staff, and Residents' Association committees is illustrated in figure 11–2). Board committees make policy recommendations to the Executive Committee, which in turn decides what will be recommended to the board. Collington's Executive Committee and board will continue to meet monthly until the policy review and monitoring functions have become sufficiently routine to consider longer intervals.

Laying the Cornerstone

This event is another opportunity to mark progress and acknowledge the roles of important persons in the achievement. There are any number of activities that can be included. Collington decided to fill a time capsule and cement the box and stone in place as a part of the ceremony.

The Residents' Association was asked to assist with the selection of items to place in the time capsule. They included information about themselves and their organization, including their biographical sketches, a description of the Residents' Association, and a resolution passed by the members in support of the Fellowship Fund. Other items were selected by the board and staff. Because of its special role helping Collington in development, the Episcopal Diocese of Washington was invited to add an item. In addition, the County Executive was present to place information about the area in the capsule. The most memorable activity, for many of the five hundred people attending, followed the ceremony. They were able to examine the stone closely, and tour framed cottages and the rest of the campus still under construction.

Planning Staff Recruitment and Orientation

What staff are needed to provide life-care services and whether people with the necessary skills are available in the area workforce are questions asked early on when initial feasibility is explored. Some proposed life-care communities will not be able to proceed with development because the answers regarding staff availability are not favorable. Later, before a financial feasibility analysis is completed, anticipated staffing must be refined if planned services were revised following the market survey. When management is se-

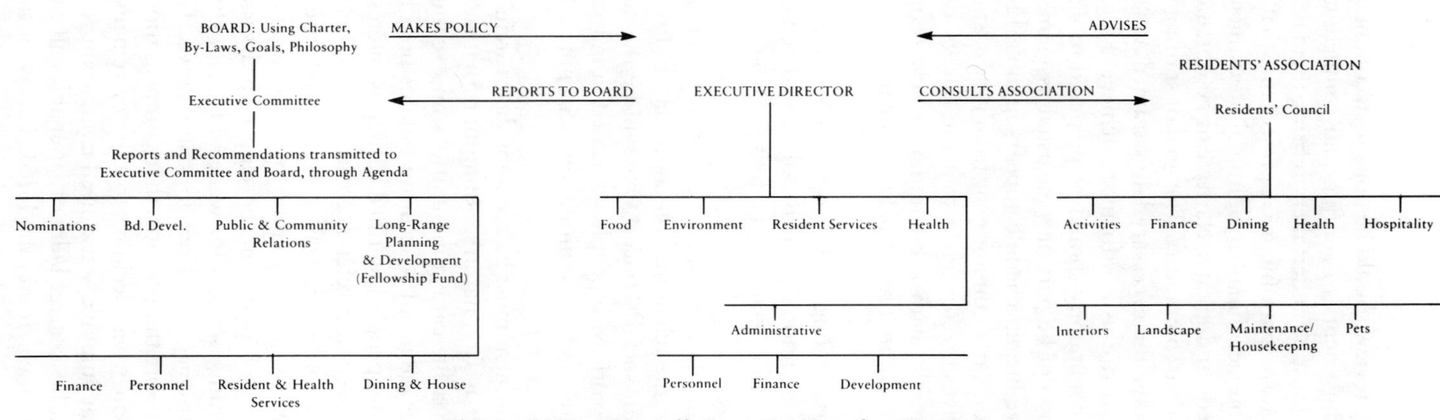

Figure 11–2. Overall Organization for Operations

lected, another staffing review should be done to accommodate the approach of that individual. Adjustments to staffing and compensation following financing of the project must be undertaken to bring them into alignment with the assumptions used to prepare financial projections that are incorporated into the postopening budget. Finally, additional adjustments must be made as construction proceeds and greater clarity can be obtained regarding resident moves to the life-care community. The goal of staffing the life-care community should be to have the necessary labor trained and ready to do their jobs when they are needed; this is difficult to achieve. Employees participating in opening of the community should be prepared to work overtime and perform tasks that may not be part of their usual assignments. A list of employees with a tentative hiring schedule appears in table 11–1.

Collington made an early commitment to minimize staff turnover. Both the board and executive director agree that the quality of services will be better if the staff is stable, with a minimum of new people recruited and trained. Making this commitment before opening has an impact on management.

First, the staff participating in development of the life-care community were selected with the intention that their skills could be transferred to other positions, if necessary, after opening. The first Collington receptionist had a certificate in gerontology and a degree in psychology. She is now the director of resident services. One of the marketing counselors is an occupational therapist who will become the rehabilitation coordinator. Two other marketing counselors will work in social services. One will be the admissions coordinator, continuing her work with people interested in independent-living residence, but also responsible for recruiting and screening admissions of nonresidents to the Health Center.

Second, staff recruitment must be accomplished carefully to identify satisfactory employees. It is Collington's assumption that working with older people, particularly in a life-care community, is an exciting prospect. Early indications are that this judgment is accurate. All positions have been posted, in addition to contacting people identified earlier as interested. Outstanding candidates are interviewed and references are secured before selections are made. The personnel coordinator was recruited and hired several months prior to initial opening. This provided time for him to establish contacts, plan the general orientation to Collington, develop record systems, recommend fringe benefits, and arrange sources for wage and salary comparisons.

Third, salaries must begin and remain competitive. There are management theories that support the position that compensation is not the most important consideration when deciding to take or remain with a position. Collington believes that employees also need comparable compensation.

Fourth, there must be a career ladder that enables all employees to reach beyond the position into which they are hired. This is particularly important with nonprofessional employees, and the majority of life-care community employees fall into this category. Collington will counsel each employee and assist each person to develop a plan for growth. There will be students among the employees; future residents already have agreed to provide academic assistance. Tuition assistance is a fringe benefit of employment, and creative staffing techniques will be used to facilitate successful completion of programs undertaken by employees.

Fifth, there must be a willingness to reorganize task assignments to accommodate individual growth and limitations. Collington does not view job descriptions as fixed. Flexibility in task assignments will allow for individual needs. Salaries will be adjusted to accommodate changes.

Collington's approach to orientation and ongoing staff education is predicated on the notion that information offered is not necessarily learned. The personnel coordinator will work with department directors to ensure that on-the-job testing validates the learning that was anticipated. As necessary, those requiring further training will be assisted.

Planning the Resident Move to the Life-Care Community

This process is one that Collington had been preparing residents to undertake for over two years. In addition to scale drawings of cottages and apartments intended to help future residents decide on the furniture they will move with them, Collington has carried on a series of activities, including:

- Regular "treasure" sales for items future residents are willing to discard; proceeds from the sales go to the Fellowship Fund and the Residents' Association. This activity is intended to help future residents to begin focusing on the upcoming move and what needs to be done to get ready.
- Opportunities to contribute furnishings and art to Collington for use in public spaces. This provides the future resident with a tax deduction and the opportunity to continue enjoying the piece.
- Presentations at future residents' receptions on home sales. Future residents were offered tips on enhancing the sale price of their home, how to select a real estate agent or attempt the home sale without a realtor, how their buyers might finance the property, and other information that was summarized and distributed. Another valued presentation on selecting a moving company and other premove activities helped future residents to plan the upcoming event.
- Setting up a system for assistance (if needed), with packing and unpacking through volunteers recruited and trained by a group of future residents and staff.

Table 11–1
Tentative Schedule for Hiring Staff

Job Title	*FTE*	*Date of Hire*
Executive Director (AD)	1.0	On Staff Throughout
Office Manager Coordinator (AD)	1.0	On Staff Throughout
Financial/Data Processing Coordinator (AD)	1.0	On Staff Throughout
Director of Resident Services (RS)	1.0	On Staff Throughout
Admissions Coordinator (RS)	1.0	On Staff Throughout
Counselor (RS)	0.5	On Staff Throughout
Counselor (RS)	0.5	On Staff Throughout
Secretary, Resident Services (RS)	1.0	On Staff Throughout
Rehabilitation Coordinator (HS)	1.0	On Staff Throughout
Personnel Coordinator (AD)	1.0	−12 weeks
Medical Advisor (HS)	0.2	−12 weeks
Director of Health Services (HS)	1.0	−12 weeks
Purchasing Coordinator (ES)	1.0	−12 weeks
Director of Dining Services (DS)	1.0	−9 weeks
Director of Environmental Services (ES)	1.0	−8 weeks
Production Manager (DS)	1.0	−6 weeks
Housekeeping Coordinator (ES)	1.0	−4 weeks
Nurse Practitioner Coordinator (HS) (7–3 shift)	1.0	−4 weeks
Personnel Assistant (AD)	1.0	−4 weeks
Dietary Technician (DS)	1.0	−4 weeks
Nursing Coordinator (HS)	1.0	−4 weeks
Nursing Supervisor (HS)	3.2	−4 weeks
Aide AM (DS)	3.0	−4 weeks
Utility Aide (DS)	1.0	−3 weeks
Security (ES)	8.4	−2 weeks
Accredited Records Technician (HS)	1.0	−2 weeks
Secretary (DS)	1.0	−2 weeks
Secretary (HS)	1.0	−2 weeks
Grounds Coordinator (ES)	1.0	−2 weeks
Secretary - Clinic (HS)	1.0	−2 weeks
Cook AM (DS)	1.0	−2 weeks
Cook PM (DS)	1.0	−2 weeks
Salad/Desserts (DS)	1.0	−2 weeks
Relief Aide (DS)	1.0	−2 weeks
Medical Claims (HS)	1.0	−2 weeks
Recreation Therapist (HS)	1.0	−2 weeks
Maintenance Assistants (ES)	2.8	−2 weeks
Secretary (AD)	2.0	−2 weeks

Table 11–1 continued

Job Title	*FTE*	*Date of Hire*
Grounds Assistants (ES)	3.0	−2 to +12 weeks
Receptionist (AD)	3.8	−2 to +12 weeks
Cooks Relief/Salad Relief (DS)	2.0	−2 to +16 weeks
Cleaning Assistants (ES)	11.8	−2 to +20 weeks
Server (DS)	9.6	−2 to +20 weeks
Laundry Aide (ES)	3.6	−2 to +20 weeks
Nursing Assistants - Comprehensive (HS)	18.2	−2 to +24 weeks
Nursing Assistants - Domiciliary (HS)	9.8	−2 to +24 weeks
Development Coordinator (AD)	1.0	+4 weeks
Cook Helper AM & PM (DS)	2.0	+4 weeks
Aide PM (DS)	4.9	+4 to +12 weeks
Bus Person (DS)	3.2	+4 to +12 weeks
Nurse Practitioner/RN (HS) (3–11, 11–7 and weekends shifts)	3.2	+8 weeks
Nursing Assistants - Clinic (HS)	2.8	+8 weeks
Cook Helper AM (DS)	1.0	+8 weeks
Trayline Aide (D)S	2.0	+8 to 12 weeks
Trayline Relief (DS)	0.8	+8 to 12 weeks
Van Driver (RS)	2.4	+8 to 20 weeks
Social Work Consultant (RS)	0.2	+8 to 20 weeks
Medical Aides (HS)	4.2	+8 to 24 weeks
Creative Arts Coordinator (RS)	1.0	+16 weeks
Registered Nurse - Comprehensive (HS)	4.2	+24 weeks

EMPLOYEES BY DEPARTMENT

Department	*FTE*
Administration	11.8
Dining Services	36.5
Environmental Services	34.6
Health Services	55.8
Resident Services	7.6
Total Employees	146.3

Note: Positions are listed chronologically by date of hire; negative numbers are listed chronologically by date of hire; negative numbers represent time prior to opening and positive numbers represent time after opening. For organizational purposes, departments are identified: Administration (AD); Resident Services (RS); Health Services (HS); Environmental Services (ES); and Dining Services (DS). The number of employees per job category is presented in full-time equivalence.

- An orientation notebook, prepared by the Residents' Association Hospitality Committee, to be presented to residents when they arrive.

As it became clear that Collington's Community/Health Center would open after the independent-living units, the opportunity was presented to move in before the health and recreation services were offered. Future residents must place the remainder of their entrance fees (usually 90 percent) in an escrow account.

Finally, Collington is not required to use the Health Center rooms solely for residents. The Health Center must be prepared to fulfill health-related contractual obligations to residents, who for the most part will not use these services heavily during the first few years, so nonresidents with dependencies can be admitted to domiciliary and comprehensive beds on a per diem basis, which will in part offset fixed costs. The Collington admissions coordinator had already begun marketing the future availability of the Health Center beds to hospitals, physicians, and other long-term care referral services in the metropolitan area. The intention is to fill the Health Center beds, aside from those reserved for resident needs, within months of opening this area.

> This chapter outlines an exceptionally thoughtful development process, where future residents are constantly involved, consulted, and kept informed. Not only is the above discussion a blueprint for an outstanding in-house development, it sets a benchmark for caring and concern of the resident's wants and needs, which should be an inspiration to all retirement housing projects.
>
> —Editors

12
Life-Care Management: Making It Work

D. Martin Trueblood

In this chapter, the author brings eighteen years experience in life-care development and management to bear on key management questions. The thumbnail job descriptions and comments on organizational relationships should be of great help to planners, sponsors, and operators.

—Editors

There are almost as many variations of life-care communities as there are life-care communities. It is therefore impossible to present a single management plan to apply to all. Changes in management organization are necessary for every variation in size, ownership, type of structure, and contractual provision of the residency agreement. The management plan I am proposing is suitable for a life-care community of approximately 240 independent units, 40 personal-care units, and 60 nursing units. This prototype community includes both single and multistory structures. It has been open approximately three years, is a non-profit corporation, provides a full life-care contract with unlimited nursing care, has outpatient medical facilities, and pays for all medical costs.

Management Requirements

There is a general lack of understanding by the public and by other professionals as to the nature of the work of a life-care community executive. It may be helpful to consider the kind of business being conducted and then to structure the management requirements. It may also be helpful to consider the organizational models that do not apply, but are often assumed by those outside the field.

First, a life-care community is not a nursing home. The job requirements of a nursing home administrator are mandated in the various state codes. The duties are specific to a nursing home and are, therefore, limited in scope. I do not mean to minimize the importance of managing a nursing home; I simply mean that managing a life-care community is different. I believe part of the confusion with nursing-home administration is that, throughout the industry, it has been common for executives of life-care communities to also be the nursing home administrator of the nursing component of the life-care community. While it may be desirable for the executive director to have a nursing home administrator's license, I believe that the executive director should not be the nursing home administrator of record. I believe this role should be filled by the head of the health care department and that the executive director should concentrate on overall management of the community.

A second comparison is with hospital administrators. There are important differences in the work of a hospital administrator and that of a life-care community executive. The most obvious difference is that hospital administrators' long-term relationships are with doctors and staff, and not with patients. A hospital administrator's primary role is in maintaining the physical operation of the hospital, including maintenance, staffing, and finance, but there is very little involvement with designing the delivery of medical care. On the other hand, a life-care community executive holds the primary responsibility for developing the system of health-care delivery.

Perhaps the best management model for a life-care community executive is that of a city manager in a rather small town. A city manager runs a number of departments with a wide variety of purposes. The city manager has responsibilities to the general public and reports to a city council. This is similar to the working relationship of a life-care executive. In a life-care community, the executive deals with most of the issues.

Qualifications of a Life-Care Community Executive

There is no consensus within the industry as to the professional qualifications for a life-care community executive. Life-care management is a new and rapidly expanding industry without an adequate pool of well-trained middle management executives qualified for promotion. Twenty years ago, all the new executives in life-care communities came from outside the life-care profession, some were related to health care, some from the ministry, and others from business and industry. I have reviewed the many life-care community executives I know and have been impressed with the absence of any clear pattern as to the best background for an outstanding executive. In fact, the group is most notable for its very diversity and wide range of previous experience. While this diversity is true, there is a great similarity among life-care community executives regarding the type of people who are successful. All have been well-grounded in management skills and nearly all are very caring and people-oriented.

If this is true, then there needs to be some serious questioning of the experience requirements commonly placed in job descriptions and in advertisements for executive directors. I submit that many successful life-care community executives would probably not meet the requirements being listed for positions that are open today. The biggest single unnecessary limitation that organizations are placing on the selection process is the requirement of a nursing home administrator's license as a prerequisite for selection as an executive director.

What then are the qualities that determine the successful life-care community executive? In my judgment, they are as follows:

- A solid background of managerial experience;
- A genuine dedication to the field;
- Great patience;
- Leadership;
- A willingness to work more than forty hours a week;
- Strong spiritual values;
- Ability to negotiate and compromise; and
- Substantial skills in public speaking.

I believe that these are the qualities that should be considered by any organization seeking a new life-care community executive. It should be noted that life-care community experience is not on the list. Realistically, when there is a choice between two candidates who fulfill the above criteria, the choice will usually go to the one with life-care community experience. In the future, most serious candidates will have this experience, but it should not be a requirement.

Management Style

Some thought should be given to the title of the chief executive. Within the industry, there are a wide range of titles in use, and there are some legitimate reasons for the differences. The most common titles in use are: administrator, executive director, and president. I believe the "administrator" title is dated, going back to the nursing-home model, and that the title of "president" is pompous and misleading. I prefer, by far, the title of "executive director."

Each life-care community inevitably develops its own management style under the leadership of the executive director and the director of the governing body. I acknowledge that management style varies dramatically from community to community and that an executive cannot administer a management style that is uncomfortable; however, I believe that most successful executives operate under a participative management style.

Participative management is necessary in a life-care community because the various department heads and others that report directly to the executive director are uniquely interdependent. The work of each functioning unit in the community has direct impact on every other unit, not only in the role of direct support, but also as a source of creative ideas. The executive director should operate in a manner that encourages creative thinking on the part of all staff members.

Participative management extends also to relations with residents. In the past twenty years, I believe there has been a significant change in the resident populations of life-care communities. Today's residents are better-educated, more articulate, and less accepting of authoritative management than those of twenty years ago. This change forces all executive directors to be more open and sharing with residents and resident associations. In many communities, the residents are demanding greater and greater involvement in community management. While there are benefits to resident involvement, there are also problems and risks. A management style that can deal with these problems is important now and will be more so in the future.

Two examples come to mind that demonstrate this point. First is the issue of wheelchairs in the dining room. As a new community opens there are residents who, while they have chosen the life-care style, are still uncomfortable with the aging process. They want the community to stay exactly as it is on opening day, and for no one to grow older or more infirm. If they are asked to set policy on walkers and wheelchairs in the dining room, they will choose to prohibit them, even though this is in direct conflict with handicap access laws. It is important for the spirit of the community in the future to resist such a move, and the executive director must stand firm on the issue. A second example is smoking in the dining room. Most residents prefer a no smoking rule and, for some, it is an essential health issue. Again, this must be a decision made by the executive director. On the other hand, in both cases, open discussion of the subject in a resident meeting is important.

One aspect of a management system is the attitude toward change. Some executives prefer to operate a status quo organization, and many governing bodies prefer no change. Personally, I believe it is a responsibility of the executive director to program change in the community and to help the governing body recognize the need for change. If we accept that each new generation of residents will have different needs and desires, then it is clear that change is essential for survival. A life-care community must be viewed in the long-term of, perhaps, a hundred years, since it is hard to see how a life-care community can go out of business except through slow death or financial failure. If a community is to be relevant to new applicants ten and twenty years after opening, it must change with the times. The realities of a developing competitive market may force change in time, but the successful community will work to keep ahead of the competition. A long-range planning committee of the governing body is probably the best guarantee of successful change. The executive director should take the lead in creating a long-range planning committee and should be an active member of it. Residents, by and large, will be against change, and their thinking will be short-term. An executive director with a philosophy that accepts appropriate change can ensure that the life-care community will meet the needs of future residents.

An important part of the management style is the staff meeting. I have found that a good staff meeting is a big help to everyone, and it is hard to see how an organization can run smoothly without it. The staff meeting should be held weekly, and at the same time each week. There should be minutes of the meeting circulated within twenty-four hours. I like to have each department head attend as well, or other key staff, and insist that, in their absence, they send a substitute. The substitute role can be rotated in a department so that over a period of time many employees have a chance to attend. The staff meeting should be for reporting significant events and actions and for announcements. It should not be used for confidential subjects or for long-range planning, but it can be used for minor planning. The staff meeting should be held with or without the executive director present.

Communication

It is hard to imagine an organization with a greater demand for communication than a life-care community. Think of three hundred to four hundred active, able people living together without employment to absorb time and energy. Add one hundred fifty to two hundred employees, who are very dedicated to their work and who care very much about the residents. Add also the governing body, the vendors, government agencies, and the general public, and it is easy to see this as a tremendous communication challenge.

I can remember an occasion when I was feeling pretty good about the communication system I had in place. It included a monthly calendar, a weekly update, a display showing the daily events, large and well-used bulletin boards, an employee's newsletter, an advance notice of menus, frequent informational programs, a monthly open forum for residents, a strong and active Resident Association, and resident observers at the board of directors meetings who reported to the Resident Association. With all of this in place, I was told that our biggest problem was lack of communication. I learned that we often fail to follow-up with a resident on an issue of individual importance, even though we are doing a good job of communicating major issues to the community at large.

I have concluded that, in a life-care community, the demand for communications is insatiable; the more you communicate, the more you need to. I do not know of any life-care community with a staff position of "director of communications," but it may not be a bad idea. Short of that, it is important to plan a communications system. This is best done by making one person on the staff responsible for communications. The right person will depend on who in the organization is most suited to the assignment. It might be the associate director, the administrative assistant, the activities director, or the head receptionist.

While there are several ways to deal with communication, the point is that it must be taken seriously. The residents' need to know is real, and failure to communicate, either one-on-one or community-wide, will result in an unhappy community.

Staff Organization

There is more agreement among life-care community executives on basic staff organization than on any other element of management. Figure 12–1 illustrates one way I have found effective to organize a life-care community staff. Of course, within this framework there are many variations. These variations will be based on the size of the community, the relative size of nursing-care units to independent-living units, the history of the organization, the presence or absence of a management contract with an outside firm, and the strengths or weaknesses of the various individuals in key positions. I will discuss each of the key positions and the variations common in each at a later point.

Appropriate titles are an important element of staff organization. Titles are a form of communication. They tell us the relative importance of a person and should clearly indicate the nature of the position. Here we have an inevitable conflict. I have found that people really respond to a more prestigious title but that, too often, organizations give out prestigious titles to routine positions. While this practice does not deceive the employee, it often deceives the public. My practice has been to use the most dignified title available that is appropriate to each position. Examples are:

Traditional Title	*My Choice*
Nurse's Aide	Nursing Assistant
Maid	Housekeeping Aide
Secretary	Administrative Assistant
Gardener	Grounds Assistant
Waiter/Waitress	Server (unisex title)
Maintenance Manager	Plant Facilities Director
Dietary Manager	Food Service Director

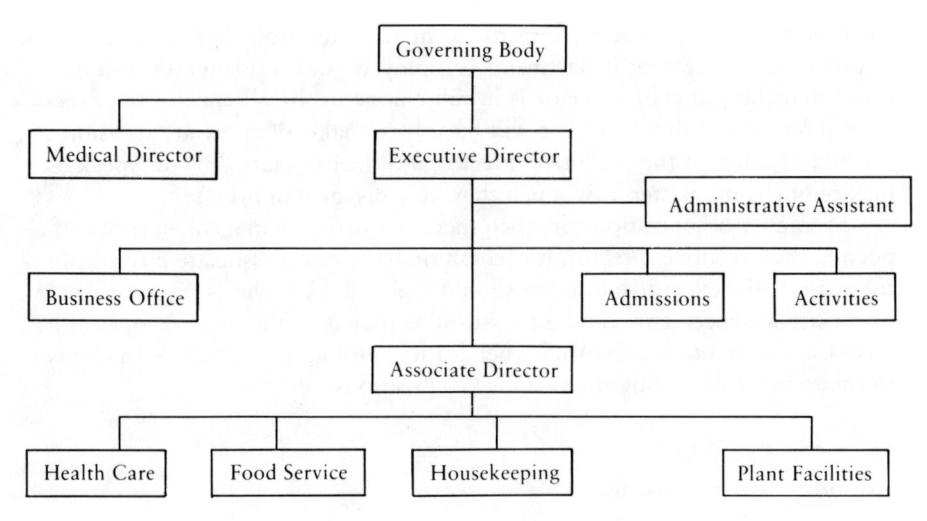

Figure 12–1. Life-Care Community Staff Organization

In addition to titles, I have also found that there are inexpensive ways to enhance the status of key employees that are greatly appreciated. Two of these that come to mind are providing business cards to all key staff members and purchasing letterhead stationery for each person who has any occasion to write business letters. This latter technique will help the life-care community executive, since it ensures that correspondence will be directed to the proper person, and not the executive director, which will happen if that is the only name on the letterhead.

Associate Director

There is great variation in how this position is structured. The best structure will depend on the relative experience and strength of the executive director and the associate director. In many cases, it is preferable to use the title of assistant director for a young or inexperienced incumbent. I believe there is a great danger if the structure is set up with a one-over-one reporting relationship, with the associate director reporting to the executive director and then each department head reporting to the associate director.

This structure will inevitably result in friction, if not open warfare. The executive has no work of his or her own and will either bypass the associate or second guess every decision. Giving the associate specific departments to manage works well; however, department responsibilities will depend on the particular skills of the associate and executive directors. In some cases, it will work better for the associate director to manage the staff departments and, in others, the operating departments. Employees and residents must understand that the associate director is in full charge in the absence of the executive director and that he or she will be able to make all necessary decisions. It is important that the executive director and the associate director speak as one, publicly, no matter how much they may disagree in private.

In smaller organizations or when there is a strong management firm supporting the executive director, it is common to have no associate director. In these cases, the executive director should make it clear who is responsible in his or her absence. This can be the business manager, the director of health services, or any other department head. I have found one good technique is to rotate this role among the various key positions.

Administrative Assistant

It is important for an executive director to have an able assistant with whom there is a comfortable working relationship. An executive director is a public figure and must often be away from the office. The assistant must be able to make appointments without consulting the executive and must be able to speak for him or her. There are many duties to be divided among a few people in the administrative office, and many of these fall upon the administrative assistant. These can include:

- Scheduling for the executive director;
- Dealing with telephone and other communications systems;
- Dealing with the postal service;
- Issuance of parking spaces or garages;
- Control of master keys;
- Control and issuance of resident lists; and
- Communicating the executive's policies and decisions.

Business Manager

The business manager is the manager of the administration department. In many life-care communities, this role of managing administration is not clearly addressed. Often the work of managing administration devolves onto the executive director, resulting in his or her concentrating on the minute details of administration, rather than focusing attention on the overall direction of the community.

In some cases, the associate director can fill the role of the administration department head, with a charge bookkeeper directing its accounting function. Whatever system is used, it is important that the administrative staff understand who their "boss" is, and who will be reviewing their performance.

The major components of administration are:

- Accounting;
- Personnel;
- Reception;
- Purchasing; and
- Control of public areas.

Other titles in common use, in lieu of business manager, include "comptroller" and "director of finance." While there are many valid variations in the organization of the administrative area, I prefer to think of administration as a functional department, no different than any other requiring its own department head. If an executive director focuses on the work of managing the administration department, then the work of management of the life-care community is likely to suffer.

The subfunction of personnel coordinator is one that has grown in importance in recent years. There are many rules and regulations concerning employees that will only be adhered to if there is a person responsible for their observance. Additionally, employees need someone to go to other than their department head or the executive director. While I believe in the open-door policy, it is not a substitute for having someone dedicated to employee concerns. I have known many instances in which a union has won an election to the total surprise of the executive. While a personnel coordinator will not necessarily prevent unionizing, in practice it is an important element in meeting employee needs. The personnel coordinator should be located physically separate from administration to give employees comfortable access and to ensure privacy.

I believe that each department head should hire his or her own employees and that the personnel coordinator should place advertisements (to ensure adherence to policies), receive applications, screen out unqualified applicants, forward qualified applicants to the department head, check references, ensure that hiring meets established policies, and orient the hired employee into the organization. The personnel coordinator usually administers the fringe benefit program.

The subfunction of the reception desk should also be treated as an important part of the organization. The style and attitude of the receptionist establishes a lasting impression on the first-time visitor. We get only one chance to establish a first impression. The business manager needs to ensure that the receptionists are pleasant, helpful, accurate, and courteous and that they understand and properly interpret the policies of the organization.

Many duties can be added to the receptionist's daily tasks that will assist in running a smooth operation. These can include:

- Controlling incoming cash transactions;
- Controlling packages, both for the organization and for residents;
- Initiating charges for extra services;
- Distributing communications;
- Giving out job applications;
- Duplicating notices in the evening;
- Typing in the evening; and
- Controlling transportation.

Director of Admissions

The director of admissions picks up the work of the marketing staff when targeted occupancy has been achieved. I like to describe the position as being responsible for admissions and transitions. Work elements include the following:

- Community promotion (public relations, advertising, open houses, etc.);
- Development and maintenance of a future list and a waiting list;
- Working with residents who are considering relocation within the community;
- Coordinating relocation to personal care and nursing care;
- Working with families following the death of a resident;
- Coordinating the reconditioning schedule for units prior to their reassignment; and
- Handling all move-in issues, including assimilation into the community.

This is obviously a key function in the continued success of the community. Many communities have a separate position of "director of resident services." I have never been comfortable with that approach, partly because I believe it tends to create a "do-for" attitude. I believe fostering independence is a proper role of a life-care community. If a community has a continuing marketing problem, then I can believe that it would make sense to separate the admissions role from the transition role, but even then, I would prefer to have the person responsible for transition report to the director of marketing.

Activities Director

Activities, in the sense used here, includes both the required activities program for nursing patients and the work of developing and maintaining a full program of events for residents in independent living. I have operated communities with this function both under the health care department and also as a separate department. After experiencing both, I prefer the latter.

There is a danger in having a "social director" approach for the independent-living areas. If there is a person whose only role is to develop and sponsor events, then the full potential of residents to direct their own programs will never be reached. Having a separate activities department can maximize the staff use in both roles and make it possible for the activities director to back away from running a program for well and able people after resident groups are organized and a full program has been developed.

Medical Director

The medical director is not truly a staff position. The role is one of advice and counsel, and it is appropriate for the medical director to be appointed by the governing body. I believe that the medical director should be independent of the executive director to ensure independent medical judgment. The role of medical director should not be confused with that of primary physician, even if the same practitioner fills both roles. In general, I prefer to have these roles filled by different people, but I have worked comfortably with a single person doing both.

The work elements of the medical director include:

- Setting overall medical and nursing policy;
- Reviewing the practice of medicine in the facility, particularly in the licensed nursing home;
- Being legally responsible for ensuring that patients in nursing are visited as required in the state code;
- Participating in mandated review committees (pharmacy, infection control); and
- Endorsing all medical transfers within the community.

Director of Health-Care Services

If the community does not have a wellness center or an outpatient clinic, then a different title would be appropriate. If the executive director or the associate director is the licensed nursing home administrator, then the title might be director of nursing. In a multifunction department, the title of director of health-care services would be more appropriate. Typically, the subfunctions of the position include:

- Nursing care;
- Personal care;
- Outpatient services;
- Social services;
- Home health care;
- Health and fitness programs; and
- Resident case management.

Director of Food Service

Organization of the food department is fairly uniform throughout life-care communities. While many life-care communities use food management firms, there is a definite trend toward self-operation. Today there are many good consultants who can provide the services traditionally provided by management firms. The typical subfunctions of the food department are:

- Food preparation;
- Food service (main dining room);
- Coffee shop or employee dining;
- Nursing food service;
- Dietician services; and
- Special functions.

Executive Housekeeper

There is little variation in the organization or duties of this department. Some life-care communities use the title of "director of environmental services," but I feel that this title is confusing to residents and to the public. Typical duties of the department are:

- Cleaning residential units (weekly or twice monthly);
- Cleaning the central building, including all public areas (usually not food service);

- Cleaning personal-care units as needed;
- Full housekeeping services in nursing areas; and
- Operating the laundry.

Many organizations have adopted a team-cleaning approach. This consists of all residential housekeeping aides cleaning the public areas and offices first thing in the morning, and then moving to the independent-living units on a scheduled, geographic basis. This technique ensures the attractiveness of the public areas, gets the cleaning in public areas done before activities of the day begin, gives more flexibility in responding to housekeeping staff absences, and delays the first living unit cleaning until residents are ready.

Team cleaning of the living units uses two aides at a time in each unit. This shortens the time for the resident, helps in training new staff, and reduces both real and imaginary theft. Changing the teams periodically reduces the dependence of residents on a particular housekeeping aide and reduces the chances of an aide developing an inappropriate relationship with the resident. Periodic and heavy cleaning tasks, such as carpet cleaning, are performed by a separate person.

There is need for providing some personal laundry service, particularly for residents in the personal-care area and in nursing care. This should be made available on an individual basis at a nominal cost. Personal ironing should not be included.

After many years of operating communities with weekly bed linen and towel service, I am now in a community that does not provide this service. I have been amazed that the residents are doing fine and that, when offered the service at a nominal extra fee, expressed no interest. I suspect that we are dealing with a generation accustomed to home automatic washers and dryers and that the need for this service has diminished. As the population age increases, it may be necessary to offer bed linen and towel service as an option.

Plant Facilities Director

The organization of this department is also fairly uniform among life-care communities. The main variations are dictated by the type of structures and the extent of the grounds to be tended. Typical functions are:

- Physical maintenance of buildings;
- Grounds care;
- Security;
- Modifications and improvements to residential units done at residents' expense;

- Transportation equipment maintenance; and
- Transportation (may be under activities or administration).

The plant facilities director position is a very important one in the community, and the quality of the person filling it has a major impact on the sense of comfort and security of the residents. If a community has a strong and able person in the position, it may make sense to combine plant facilities and housekeeping under a single leadership. This is particularly true in single-structure communities with very small acreage. If this is done, care must be taken to ensure that a subdepartment is not created and one more person added to the payroll.

Relationship With Governing Body

An important element of life-care community management is the relationship between administration and the governing body. The governing body may be a church-related board whose members represent many constituencies, a nonprofit corporation that is self-perpetuating, a multifacility corporation (profit or nonprofit), or a single-owner company. In each case, the executive director is responsible for managing the community as directed by the governing body and also for educating the governing body to issues they should be aware of and consider. Issues that should be brought to the governing body include:

- The need for long-range planning;
- The need for adequate legal counsel;
- The state of the community, both physical and emotional;
- Trends that may adversely affect the community;
- Potential conflicts of interest;
- Industry trends; and
- Competitive trends.

Resident Relations

A life-care community exists to serve the needs of its residents. No matter what the ownership structure, an executive director must focus the work of the entire staff on appropriately serving the residents' needs within the definition of the Residency Agreement.

I believe that a well-organized Resident Association can be a help in administering a community by providing an organized system for dealing with the many concerns of a wide variety of residents who often represent conflicting objectives. Residents can totally exhaust the administrative staff with issues, observations, new desires, and complaints, if no alternative is available.

The Resident Association should in no way be a captive of the administration, but, on the other hand, the executive can and should be a catalyst in developing a Resident Association in a new community. It is usually possible to bring a group of able and responsible residents together and help them organize a single democratic representative government that can be an umbrella organization for all resident groups. It is common for resident groups to organize for specific purposes (such as nursing volunteers) before a strong association is formed. Planning for an association prior to the opening of the community can provide a structure that can encompass all resident groups.

The executive director should develop a close working relationship with the president of the Resident Association, possibly through planned meetings. In most cases, the Association will invite the executive director and others to attend at least part of their meetings. It should be kept in mind that attendance is at the pleasure of the Association and that the Association has the right to meet alone.

Conclusion

The management of a life-care Community is a complex and difficult job. Like rearing children, there are a lot of ways to do it wrong. On the other hand, there are many ways to do it right, if there is a clear system administered fairly. Fairness is the best test for decision making as it applies to all constituents: the residents, the employees, the governing body, and the public.

The job of executive director is not for the faint-hearted. Criticism is common and often unfair. A good executive director is sometimes placed in a situation in which continued tenure is neither possible nor desirable. It seems that very few executives are able to continue in one position for over ten years unless the organization is expanding significantly. While a series of short tenures is bad for a community, an exceptionally long tenure may be equally bad. Change can be good for both the executive director and the community. I feel it is appropriate to say a word about successions. While the idea of promotion from within sounds good, in practice it almost never happens. Young people moving up in the field should expect to change locations rather than wait for the top job to become available.

Good management is critical to the success of a life-care community, just as it is to any other enterprise. There have been a number of failures and near-failures of life-care communities, which I feel have been ascribed to the wrong reasons. I have heard of failures attributed to the fact that the average life expectancy was longer than expected, or that the health-care costs turned out to be higher than expected. In fact, in every case I know, those failures have, in fact, resulted from poor planning or poor management or both. Now is the time to develop our own literature on the planning and management of life-care communities.

> While every sponsor will wish to play with job titles and organizational structures, the above comments offer a tested and strong basic framework for an efficient and effective life-care organization.
> —Editors

13
Life Care at Home: Is It an Affordable Option?

Donald L. Moon

The following chapter describes the first full-scale Life Care at Home (LCAH) program in the U. S. There are currently three more somewhat similar projects funded by foundation grants, and also involving the author's advice and consultation. This is an ideal case study of options for life care in a home setting that encourages the notion of aging in place in one's own community. Similar programs exist in other developed countries where public policy encourages the elderly to remain at home by providing community based home-making, homehelp, and health-care support services. As the first major U. S. project, the LCAH program serves as an important reference point for further development and refinement, and highlights the most important issues of providing life care off-campus, with considerable clarity.

—Editors

The life care at home plan (LCAH) is designed to allow the elderly to maintain their own living arrangements for as long as possible, while providing a life-care contract similar in many respects to those offered in many existing life-care or continuing-care retirement communities (CCRCs). A full-guarantee CCRC (type A, or life care) offers a contract to retirees usually for the rest of their lives. The costs of housing, services, and health care are spread among all residents, minimizing individual risks of unmanageable health-care expenses, especially those associated with long-term nursing care.

Like a CCRC, an LCAH will provide for a continuum of services and, most important, guaranteed health care. Yet unlike the CCRC, the LCAH is designed for people of retirement age who will not live initially on a specific campus, but rather, who will maintain their own housing arrangements, at least upon entry into the LCAH, with a number of services available that will allow them to continue to live independently for as long as is practical.

The LCAH member will hold a contract that will provide for a more or less comprehensive range of services under the management of the LCAH. These services will be guaranteed for as long as the contract remains in effect or for the lifetime of the member.

The first LCAH in the nation is now (1988) being marketed in northeast Philadelphia by the Jeanes/Foulkeways Corporation, a nonprofit corporation formed as a joint venture between Jeanes Health System and Foulkeways Retirement Community. Jeanes Health System (Jeanes Hospital) is a Quaker-oriented health-care system in northeast Philadelphia that owns and operates an acute-care hospital, a skilled nursing facility, and a Medicare-certified home-care agency, among other health-care and social entities and programs. Foulkeways is a Quaker-oriented life-care center that has been offering full-guarantee life-care contracts for over twenty years. Foulkeways was one of the first life-care communities on the east coast.

In addition to the Jeanes/Foulkeways LCAH, a number of other institutions are in the process of conducting feasibility studies and market surveys to determine the advisability of establishing an LCAH in their own area.

Purposes of the Life Care at Home Plan

The purposes of the LCAH are twofold. First, it is designed to provide a lower-cost alternative to the CCRC life-care model, so that it will be available to a much broader economic spectrum of the elderly than those who are now finding the CCRC to be the preferred option for retirement living. The second purpose of the LCAH is to make an optional lifestyle available to the elderly that is not currently in place.

A Lower-Cost Alternative

The LCAH is designed to reduce the costs of the life-care contract by eliminating or reducing normal CCRC costs, such as housing, food service, and other campus-oriented components. By eliminating or reducing these expenses, it is anticipated that the costs of the LCAH can be reduced significantly. It should be noted, however, that the reduction of these items from the list of services offered by the LCAH necessitates the addition of other services not being offered in the traditional CCRC (e.g., a home emergency response system, home-delivered meals, and adult day care). It should also be noted that reducing these costs from the LCAH contract does not necessarily eliminate them from the total expenses of the retiree. Further, servicing clients in scattered locations is neccessarily less efficient and carries some extra expense.

The LCAH also functions to spread the risk of providing health-care services over a relatively large number of people, in a manner similar to the traditional CCRC, Health Maintenance Organization (HMO), and some long-term care insurance plans. Hence, the LCAH borrows elements from both the CCRC concept and the insurance industry to effectively manage the health-care risks of the system through cost-pooling. The result should be protection against catastrophic health-care expenses for the individual member of the LCAH.

An Optional Lifestyle

The LCAH, however, is much more than an insurance concept. It is also a methodology of health-care provision that guards against overutilization of institutional health care. There tends to be a bias within the health-care system of the United States toward institutional care; not necessarily because of explicit choice, but largely as a result of the reimbursement system. Medicaid, the primary source of public funding for long-term health care, has become the long-term care insurance of choice or necessity for many Americans. Yet its reimbursement system goes almost exclusively for institutional care. Many elderly, however, would prefer to spend as many of their retirement years as possible in a noninstitutional setting. They view the institutionalization predilection as one that dehumanizes and detracts from the dignity and independence they desire.

The LCAH seeks to utilize the least restrictive environment for the elderly, commensurate with their health-care needs. The CCRC goes far toward maintaining people outside an institution through the use of a careful case-management system and a comprehensive system of services that supports residents in their own living units within the campus. The LCAH carries this one step further so that individuals can live independently in their own accommodations for as long as possible with support services provided as they are needed.

Philosophical Basis for the Life Care at Home Plan

The maximization of functional independence for all members is a philosophical tenet upon which the LCAH is based. The emphasis of the LCAH is on providing long-term health-care guarantees through a pooled-risk arrangement to a population of elderly who want protection against the catastrophic expenses of long-term health care and who prefer to remain in their own homes. In addition, a variety of amenities not normally found in the traditional CCRC will be added to the LCAH in order to maintain the member in his or her own living accomodations as long as is possible or practical.

In a campus-based life-care program, the financing for long-term health care is provided through a pooled-risk arrangement from resident entry and monthly fees. These arrangements vary between CCRCs, but in true life care, many individuals pay no more for living in the facility's nursing home than they paid to live in their apartments. In this manner, no individual needing long-term health care should suffer an unmanageable medical expense.

Insurance Concepts

There are a variety of insurance concepts inherent in the LCAH (as well as in traditional CCRCs). Like most insurance and pension plans, LCAH revenues are largely received in advance and accumulate prior to the time that promised benefits are delivered. LCAH entry and monthly fees are actuarially determined and are designed to advance-fund the costs of future health care for LCAH members. However, consistent with the concept of pooled risk, only a relatively small portion of members (estimated to be between 5 and 20 percent) are expected to need medical or nursing-care benefits at any one time. Similarly, only a portion of those who pay health insurance premiums actually suffer losses for which they receive benefits.

While the probability of a lengthy period of institutionalization for any LCAH member is low, the expenses associated with such a stay could be high. In many areas in the United States, nursing-home costs can be $35,000 per year or higher. One of the objectives of the LCAH is to insure elderly members against the possibility of an expensive institutional outcome. In this respect, LCAH will function as an insurance-like product. Under such a plan, the risk of a high-cost, low-probability outcome is spread over a large number of people through cost-pooling. Since the objective of LCAH is to design a retirement option that is affordable to a larger portion of the elderly population than can now afford a CCRC, the cost of the plan will need to be kept as low as possible. LCAH accomplishes this through careful selection of its membership and the use of various risk-management and screening techniques.

As in the insurance industry, an LCAH must be concerned with avoiding adverse selection. Risk-management controls employed by the LCAH include: entry and admission restrictions; benefit and service restrictions; and within-system utilization controls. The following are techniques incorporated into the LCAH:

- Health status screening at entry will be conducted. LCAH members must be capable of a certain degree of independent living, since they are expected to remain in their own living accommodations upon enrollment. The population mix of the LCAH will be managed to admit only those who are free of activities of daily living deficiencies (ADL). This will be accomplished generally through health status screening, as well as ADL assessments prior to entry into the plan.

- Financial status screening will be conducted at entry. Although the LCAH is aimed at a broader income segment than traditional CCRCs, it will still be important to ensure that the population can afford the entry and monthly fees for a specified time period. In addition, it is important to ensure that prospective members are able to afford the necessary copayments associated with the institutional long-term nursing care and other services, if they should be required.
- To encourage members to enter at a younger age (more in advance of the time when benefits are needed), monthly or entry fees are varied based on age. A similar approach is often used by long-term care insurance companies. Pricing schemes that encourage the enrollment of couples are also advantageous to managing risk within the LCAH, since couples in the general population tend to experience a reduced risk of institutionalization because of their mutual support.
- Benefit and service restrictions are included in the LCAH by applying a surcharge (exclusion) for the use of services related to certain costly preexisting conditions. Cost-sharing (copayments or deductibles) is also used to control utilization of certain services. The LCAH will also establish eligibility requirements for the receipt of many services as well as benefit restrictions on many noninstitutional services.
- Perhaps the most important controls within the LCAH are the extensive use of case-management services to ensure the most cost-effective and appropriate use of services being guaranteed.

Delivery Concepts

In addition to being an insurance-like plan, the LCAH is also an efficient and comprehensive delivery system. An important aspect of the LCAH is the delivery and coordination of a wide selection of services necessary to maintain members in their own living accommodations as long as possible, while still providing the security of needed services. For this reason, the LCAH incorporates services that cross traditional boundaries found in other concepts. These include comprehensive health care (prevention, acute, and long-term care), social and recreational services, home-delivered meals, assistance with activities of daily living, and others.

Members of the LCAH receive the full spectrum of care, based on needs-assessment methods to be incorporated into the delivery and coordination of services. While services will be provided that are commensurate with population needs, this will be balanced against concerns with cost-effectiveness and the appropriateness of care for the needs present.

Careful case management is essential to the success of the LCAH and to the assurance that members receive care when they need it. Case management becomes more important in the LCAH as compared with traditional CCRCs and other retirement options because its members are geographically dispersed and may have more difficulty arranging for various services themselves. In addition, because of this geographic dispersement, it will be difficult to monitor the health status of members to ensure the appropriateness and timeliness of services. Adequate case management will ensure that members receive the proper level of services and will also ensure the LCAH that services are being delivered at the lowest reasonable cost. A balance must be struck between members' needs and cost-effectiveness. The goal of the case-management function is to incorporate these two concerns into the member-placement process.

The Service Package

The LCAH is designed so the member will hold a lifetime contract that will provide for a wide range of services under the management of the LCAH. These services will be guaranteed with varying degrees of copayments for as long as the contract remains in effect. For the most part, this means the services are guaranteed for the lifetime of the member.

From the objective of retirement security and, in particular, financial protection against substantial long-term health-care expenses, arises the need to have a comprehensive and efficient benefit package within the LCAH. However, the benefits must also be predictable enough to ensure fiscal integrity for the LCAH.

In order to distinguish the benefits for which individual participants pay the full cost from those for which they do not, the benefit structure is designed to include "covered" services (with or without copayment) and "brokered" services. Copayments may be used within the plan to reduce demand, to distribute costs closer to use, or to increase the revenue of the LCAH.

In those instances in which there is little reason to subsidize the service, but the service is still desired by the plan's managers or members, the LCAH may choose to offer the service, with the members paying the entire cost. In such an instance, the LCAH need not worry about the financing or predictability of the benefit, but will simply "broker" the service to the member at cost.

Benefits Provided in the LCAH

There are a number of reasons for providing a benefit or service under the LCAH. These reasons point to the need to provide a service package that is both comprehensive and efficient in its delivery. The services must be comprehensive in order to provide for a full range of services that are marketable, but also in order to maintain members outside of institutional health-care situations for as long as is possible or practical. The LCAH must be efficient in the delivery of services in order to maintain the costs of the plan for each member at a manageable and affordable level. The specific reasons for providing a benefit or service under the LCAH are:

Services Provided for Financial Protection. One of the basic objectives of the Plan is to provide financial protection to its members against catastrophic health-care expenses that have a small probability of occurring for any one individual. By pooling those costs over the entire group of participants (e.g., long-term skilled nursing care), the plan reduces the costs per member to a manageable level so that no one member is faced with the full costs of providing the specific service.

Services Integral to the Plan's Comprehensive Concept. In developing a comprehensive package that will allow individual participants to stay out of long-term care institutions, various medical, long-term health care, and social service benefits in the broader community will be included, such as home health care. While in and of themselves, these services can be costly to provide, when pooled over the entire membership, they provide the ability to keep members in their own homes longer and thus help avoid the even more costly institutional care that might otherwise be necessary.

Services Provided for Cost-Effectiveness. Some services can be provided to coordinate and manage the entire LCAH system in a more efficient and less costly manner, such as case management.

Services Contributing to the Marketability of the Plan. There are some services that prospective members would like provided. These benefits do not have high cost-variation, do not necessarily fit into a comprehensive long-term health-care system, and will not reduce the system's cost. However, they are desired by potential members and, therefore, may make the plan more attractive and hence more marketable. Examples of these services are lawn and snow removal.

Services Adding to a Sense of Community Within the Plan. While the plan is designed to provide retirement security, older individuals gain security by being part of a community. One way to build such security will be to offer services that yield immediate benefits to the members, such as home inspection and social and recreational events.

The covered and brokered services, as well as the features of the copayment system and any limitations of services that will be used in the initial LCAH, are listed in tables 13–1 and 13–2. It stands to reason that the list of services offered will vary with each LCAH, depending on specific local factors that are impacted by the availability of services, the character of the

Table 13–1
Covered Services for the Life-Care-at-Home Plan

Benefit	*Copayment/Limitations*
Acute care (Medicare supplement)	Medicare A & B coverage required. Benefit is limited to those medical services covered by Medicare A & B, plus a group Medicare supplemental insurance policy purchased by the LCAH.
Physician coverage	Benefit is limited to those services covered by Medicare A & B and a group Medicare supplemental insurance policy purchased by the plan. One routine physical examination by a plan physician per year is provided, exclusive of laboratory tests.
Skilled nursing care—short-term	No copayment for 1st 100 lifetime institutional days (personal, skilled, and/or intermediate nursing care combined).
Skilled nursing care—long-term	No copayment for 1st 100 lifetime institutional days (personal and nursing care combined), 30% of semi-private per diem rate copayment charges thereafter. Member may choose to pay extra charges for private room.
Personal care—short-term	No copayment for 1st 100 lifetime institutional days (personal and nursing care combined).
Personal care—long-term	No copayment for 1st 100 lifetime institutional days (personal and nursing care combined), 30% of per diem rate copayment thereafter.
Home health care for skilled and intermediate levels	No copayment.
Home health assistance/ homemaker service	No copayment.
Emergency response system	No copayment.
Respite care	No copayment for 1st 100 lifetime institutional days (personal and nursing care combined), 30% of per diem rate co payment thereafter.
Day care (social and medical)	$5.00 per day copayment.
Home-delivered meals	$1.00 per meal copayment.
Pharmacy	$130 annual deductible; $3.00 copayment for generic drugs; $4.00 copayment for name brand drugs.
Social/recreational activities	Some recreational services offered without copayment, others determined by individual activity.
Biannual home inspection	No copayment.

Table 13–2
Brokered Services for the Life-Care-at-Home Plan

Benefit	*Copayment/Limitations*
Home maintenance	100% copayment
Lawn service & snow removal	100% copayment
Travel club	100% copayment
Financial & legal planning	100% copayment

market, the costs associated with the service, and the degree of risk the sponsor is willing to accept.

The services listed in tables 13–1 and 13–2 are essentially for members while they are physically located within the targeted service area. However, it may be that individual members will be out of the area (e.g. on vacation, etc.). In those cases, routine medical and acute care would be covered by Medicare and the Medicare supplemental insurance, subject to the limitations cited above. Any institutional nursing care outside the geographic area by more than one hundred miles will be covered in an approved facility up to an aggregate amount of $500. Any additional costs will be covered only when the member returns to the area and enters the LCAH's own health-care facilities. All other services will only be provided within the targeted service area.

There are several eligibility and limitation requirements for the services offered through the LCAH. One of the challenges for the LCAH is to structure the benefits offered in a manner that is both equitable and efficient. This requires conscious decisions in terms of limitations on total service costs for members. The copayment structure is designed to reduce unnecessary utilization and thus limit the LCAH costs. However, there also must be limitations upon the services provided to members in order to manage care and control costs to the plan. While the LCAH is committed to maintaining members in their own homes when appropriate and when it is the member's desire generally, home care often can become more expensive than institutional care for some more severely impaired individuals.

In order to effectively manage the costs associated with the provision of health care, members will be nominally eligible for many health-care services only when they display one or more ADLs. The individual case manager, however, will have a great deal of flexibility in determining eligibility for the services. All final eligibility decisions will be made by a care coordination team composed of health-care professionals and members of the administrative staff of the LCAH.

In addition, the LCAH will be responsible for community-care costs only up to the costs of alternative institutional care. That is, when the cost of care in a member's own home is equal to or greater than the cost of maintaining that member in an institutional setting, the member will no longer be eligible for the home-oriented service. However, members who choose to pay the actual per diem costs for the additional home-oriented care will be allowed to be maintained at home.

The LCAH will exclude from membership anyone who possesses one or more ADLs upon application for enrollment. This excludes applicants who need personal assistance, those with Alzheimer's disease or any type of dementia disorder, those who are bedbound or homebound, or those who need special equipment to ambulate. In short, the LCAH will enroll only those who are relatively well and independent.

The Pricing Mechanism

There are two basic elements to the price of the LCAH: the cost of providing long-term nursing and personal health care and the cost of noninstitutional support services. The actual charge to participants will represent the sum of these two elements as determined according to a per-member, per month formula. To determine the actual costs of both elements, one must project the levels of utilization for specific services. The estimates for the long-term health-care component figure are derived from an actuarial estimate of the future liability of providing both personal care and skilled nursing care to the entire body of participants throughout their assumed lifetimes. The noninstitutional support services component figure revolves around various utilization assumptions for each service provided. Those projections are based with experiences of mature CCRCs and other providers of the same services throughout the United States and represent the best estimate that can be made according to the experience of those institutions.

The fee calculations for the LCAH are based on several principles that impact on the specific amount of the various fees. For example:

- The fees are based on the principles of prepayment and cost-pooling. Hence, an individual member pays a fraction of what the actual cost might be for both the institutional nursing care and the noninstitutional portions of the plan.
- The fee structure includes both an entry fee and a monthly charge. The entry fee is charged in order to both prefund a portion of the plan and to discourage disenrollment. It is thought that individuals will be more reluctant to leave the plan if by doing they would lose a significant portion of an entry fee. Hence, the LCAH would be able to avoid the adverse effects of significant numbers of participants coming into the plan at a time when required services would be imminent, receiving those expen-

sive services, and then disenrolling after they had received the services. Entry fees are a one-time fee and will only be adjusted in subsequent years for new members.

- Monthly fees may be increased over time to reflect increases in expenses within the LCAH. This principle is necessary in order to provide protection to the plan from both foreseen and unforeseen inflationary increases as well as for changes in the service package or errors in utilization projections. Of course, the provisions for these potential increases must be clearly delineated within the Participation and Care Agreement executed with each member.
- There will be no refund of the entry fee or monthly charge upon the death of a member. There will be a refund of the entry fee upon early withdrawal from the plan. A portion of the entry fee will be refunded according to the length of time the person has been a member of the LCAH. The amount of the refund will be the entry fee paid, less a sum equal to 2 percent per month of the principal amount of the entry fee for each calendar month of membership. In other words, a member will "use" the entry fee over a fifty-month period.
- Since there is some concern about marketing the LCAH during the beginning enrollment period, both the entry and montly fees will be discounted during the first generation of enrollment. Actuarially, this approach will have virtually no long-term impact on the plan.
- The amount of the entry fees will be age-related. In particular, there will be two age categories for entry fees: sixty-five to seventy-four and seventy-five to eighty-five. At least initially, the plan will not admit members over the age of eighty-five. This is done for two specific reasons. First, the LCAH hopes to attract the younger elderly into the plan. It is thought that such a price differential will help in that encouragement. Second, the actuarial projections made for the LCAH indicate that the costs of long-term health care increase dramatically for entrants over the age of eighty-five. Therefore, it is felt this additional cost liability would recommend the initial limitation to entrants under the age of eighty-five.
- For purposes of determining fees, there will be no sex differentials. Thus, all entry and monthly fees will be unisex-determined.
- The LCAH will maintain a couples entry fee that is approximately 10 percent less than two singles rates. It is anticipated that this will not only reflect projected expenses more accurately, but will also be an effective marketing tool.
- In order to provide a further marketing tool, there will be two specific pricing options available to members. One option will have higher entry fees and lower monthly fees, and the other will have lower entry fees and

higher monthly fees. This will allow the member to structure payments to the plan in relation to the specific circumstances of his or her financial situation. Once the member chooses the payment option upon entry, that option remains for the length of time the member is in the plan. Both payment options are actuarially determined, so it makes no significant difference to the plan which option is chosen.

- There is concern that some members may experience depleted resources over time and thus would find it difficult to meet the ongoing monthly fees of the plan. This is especially so given the probability of increased monthly rates over time and the necessity to pay a 30 percent copayment upon entry into the institutional health-care facilities. A thorough admissions test will be given to each prospective member to make every attempt to avoid this eventuality. However, there is the possibility that a limited number of members may find their funds insufficient for the accelerating costs of living the subsequent increases in the monthly fees of the plan. Therefore, a $2.00 per month amount is built into the monthly fee structure, to be placed in a separate "assistance fund." This fund will then provide financial assistance to those members who run out of funds. The funds will be distributed with the understanding that, should there be any funds left in the assisted member's estate, an amount would be returned to the assistance fund to the level that funds were dispensed by the LCAH.

The long-term institutional health-care component and the noninstitutional support services component are built according to specific guidelines, as follows.

Long-Term Institutional Care

The calculation of entry and monthly fees charged to LCAH members to cover both short-term and long-term nursing-care expenses consists of two steps. The first step is to estimate the actuarial liabilities (i.e., present value of future expenses) associated with providing the guaranteed personal and skilled nursing care. These estimates will vary with the members' age, sex, marital status, and health status. Using these actuarial liability estimates, the second step calculates the combinations of entry fees and monthly fees that are required to fund the expenses' present value according to both payment options.

Age and sex distinct actuarial liabilities are calculated based on an intial set of assumptions. Of course, these assumptions must be adjusted once the actual experience of the LCAH becomes evident. The following are preliminary assumptions used for the LCAH:

- A unisex pricing modality was used for all single members with the plan. That is, both single males and single females are priced at the same rates.
- Traditionally, a couple (i.e., two or more individuals sharing a single household, whether related or not) has been considered as a combination of two single residents in a CCRC. However, an analysis of the data indicates that there is interaction between couples that reduces their expected utilization. Thus, it was felt to be prudent to assume that couples represent the same liability as a single female whose age is the same as the female member of the couple, for purposes of making actuarial projections.
- It is assumed that approximately 50 percent of the total members of the LCAH will be couples (i.e., 67 percent of the total members will be single and 33 percent will belong to a two-member household).
- The utilization projections for both personal care and skilled institutional nursing care are based on the specific experiences of CCRCs. It is assumed that the actual experience of the LCAH will be most similar to these institutions, since the plan will be case-managed in a similar manner.
- The pricing structure is based on the assumption that each member who utilizes the long-term institutional health care will pay a room and board charge equal to 30 percent of the per diem daily charge for the appropriate facility when the member enters the long-term care facility. It is assumed that the copayment will begin after the individual has received one hundred lifetime free days in the long-term care facility.
- The actuarial projections are based on specific inflation-rate and investment-yield assumptions. The real rate of return is represented by the spread between these two rates.
- In the northeast Philadelphia LCAH, no contingency loading factor was built into the projections. Future LCAHs may wish to include loading factors in the neighborhood of 2 to 5 percent in order to cover unexpected adverse utilization experiences.

Noninstitutional Support Services

The noninstitutional support services component of the pricing mechanism is built from a zero base, that is, costs are directly calculated upon the costs and utilization rates projected for each individual service within the plan, including administrative, marketing, case-management, and assistance-fund costs. Once the utilization and cost assumptions for each service are made, a cost per member, per month figure is derived for each service, with the total of all services added to the institutional monthly fees to arrive at the initial monthly charge to members.

In order to be as conservative as possible, the LCAH assumes that the cost experience of the fifth year (i.e., using the utilization projections of the fifth year) would be the costs to the plan used for pricing estimates. Actual expenses will undoubtedly be significantly lower during the early years of the plan, since only those free of ADLs will be admitted. However, it is anticipated that calculating costs in this manner will mean that a cash surplus will be built into the plan during its earliest years. This surplus can then be used as contingency loading for future service costs, should the projected utilization figures for either the institutional or noninstitutional support services prove too low.

The Targeted Market

Enrollment Size

The ideal or most efficient size of the LCAH is dependent on a number of factors, including basic pricing assumptions and variables. Some of these are controlled by the sponsor, while others are beyond the sponsors' control and subject to various interpretations. One consideration pertains to economies of scale. For a variety of services, the concern is with selecting a size that makes the most efficient use of resources and fixed assets. The LCAH has slightly different concerns in this regard than a traditional CCRC, since it will not be maintaining a large physical plant. However, there are still economies of scale that must be considered. For example, a larger plan has more leverage in negotiating discounts for services. Administrative costs can also vary with plan size, although a certain minimum number of members would be needed to support those costs economically.

The size of the LCAH also will depend on the number of elderly and their economic and demographic composition in the targeted market area. That only a small percentage of the population in the market area can afford and is interested in the LCAH places a specific limit on the number of members in the LCAH, unless the plan's marketability can be significantly changed or its service area expanded.

Another factor in LCAH size is the availability of resources in the community to meet members' needs. Although the availability of home care needs to be considered, as well as transportation and medical resources, undoubtedly the most crucial consideration will be the availability of long-term care beds. A limited supply requires a smaller LCAH. For example, it is estimated that an LCAH enrollment of 500 would require about 60 long-term nursing care beds in the mature plan, compared with 120 beds needed to support an enrollment of twice that size. However, better control of long-term health-care utilization rates and greater reliance on alternatives to institutional care, where feasible, might mitigate this limitation to some extent.

A final consideration in selecting the ideal or nominal size of the LCAH pertains to the actuarial risk that is known to vary indirectly with the number of members. Specifically, research suggests that for a population of 500 members, it is estimated that 12 percent of projected actuarial costs must be added as a risk factor. In contrast, a population of 1,000 reduces the added risk premium to 4 percent. A confidence interval around the estimate of 90 percent or better is recommended for the LCAH. Thus, if the LCAH can attract and support an enrollment of 1,000 members, it can significantly reduce the per member lifetime expenses by up to $4,000, if one assumes a lifetime cost of $40,000 for the institutional long-term care portion of the LCAH guarantees.

Who Will be Served?

It is important to develop a projected membership profile for the LCAH for a number of reasons. Actuarial and utilization projections are based on the projected profile. The development of a marketing strategy is dependent on an understanding of the composition of the potential market. The composition and extent of the various services is in direct relationship to the age and health status of prospective members. Thus, the LCAH must make various assumptions regarding the composition of the plan's membership.

Minimum and Maximum Ages at Entry

The LCAH is intended to follow the prevailing practice of CCRCs by limiting entry to individuals over age sixty-five. Supporting this practice are the actuarial cost estimates for the institutional long-term care portion of the plan, which indicate that a lower entry age does not greatly influence lifetime long-term care costs, since younger members will be paying monthly fees longer to offset their larger initial liabilities as a result of their greater life expectancy (i.e., more years during which services are to be provided). In addition, experience indicates that health status and functional ability are more important predictors of long-term care costs than is age. Thus, managing the LCAH population mix in terms of health status and disability will be more important than imposing explicit minimum-age criteria for admission.

There is an additional practical reason behind the decision to impose a specific minimum admission age on the plan's members. In order to provide a number of the services, the plan will require that each member maintain full Medicare coverage. For the most part, this coverage is not available to those under the age of sixty-five.

The actuarial projections concerning the LCAH also indicate that the costs of long-term care accelerate rather rapidly once the member reaches age eighty-five. If a member is admitted to the plan after that date, he or she would be expected to utilize institutional long-term care sooner and at a much more concentrated level. Thus, there is a great deal of evidence to support a decision to impose a maximum entry-age of eighty-five on the LCAH. Without such a maximum entry-age, there could be more immediate need for long-term care capacity, since older entrants have a higher probability of needing long-term care in the nearer future.

Average Age

People in CCRCs are generally older on average than the elderly population as a whole. The average age for new entrants in a CCRC is between seventy-six and seventy-nine years old. The average age of CCRC residents nationally ranges from eighty to eighty-four years old. Average resident age increases with the maturity of the CCRC. It also varies across the levels of living units, from an average age of 80.2 years in independent living units to an average of 84.7 years in the skilled nursing-care area. How long a community has been in operation and the proportion of residents at various levels of care are factors that help to determine the CCRC's overall average age.

It is not yet known what age groups will be attracted ultimately to enroll in the LCAH. On the one hand, the younger elderly are probably better able to afford the entry fee and monthly charges anticipated by the LCAH. In addition, the population that is capable of and interested in remaining at home is also likely to be a younger elderly population. On the other hand, like CCRC entrants, it is likely to be the older members of the elderly population who are most aware of and concerned about insuring against the costs of long-term health care.

For these reasons, we have assumed that the average entry age and average resident age in the LCAH will follow essentially the same pattern as exists in CCRCs in general. Specifically, it will be assumed that an average entry age of seventy-five years and an average member age of eighty-two years within the mature plan (after, say, six to eight years of operation) represents an accurate estimate. These assumptions are built into the actuarial projections for the plan for institutional long-term health care as well as in the utilization assumptions for the noninstitutional support services.

Age Distribution

Assumptions regarding the distribution of entrants by age, sex, and marital status are even more important for financial planning in the LCAH than average entry age. CCRCs may have similar average entry ages and yet have a different distribution of their resident ages. It is felt that more accurate forecasts of health-care utilization within the LCAH will result by using estimates based on entry-age distributions. These specify the percentages of participants who enter from different ranges of ages. The age distribution being assumed for the northeast Philadelphia LCAH reflects the experience of the five Quaker CCRCs in the Philadelphia area. These assumptions have been incorporated into the actuarial and utilization projections made for the LCAH.

Other assumptions regarding new entrants into the LCAH that must be considered are the gender distribution and the distribution of the entrants by marital status. In part, these will relate to the average age assumptions that have been made, since the probability of being married varies with age. For example, while 63 percent of the elderly population between ages sixty-five and seventy-four are married, only 39 percent over age seventy-five and married.

Similarly, it remains to be seen whether the LCAH will be more attractive to married people or to people living together than to singles. This is likely to be true since couples are more likely to be able to afford the LCAH charges and more likely to be able to live independently in their homes for a longer period because a second person is present. On the other hand, single individuals may be more concerned with their ability to finance future long-term health-care needs and thus be more willing to purchase protection against those costs. Both the gender and marital status assumptions that have been incorporated into the LCAH actuarial assumptions are cited in table 13–3.

Income Level

To determine the feasibility of the LCAH from the point of view of the consumer, it is important to estimate the income, assets, and discretionary resources of the elderly to be served. Such an examination would indicate whether the costs projected by the LCAH pricing mechanism are within the purchasing power of those elderly. In addition, certain demographic variables, such as age and marital status, may be associated with different levels of purchasing power among elderly subgroups. Identification of these variables will aid in the marketing as well as the pricing of the LCAH.

The level of income necessary to support the LCAH will obviously depend on how much the plan charges for its services. It is assumed that the elderly will consider purchasing the LCAH only after their current routine needs are met. Thus, the amount of income that could theoretically support an LCAH purchase is that amount remaining after expenditures for standard necessities are subtracted from an assessment of the elderly's combined income, transfers, and assets. This amount is defined as their "discretionary resources." It is assumed that the elderly will be willing to spend some portion

Table 13–3
Initial Assumptions Regarding Distribution of LCAH New Entrants by Age, Sex, and Marital Status

Sex Distribution	
Female	75%
Male	25%

Marital Status Distribution	
Married	75%
Single	25%

Age and Sex Distribution

Age Range	*Female*	*Males*	*Combined*
Average	74.8	75.8	75.1
64 & younger	7.2%	5.3%	6.6%
65–69	18.1%	16.3%	17.5%
70–74	24.2%	22.4%	23.6%
75–79	25.5%	23.2%	24.7%
80–84	15.9%	20.8%	17.5%
85–89	6.9%	8.8%	7.5%
90–94	2.2%	3.2%	2.6%

of their discretionary resources on the monthly charges of an LCAH, probably between 10 and 25 percent.[1]

Using this assumption, in order for an individual to purchase an LCAH plan costing $200 per month, he or she would have to have an annual income of $9,600 to $24,000. Therefore, using a midpoint, it can be assumed that those eligible for the LCAH will have a household income of at least $15,000. While the income level of those actually interested in joining the LCAH is unknown at this time, it is felt that the $15,000 level represents a reasonable projection.

Major Marketing Issues

An important challenge in the efforts to develop the LCAH concept has been to determine whether the model is marketable to the elderly. While research has shown that the elderly are interested in some kind of long-term care insurance, their knowledge and understanding of the issues involved are somewhat limited. Therefore, it is still not known if the elderly will be interested in this LCAH model. Will they understand the advantages of a comprehensive program such as this, which not only guarantees health care and other related services, but also delivers and manages those services? Do the elderly wish to remain in their current homes while receiving these services, or would they prefer the change of lifestyle and living arrangements found in a traditional campus-style CCRC? Can the cost-pooling and health delivery components of a CCRC be marketed separately from the campus features, as this particular model attempts to do?

To address these questions and to help further refine various design features of the LCAH, a market research effort was designed that consisted of four related studies:

1. A mail survey to over 2,000 CCRC residents and applicants to better understand why people join CCRCs and to learn whether the aspects of a CCRC emphasized by the LCAH are the main ones attracting residents;[2]
2. Focus groups held in Boston and Philadelphia designed to assist in the development of the telephone survey and to determine qualitative features of the LCAH that might be marketable;
3. A telephone survey of 2,000 age- and income-eligible elderly in five cities to test interest in the LCAH; and
4. A mail survey of 2,000 age- and income-eligible elderly in northeast Philadelphia.

The market surveys conducted during the feasibility studies for the LCAH discovered several key issues that will have major impact on the marketing strategies of the LCAH. Early experience in the actual marketing process also verifies the extent of these concerns. It should be noted that different issues than those now anticipated will present themselves throughout the marketing process itself. Obviously, the LCAH marketing efforts must identify these when they appear and adjust marketing strategies accordingly.

It is anticipated that the following issues will have major implications for the successful marketing of the LCAH.

Misinformation Regarding Health-Care Benefits

The LCAH surveys and a survey conducted by the American Association for Retired Persons clearly show that seniors are either unaware of or misinformed about their long-term health-care coverage. Many (39 percent) within the LCAH surveys believe that Medicare or their supplemental health insurance policies will cover all the costs of long-term custodial nursing care. They are unaware of their potential liability for such care and see no impending reason to further protect themselves from the catastrophic expenses of nursing-home care. One of the major functions of the LCAH is to provide adequate protection against the eventuality of such an overwhelming expense. Therefore, the plan must address this lack of information concerning potential liablity. It must also convince the eligible public that the LCAH is an adequate, cost-effective, and attractive way to cover long-term nursing expenses.

Avoidance of the Need for Long-Term Nursing Care

The marketing surveys, focus groups, and the long experience of CCRCs have made it obvious that many seniors practice avoidance techniques regarding the eventual need for long-term nursing care. A phrase heard quite often within the focus groups was: "I think the LCAH is a good idea for those who need it, but I'm healthy and will never need a nursing home." Implied within that statement is the belief that the LCAH would not be a good value, since the individual would never need its most central service. For the healthy sixty-five-year-old, the perception of the eventuality of ever being in a nursing home is remote. In fact, the subject is often avoided vigorously. The nursing home is the symbol of deterioration; an eventuality no one wants to consider. Yet, the plan hopes to attract the healthy elderly and is, in fact, only open to those sixty-five- to eighty-five-year-olds who are fully capable of living independently. This group of prospective members must be shown that there is a possiblity they will need long-term nursing care.

Participants Are Asked to Purchase a Product They Will Use in the Future or Not at All

Members will be asked to pay what some would consider a substantial entry fee plus ongoing monthly fees. Yet the services they will immediately receive are limited and, in fact, form a very small percentage of the total benefits of the plan. Therefore, the marketing strategy must develop ways to show the value of the LCAH under these conditions. This issue speaks of perceived value and the recognition of the future benefits of the program for each individual. In many respects, this issue is similar to that faced by CCRCs. However, the CCRC has a campus with which a resident can identify immediate benefits. Our model LCAH does not have such an immediately identifiable entity that can symbolize immediate access to services.

LCAH Is an Innovative Yet Unknown Concept

In many areas, the CCRC and HMO concepts are well-known. For the most part, both are respected and recognized as viable ways to provide retirement living and health care. However, the LCAH is completely unknown and untried. In many respects, the plan is in the same position in which CCRCs found themselves several years ago. There is the possibility that many will wish to wait to enroll until they are convinced the new concept will work and will be viable economically. In addition, the plan must mount an effective campaign to educate the public about the concept itself. One of the largest difficulties faced by the market surveys was finding an adequate definition of LCAH that could effectively inform the respondents of its features. This also will be a major issue facing the plan's sales efforts.

Perceived Value Versus Cost

The potential member has no real benchmark by which to determine if the plan has a value equal to its cost. A few may know the costs associated with nursing homes in the area. Some may be aware of the expenses associated with CCRCs. However, since the LCAH is an entirely new concept, few will have the means to make a judgment as to the relative value of its services. It may be that many elderly of the area will see the entry fee and monthly fees as excessive in relationship to the perceived value of the plan.

A Perception by Participants That They Are Not Getting Services for Which They Have Paid

To gain sales, the Plan must emphasize the services it is offering to members. However, the entire plan is based on the premise that not all members will use all the services provided. The services will be carefully case-managed; there will be eligibility requirements to receive them, and there will be limitations on the amount of services any one individual can receive. Therefore, it could be perceived by some members that they are not receiving all the services for which they paid.

A companion perception could be that members will have a sense of losing control over their lives. Service eligibility and limitation decisions will be made by a case manager and a case-management team. This team could be regarded as disinterested or disconnected and perceived as only trying to protect the corporation from any drain on its assets. Members must somehow be convinced that the service limitations and the case-management system are for their own well-being and that the plan will not be capricious in its assignment of service eligibility.

Difficulty in Attracting the First Generation of Members to the Plan

The LCAH actually will begin offering services only after a sufficient number of members have enrolled to ensure its financial viability. This means that members will be required to pay a significant deposit and processing fee and then wait until sufficient members have done likewise before they see any services. Conceivably, potential members would be reluctant to make deposits until the services are ready to be offered. Thus, the first generation of deposits could be very difficult to obtain. The plan must have some method to encourage early enrollment prior to actually receiving services.

Conclusions

Based on the initial analysis of responses in northeast Philadelphia, there appears to be a sufficient market for the LCAH among the eligible and interested elderly in the area. Thus it would appear that the plan is both affordable and attractive. The ultimate test of its attractiveness will have to await the full conclusion of the marketing attempts in northeast Philadelphia and in other sites throughout the United States.

Analysis of peoples' worries and concerns suggests that there is a market for a plan that enhances access to quality long-term health-care services and provides financial protection for nursing-home and in-home services. However, to facilitate marketing efforts, it is obvious that the elderly will have to be educated as to their lack of coverage and their vulnerability to long-term care costs.

Drawing from the experience outlined above, other approaches to life care should also be considered. One option is a life-care–at-home program "wrapped around" a new campus-based life-care center. It might be smaller, less expensive, and much more marketable because of the access to attractive club-like facilities. Access to "campus" facilities, such as dining, educational, recreational, and social programs, clinic, pool, etc., would meet the need for a tangible, immediate benefit, akin in some ways to joining a country club, a health club, and an HMO all at once. Priority future entry, if desired, to the life-care center, including nursing services, with the LCAH entry fee credited to their life care entry fee, would offer LCAH members more meaningful options for their future needs.

For new life-care centers looking for support to obtain zoning approvals or variences, linkage with the more affordable and otherwise unavailable LCAH programs can be a plus for the life-care project and for the community as a whole. Such integration will no doubt benefit local seniors who may not at this time desire to relocate to a full life-care facility. This option can build a much broader base of support for life care than has been offered previously.

—Editors

Notes

1. Cohen, Marc A., Tell, Eileen J., Greenburg, Jay N., and Wallack, Stanley S. "The financial capacity of the elderly to insure for long-term care." *The Gerontologist, 27(4),* August 1987, pp. 494–502.

2. Tell, Eileen J., Cohen, Marc A., Larson, Mary Jo, and Batten, Helen L. "Assessing the elderly's preferences for lifecare retirement options." *The Gerontologist, 27(4),* August 1987, pp. 503–509.

14
Insurance for Long-Term Care: Implications for the Life-Care Industry

Mark R. Meiners, Ph.D.

The following discussion on long-term care expands the scope of this book as it points to policy decisions and incentives on the national level. Although it would require the power of Congress or the I.R.S. to achieve these goals, there is clearly a role for all concerned citizens in their promotion.

—Editors

The emergence of long-term care as an insurable risk has focused new interest and attention on the life-care concept. Life-care or continuing-care retirement communities (CCRCs) were for many years the only form of long-term care insurance available. As little as ten years ago, health insurance was generally perceived as not applicable to long-term care. Except for the relatively few people who were willing and able to afford a move from their home to one of the limited number of retirement communities offering a full chronic-care guarantee, there were no options. The burden of long-term care expenses fell first to individuals and their families until their resources were exhausted and then to the Medicaid program. Then as now, Medicare did not address the long-term care problem.

Private insurance options have now begun to appear on the market, and there is a wave of renewed public policy interest in dealing with the long-term care financing problem. The implications of this for the life-care industry are unclear. There are at least several possibilities, all of which seem more or less positive.

Positive Implications

Relatively few CCRCs offer an unlimited chronic-care guarantee.[1] For some, this may simply reflect intended limits to the scope of the benefit package. For others, however, the limited guarantee is related to the difficulties of insuring the long-term care risk, especially with the small risk pool that most communities represent.

As discussed in chapter 15, some CCRCs are actively exploring joint ventures designed to put the long-term care (LTC) insurance component with an established insurance company, and a number of insurance companies are marketing products to meet this demand. This type of arrangement eliminates the need for the community to act as its own small insurance company. By reinsuring with a company that specializes in long-term care insurance, the opportunity exists for creating a broader risk pool, which can have the effect of reducing the reserves needed to maintain viable coverage. This type of arrangement has the potential of increasing the number of retirement communities that are willing to offer some form of long-term care protection.

CCRCs also represent an opportunity to market long-term care insurance protection on a group basis, where all parties can work together in a managed care environment to control the risk. The direct link to sheltered housing, a critical but often overlooked component of long-term care, facilitates the management of services. This may reduce the difficulty of controlling the home-care and community-care utilization and encourage insurers to offer these services. Since home and community services are preferred by consumers over institutional care, this should help the market for retirement communities that offer such insurance.

Market Definition

The recognition of long-term care as an insurable event has also spawned competition for the life-care industry that did not previously exist. While CCRCs are no longer the only long-term care insurance option around, on the whole, this can be viewed on the positive side. The market for such protection in whatever form can benefit from the distinctions that can now be made in the types of options available.

Alternatives to CCRC model include free-standing indemnity products, social-HMOs, and life care at home (LCAH). Each of these models differ along a variety of dimensions, including the comprehensiveness of the benefit package, the management of risk, and the organizational structure. Each is undergoing testing, revisions, and further development.

The free-standing indemnity model typically focuses on the long-term care risk alone, with emphasis on nursing-home benefits and more modest coverage of home health care. The social-HMO model expands the concept by integrating a broader array of chronic-care benefits with acute-care benefits in a managed-care environment.

The LCAH model is a direct attempt to adapt the life-care concept to the needs of a broader population. It synthesizes concepts involved in free-standing LTC insurance, social-HMOs, and CCRCs, encouraging participants to buy into a risk pool arrangement that has a managed-care component. Unlike traditional CCRCs, however, enrollees are not required to move to a campus.

According to its proponents, the LCAH accomplishes two purposes. By eliminating the housing costs of traditional CCRCs, similar retirement security can be achieved at a lower cost, thus making it affordable to more people. In addition, this alternative may appeal to people who can afford a traditional CCRC, but who prefer to remain in their home.

Today's Changing Market

The market for all forms of LTC insurance is still new and developing. The free-standing type of product captured much of the initial interest in dealing with the problem of financing long-term care. However, features of the social-HMO and CCRC approach are receiving close scrutiny, particularly by insurers interested in gaining experience for the group market.

Initially, most of the insurers involved in selling long-term care insurance were small companies. This has begun to change, however, and some of the largest insurance companies are actively marketing their own products. Most are sold on an individual basis, but there is strong interest in developing group marketing strategies.

Strategies for market expansion might also involve links with other financing vehicles, such as home equity conversion, life insurance, or pension annuities, to take advantage of offsetting risks while promoting recognition of the need for long-term care protection. Other strategies being discussed involve tax preferences for individual savings accounts dedicated to the purchase of LTC insurance or for encouraging employers to offer such protection as a retirement option. There is little reason to see these strategies as limited to one form of insurance over another with the possible exception of equity concerns. Special tax breaks for high-income people may not be warranted.

Affordability Versus Appeal

A basic barrier to further development of the long-term care insurance market is the conflicting goals in product design. Insurers are faced with the need to improve the current offerings. At the same time they must make their products more affordable. Both affordability and appeal impact on demand, and the delicate balance between these factors is still being determined. It is a difficult task because improvements such as offering more benefits or assuming more risk generally increase the cost, which serves to limit the market more than is desirable.

In the past year, several insurance companies have actively begun to work with employers to facilitate the marketing of affordable options for their workers and retirees on an employee pay-all basis. Often the same insurers interested in the employee group market are interested in business with CCRCs because they see this as an opportunity to learn the group business on a smaller scale before expanding too far.

Expected Developments

In addition to reinsuring retirement communities for their chronic-care guarantee and developing similar risk pools among community members preferring to stay in their own homes, other market strategies are being discussed. One option is to offer Medicare supplemental insurance that includes long-term care benefits. The interest on the part of some Medicare-HMOs in offering LTC insurance to their members is a move in this direction that should be encouraged. Revisions to Medicare may encourage Medigap insurers to adjust their products by providing long-term care benefits. This type of development fits well with marketing to CCRCs, since many communities require residents to have Medicare supplemental insurance.

The appropriateness of the size and composition of the market, however, may be in the eye of the beholder. Currently the life-care industry seems mostly oriented toward an upscale cliental. The CCRC model of long-term care insurance seems to emphasize product appeal over concerns about affordability. Large segments of the at-risk population will have to look to one of the other options to meet their need for LTC insurance protection. Even then, there is need for improvements on both product appeal and price. It is in this context that public policy concerns enter the picture.

Possible Public Policy Roles

One intriguing aspect of LTC insurance that has fueled interest in public support for market development is the potential it holds for relieving some of the pressure on Medicaid. Government payors will benefit if private insurance can reduce the role of Medicaid as a source of payment for middle-income elderly by delaying or avoiding the need to spend down their resources. It also may be viewed as an alternative to the current incentive to transfer assets to gain eligibility. The possibility that there could be savings to public budgets as well as benefits to consumers suggests that there is a public role in encouraging the market.

In August 1987, the Robert Wood Johnson Foundation (RWJF) took a major step toward exploring this potential by initiating a grant program for the development and evaluation of public and private partnerships in the creation of LTC insurance programs and funding a National Program Office at the University of Maryland Center on Aging to provide technical assistance and direction to selected states. The purpose of the program is to provide those states that have demonstrated a commitment to reforming long-term care financing with the resources to evaluate the potential of private market products and to design demonstration models in which the state will work with insurers to expand the role and comprehensiveness of their products. Eight grants have been given (California, Connecticut, Indiana, Massachusetts, New Jersey, New York, Oregon, and Wisconsin) under the RWJF Program to Promote Long-Term Care Insurance for the Elderly.

By locating the grants in the states, the program takes advantage of the only substantial body of experience with all aspects of long-term care, including benefit determinations through nursing home screening programs, eligibility determinations through the Medicaid spend down process, and initiation of a wide variety of community-based services through 2176 and other waiver programs. This experience, combined with the variation in approaches to long-term care, makes the states an ideal laboratory for the development of new financing options. Given the large proportion of the states' budgets that are devoted to long-term care, there is a clear incentive to explore new financing methods while maintaining their well-established commitment to long-term care.

The grant program is structured to encourage individual states to select conceptual models that best complement their existing financing and service delivery systems while remaining consistent with the program's five overall goals:

- Restructure current public and private partnership to avoid requiring elders to impoverish themselves before becoming eligible for public benefits;
- Ensure access to quality long-term care services;
- Cover the full range of home and community-based services;
- Establish a case-managed benefit structure; and
- Design the program so that it provides for the participation of all income groups.

Working within these goals, states are considering a number of the strategies for the development of partnerships with private insurers. Options that involve reorientation rather than expansion of current public responsibilities include educational campaigns to enhance public awareness, regulatory review to encourage market flexibility while promoting consumer protection, support for improved data development and sharing to minimize uncertainty, and coordination of public cost and care-management mechanisms (e.g., preadmission screening, utilization review, case management, benefit coverage, and rate regulation) with those of the private market. More aggressive strategies involving direct market subsidies targeting those at some risk of needing Medicaid to help pay for their long-term care are also being considered.[2]

The grant program provides a method for states to benefit from an insurance perspective on the delivery and financing of long-term care and for private insurance companies to benefit from the experience that the states have gained through years of long-term care system experimentation. Through the course of the planning phase and subsequent demonstration phase, a broad array of insurance components will be evaluated and tested. The results from these grants should be a great assistance in furthering how to make LTC insurance both affordable and appealing.

Further Links With Housing Needed

The fact that housing is a key component of long-term care is often overlooked. Only the life-care industry has made the link explicit. Nonetheless, housing is a basic ingredient in the package of services comprising long-term care. Noninstitutional housing is a critical ingredient in keeping the elderly in the community and out of institutions.

The housing component of long-term care, however, is typically not part of the agenda when rethinking long-term care financing. The problem is one that is at the heart of why long-term care is such a difficult public policy issue. People of any age may need long-term care because they are temporarily or permanently ill or disabled. However, long-term care is needed mostly because of conditions related to old age. The needs of those aging in place are largely nonmedical and cover a broad range of health-related, social, and personal-care needs. This means that virtually all aspects of an elderly person's daily living needs are potentially eligible for public assistance unless some limits are established.

This is a concern in the context of tight budgets, uneven personal resources among the elderly, and the need or desire for both personal preference and personal responsibility. Long-term care financing programs, both public and private, have struggled to control expenditures. Typically, the result has been to limit the definition of long-term care to health-related assistance, with heavy emphasis on the medical model. Not only are housing considerations not included in such a definition, but home and community services have been severely restricted.

There are signs of change, however. Home-care and community-care benefits are in demand, and both public and private program development has been underway to meet that demand. How to structure and finance these benefits has been the source of considerable debate. The life-care industry should look for opportunities that build on this interest. In particular, it will be important to extend the concept to a wider market than that viewed as upscale if it is to be viewed favorably in the public policy debate on how best to ensure our citizen protection against the catastrophic costs associated with long-term care.

Rethinking Housing and Long-Term Care

Federal assistance for housing through our current tax structure is a major benefit enjoyed by older Americans. Formalizing the links between our efforts to support housing as a major societal benefit and financing long-term care should be considered. This will require widespread availability and acceptance of home equity conversion mechanisms as a means of helping pay for long-term care in residential environments. Success in this area will allow better targeting of limited resources for those segments of the population unable to afford to participate in these benefits.

The link between housing and long-term care for the elderly is ripe for rethinking. Consider the following:

- Housing is by far the most significant asset of the elderly. An estimated 73 percent of the elderly own their own homes, and most of them have no mortgage debt.[3] In total, the equity value has been estimated to be between $548 billion and $700 billion. Without effective means for freeing this equity for their own use, the elderly are "house rich and cash poor," leaving their heirs as the major recipients of these resources.
- Under most circumstances, the home is effectively exempt from any claim by Medicaid.[4] Therefore, the most significant asset of the elderly is not available to help pay the long-term care bill, leaving Medicaid as the payer of last resort even when the elderly recipient may have had significant means to contribute.
- It is becoming increasingly difficult for young people to afford to enter the housing market. According to the National Association of Home Builders, the rate of home ownership has begun to decline with the most noteworthy decreases registered among those 25 to 34 years of age.[5] This has prompted numerous proposals to assist first-time home buyers, including allowing funds accumulated in IRAs to be used as a down-payment by first-time home buyers.[6]
- Homeownership tax deductions valued at $38.8 billion in 1988 are beginning to be a more frequent topic of discussion as a potential source of tax revenues to help broaden the distribution of tax benefits to address

> the growing needs of the poor or at least to help reduce the federal deficit.[7]

What these represent is a mix of factors that may offer an opportunity to make progress in establishing creative linkages between our public policy on housing and long-term care. For most people, the best vehicle for saving is the purchase of a house. It reflects an appealing form of consumption while at the same time acting like an investment that can accumulate additional value. Linking housing investment to long-term care needs may serve to reinforce housing as an important part of long-term care both in terms of the services it provides and the asset accumulation it represents.

These factors could be used to reinforce the need for such linkages. Current or future tax benefits designed to facilitate housing purchases could be predicated on tieing some of the equity value in the home to the purchase of some form of long-term care insurance. This would serve multiple purposes, including investment in housing, saving for long-term care, and reduction of resistance to requiring home equity to be a source of funds for the elderly in need of such care. Creative linkages can be imagined that would help to balance the concerns implicit in these issues.

A key assumption behind home equity conversion strategies is that people feel strongly about staying in their current home. If this preference is not widespread and strongly held, then it may be as economical and appealing for people to sell their current home and use some of the proceeds to buy or rent a less-expensive home, freeing the remainder for other uses. This would represent new opportunities for extending the basic life-care concepts to a broader population. Several proposals made elsewhere in the context of facilitating aging in place are relevant to this line of thinking[8]

Linking Long-Term Care With Capital Gains

One adjustment to current practice that could have an immediate impact would be to require that the savings from the exclusion from taxes of up to $125,000 in capital gains on the sale of a home for people age fifty-five and over be set aside for long-term care needs. Under current tax law, the maximum tax savings from this exclusion range from $18,750 to $35,000. Even at half this amount (more in line with the median home value), a significant dent in long-term care costs could be made; especially if the tax savings are used to help purchase insurance. Targeting these savings to long-term care needs represents no additional tax loss to the Treasury. For consumers, it is certainly more appealing than having this tax break eliminated. It simply reinforces the use of those funds for long-term care needs, something that is otherwise easily overlooked.

Linking Long-Term Care with Down-Payments

Another idea would be to allow the use of funds accumulated in an IRA for first-time home buyers in exchange for a commitment to devote a proportion of the accumulated value to help pay for long-term care if it is needed. One of the challenges in the development of a market for long-term care insurance is getting people at younger ages to save for such expenses. One of the concerns about allowing for the use of IRA funds for home purchases is it involves trading of housing for retirement income. This link might help on both issues.

Linking Long-Term Care with Principal Payments

Additional support for multiple societal goals might be accomplished by allowing monthly contributions to the payment of principal to be treated like IRA accumulations, in exchange for a commitment similar to that suggested previously on long-term care from current home owners. The deduction could be targeted to lower- and middle-income people along the lines of the current IRA rules, or broadened some by allowing the deduction for everyone up to some limit, such as paying off the first $100,000 on a mortgage.

The incentives for saving in this form are more than just the tax deduction. On a $100,000, 30-year, 10.25 percent mortgage, a payment of $25 extra per month can cut the life of a loan by four years and save nearly $39,000 in interest. Even before the recent change in the rules, participation in IRAs was low and skewed toward the higher-income brackets. The link to housing equity accumulation and earlier mortgage payoff may be a relatively appealing form of saving for low-income people because the value of tax write-offs from interest payments is lower for them than for people in high-income brackets.

Also, for lower-income people, the savings are more likely to be new rather than just shifted from other sources (as has been suggested is the case with higher-income people). Encouraging an increased savings rate may be especially important for this proposal to receive serious consideration in the current tight fiscal environment. Any tax break to encourage savings in some form of long-term care account represents a drain on the Treasury now in exchange for benefits in the future. This type of benefit–cost comparison will give discouraging results unless there are externalities (such as enhanced economic growth from increased savings and investment rates) that can be introduced into the calculations.

Conclusion

The need for long-term care is the single most important cause of catastrophic health expenses for the elderly. The recent push to develop protection against catastrophic health-care expenses has helped to focus attention on the need for better long-term care financing options. New private financing initiatives have begun to show how the risk can be shared in a way that encourages individuals with resources to participate in risk-pooling and, in the process, help clarify those areas where there will be a need for public involvement on behalf of individuals without adequate resources.

The life-care industry can benefit from the emergence of long-term care insurance options. Alternatives to traditional CCRCs help to better define the market and assist in creating greater public awareness of the need to prepare financially for long-term care. By reinsuring with a company that specializes in long-term care insurance, the opportunity exists for CCRCs to share in the benefits of a broader risk pool, thereby increasing the number of retirement communities that are willing to offer some form of long-term care protection.

Long-term care insurance product development can also benefit from what CCRCs have to offer. CCRCs represent an opportunity to market long-term care insurance protection that emphasizes home and community services. Since these are preferred by consumers over institutional care, this should help the market for retirement communities that offer such insurance.

Although the current fiscal environment is not encouraging for tax incentives, the need for protection against the catastrophic expenses associated with long-term care may lead people to conclude that these strategies may warrant special consideration, particularly if they can be targeted to those most likely to need public assistance if they are not encouraged and assisted to set aside resources for long-term care needs. In particular, consideration should be given to the fact that housing is a key component of long-term care. Formalizing the links between our efforts to support housing as a major societal benefit and financing long-term care should be considered. This is a strategy that could serve the needs of the country as well as those of the life-care industry by ensuring that long-term care options are financially feasible for a broad segment of the population.

> The suggested options at the end of this chapter deserve the broadest consideration. Related proposals are starting to surface around the country, where land or project approval expediting may be offered by a town or city in exchange for privately generated internal subsidies of some residents or other socially useful concessions.

These ideas, proposing nearly "free" tax and other incentives to help older people use their own assets to guarantee their own housing and health care, can be a great boon to our society. They deserve to be promoted by all. They can be introduced locally, in nearly any municipality, and should receive broad support as a means to reducing the overall tax burden of society.

—Editors

Notes

1. Winkelvoss, Howard E. and Powell, Alwyn V. *Continuing Care Retirement Communities: An Empirical, Financial, and Legal Analysis.* (Homewood, IL: Richard D. Irwin, 1984).

2. Meiners, Mark R. "Enhancing the market for private long-term care insurance." *Business and Health, 5(7),* May 1988, pp. 19–22.

3. Jacobs, Bruce. "The national potential of home equity conversion." *The Gerontologist, 26,* October 1986, p. 498.

4. Office of Inspector General, Office of Analysis and Inspections "Medicaid Estate Recoveries: National Program Inspection." Report Number OA1–09–86–00078, June 1988.

5. Apodaca, Patrice. "Homeownership declines despite sales boom." *Investor's Daily,* February 20, 1988, p. 7.

6. Harney, Kenneth R. "A bumper crop of (election year) bills." *Washington Post,* October 1, 1988, p. F28.

7. Mariano, Ann. "Affluent get thousands in subsidies." *Washington Post,* October 15, 1988, p. E1.

8. Meiners, Mark R. "Financing Long-Term Care in Residential Environments." Paper prepared for Conference on Aging in Place, July 1988.

15

Self-Insurance Versus Private Insurance: A New Option for Life-Care Communities

Larry M. Diamond, Ph.D.

This chapter gives a rare, clear look at the new and rapidly evolving life-care insurance scene. Insurance companies are finally offering alternatives to the self-insurance programs most life-care centers worked out for themselves until the mid-eighties. Many still choose to self-insure, and enjoy less costly overhead plus greater control. This chapter helps to clarify the issues for sponsors, developers and operators faced with one of the most critical decisions a life-care community will make.

—Editors

A year ago, this topic would not have been included in this volume. At that time, there was no clear indication that the private insurance sector had any commitment to include retirement communities in their marketing plans for new long-term care insurance products. This lack of commitment seemed well-warranted: why should insurors adopt a policy that seemingly violates all of the basic principles of insurance, that is, to market specifically to the target population that is most at risk of using the benefits that are covered under the policy?

Today, the direction for private long-term care insurance has changed. Retirement communities, along with HMOs, large employer groups, and associational groups, represent an important part of the target group market selected by the major insurance carriers. At least twenty-six facilities or chains of facilities, including both full and modified life-care facilities, have purchased custom-designed group long-term care insurance policies that place the insurors at risk for the nursing home benefit, and many more are under negotiations. It is possible that soon about 4 to 5 percent (some twelve to twenty sites) of all life-care facilities will have private insurance policies fully covering their benefits. Thus, the first serious option has emerged to the current choice of prepaid, self-insured financing among life-care communities, or offering benefits largely on a fee-for-service basis, as observed in the rental model.

This significant new option for retirement community sponsors deserves some examination. In particular, several critical questions about the private insurance option warrant close scrutiny:

- Why are insurors writing group policies for life-care communities?
- What types of facilities are being targeted by the insurance sector, and what criteria are being applied in the selection process?
- What do these policies cover, and what do they cost?
- What is the nature of the financial and administrative relationship between the facilities and the insurors?
- What are the costs of risks or insurance coverage in comparison with self-insuring?
- Which facilities might benefit the most from insurance coverage? Which might benefit the least?
- How should facilities evaluate the potential risks and rewards of purchasing group insurance coverage versus self-insuring?

These seven questions are the focus of discussion in this chapter; each will be treated in turn in the sections that follow.

Why are Insurers Interested in the Life-Care Market?

It was noted previously that long-term care insurance in the life-care marketplace appears to be contradictory. Why would insurors want to sell a new, untested product in this high-risk environment?

The answer lies in part in the problems that the insurance carriers have encountered in marketing individual policies to the elderly market—some of which were noted by Dr. Meiners in chapter 14. Generally, insurors have experienced high marketing costs and modest sales and premium revenues in their pursuit of this market. The high sales costs reflect the high level of professional labor costs required to sell a complex, unknown product to a market that remains in large part ignorant of the need for insurance protection for long-term care. In contrast, life-care communities represent a defined group that does understand and feels the need for such protection and is willing to pay a portion of their fees to secure it as part of their contractual agreement.

A second important factor is the critical need among insurors for data in pricing their new products: unlike the medical sector, where national data bases on services utilization (Medicare and private insurance) are available, there is no reliable data base for long-term care services utilization, particularly for services that are paid for by private funds, which represent half of the total reimbursement.

Life-care facilities, by contrast, represent groups for which utilization data is usually readily available and, in turn, groups for which utilization and cost data and management can be controlled under a single organizational umbrella. Furthermore, through the efforts in recent years of Johnson and Higgins, working in a joint partnership with the Provident Life Insurance Co., Laventhol & Horwath, and other actuarial resources, reliable national data bases on life-care facilities have been developed.

The shift in the insurance sector to include life-care facilities as a primary group market for new long-term care policies is perhaps best understood as a transition phase toward the employer and membership association markets, where insurors currently sell most of their health-care insurance products. Seen in this context, the level of risk and venture capital required to write a finite number of life-care contracts in order to establish an experience base is relatively small.

Which Insurors Offer Group Policies for Life-Care Communities?

The major insurance carriers in the retirement community market are Aetna, Metropolitan Life, Provident Life and Accident Company, and UNUM. The first CCRC policy was developed by Metropolitan Life in 1986 at Williamsburg Landing in Virginia. Since that time, Aetna, Provident, and UNUM have signed agreements with an additional two dozen facilities, including both operational and developing facilities or groups of facilities.

There is evidence that competition in this market will grow in the near future, with the possible addition of the John Hancock and the Travelers companies and others to the current field of carriers. All the current companies in the field plan to expand their market share in the near term. It is conceivable that 5 to 10 percent of all life-care facilities could have private insurance underwriting for their long-term care benefits in the next year or two.

How Do Insurors Screen Potential Life-Care Sites, and Who Is Eligible to Purchase Their Policies?

Insurance companies that sell group policies to life-care communities have approached the market in essentially the same manner: priority has been given to upscale facilities or chains that offer life-care benefits on a prepaid basis. This targets a group of somewhat younger and affluent residents, and the availability of such a policy represents a potential competitive marketing advantage for the sponsor. In a few cases, however, policies have been negotiated for established facilities with many older residents, in their middle and upper eighties.

Purchase of the policy is mandatory at each facility. Group size requirements vary somewhat; however, Aetna requires buy-in by at least fifty residents to write a policy and a minimum enrollment potential of two hundred. Provident also considers groups of two hundred or more. Aetna allows individuals on facility waiting lists to purchase the policy as a mechanism to facilitate policy coverage at the time of initial operations. The policies are uniformly guaranteed renewable, but premium rates are negotiated annually. Provident differs from the other carriers by requiring that their contract facilities conduct benefit determinations and provide ongoing case-management services for utilization control and monitoring purposes. This allows for the possibility of a more balanced and possibly richer home-care benefit to be covered, as is shown in the following section.

Policy coverage through all three insurors is open to residents of all ages at the retirement community, except for those who are already using long-term care services or who have existing serious health problems, such as active cancers or heart conditions under treatment. This is a significant difference from individual policies in which age cut-offs are observed—usually at age eighty or eighty-four. There is usually a six-month wait period for eligibility for coverage for people in this category. The following lists summarize these major facility screening criteria that are applied by the insurors.

Uniform criteria applied by all insurors in the market are:

- Entrance fee requirement (modest–high);
- Monthly fees (modest–high);
- Wide range of service amenities;
- At least two hundred units;
- Policy is mandatory for all residents;
- Age cohort of the residents;
- Nursing home beds or home-care on-site or nearby;
- Staff resources on-site; and
- Track record of the sponsor or developer management group.

Other criteria applied by one or more insurors are:

- Local case-management resources available;
- Expansion potential of the local resident base;

- Assisted-living units provided;
- Part of a chain;
- Benefit design option desired; and
- Local market factors.

What Do Private Group Long-Term Care Insurance Policies Cost and What Benefits Do They Cover?

Scope of Policies Currently on the Market

Most of the long-term care policies in effect among retirement communities look, on the whole, very different from the individual policies that are sold on the market. This is because their common characteristic is custom design, tailored to the needs and resources of each local facility. In most cases, this involves full or nearly full lifetime coverage and more expansive home-care benefits, often including personal-care services, both of which are unavailable through any individual policy.

The major difference found among the carriers in the scope of benefits included is that Aetna limits its coverage to a maximum of five years of nursing-home benefits and two years of home-care benefits, while provident and Metropolitan offer full lifetime coverage. UNUM offers both limited as well as full coverage options. Provident and UNUM offer personal-care services as benefits options, the other carriers do not. Unlike the individual policies, there is no prior hospitalization requirement for nursing-home placement, and the nursing-home requirement for home-care services eligibility is eliminated.

Premium prices among the policies vary dramatically in direct relation to: the age and sex of the residents; the scope of the benefits included; and the maximum daily rate schedule for the nursing home. Age and the scope of benefits offered are the most critical variables in rate determination. Rates are almost uniformly age-graded, and the benefits are fully prefunded, utilizing group underwriting principles. On average, commercial insurance will cost 20 to 30 percent more than self-insurance, encompassing administrative fees, profit, and reserves margins. Table 15–1 presents a profile of the types of policies that have been sold to life-care facilities to date.

There are some potential advantages to the resident of private group insurance coverage for the facility's long-term care benefit. They include the following:

- Guaranteed protection of the life-care benefit through the insuror's large base of pooled reserves; and
- Rebates if costs incurred are less than the amount of premiums collected and reserve requirements are maintained.

Table 15–1
An Overview of the Private Insurance Policies Among Existing Retirement Communities

Name of Carrier	*# of Life Care Policies in Effect*	*Size of Group(s) Covered*	*Scope of Coverage*	*Wait Period*	*Monthly Premium (1988)*
1. Metropolitan	1	254	Unlimited nursing home care (all levels) plus limited home care	60 days	$95
2. Aetna	6, three of which are part of a chain	200–300	Nursing home care (all levels), ranged from 2–6 years, home care—2-year limits, prior nursing home care required	20–100 days	$60–$300
3. Provident	19 facilities, through 6 organizations, two of which are large nonprofit chains	200–350 +	Unlimited nursing home care (all levels), home care (30-day annual limit) and personal care services ($20 day maximum—unlimited units of service—at 4 facilities)	20–100 days	$98–$325
4. UNUM	1 (several others in process)	200 +	Any combination of nursing home and home care from a few years to lifetime coverage, on either a disability or managed-care services payment model	20–100 days	$125 + (depending on age and type of plan)

Note: Most facilities have maximum or near maximum nursing home care; a few also offer home care.

The facility, in turn, could stand to gain these potential advantages:

- No need to maintain a large reserve account for life-care services;
- A potential competitive advantage with similar facilities in the local marketplace;
- Financial protection for unexpected occurrences;
- Access to the actuarial base and knowledge of the insuror in estimating future utilization; and
- Access to comprehensive utilization and cost data reported on a regular basis.

What is the Relationship Between the Insuror and the Facility?

Group long-term care insurance policies are contractual agreements between the insurance company and the facility's management entity. The monies collected in premiums and paid in claims flow between the two parties. Individual policy certificates are issued to the residents by the insurance company.

Benefits eligibility determination is conducted by the insurance companies, although it is possible for facilities with appropriate staff resources to share this function, as is the case among the facilities covered by Provident. The criteria for benefits eligibility are specified in the policy certificate and are related to defined disability levels.

A portion of entrance fees collected can be used to reduce the monthly premiums. These funds are placed in reserve accounts and are applied as needed.

The facilities are paid, in addition, by the insurance companies, a monthly administrative fee for the services they perform in premium collections and in related oversight of policy-related matters among the residents. These fees are normally in the range of 2 to 3 percent of total premiums paid. This yields revenues of about $1,400 per month for a facility of 240 units, with 300 people covered under the group policy, and monthly premiums of $150 for each person. The facility might also receive dividends on the reimbursement for any case-management services provided on a negotiated rate basis.

The insuror's financial obligations under these contractual agreements include the following:

- The cost of staff time incurred to plan, price, and design the benefits package and to negotiate a contractual agreement with the facility;
- The cost of any marketing materials produced and of on-site marketing and education activities;

- The cost of claims processing and preparation of monthly and annual reports for the sponsor; and
- The full amount of any losses incurred.

These obligations are counterbalanced by the following revenues accruing to the insuror. These include:

- A yearly administrative fee—usually up to 10 percent of premiums collected;
- A profit margin—usually at least 10 percent; and
- The ability to renegotiate rates annually linked with the prior year's utilization experience.

The insurors in this market are attempting to pool their total risk across a number of life-care facilities in order to avoid sharp premium increases for high utilization at a selected site.

What Are the Costs and Risks of Private Insurance Versus Self-Insurance?

The cost to establish life-care facilities of the nursing home benefit provided is substantial, perhaps as much as 10 to 15 percent of the annual operating budget. This obligation is significant, since this model has traditionally self-insured against this risk. Reinsurance is not yet available in this area.

Estimates vary on the number of life-care facilities that have closed down or broken their contracts because of the drain on revenues created by higher than expected nursing-home utilization; at least a few dozen facilities may be in this category. However, life-care communities are reluctant to shift their health-insuring responsibility over to insurance companies because this is costly, is usually seen as imprudent, and runs the risk of policy termination at some future time. Developing life-care communities might give the private insurance option some more consideration.

The evolving market for private insurance is among rental facilities and modified life-care facilities. Here, the benefits offered are limited, and the resident assumes the obligation to pay for the services needed out-of-pocket, over and above what he or she pays in entrance fees and monthly fees. A private insurance policy could offer greater protection at potentially cheaper costs to the facility while concurrently eliminating any risk assumed by the facility's sponsor.

Let us examine two hypothetical situations. In Facility A, the current nursing-home benefit is sixty days annually after a thirty-day wait period, accumulating to a maximum lifetime benefit of two years, or 720 days. The daily rate is $70. The average age of residents is just under eighty years, and the facility has three hundred residents. Under this scenario, the resident has a $2,100 out-of-pocket liability, and the community has a $48,300 total liability per resident, $1.26 million annually.

What would happen if the management of Facility A decided to purchase insurance to cover this benefit? It is quite likely that a monthly premium of $150 to $200 per resident would cover a policy of at least two years of nursing-home benefit, and perhaps some limited home-care services as well. This represents considerable savings to the facility. The wait period could be shortened to twenty days, removing one-third of the resident's financial risk, and a small monthly cash flow of $1,400 to $1,800 in the form of an administrative fee would be generated.

At Facility B, all home-care and nursing-home services are offered on a fee-for-service basis, set at $30 and $60 respectively. The resident is at 100 percent risk to a maximum of $21,900 annually, and the facility is at no risk. There is at least a 20 percent chance of a resident in Facility B incurring a nursing-home obligation of at least $21,900.

If, instead, these residents were asked to pay up to $2,000 annually in premiums over their expected five to ten years in residence to protect themselves against this obligation, they would probably do so. This facility would not only gain incrementally in revenues, but could gain greatly in stature and competitive advantage by considering such an approach.

Both of these examples assume that private insurance covered all of the benefit and that self-insurance covered none. These options are not necessarily mutually exclusive. For example, nursing-home care might be covered under the policy while a modest home-care benefit could remain self-insured or available on a fee-for-service basis.

How Should Life-Care Communities Evaluate the Private Insurance Option?

Some of the important factors in weighing the private insurance option against the self-insurance option were highlighted previously: the degree of risk exposure for the facility and for the residents; the ability to off-load risk and reserves requirements; and potential marketing advantages accruing through such an arrangement with a major insurance carrier.

These must be weighted against some serious potential obstacles, including the following:

- The considerably higher cost of the product that would be passed on to the residents;
- The flexibility, responsiveness, and good will of the insuror in covering the services that you offer to the level and benefit amounts desired;

- The credibility and capabilities of the insuror;
- The insuror's track record in this market; and
- The insuror's approach to benefits eligibility determination.

It is very important that life-care communities do not trade-off risks reduction for any of these other risks as the price paid for private insurance coverage.

> When new life-care projects look at full long-term-care insurance coverage for residents, and are uneasy about self-insurance, an insurance company group policy may be a very attractive option. It may be "marketable," and with some policies, unexpended reserves which are drawn from entrance fees will be returned to the sponsor should they decide to self-insure in the future. Further, while there may be a premium paid for the cost of dealing with an insurance company to cover its administrative costs and profit, the prestige of a large company and the services it offers will become a special sales feature for the life-care facility. For those facilities concerned about size, the premiums for small groups may well be less when part of a pool than when self-insuring a resident group of say two hundred or less. It is clear that every new program further enhances choice, competition, and future options.
>
> —Editors

16
Promising Life-Care Trends in the United Kingdom

George Cochrane, M.D., FRCP

In this chapter the author provides a survey of the history of the National Health Insurance Act in the United Kingdom and its impact on health-care services for the elderly. He informs us of current issues and concerns in caring for the frail or severely-disabled elderly. We are introduced to innovative trends in monitoring and maintaining one's independence, be it in a life-care center, sheltered housing, or in living alone. We are also introduced to a wide variety of technical aids available in the marketplace, or in research and development, which can provide additional encouragement to both the elderly and their caregivers.

—Editors

In the last forty years of Britain, momentous changes have come about in the organization of the nation's health care, not least in respect to older people. The concept of the "welfare state," propounded by William Beveridge in his famous report of 1942,[1] was acclaimed for its attack on the five evils of Want, Disease, Ignorance, Squalor, and Idleness and for its recommendations of a minimal income for all through an effective system of Social Security.

In 1945, a substantial majority of the British people voted for a socialist government, and the welfare state was born. Aneurin Bevan's National Service Health Act[2] was a landmark in social policy, providing health care on a universal basis in response to need and regardless of income, age, sex, occupation, or area of residence. Women and children in particular gained from its introduction, removing a fundamental injustice.

The health care provided has been predominantly curative and hospital-based; next in importance has been the primary medical care provided by family doctors, dentists, pharmacists, and opticians; and of least importance has been the local authority sector, which is responsible for preventive medicine, environmental health services, midwives, health visitors, and home helpers. Costs of services are borne by national insurance; compulsory contributions are paid by workers in relation to their earnings.

Salaries, always accounting for approximately 70 percent of the costs, have increased about twenty-five fold during these forty years. Scientific medicine generates its own momentum and its own resource demands. Advances have lifted the expectations of providers and of the population, with soaring costs from supporting lives that would have ended. The gathering forces of advancing technologies and rising expectations had not been foreseen. The increasing annual allocation to the National Health Service (NHS) is not keeping pace with the ever-increasing revenue expenses, not giving rein to the expanding opportunities in curative medicine, and not providing adequate support for increasing numbers of the old and chronically ill. The pattern of disease has shifted from acute illness toward chronic impairments, requiring caring rather than curing. The NHS is under severe strain. Bed, ward, and hospital closures, combined with growing waiting lists and strike action by NHS staff, compel a fundamental review.

The first reorganization of the administrative structure in 1974 aimed at management by consensus, and the second in 1983 replaced participating democracy by giving managers and small executive committees authority for decisions. Through competing interests, the welfare state is seen by capitalists as too expensive to support. The NHS is being overhauled radically. Changes are everywhere, with hectic debate in Parliament.

The answers to three big questions must follow: "How much should Britain be spending?" "How should this be raised?" "By what mechanism should it be spent?" On the share of national wealth spent on health, in 1984, Britain's public spending was 5.3 percent of its gross domestic product (GDP), and with its small but growing private sector, 5.9 percent of its GDP. Italy spent 7.2 percent, Germany 8.1 percent, France 9.1 percent, Sweden 9.4 percent, and the United States spent 10.7 percent. The money is coming from encouraging private health insurance. Because of the closures of NHS hospitals and wards, delays in obtaining outpatient appointments, and long waiting lists for admission to hospitals, private health care is booming.

The growth in personal health-care insurance is particularly large in plans for retirement and private hospitals. People reaching age sixty-five can take out insurance for the first time, making sure that they get private treatment if they have to wait six weeks or longer for an NHS hospital bed—and they are eligible for this insurance until they are seventy-five. New companies are entering the market. The Social Services and NHS may become a safety net for those who are less well-off and for medicine's tragedies through chronic illness and major injuries. For all who can afford additional insurance coverage, tax relief may be offered as an inducement. Health authorities are encouraged to generate income from partnerships with private companies, from selling exceptional skills and treatments, and from shorter waiting lists. Most thoughts are focused on the acute service, waiting lists, and consumer choice, and few on planning services, control of costs, and such hard choices as balancing the need to care for confused, incontinent elderly people against such expensive procedures as heart transplants. The test of any change will be how it copes with the disasters, the inherited defects, the brain and spinal injuries; and the long-term debilitating diseases—calamities that no amount of self-help can prevent.

The demands on an aging population on the Health and Social Services will continue to increase, and if the dichotomy of curative medicine and caring is forced, the elderly will be in disputed territory. If cost-efficiency becomes the general objective of the NHS, it is likely that there will be diminishing commitment to the care of elderly people, the chronically ill, the disabled, and the mentally impaired.

A new community-care strategy is needed urgently. Approximately 3.7 million elderly people, 1.5 million mentally ill, and 1.5 million physically disabled people living at home are currently getting help for private nursing homes from the NHS, from Social Services and through Social Security payments. Care for a sick person at home costs less than £100.00 per week; for the same person in a private nursing home the cost is nearly twice that, and in an NHS hospital the cost is approximately three times greater.

Most elderly people care for themselves or rely on a network of family friends and neighbors. In an era when "we grow three grannies where once we grew one," commonly the younger members of their families are employed and less-inclined to assume the responsibilities of looking after an invalid relative. People most at risk are over age seventy, living alone, recently bereaved, disabled by locomotor disorders, and lately discharged from the hospital. Very old people live precariously, unreliable in their activities, frail, and at risk of injury. When illness, accident, malnutrition, apathy, and neglect can be avoided, more elderly people survive. The elderly report ill health at a relatively late stage and do not bring to their physician's notice such symptoms as painful feet, difficulty in walking, trouble with micturition, anemia, and confusion. Many of the disorders, such as cardiac failure, deafness, failing sight, and inadequate diet, are remediable, but half these disabilities may not be known to the family practitioner. It is certainly better to keep people healthy than to treat them when they are ill. The relevance of preventive medicine is startlingly clear.

Preretirement courses give information about personal savings, state benefits, balancing one's budget, health, diet, safety, physical exercise, and local amenities. Many men dislike retirement and want part-time employment, and in some localities voluntary agencies introduce would-be employers and employees. In the Link Opportunity Study,[3] local schemes enable elderly people to exchange their skills, which they make available to others for stamps they can use to receive services they require. In some industries, comradeship is prominent and continues after retirement, with people who have worked together meeting regularly, supporting one another, and visiting friends who are ill or bereaved. Luncheon clubs and day clubs for the elderly entice lonely older people and particularly widowers for a good midday meal. Volunteers arrange regular visits to the home of an elderly person, and a short training course for voluntary visitors advises about services available for the elderly and improves the volunteers' ability to detect early deterioration. The local authority alone or jointly with the health authority may employ organizers of volunteers, wardens of sheltered accommodation, and street wardens to visit elderly and disabled people once or twice every day. Friendships can be fostered by telephone calls.

It is the isolated elderly person who increasingly relies on the voluntary or public services and now the private sector. Most elderly have the earnest wish to retain charge of their own lives, to be cared for in their own homes, and to tap the health and personal social services as they require. With the closing of institutions, unqualified and unprepared family members are becoming front-line caregivers. If, because they are tending a disabled person, they are unable to work, they may receive financial assistance from the state as Invalid Care Allowance. Usually the female members of the family become the caregivers. Too often these caregivers lack basic training, emotional support, information, demonstrations of basic procedures, practical assistance, and time. Caregivers too must be cared for. Besides the assistance of home helpers, community nurses, and meals-on-wheels, elderly people and their caregivers may welcome a "shared care" split between home and hospital or nursing home.

The Crossroads Care Attendant Scheme[4] concentrates on caring for the caregivers, providing nursing assistance and domestic help. The care attenders have basic nursing experience and take on the duties of a relative, giving the help that is needed early in the morning, late at night, and, in some cases, overnight, thus preventing a breakdown in the care arrangements. Since the first scheme began in 1974, the notion has caught on, and each local scheme is autonomous, raises its own money, and may be helped by the health and local authorities, joint financing, and Urban Aid grants.

There are seven possible ways of enabling elderly people to live in the community before deciding on institutional care:

1. The person's own home may be altered. An attractive alternative to relying on a private builder or the maintenance staff of the local authority has been the employment, through joint funding, of a domiciliary rehabilitation engineer, provided with a fully equipped van, to undertake home improvements quickly and cheaply.[5] Another alternative is "community service," which has its roots in the 1970 Home Office Report of the Advisory Council on the Penal System. Offenders are ordered to perform unpaid work, as an alternative to custodial sentence, as punishment, rehabilitation, and reparation. Those with manual skills might adapt homes of the elderly and disabled.

2. When their children have gone, many elderly people live in a few rooms downstairs, leaving upstairs unused. Homes can be converted to provide the accommodation that the elderly person wants on the ground floor and separate accommodation above. This preserves contact with the past and with neighbors, and companionship with the upstairs tenants may give certain personal and domestic services.
3. Some elderly people share their homes with a companion who may be paid to provide personal and domestic services. There is scope for agents to encourage and arrange home-sharing when two elderly people can give companionship and mutual support.
4. Schemes similar to fostering children may be developed for elderly people so that each may become a member of a family, the family receiving fostering allowance and caring allowance.
5. There is an extending range of sheltered accommodation provided by local authorities, increasingly in cooperation with housing associations, and by charitable organizations with varying amounts of personal support by the warden, home care aide, or volunteers.
6. Elderly people may move to a private accommodation that has been specially designed, either within a condominium or often on the ground floor as an annex to the home of a close relative. Around the time of retirement and in later years, people who could afford to have been inclined to move to a home that is smaller, more easily run, and in a district that is more convenient and attractive, where the climate is softer and closer to one or more members of their family. About a generation behind the United States, Britain is witnessing the rapid expansion in building for retirement living. People are being persuaded to sell their homes and buy or rent retirement apartments that are easy to run, cheaper to heat, well-planned, comfortable, on the ground floor or with lift, and include security features, such as entry telephones, spy holes in the front door of the apartment, and intercommunication links to a resident house manager in case of anxiety. In some developments, facilities are available for communal dining and recreation. In town centers where land is scarce, family houses in large gardens are being replaced by blocks of apartments specially designed for retired people, and some large country houses, set in several acres of land, are being adapted internally for secure retirement in elegant apartments.
7. Schemes are being set up to give families a break from the demands of caring for elderly relatives by offering regular stays of one or two weeks with a substitute family.[6] Part of the success of this program is its ability to match the elderly person to a family with similar interests and social status.

The frustrations that are common among older people, often leading to their moving from their own home into residential care, are:

- Urinary and fecal incontinence;
- Confusion and forgetfulness;
- An adverse environment, frailty, and need for frequent personal services;
- Immobility and difficulties in transferring between bed and chair and lavatory;
- Pressure sores;
- Loss of use of the upper limbs; and
- Inability to speak and communicate, yet an earnest desire to direct one's own life.

Incontinence is particularly common among the elderly. In the United Kingdom, 11.6 percent of women and 6.9 percent of men over the age of sixty-five are incontinent of urine.[7] Prevalence increases appreciably with age. Fecal incontinence is underestimated, underresearched, and isolating. Rectal incontinence is predominantly a disorder of women, and its frequency increases with age. Nerve damage that has usually come about through childbirth or through chronic constipation results in weakness of the sphincter musculature so that feces are passed inadvertently, as for example, when standing up.

A continence advisory service must be accessible to all in need, with facilities for thorough urological and lower bowel investigations, with opportunities to admit, and facilities for the display and supply of basic equipment to restore self-confidence and self-esteem.[8] By attending to underlying causes, much incontinence can be cured or alleviated.

In the United Kingdom, over three thousand different continence aids and appliances are marketed by over a hundred companies, and there is little objective evidence to help one select from the plethora available.[9] The dearth of information is matched by ignorance of how to interpret the findings of such studies. Information from functional evaluations must be immediate and accurate, and the best use made of it, for it can soon be out of date.

For women, body-worn absorbant pads are the most commonly used. Subjects fall into three groups: the first experience minor daytime loss, are mobile, dextrous, independent, and mentally alert; the second have heavy daytime losses; and the third have heavy nighttime losses as well. The type of pad should be chosen to match the severity of incontinence. Pads leak partly because urine may not enter the pad fast enough through the cover stock, and because the absorption capacity of the pulp has been exceeded. Pad width and lateral compressibility determine dry comfort, narrow compressible pads being the most comfortable.

For women who dribble small amounts, a pair of pants having an insewn absorbent patch is recommended, with a hydrophobic surface of brushed polyester so that the surface against the perineum remains dry.[10] For women who have heavy daytime incontinence, an appliance has been developed with a perineal receiver and a suction pump with a charcoal filter so that urine is removed almost as rapidly as it is voided and contained in a reservoir on a waist strap.[11]

Deterioration of psychomotor function, confusion, and forgetfulness often make elderly people incapable of protecting themselves from common dangers. Their discharge from hospital may be obstructed by doubts about their remembering to take medicines and to conduct every-day personal care. There are dispensers correctly packed for each day (figure 16–1), and a personal prompter can be made with taped instructions as detailed as necessary, even to guiding in dressing, taking medicine, preparing meals, and going to

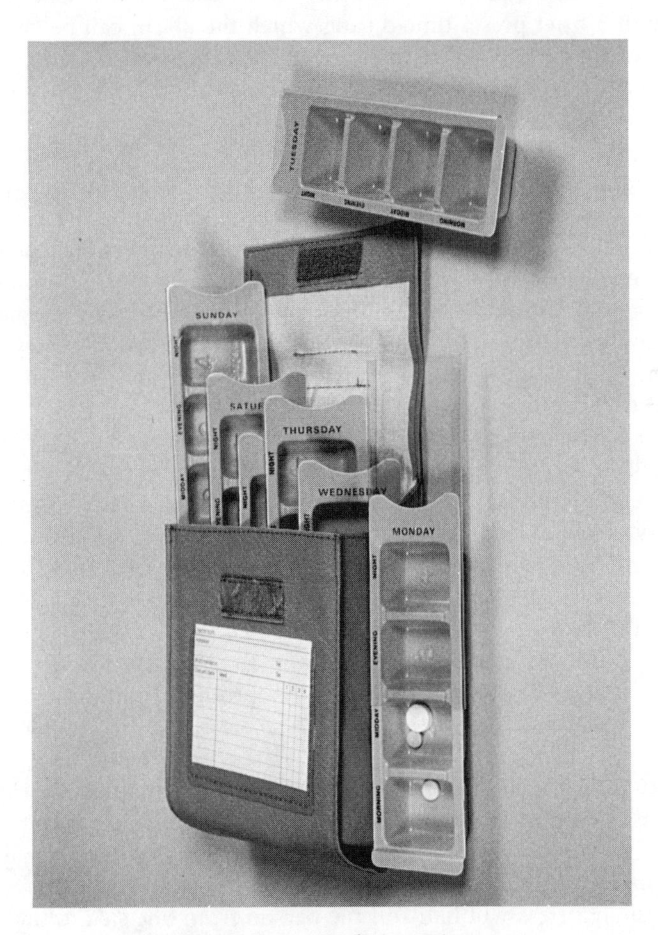

Figure 16–1. Medicine Dispenser

the bathroom. By requiring some response from the person before the program can proceed, it is possible for a caregiver to be alerted if the response is too long delayed.

Frail elderly people may need frequent personal services. Alarm and call systems are only as good as the certainty of appropriate response and the users' confidence that desired action will follow. Knowing that assistance can be summoned will allay the fears of an elderly person and of the relatives. The range of call systems is wide, evolving from the simple two-day listening devices to the pointing of an infrared transmitter at an alarm point, connected by a fiber-optic cable to a distant receiving point, and an emergency call system with a constantly manned station. When the user operates a neck pendant, wrist, or pocket transmitter, a radio signal is sent to the telephone autodialer. Visual and auditory signals inform the user that the alarm has been passed, with a brief preset time during which the alarm can be cancelled. If the alarm is not cancelled, the operator at the center has on the computer a full account of the person's circumstances, medication, special risks, and the people to contact.

Environmental control systems allow elderly and severely disabled people to exercise control over a wide range of domestic appliances by using movements under their control to operate special input switches. The demand for environmental controls is growing as the number of elderly and disabled people in the population increases, many living alone. Twenty-eight percent of the 8 1/2 million pensioners in the United Kingdom live alone. They want the best alarm, telephone, and intercommunication facilities, and the best domestic electrical equipment.

The first patient-operated selector mechanisms were hard-wired electromechanical, bulky, inflexible systems, with the operator selecting from the slow, sequential scanning of characters on an indicator panel. Remote control, achieved by infrared, ultrasound, or voice signaling, allows the user and others in the house freedom from the inconvenience of trailing wires, and because it does not demand precise direction, it is suitable for the blind. With newer input devices, encoded or direct selection becomes possible.[12] A microprocessor-controlled voice recognition system can be trained to respond to any voice or to any sound that can be reproduced faithfully. (See figure 16–2.)

Immobility and difficulties in transferring can be simplified by electrically operated air sacs that inflate to lift the head end of the mattress, raising the person to a sitting position in bed, or raise the seat cushion of a chair, assisting the person to stand from sitting. A pair of inflatable sacs under the full length of the mattress will half-roll the person from one side to the other by

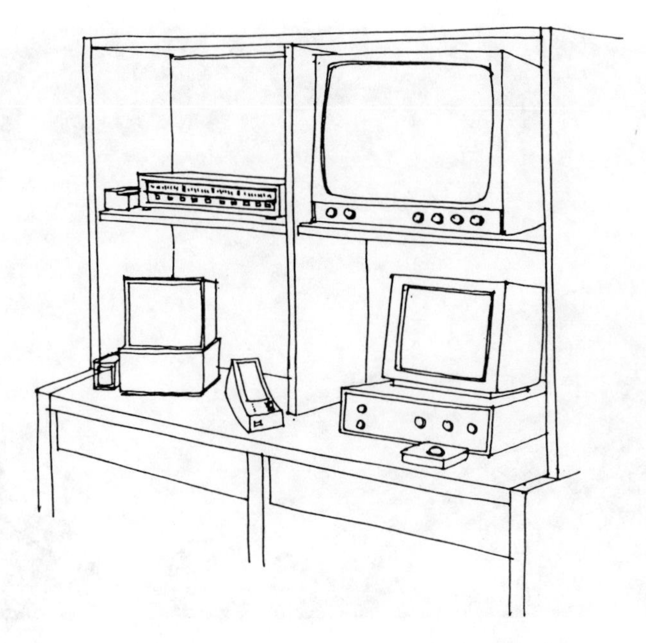

Figure 16–2. Environmental Control System with Word Processor—PSU6

filling and emptying alternately, either automatically at preset intervals or by operation of a switch. (See figure 16–3.)

The gap between bed and chair for those unable to move safely can be overcome by a low-friction bridge, an electrically operated sliding board (figure 16–4a), or an electric hoist with a traversing motor running on an overhead track (figure 16–4b).

Electrically powered wheelchairs can be operated by those only able to make controlled movements of the chin, tongue, or head. The Oxford Optical Pointer (figures 16–5a, 16–5b) behaves as a noncontacting joystick emulator and is small, low-cost, and unobtrusive. From a remote infrared emitter, the proportion of radiation falling on each of the detector's photosensitive quadrants is determined by the orientation of the head with respect to the emitter. Signals from each quadrant are processed to provide electronic outputs.[13] Raising the head causes the chair to advance, lowering the head reverses the chair, and turning the head to the right or left causes the chair to move in those directions. Sensitivities can be individually adjusted. A means of engaging and disengaging the control is provided by a microswitch to suit the user, and only when the head attains an approximately neutral position is the control engaged.

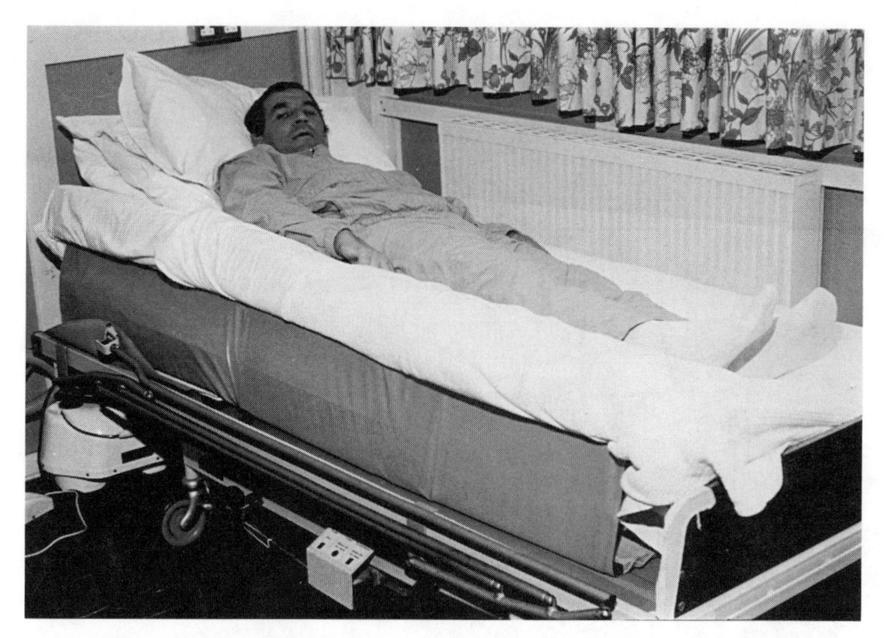

Figure 16–3. "Unibed" Under-Mattress Pneumatic Tilting Device

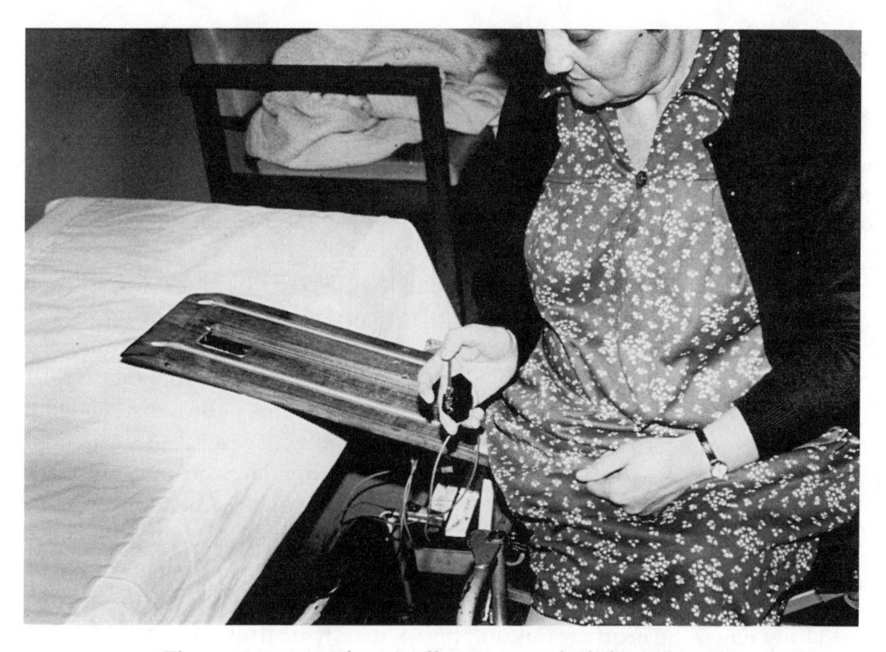

Figure 16–4a. Electrically Operated Sliding Board

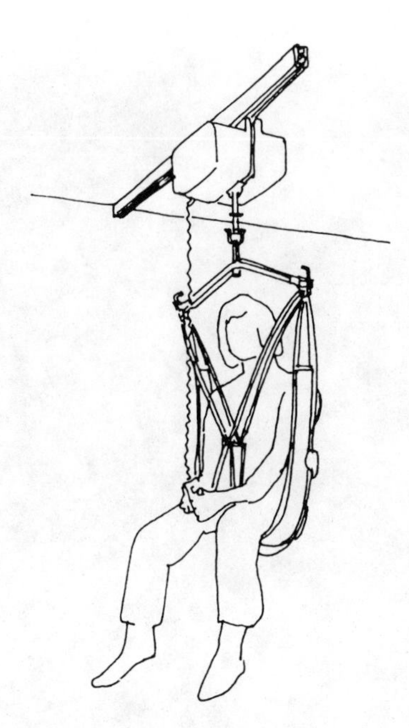

Figure 16–4b. Electric Hoist with a Traversing Motor

Decubitus ulcers are an ever-present threat to those who are frail, in poor health, immobile, and lacking sensation, but they may be prevented if corrective action is taken in time. We are currently engaged in developing a device that will give warning when the critical thresholds of pressure, temperature, humidity, time, and acidity or alkalinity have been reached.[14] A monitor records precisely the interface pressure at that moment in twelve adjacent flexible air cells that can be positioned at the areas of the body that are vulnerable. The thresholds of other extrinsic factors that cause blood flow in tissue to be reduced will be measured so that by timely warnings the dangers can be averted.

Loss of use of the arms can make people totally dependent on others for the simplest tasks. Parallelogram links added to mobile arm supports allow gravity-eliminated movements on horizontal and vertical planes, and the spoon will not decant its contents when it is close to the mouth (figure 16–6). Those with certain diseases have no use of their arms, yet retain willed movements of their legs. Four independent leg and foot movements can be translated into four movements of a manipulator by simple mechanical linkages and cables.[15] The foot-operated manipulator has proven its success in feeding, typing, shaving, and reaching (figure 16–7).

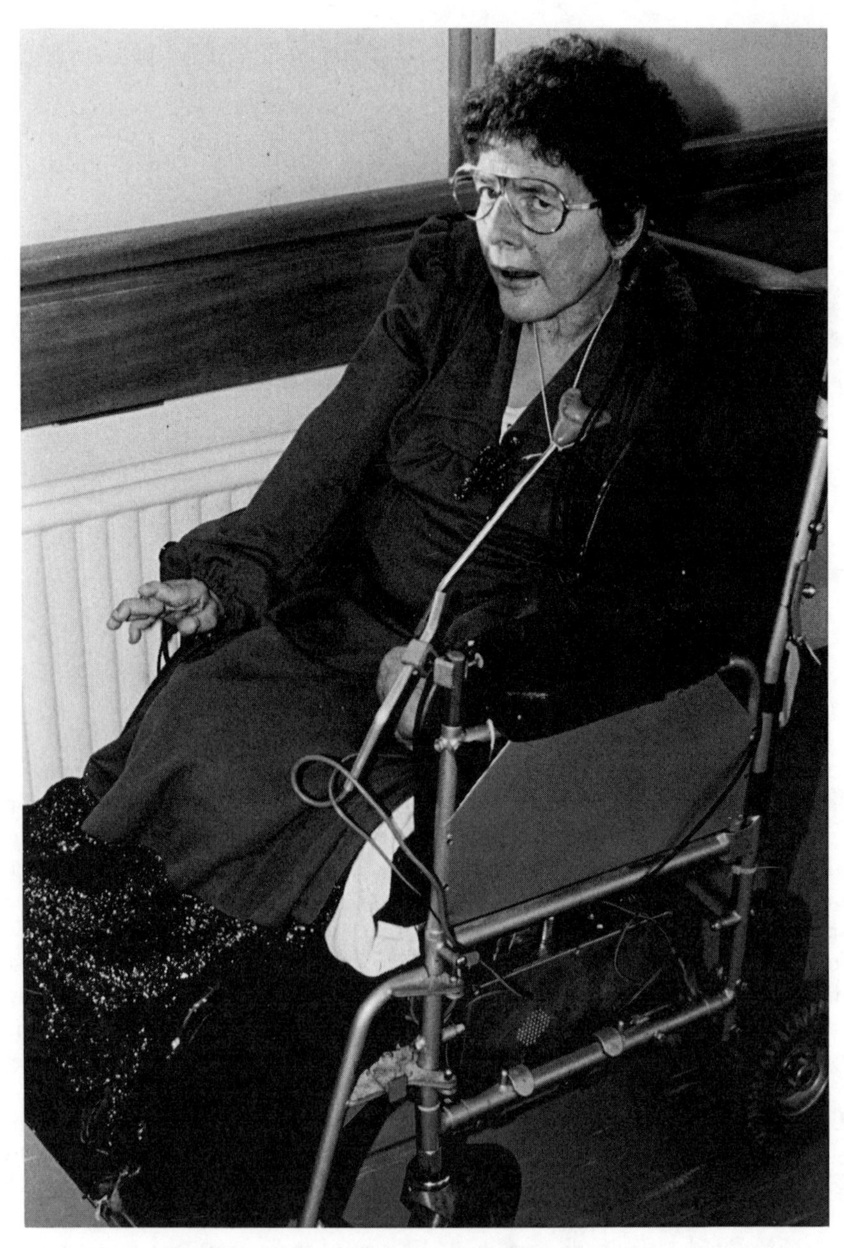

Figure 16–5a. Oxford Optical Pointer: View I

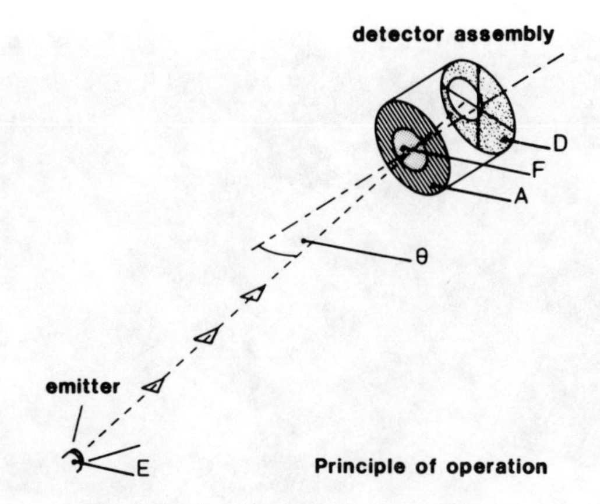

Figure 16–5b. Oxford Optical Pointer: View II

Inability to speak—to make one's basic needs known, to express emotion and exchange information—is frustrating and isolating. The increasing processing power and memory of microcomputers, together with their diminishing costs, size, and weight, have made powerful means of handling information widely available. A range of devices can be connected to a computer, including printers, monitors, alternative keyboards, speech synthesizers, and modems that enable messages to be sent by telephone wires. Further miniaturization, more efficient use of power, and alternatives to conventional monitors have made possible the development of portable or "lap" computers. Lap computers usually have a word processor program built in and may be used by a person in a wheelchair to communicate through writing. Digitized speech is produced by recording a human voice and storing it on a memory chip. Individual words can be selected by a computer and uttered one after another to form phrases and sentences. The quality of the synthetic speech is usually acceptable, but the vocabulary cannot be changed and is restricted to what has been recorded and the amount of memory available. In text-to-speech synthesis, the computer analyzes the typed words into phonemes, which are converted into speech according to rules stored in the speech synthesizer. The vocabulary that can be spoken is therefore unlimited, and it is possible to alter the spelling of the word to improve the pronunciation.

Technical aids for the elderly and disabled are their tools for living, yet research studies have shown that of the aids supplied by social service departments in Britain, nearly half are not used.[16] We need well-designed aids, better quality information, and better matching of aids to people as a continuing service. If the aid is not used, the money is wasted, and the problems remain unsolved. There are enormous cost implications. A standardized tech-

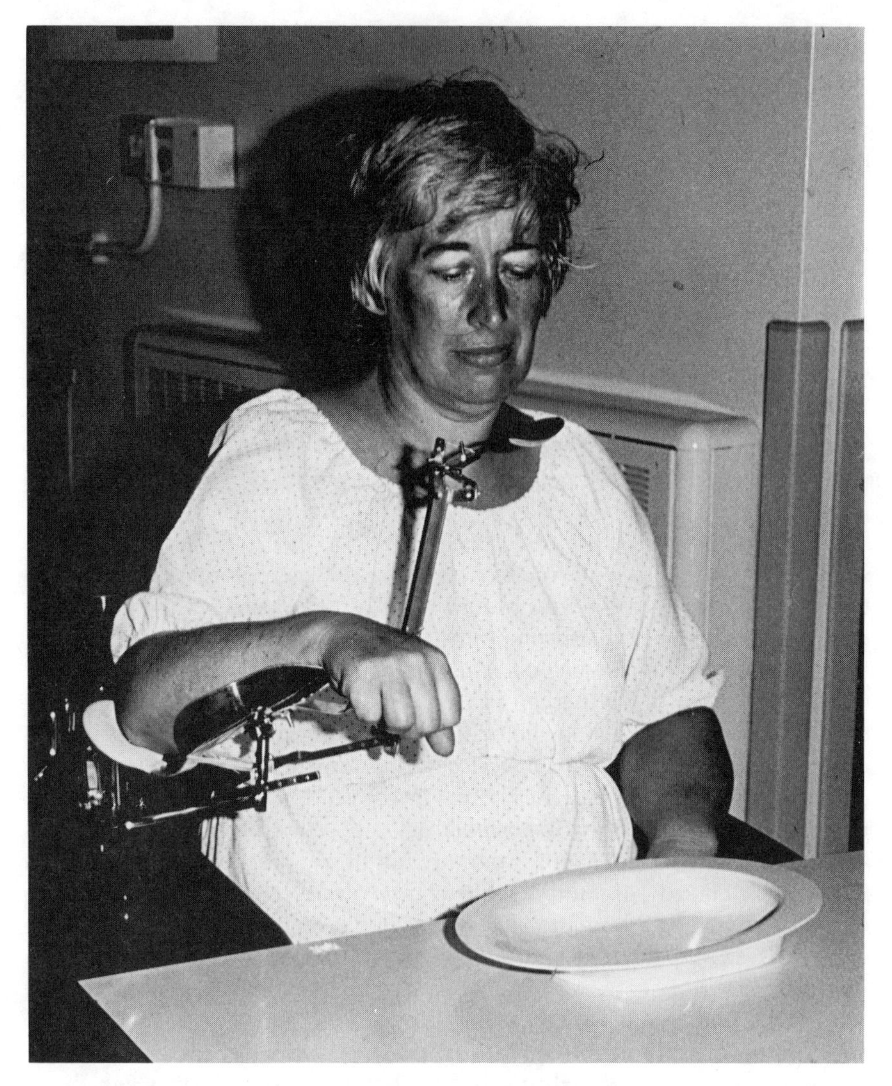

Figure 16–6. Mobile Arm Support With Parallelogram Linkage

nical and functional evaluation of aids is needed that will be comprehensive so that those who purchase and those who prescribe will have more and better quality information upon which to base their judgments.[17]

When the following four conditions are satisfied, even people who are severely disabled and totally dependent on others can live alone.

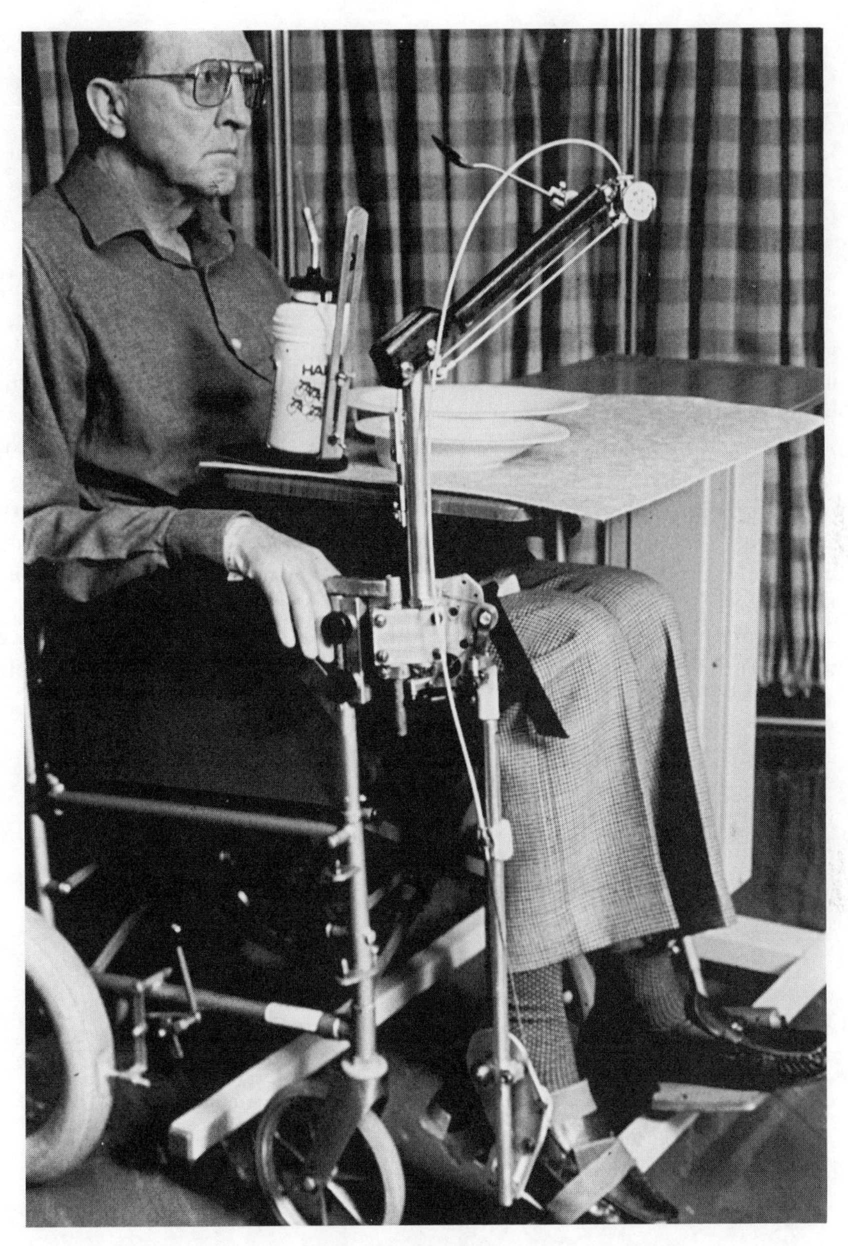

Figure 16–7. “Magpie” Food-Operated Manipulator

1. The person is determined to succeed whatever the odds.
2. The person's intellectual, emotional, behavioral, and physical characteristics are attractive to others.
3. The health and personal social service agencies are committed to the success of the endeavour.
4. There are sufficient friends, neighbors, and paid attendants to guarantee care early in the morning, many times during the day, and at bedtime.

It should be our undertaking that, by every means we have and can develop, elderly and disabled people should be encouraged and enabled to be actively involved in finding the solutions to their own problems as intelligent and discriminating consumers.

Holidays and living in sunny countries away from the cold and damp of Britain are no longer only the prerogative of the wealthy. Each year, more people who have enjoyed higher incomes are buying property in southern Europe as a second home for holidays, retirement, and occasional renting, and developers are building time-sharing units for the elderly in Spain, Portugal, and the Canary Islands. When Britain's welfare state is being lost to competitive marketing and everything is known of costs and less of value, we must be especially vigilant about protecting those who are most vulnerable among the elderly and disabled.

> A wide range of examples were given in this chapter on innovative technical aids that help create a supportive environment for even frail elderly with severe disabilities. Not only do such aids assist the elderly to maintain their sense of freedom, privacy, and self-esteem, but they reduce the stress and strain on caregivers and help reduce the accompanying cost of health care. A considerable amount of information is presented on problems of incontinence, with examples of various products to help those suffering from this condition maintain a more normal existence. Conditions which impede independent living were discussed, such as lack of mobility and inability to communicate, confusion, and forgetfulness. We are fortunate to have the opportunity to learn about the author's outstanding research and use of technical aids for the elderly and disabled in Great Britain. Through exchange of information on work accomplished in other countries and ourselves, we can help shorten the time and effort in research and development of new products, and bring such concepts and products to the consumer in a more timely fashion for the benefit of all.
>
> —Editors

Notes

1. Beveridge, Sir William. *Social Insurances and Allied Services*. London: H.M.S.O., 1942.

2. National Health Service Act. H.M.S.O., London, 1946.

3. *Link Opportunity Study.* Information from the press officer, Link Opportunity Study, Flat 6, 40 Sheperd's Hill Road, London, England, 1975.

4. Association of Crossroads Care Attendant Schemes Ltd., 10 Regent Place, Rugby, Warwickshire, U.K.

5. Cochrane, G.M. "Hidden resources for rehabilitation and care of the disabled." *J. Roy. Soc. Med., 75,* 1982, pp. 89–95.

6. Thornton, P. and Moore, J. "The placement of elderly people in private households: An analysis of current provisions." Leeds, U.K.: Department of Social Policy and Administration, University of Leeds, 1980.

7. Thomas, T.H., Plymat, K. R., Blannin, J., and Meade, T.W. "Prevalence of urinary incontinence." *Br. Med. J., 281,* 1980, pp. 1243–5.

8. Barnard, R.J. "The management of urinary incontinence." *Int. Rehab. Med., 4,* 1982, pp. 21–26.

9. *Directory of Continence and Toiletting Aids.* Association of Continence Advisers, 380–384 Harrow Road, London W9 2HU, 1988.

10. Cottenden, A. and Philip, J. "Innovation for incontinence." *J. District Nursing,* Oct. 7–10, 1988.

11. Cottenden, A. Personal Communication. St Pancras Hospital, London, 1988.

12. Gunderson, J.R. "Interfacing the motor impaired for control and conversation aids for non-vocal physically impaired persons." In Webster, J.G., Cook, A.M., Tompkins, W.J., and Vanderheiden, G.C. (eds.): *Electronic Devices for Rehabilitation.* London: Chapman and Hall Medical, 1985.

13. Tew, A.I. "The Oxford Optical Pointer: A direction sensing device with proportional electrical output." *Med. and Biol. Eng. and Comput., 26,* 1988, pp. 68–74.

14. Cochrane, G.M. "Pressure sores—A practical problem in severely disabled people." In Bader, D.L. (ed.) *Pressure Sores: A Clinical Problem.* London: MacMillan Press, 1989.

15. Evans, M., Cochrane, G., Osborne, M., and Harris, J.D. "Magpie: A foot operated manipulator." *Oxford Orthopaedic Engineering Centre Annual Report, 14,* 1987, pp. 85–89.

16. Page, M., Galer, M., Fitzgerald, J., and Feeney, R.J. In *The Use of Technology in the Care of the Elderly and Disabled: Tools for Living,* Bray, J., and Wright, S., eds. London: Pinter (for the Commission of European Communities), 1980, p. 119.

17. *Equipment for Disabled People,* 6th Ed. Titles in the series Communication, Clothing and Dressing, Home Management, Outdoor Transport, Wheelchairs, Gardening, Incontinence and Stoma Care, Personal Care, Hoists and Lifts, Walking Aids, Housing and Furniture, Disabled Parent, Disabled Child, 1987–89.

17
The State of the Art in Life Care in Denmark

Bjarne Hastrup, M.A.

This is an inspiring chapter on "The State of the Art of Life Care in Denmark" by the energetic managing director of Denmark's EGV Foundation, and the old people's association *DaneAge*. The author provides a background on the organization and workings of Denmark's unique, private, non-profit association of companies devoted to the creation of services and housing for the elderly. This hybrid group works on various levels, including the provision of grants for research and development of services and housing, advocacy for the elderly and protection of their rights, the operation of a travel agency offering discounts to younger people accompanying elders on holiday trips, continuing education programs, the development and management of housing and adult day-care centers, and consultation on planning and programming of facilities to self-governing institutions and municipalities.

—Editors

The Ideology of EGV

EGV is a nonprofit organization, founded in 1910, with the objective of helping the elderly in Denmark to manage as happy and active members of society in the type of dwellings and environment they prefer, and to help to provide them with adequate housing and care. EGV is an organization of the elderly—a consumer's organization—made up of voluntary initiatives, a pioneer organization, and a service organization for municipalities.

EGV is not linked with any special political or religious ideology, but takes its starting point in the assistance offered to the individual. We take active part in the development of Danish social policies concerning the older generation, endeavoring at the same time to influence society's attitude toward elderly people in general.

We are convinced that with more and more democratization of all the decision-making processes, we shall be faced with quite definite demand from the older generation to make their own life decisions. This development, combined with our basic philosophy of "help to self-help," has resulted in our trying to encourage the elderly to influence the decision-making processes at all levels within EGV.

The EGV Family

During recent years the EGV organization has undergone substantial changes:

- EGV's contact with the elderly has been intensified;
- EGV's influence in Danish society has increased; and
- EGV has developed a strong dynamic structure to meet the demands of the 1990s.

Many organizational changes have been introduced in the last two to three years. The organization now comprises three independent main bodies.

EGV–Foundation (DaneAge)

The foundation is concerned with development, research, and initiatives concerning the elderly in Denmark. The objective of the EGV Foundation is to subsidize activities for the elderly, carry out research and development, provide information, publicize elderly concerns, implement "help programs," and organize travels and holidays for the elderly.

Today, EGV–Foundation has an annual turnover of approximately 40 million Danish kroner (equivalent to about $6 million U.S.) and vested interests of approximately 100 million Danish kroner. The staff comprises about twenty-five people, of whom the majority work in the Senior Travel Centre. The Senior Travel Centre served approximately 25,000 elderly people in 1988.

EGV–Services Ltd.

Within the last twenty-five years, EGV has assisted Danish municipalities in the areas of building, service, and consultancy aid through self-governing institutions for the elderly. To continue these activities, EGV–Services Ltd. was founded. EGV–Services Ltd. is a nonprofit organization working to build housing, centers, and planning programs for the elderly in Denmark and abroad, usually in cooperation with local and central governments.

EGV–Services Ltd. has a turnover of approximately twenty-five million Danish kroner and a staff of about sixty people. It works in close cooperation with eighty self-governing institutions and has a number of consultancy functions and assignments in Denmark and also in the other Scandinavian countries. The organization employs 4,000 people at its centers and is responsible for the administration of 5,000 dwellings for the elderly, including about thirty residential nursing homes. (See figure 17–1.)

The National Association for Elderly (DaneAge)

The National Association for Elderly is a member-based association, and its main task is to provide active support for elderly people in a wide variety of fields, act as a voice for the elderly, arrange activities, and provide consultancy aid for members. The organization has 180,000 members after just two years. Membership is open to all over the age of eighteen. The Association employs about ten people and works through local voluntary committees.

As an example of private and public collaboration, I will concentrate on the functions that the EGV organization performs in cooperation with municipalities in Denmark and abroad, that is, the activities of EGV–Services Ltd.

The Role of EGV in Denmark

In Denmark, 14 percent of the five million inhabitants are over sixty-five years old. By Danish standards EGV is a large organization. We operate eighty centers for elderly people all over the country, of which thirty are large centers with nursing homes, day centers, and congregate housing. At the moment we have a staff of approximately 4,000 salaried employees and 1,000 voluntary workers.

EGV operates 5 to 6 percent of Denmark's specially equipped homes for the elderly, including nursing homes. We employ approximately 4 percent of the total staff within the elderly sector, administer approximately 4 percent of the total public expenditure for the operation of institutions for elderly people, and expect to build 500 to 1,000 dwellings for elderly people in 1989. Our turnover amounts to 1,000 million Danish kroner, or just over $153 million U.S., and the annual investment program is for approximately 500 million Danish kroner, or $76.5 million U.S.

The part played by EGV in connection with the care of elderly people must be seen in comparison with the United States. Unlike the United States, all health services as well as all social-service activities in Denmark, both within institutions and outside them, are financed almost 100 percent by taxes and managed by the municipalities.

You could ask, then, where does EGV belong in this system? Is there any justification for EGV or other voluntary organizations, when we have just

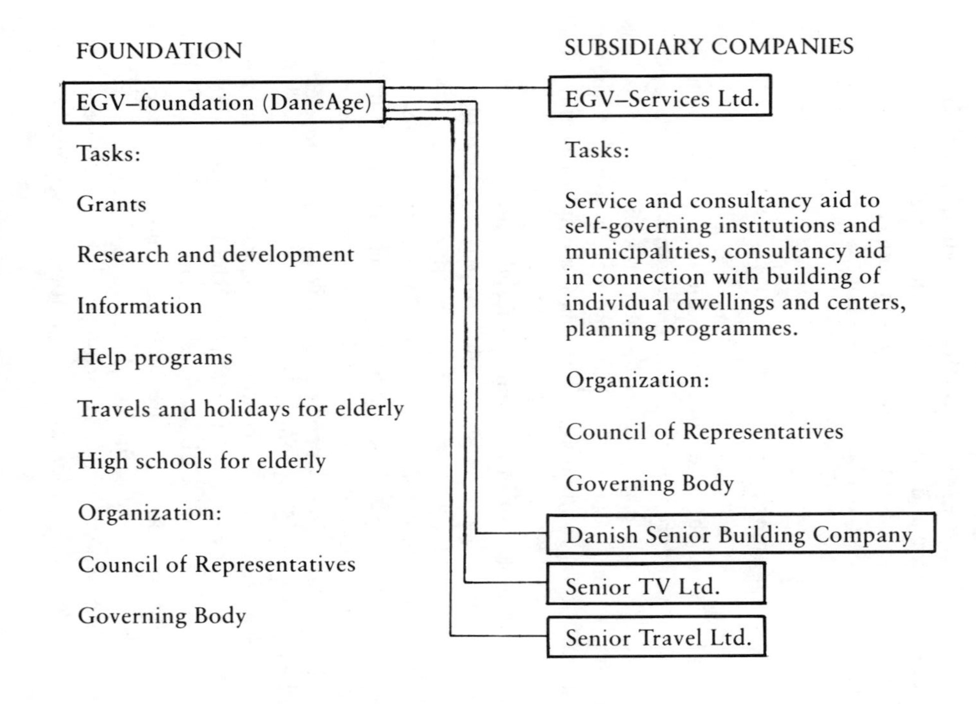

Figure 17–1. The EGV Organization

Via its activities, the EGV organization is in contact with 220,000 people in Denmark. Of these, approximately 180,000 are members of the National Association for Elderly. The remainder of 40,000 are covered by the activities of EGV–Foundation and EGV–Services Ltd.

seen that with the Social Assistance Act in your hand, you are apparently able to solve any economic, and perhaps psychological, problem of Danish citizens? The Social Assistance Act might, by way of example, pay the installments on luxury villas or support people who are striking illegally.

In our opinion there are two basic reasons why nonprofit service organizations will continue to operate in Denmark and elsewhere in the future. First, the Gallup (Market Research Institute) and other polls have examined the population's attitude toward private nonprofit service organizations and show that 76 percent of the Danish population is in favor of social work based on private initiative. Second, private social work must naturally offer certain advantages. Voluntary service organizations have a *raison d'être* if they continuously offer advantages to society and help to solve social problems.

As far as EGV is concerned, the four main advantages to society are:

1. Renewal of ideas and energy;
2. Influence of attitudes;
3. Development of social engagement; and
4. Lower costs.

Implementation and development of new kinds of assistance in the social sector have always been the result of private initiative. This source of renewal continues with undiminished strength in our day and age. As examples of renewals implemented particularly by EGV, we can mention: day centers; pensioners' high schools; congregate housing; nursing centers; alarm systems in private homes; and pensioners' workshops. As examples of new attitudes promoted by EGV, we can mention: help to self-help; pensioners' self-determination; and active consumers.

Residents Served by EGV

EGV and the Public Authorities

In Denmark most costs for the care of elderly people are covered by the state and local municipalities. Consequently, it is also the state that in many ways, through rules and regulations, prescribes what conditions individuals have to comply with in order to qualify for some kind of activity within the senior citizen sector.

All such rules and regulations are collected in the Social Assistance Act of 1976. This Act was a result of the Social Reform Commission's restructuring of the welfare system, consolidating previous public assistance acts.

The Social Assistance Act relates directly to Section 75, Subsection 2, of the Danish Constitution: "Any person who cannot provide for himself or for his family, and whose maintenance is not provide by any other person, is entitled to public assistance, but subject to the obligations which the Law prescribes thereto." Assistance is granted according to an evaluation of the so-called principle of need of the individual citizen, but with certain maximum limits.

For nursing homes, protected housing day-care centers, and most day centers, for example, public screening is required. This is an overall evaluation of a person's state of health and social situation. Something similar takes place in connection with other special types of dwellings for elderly people, although this is not required by law.

These screenings serve to ensure that the available resources are really used for the most needy. This means that the most of those living in EGV homes suffer from severe physical handicaps, often coupled with relatively severe mental handicaps. This solution for the use of resources, which the public authorities have laid down up until now, has some extremely weak points when viewed from an environmental angle and with regard to our philosophy of help to self-help.

Dwellings for Elderly People

Before going into detail regarding methods of determining people's health status and the use of such methods as a control tool in the daily operation of institutions, let me explain EGV's attitude to the solution of what may be the greatest problem for senior citizens: housing.

The objective of a housing policy for elderly people may be said to be that elderly people should be allowed to manage as well as possible and as long as possible in dwellings and environments of their own choice, without outside help, and on their own terms to the greatest extent possible, as equal members of a society. Housing policy for elderly people must start from the person's need for self-help plus self-determination and equality with the remaining population. For humane reasons as well as for economic reasons, it is preferable for elderly people to manage on their own, rather than being dependent on public assistance. The policy for elderly people must therefore consider as one of its main objectives the creation and maintenance of the necessary prerequisites and incentives, so that they can cope on their own through self-supporting networks.

Based on these principles, the following efforts should be made within the housing field:

- Elderly people should have suitable housing conditions enabling them and inviting them to manage their affairs in and around their homes, preferably unassisted;

- There should be latitude for the elderly people's self-determination regarding their choice of dwelling and their command of it; and
- Elderly people should enjoy a standard of housing comparable to that of the population in general.

The ideal dwelling for elderly people does not exist because elderly people have completely different wishes, needs, and backgrounds. Life care may come closer than most solutions, but it will never be the choice in all cases. There are a number of factors of importance for the elderly's choice of dwelling and for their ability to manage in the dwelling. For the old as well as for the young, the dwelling must satisfy a great many elementary human needs. Physiological needs (sleep, food, light, sun), plus the need for safety, and psychological needs (contact with other people). The better such elementary human needs are satisfied in and around the dwelling in accordance with the individual wishes of the resident, the better the dwelling will also function for the older resident.

The aim for a housing policy for elderly people should be that there are enough housing units that are suitable and that function satisfactorily for elderly dwellers, with respect to size, arrangement, equipment, location, and the qualities of the surrounding local district. EGV has thus pioneered attempts to prevent the concentration of all frail elderly people in institutions. That our thoughts have met with sympathy is demonstrated by the fact that the chairman of the Danish Government Commission on Aging has stated that he does not believe nursing homes as we know them today will exist twenty years hence. The former Danish Minister of Social Affairs, as well as the present Minister, have in more careful terms stated that no more nursing homes are to be built.

Health Status

Following these principles, I will now describe the EGV method of evaluating the health status of the residents, first with some general comments and then by studying a particular case.

As an element in the development and control of the operation of care centers, EGV makes an evaluation of all residents and day-care visitors, as required. On the basis of a classification model and studies of normative periods of care, it is possible to calculate a minimum norm. In this way a control of the management is obtained, inasmuch as both the approved budget and the actual utilization of it are checked. The preparation of a study of the residents' degree of handicap involves a nursing–technical study of a center's functions. It is furthermore a pedagogic means of consolidating the staff's ability to evaluate the residents' needs and the assistance required to cover them.

As a case, I will use EGV–Strandlund, which is situated in Charlottenlund in the municipality of Gentofte. EGV–Strandlund consists of 210 congregate housing units and an activities and administration center. The development was completed in 1978. The congregate housing has been designed and arranged in such a way that the residents have suitable housing conditions and receive assistance when necessary, thereby encouraging them to manage on their own and to stay in the dwelling, even if they should require a great deal of care later on.

It should be pointed out that no nursing home or nursing department has been included in the project, thus providing us with particularly good possibilities to check the objective of our congregate housing, namely that the residents may stay in this type of housing, even if a substantial need for care should arise.

In addition to the normal staff, there is a head nurse who is fully responsible for the operation of the care center. It is a prerequisite for the flexible type of operation with a care center, where the assistance offered is constantly adapted to the actual requirements, that there is a suitable margin between the calculated standards and the budget. It will be seen that this prerequisite has been complied with, as there is in fact a reserve of nursing capacity.

Different Types of Facilities

Is your present housing the place where it would be most suitable for you to continue your life as an elderly person, and would it be most suitable for society that you do it? Good housing conditions are a basic prerequisite for our well-being, and this is true at all ages. But we do change our demands for facilities and our attitude to a lot of things as time passes. After we become pensioners, we will probably be spending a much larger part of the day in our homes than before. Housing will therefore be of increasing importance for our lives and well-being.

Most of us stick to the dwelling we have been living in for a large part of our life as long as possible, whether or not it and the surroundings are suitable for us because, especially as we grow older, it is difficult to make a decision to move to new surroundings. One of the chief reasons for this may be that society has had no attractive alternatives to offer us when we grow old.

As equal members of society, elderly people must be entitled to reasonable housing conditions, commensurate with the general housing conditions for the whole population. On the basis of the objective set, it should be ensured that elderly people may stay in the general housing stock together with young people, or move to another dwelling, if they so wish. The best prospects for providing improved facilities for elderly and handicapped people are found in new buildings and in a radical reconstruction of old housing areas. The question as to whether elderly people should be integrated in the general housing stock and mixed with younger people or be brought together in more efficient special developments cannot be given an "either . . . or" answer when the elderly's right of self-determination is taken as the starting point.

The vast majority of elderly people today live in ordinary houses and flats, and most would undoubtedly prefer to keep it that way, even if other and more suitable housing might be available. Among elderly people there is also, however, a strong interest in moving into suitable developments for the elderly where they have contact with other elderly people and with the special facilities that can be incorporated into such programs.

As mentioned previously, it seems that the nursing home in its present form is a phenomenon that, like the old people's homes of the past, will sooner or later disappear. With their strong institutional character—the small identical rooms with little or no possibility of private life, the concentration of elderly people who only have the need for extensive care in common—nursing homes are far from suitable housing for elderly people. In the long-term, a phasing-out of nursing homes in their present form should be planned, the intention being that elderly people requiring extensive care instead be placed in small congregate housing projects that have a more residential nature, where in daily contact with other residents who are hale and hearty and with people from the outside, the elderly may be stimulated to self-help, to self-determination, and to a feeling of equality.

A place apart is occupied by the psychiatric nursing homes whose integration with the mixed settlements for elderly people may not always be free from problems, due to the mental state of the residents. Without doubt, there is a great lack of psychiatric nursing homes, and it would possibly be an advantage if some of the present somatic nursing homes could gradually be converted into psychiatric nursing homes.

It is implied in the objective that special housing for elderly people should be part of more general programs available for elderly people, but also that such special housing should not have the character of "ghettos for the old," where the residents feel almost alienated. For an example of a community-integrated congregate housing center with independent apartments and supporting services, see the aerial sketch in figure 17–2.

Danish congregate housing appears and functions in every respect as an ordinary dwelling, and usually consists of two rooms in addition to kitchen, bathroom/lavatory, and hall. However, as opposed to general housing, congregate housing contains special facilities for handicapped people. A typical apartment layout in special housing, expressing current Danish design, is shown in figure 17–3. Residents can manage on their own to a large extent with this layout, even if they are, for instance, in a wheelchair. There is a 24-hour alarm system to call help in an emergency situation through a service center. There is also access to common rooms, where it is possible to obtain

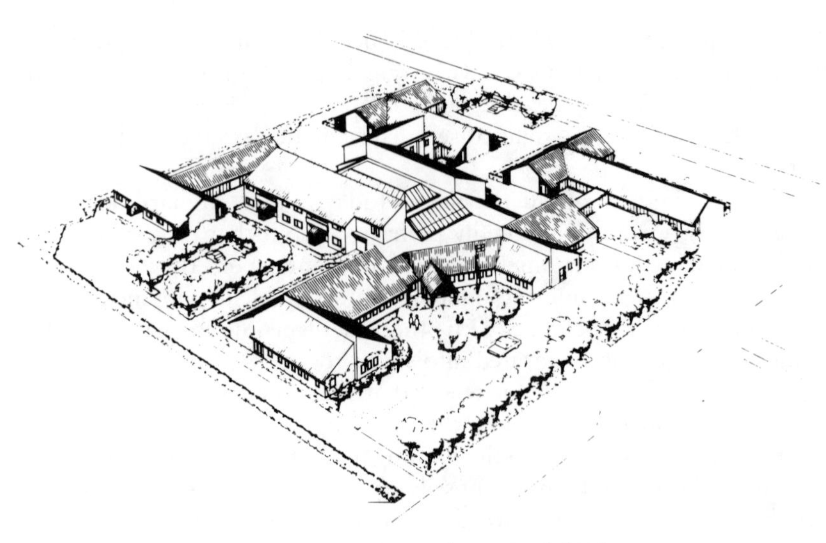

Figure 17–2. Degneparken: Aerial Diagram

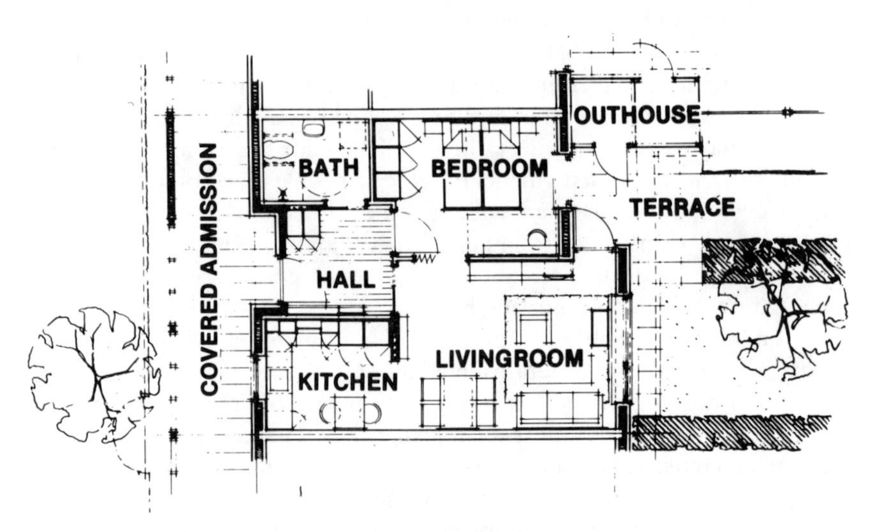

Figure 17–3. Degneparken: Sample Apartment Floor Plan

service, take part in various activities, and make contact with others. The size of the developments varies, but they usually comprise units of six to twelve houses scattered in the municipality, often with a common service center that may be located at a nursing home or at the local fire station. These small units are operated by the local home help, whose officer-on-duty can be called to the center in an emergency. Larger and more differentiated developments are usually combined with day-care centers, day centers, and a small nursing

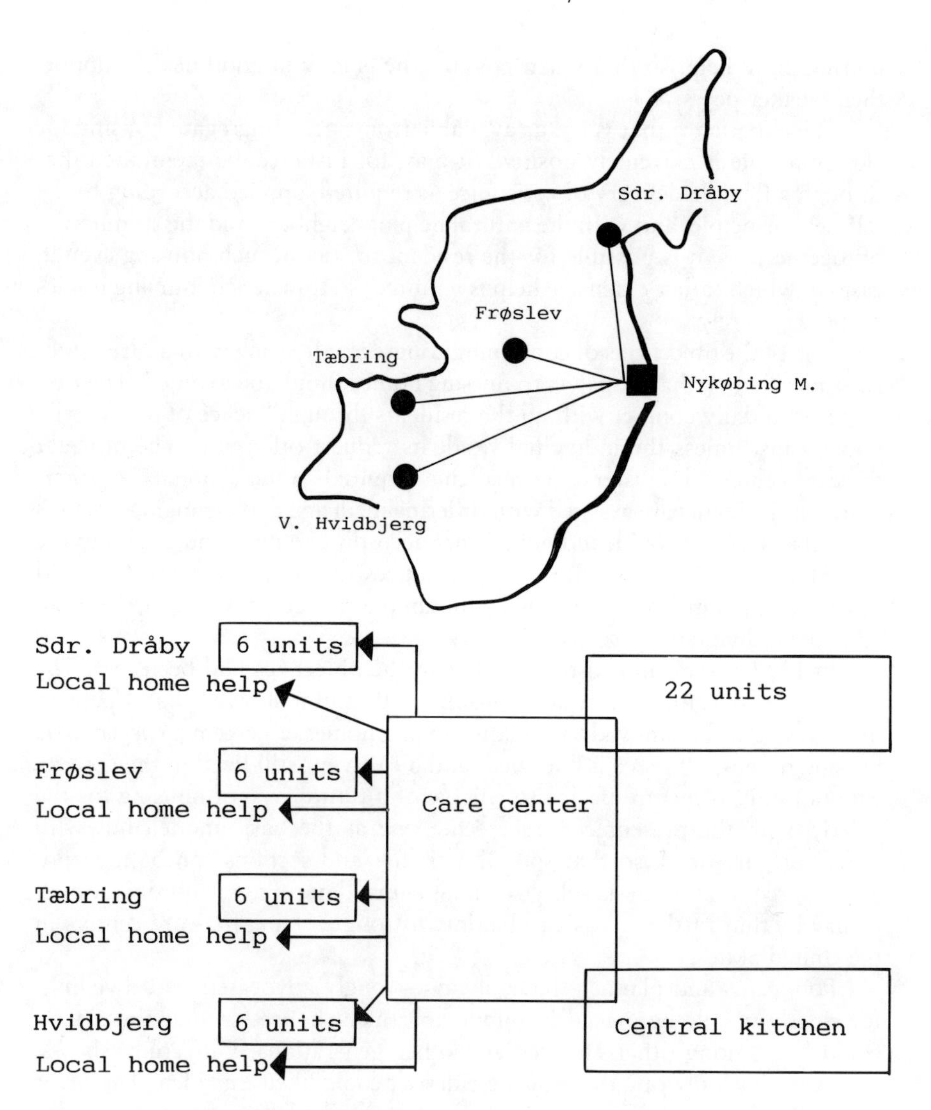

Figure 17–4. Functional Diagram Locating Congregate Housing in the Rural Districts of Mors

ward, but with a preponderance of congregate housing, so that the built-up area assumes the general character of an ordinary housing district. Figure 17–4 presents a functional diagram locating congregate housing in the rural districts of Mors.

The legislation does not stipulate that moving into congregate housing is necessarily conditional on any current need for assistance. In order to stimulate the residential environment, one may, in the letting of the housing, seek to obtain a suitable mixture of resourceful elderly people and pensioners requiring more help, so that when possible the elderly in good health support their weaker peers.

The experience that is so far available from such congregate housing for elderly people is extremely positive. It may, for instance, be mentioned that through a flexible delivery of assistance as required, applied according to the self-help principle, and with the natural help of neighbors and the stimulation of togetherness, it is possible for the resident to stay in such housing even in cases in which rather extensive help is required, so transfers to nursing homes occur very rarely.

One of the objections of combining congregate housing with a care center is, as mentioned, that transfers to nursing homes should be avoided. The care center is in daily contact with all the residents through "peace of mind" telephone calls, unless the individual residents request otherwise. The nurse at the care center administers any medicine required to the residents. Furthermore, the residents are assisted with ordering medicine and arranging doctor's visits. The nurses provide individual care according to need and attend to the frail elderly in cases of acute illness. Changes of bandages, injections, and other nursing duties are performed either in the care center's consulting room or in the individual houses.

In 1982, we examined to what extent the objectives had been met. The study covered 1,400 congregate housing units, and it showed that 4 percent of the residents had moved to somatic nursing homes, 2 percent to psychiatric nursing homes, 10 percent had died, and 84 percent still lived in the congregate housing. A picture begins to emerge of a future type of housing for the elderly, with the present congregate housing as the basic model, but with scope for variations, so that special activities and sections can be incorporated as required, such as self-governing clubs, day centers, and day homes. It may be that further ideas can be drawn from evolving life-care centers in the United States.

Politicians and planners have always strongly advocated that dwellings for elderly people be placed in public apartment houses so that the elderly could live among other families and other generations. Our study shows, however, that only one-third of the elderly people liked this idea. The older the senior citizens were, the more they wanted to be left on their own.

Contact with the family seems unaffected by a move to congregate housing. While 42 percent indicated that they have better contact with their surroundings now than before; 8 percent stated that they were worse off. The contact between residents was surprisingly good.

Founding of Facilities

Danish municipalities are responsible for the care of elderly people, and for EGV it is therefore natural to place our know-how and experience at the disposal of the municipalities, and also to take on the problems the municipalities ask us to solve. In this way, EGV acts as a service organization for the municipalities, both regarding building and operation and as consultants. Currently, EGV cooperates with more than eighty of Denmark's 275 municipalities. The number of cooperating municipalities grows by five to ten each year.

Usually the cooperation between a municipality and EGV starts with a noncommittal mutual briefing. EGV gives an account of its structure, bylaws, objectives, and means of the institution. The legislation, housing concepts, and the related economy are explained. Often such an informative meeting is linked with a conducted tour of one or more of EGV's centers.

The municipalities, in turn, inform EGV of the population basis and age distribution, existing housing and care facilities, their plans for extending social services, geographical possibilities, and budgets. Following the introductory round, EGV will be able to offer the municipality a strategic planning program for development of care for elderly people.

If there is continued interest in cooperation after this, the normal course of events is usually as follows:

Planning

A. Analysis of the Residents. EGV performs a complete analysis, in close cooperation with the municipality, of the municipality's existing facilities for care of elderly people. A study is made of population forecasts distributed by age groups, inhabitants placed in institutions, housing potential, health status of the population, health visitor arrangements, home help, and delivery of meals. Each development for the elderly in the municipality is evaluated with respect to its technical as well as its administrative function. The analysis results in general and specific conclusions, where solution models are offered. Such a demand analysis is an important tool for politicians when they have to make the correct decisions concerning the care of the elderly.

B. Proposed Solutions and Economy. The economy of the proposed solutions is examined. Sometimes the proposed solutions are accompanied by sketches illustrating the presentation of ideas. On the basis of the analytical work done, solution models are normally offered within the following sectors: nursing homes, congregate housing, day homes, day centers, meals on wheels, therapy, evaluation criteria, and possible renovations of existing nursing homes. Following this, a political decision may be made.

C. Building Organization. When the adopted project has to be implemented, it is usually by a local nonprofit organization. In addition to the local representation of the municipality and professional and industrial bodies, EGV takes part in the local organization's board of directors, thereby ensuring that the project benefits from EGV's great experience and know-how within the elderly field. EGV manages the building administration in its capacity as business manager.

D. Installations. In order to create a good environment for residents as well as staff, EGV has its own consultants who, on the bases of aesthetic and functional requirements, will provide the best possible environment at the centers.

E. Working Organization. An important part of the planning phase is the assignment of staff to the project. EGV utilizes its experience and skills when organizing and planning descriptions of functions for each employee of the organization. A staff standard and size is worked out that is related to the expected or desired classification of the residents. Combining this information with details from the building project, the working budget is elaborated.

EGV participates in the appointment of managerial staff and also undertakes to give them the necessary specialized training. In connection with the moving in of new residents, EGV provides help with informative brochures, application forms, tenancy agreements, and regulations.

Project and Building

A. Project. The local nonprofit organization hires EGV as business manager for the project. Based on the analytical work carried out earlier, the board of directors of the local organization in cooperation with EGV defines the specifics of the building project. This results in a building program containing all the wishes and requirements of the project's sponsors.

B. State Approval. When building projects receiving public funding are involved, work is carried out within the so-called expense frame per dwelling unit fixed by the Ministry of Housing. EGV prepares a detailed budget for the building project, plus a working budget, and submits the budgets to the board of directors for approval.

C. Technicians, Planning, Management. When the technicians have been selected, a contract is drawn up, and the planning work can begin. This planning work is carried out in close cooperation with EGV, and is also based on the building program that has been prepared and that contains EGV's complete knowledge of housing for elderly people. EGV sees to it that the program is carried out according to plan.

When the project has been worked out and approved by the board of directors, construction bids may be invited in coordination with the builder's wishes. The business manager offers advice and guidance about different conditions and specifications for tenders. In its capacity as business manager, EGV supervises the preparation of the necessary building contracts and required guarantees.

Management of the building project will be handled by responsible technicians hired for the specific job. EGV will supervise the management and make sure that the time schedule is complied with and that the level of quality and building program are carried out as planned.

Control of the economic management in connection with the building project is handled by EGV. The administration of building loans, letters of hypothecation, insurance, deed, financing, public rent subsidy, and reports to authorities and to those who will later be responsible for the operation are likewise handled by EGV. If the project comprises care-center facilities, EGV undertakes to work out an arrangement and installation plan with accompanying budget. The builder may receive financial support from EGV to cover this expense. EGV also takes on the actual installation work, comprising, for example, physiotherapy and ergotherapy facilities, care center, central kitchen, and other communal premises. When the project is handed over, a general maintenance plan is also included to facilitate the future operation of the settlement.

Management of Facilities

On account of the general development in society, with an ever-increasing degree of democratization in all decision-making processes, it is to be expected that in the course of ten years one will reach the point where there is an undisputed demand—also from the older generation—that elderly people be allowed to have more say in their own lives. Comparing this expected development in society with the basic attitude that we hold at EGV, to help to self-help for the older generation, and the fact that we shall act both as spokespeople for the older generation and as a service organization for the public sector, it is natural for us to evaluate, continuously, two questions: How can we, internally in our organization, create the best possible democratization of the decision-making processes? How can this contribute a higher degree of influence in the public decision-making processes for the older generation?

From our point of view, there is a considerable risk that the older generation's influence on the decision-making processes in society will be minimized as, in different ways, barriers are raised that restrict the elderly from continuing to contribute on an equal footing with others.

It is therefore only natural to begin to raise the level of consciousness for participating in decision-making processes in order to train the older generation to accept responsibility and influence decisions.

Representation on EGV's Advisory Council is strengthened through revisions in local governing structures in each of EGV's centers. The chair of the locally elected Center Senior Council, for example, now serves as the center's representative on the Advisory Council. This is also true of the chairs of local Volunteer Staff Councils.

At the start, EGV's central personnel department helps appoint the right director of the specific center on the basis of special personnel tests. After that, the person appointed takes part in a four-month introductory program as well as a number of special courses to ensure that he or she is fully acquainted with the basic philosophies of EGV and has learned to use the management tools employed at all EGV centers. At the same time, the standard EGV control system for the center is worked out so that everything is ready and tested when the first consumer arrives at the center.

Our control systems follow normal management principles. Beyond having to cope with the management of economy in the normal businesslike fashion, we must also be able to control the economy adapted to the municipality in which the center is located. In short, EGV has to supply a product that is better and cheaper than the competitors' and at the same time must ensure that our basic objectives are met in practice. This requires a constant product development and very great efforts on the part of our staff, the aim being to constantly influence attitudes and to offer a good supply of relevant training courses. These efforts are directed toward the consumers as well as toward the voluntary workers and the salaried staff.

By way of example, our training department arranges twenty-five courses and conferences in the spring and autumn months. Add to this short evening courses and lectures that are arranged locally for all the groups, as required, with especially large conferences for the consumers. For this work alone we employ nine people.

Research and Development

It is of paramount importance that EGV can contribute to a constant development and renewal within the senior citizen sector. We try to accomplish this in many ways and on many levels, and we use a great deal of resources for it. We distinguish between what we understand by research (not basic research) and what we call development. All the results of EGV's endeavors in this field are published in research reports and books that are distributed to ministries as well as to all municipalities. EGV–Foundation has an independent research and development department that, apart from individual research projects of a more general socioeconomic nature, works closely with EGV–Services Ltd. and DaneAge on concrete projects. Examples of these concrete projects are: development of service demand analyses at local authority levels, service organization, and member analyses.

The main ongoing research project is a broadly based future study designed to provide a tentative picture of the situation of the elderly in Denmark around the years 2000 to 2010. The study comprises all age groups over sixty years at the beginning of the next century. However, as the study is concerned with the future aspects, it is logical that special emphasis is placed on the coming cohorts of elderly, whose background and attitudes are likely to differ in many respects from those of previous generations of elderly.

The majority of the present elderly have lived the larger part of their lives under fairly modest conditions that are quite different from what has been the experience of the coming cohorts of elderly, who have been used to a higher standard of living, better housing, and other consumer habits, including a private car. They have experienced more frequent changes in their family life, and they have had fewer children.

The health of the future elderly generation is generally better than that of the previous generations. Their attitudes toward work and leisure time and toward freedom of the individual will probably be different from the attitudes of the older generations. The coming cohorts will have had longer schooling and often higher education. Most of the women have joined the labor market, and the majority have been in the public and private service sectors. Differences between the cohorts will be especially pronounced after the year 2000. The different backgrounds and attitudes will play an important part in the elderly's personal development and in their requirements in old age.

In order to test a number of hypotheses on cohort differences with regard to attitudes toward and wishes for old age, an interview survey has been carried out. The survey comprises a representative sample of 1,200 people in the age groups of forty to forty-four, fifty to fifty-four, and sixty to sixty-four years. In addition to more general questions about attitudes toward private life and the Danish society, there are questions about attitudes and wishes within the special areas covered by the study. Finally, there are questions designed to elucidate the respondents' health, education, work, dwelling, financial status, family and friendship relations, leisure time, and community engagement.

Just as we expect the future elderly to differ quite a lot from their predecessors, we also expect Danish society to undergo changes that will be of importance to the situation of the elderly, including the following:

Demographic developments may increasingly affect contact and assistance patterns. There will be fewer young and middle-aged people to assist the elderly, and the four-generation family will become more common. Changes in the composition of the senior citizens' civil status may be expected, such as more widows, divorced, others living alone, and more people living together without being married. Further, it is probable that elderly people will live longer.

Technological developments will make everyday life for the elderly easier and medical treatment more effective. However, technological developments may also lead to a feeling of resentment toward the new phenomena that individuals are confronted with not only at work, but also in the area of information, and in participation in society in general. The impact of new information developments on the elderly is also studied.

A decisive factor in determining the development of the elderly's conditions is the future attitudes of the younger generations toward the demands that the coming generations of elderly will make. Will there be generational conflicts? If so, in what way? It is not possible here to provide a satisfactory impression of the multitude of questions that are considered in the various parts of the study, so it shall suffice with a few examples:

Health: What changes will there be in the morbidity and mortality rates? What percentage of the elderly will need nursing and for how long? Will the coming elderly be more health conscious? Will more elderly try alternative methods of treatment?

Working conditions: The following factors affecting retirement in the future will be considered: the employment situation, new technology, qualification demands, health and mobility of the elderly, attitudes of employers and colleagues toward elderly labor, the elderly's own preferences, and the pension system.

Financial aspects: How will the incomes of the elderly develop? To what extent will they have savings, insurances, private pensions? What structural change in the income distribution can be expected? How will alternatives within the area of pensions policy affect incomes?

Housing: How will the elderly's housing condition develop if there are no appreciable changes in the present housing policy? What sort of housing will the coming elderly prefer (type, situation, cost)? Will the elderly, given the opportunity, be more mobile as far as housing is concerned?

Use of time: What leisure time activities will the coming generation of elderly have? How will they use the media, and what will be their demands for entertainment, education and studies, sport, and travel facilities? Will they be more active in the community? Will the demand for special leisure-time programs for the elderly increase or decrease?

Service delivery: What will be the elderly's need for and use of public and private service, including transport and shopping facilities in the future?

Reports on the different parts of the study are expected to be completed in the near future. A cross-sectional report will be published at the end of the study, including a discussion of initiatives required if the situation of the future elderly should be brought closer to their wishes.

The first report on housing is now complete and reveals that elderly mobility is restricted seriously by the available alternative housing. The coming generations of elderly have given their future housing requirements a great deal of thought and would prefer, all things equal, to remain in their present homes. This would in itself lead to housing problems, not for the future elderly, but for the young in search of their first home.

Development of EGV's comprehensive know-how in the elderly field is an essential element for the continued success of the organization with existing centers. New forms of service are implemented and appraised, and the views of the elderly and coming elderly are investigated. An essential feature of the research and development activities of EGV is to maintain the pioneer dynamics of the organization at their peak.

> We have been introduced to the philosophy in Denmark, of old people's right of self-determination, as the starting point of public policy and self-help programs. This chapter emphasizes the notion of non-institutional care, and focuses on helping the elderly to maintain their independence with the backup of community-based support services and home renovation programs. It is considered that this policy of encouraging the elderly to maintain their independence helps foster health and well-being, helps promote continued participation in community affairs, and reduces the overall cost of health care and housing. These ideas may encourage developers and sponsors of life-care centers in the United States of America to creatively broaden their services to residents both in their life-care centers and in the community at large.
>
> —Editors

18
Aging and Comprehensive Care in the Twentieth Century and Beyond

Robert Morris, D.S.W.

In this chapter, the author sets a broad stage for his lively reflections on how the delivery of care has changed over the years. An interesting observation is whether the middle class may come to see life-care retirement communities as a way, at least in their golden years, to enjoy a lifestyle once only available to the very wealthy. The chapter also reviews the growing complexities of our service delivery system, and discusses the ability of elderly to afford life care. It finishes with some stimulating questions and futurist answers which will be of wide general interest.

—Editors

The life-care community, or continuing-care retirement community (CCRC), has become a widely publicized way to meet several needs, or events, of an aging population in an integrated or comprehensive fashion. Promotion of the idea has variously emphasized: more carefree living for the active elderly; new ways to explore leisure; protection against some future and feared disability and physical dependence on others; prolongation of good health; and the discovery of a new community. The public response, at least by those with adequate incomes and assets, has been positive and welcoming; hundreds of these communities are being developed, a new cadre of entrepreneurial developers and inventors has emerged, and ideas about insurance against illness are being broadened.

The life-care community is viewed by many as a major breakthrough in the search for ways to fulfill the expectations of an aging society in which the elderly demand better ways to live and to occupy time, more years of intellectual and physical capacity, more leisure, and greater awareness of potential ability. While the large numbers of active, unoccupied, economically secure aged people is a relatively new phenomenon, other problems are very old: how to integrate medical and social provision; whether to build age-segregated or age-integrated communities; how to organize and pay for long-term health care; and how to handle physical or social dependency in old age.

In an attempt to understand the longer-term significance of life-care communities, the following discussion examines first the long prehistory of efforts along similar lines and then probes several of the as yet unanswered questions about this approach to an integrated provision of health or other services for an aging society.

From Community to Institution to Life-Care Community: 1600–1990

The phrases "life-care community" and "continuing-care retirement community" are examples of how language changes with new social conditions. The recurrent use of the term "community" is instructive. If we ask how it all began, we have to ask what the term "community" implies. We think first of our neighborhood or district or town as being "ours." It ensures all its members, by formal or informal means, the basic necessities of life, or at least those that lie beyond individual or family self-sufficiency.

Today's use of the word "community" in life-care or continuing-care retirement communities probably represents: (1) only the latest in a long series of efforts to replace the older natural and informal ties of a primary community with the creation of new artificial communities; and (2) a desire to reverse a century-old evolution of splintering into specialized and fragmented health-service organizations.

For much of world history, primary communities did in fact look after all members in some fashion. As far back as 100 B.C., formal institutions were developed to look after needs that were beyond family capacity. The ancient Greeks even built institutions (including Asklepieia with its "dreaming halls") where a full range of needs could be met for individuals sick or approaching the end of life's course.[1] The Romans also had some sophisticated solutions to housing and health needs.

After centuries of local, ad hoc solutions, by the sixteenth century, governments again began to develop more specialized forms of care for the aged, the disabled, and children for the same reason we do today—because of a breakdown in the cohesiveness of the small face-to-face community, population movement, and social, technological, and economic upheaval and change. In part, life-care communities are a response in our time to similar forces. By the mid-twentieth century, our concepts of community were radically transformed. Families are not only smaller but often "unbundled," and members may live far from each other; most adults, except for the minority poor, probably are out of the home, at work during the day; and neighboring is much attenuated so that even those who are at home are unlikely to take on much serious caring responsibility for others.

Our sense of community has shifted to wide networks of specialized interest groups: the workplace, professional group, union, and church. We have built up a most complex network of formal organizations to look after many human needs. The network is distinguished by its tendency to proliferating specialization, following the pattern of economic life. There is little rationalizing of these specialties in their relationship to each other, so additional agencies have been added to the complex in the hope that the numerous specialties will naturally come into some conformity with the more holistic needs of human beings.

One can conclude from such a history that life care once meant (although the exact phrase was not used) caring for all needy community members, by all other members in some face-to-face association. With such a community much reduced, if not lost, these new specialized forms of community began to develop. Instead of trying to restore the older sense of community care and living in which everyone cared for someone in the neighborhood and area where they lived, we try to build specialized new communities from scratch. It is only a slight exaggeration to suggest that the main function of modern life-care communities is to create new communities that are partly, if not wholly, removed from the larger, less personal community of modern life. A good life-care community organizes housing, food, medical, nursing, and physical care in some form, along with opportunities to make new friends and to socialize in a closed and protected environment—usually a campus or congregate living setting.

It may be an outrageous interpretation, but it seems to me that such a life-care community shares one or two characteristics of the seventeenth century poor houses and nineteenth century asylums for the mentally ill. (Of course they are more different than alike, but the few similarities may be instructive). The poor houses combined under one management and in a closed environment shelter and food, and the best of the early ones also offered medical care, at the charity standards of that day.[2] Such houses often provided some communal living in which mutual help probably was more meaningful than management.

Today's life-care communities also combine housing, food, some social life, and modern medical care or protection as well as craft activity and recreation. Of course, the objectives are different: the life-care community aims to offer a carefree life to elderly while they are still active, with security in case of illness or disability, and leisure without daily management chores; the poor house relieved residents of all ages of care but under harsh conditions, and any generosity in care was directed at returning the sick and poor to productive work.

The implicit aim of a life-care community is also akin to, if not exactly like, the aim of the early nineteenth century asylum. Its creators envisioned an enclosed, more perfect community for the mentally ill and chronically sick, where bodies and minds could be restored in circumstances more ideal than could be found in the harsh environment of a newly industrializing America.[3] In other words, a scientifically ideal mini-world was to be created by experts.

This process, in its initial motivation, was not so different from that which imbued the first designers of poor houses in the 1600's. One major difference is that these early attempts to create protected communities were directed at the already sick, the handicapped, and those who were usually poor. The modern life-care community appeals to those still active, able to function, and reasonably well-to-do financially, but who are preparing, and are able to prepare for, that future date when they may be disabled—but all directed toward a life of comfort and not one with harsh charity standards.

In both past and present periods, a campus-like facility under administrative and professional management sought and now seeks to provide for a cluster of human needs: shelter, nutrition, medical care, physical care and protection, rehabilitation, and restoration of ability to live according to prevailing expectations. In both the old asylum and contemporary life-care arrangements, much of life's management problems are turned over to professional staff, although life-care residents retain more personal control over more decisions, and have a greater range of choices, than was ever true in the nineteenth century.

It is of special interest that today professional attention to life care is excited by the wants and needs of the relatively well-to-do who, as a matter of individual choice, decide to move into a new world that promises more comfort and security than they find in the wider world of independent living. In so doing, individuals also willingly surrender much decision making, either because it became too onerous for them in a modern environment or because they are convinced that professional management is, or will become, superior to their own judgments. Within limits, decisions are transferred from self to management about shelter, maintenance, food and nutrition, security, environmental comforts, access to some recreation, and some socialization.

This shift from poor to well-to-do leads to another speculation. Do life-care communities represent a middle-class effort to retrieve one lifestyle of the past? Probably until the eighteenth century, the very rich met all their needs and comforts in their own homes. They could command such medical and physical care as they needed from a generous supply of servants and workers at low pay. Medical care was delivered at home. Hospitals were only for the very poor. By the mid-twentieth century, the supply and cost of labor had changed so much that not many could afford to have nursing and other services at home. Leading a carefree life with most chores handled by servants who were dependent on one employer was no longer possible. But even then, health spas and baths, from the eighteenth century at least, provided short-term attention to health, social, and daily living wants in congregate settings for more people, reminiscent of the individualized attention once available in the privacy of one's home.

In this evolution, pioneering scientific and professional interest shifted from improving the life of the most vulnerable poor, sick, and helpless to attending to the needs of the well and well-to-do, often in a new life-care community. In the nineteenth century, the poor accounted for over one-half of the American population. By the late twentieth century, the needs of the middle class became dominant as the very poor population shrank to approximately 15 percent. Did public and professional interest in the poor erode? Or do we simply recognize how much the economic and social profile of the nation has changed, with 85 percent or so of the population either locating itself in a middle-class position or believing that it will enter that position before long? It is a recognition that so much of the population can now claim a right to lifestyles once reserved for the most affluent few?

This evolution has been matched by a major change in how we manage public spending. We now design our major public social care programs with a combination of direct money transfers and tax expenditures. It is commonly estimated that at least half of all we count as welfare spending benefits the middle-class directly, justified by some as an example of universal social provision, and attacked by others as exploitation of public resources for the well-to-do.[4]

This shift in thinking is of more than intellectual or historical interest. The old asylum was clearly a public charity. The new life-care community is a private venture that depends on favorable tax treatment of capital investment, savings, administrative costing of service, and the like. If these tax benefits become substantial and benefit the presumably most self-reliant of our population, then our views about public responsibility and obligation for the dependent will come under close scrutiny. If financial resources are limited, how will they be divided? And will, over time, the cost of tax expenditures to individuals rise so much that a new tax payer rebellion will take place?

The Search for Order with Increasing Fragmentation and Specialization

Technical specialization and the ensuing complexity of social organization is another persisting strand in the evolution of elderly care. Originally, most care of individuals rested within the family, or if a family was lacking, in the generosity of neighbors. Simple communal formal organizations gave way in the Middle Ages to church organizations; there was a growth of public poor houses, poor laws, and secular charitable foundations in the fifteenth and sixteenth centuries.[5]

For a long time, the well-to-do continued to look after their social and health needs in their own homes. Hospitals were soon developed, but were used mainly by and for the poor. In the nineteenth-century, specialization began to pick up speed. Special institutions for the mentally ill, for the chronically ill, and homes for the aged only (congregate living facilities) proliferated. In the succeeding years, hospitals slowly became acceptable to the well-to-do, and most medical care shifted to them. Old age pensions and later social security began to provide minimum income security, followed by added occupational health and welfare benefits for more fortunate workers. Boarding homes for the well and feeble but not too disabled evolved, followed by the several levels of nursing homes with which we are now familiar. Then came adult day care and social day care centers and independent-living arrangements for the aged.

During the nineteenth century, homes for the aged, usually under religious and later secular auspices, began to spread. They offered sheltered living mainly for elderly, economically or psychologically dependent individuals, who were often widows and widowers. At first, they offered only shelter and food and were charitable in nature. As time went on, their managements demanded that individuals surrender whatever financial resources they had accumulated as the price of admission: a kind of nonprofit spend-down. Accommodations were shared, there was little privacy, and few mementos of ones past life could be brought in.

As the income position of the elderly and their families improved, these homes were less acceptable, and their occupancy began to decline. The trend to long survival for the aged, along with more chronic illness, set in. These homes began to feel the pressure to provide nursing-home care, which they resisted. The original homes refused to keep individuals who became ill or who needed much physical care; these residents were, in effect, evicted or transferred to hospitals, nursing homes, or to their families. Paradoxically, the next wave of independent-living apartment houses adopted the same policies and resisted the introduction of services to help progressively enfeebled residents remain in their own apartments.

Slowly, the force of economics and demography became irresistible, and these homes began to split along two lines. Most of them began to offer substantial health and nursing care and became nursing homes; some added accredited chronic hospital units. These became more and more medically oriented, although they still retained some conventional living facilities for the more feeble yet independent individuals.

The matching development was that of housing for the elderly with independent-living apartment units. These sometimes offered socializing activity, but not much else. As the residents' health became progressively worse, they had to move out.

Early in this development, a few general hospitals tried to meet the growing need for attention to long-term chronically ill patients, especially among the elderly. Some, as in Philadelphia, built chronic units on their grounds and administered them for the hospital. Others, like Montefiorie in New York, pioneered by creating home-care units to deliver sustained medical and social care from a hospital to long-term patients living in their own homes. These experiments built on the much older extern medical services to deliver acute medical care to poor people in their own homes, such as the program at Boston University Hospital. This concept of a broader, medically based, long-term care system did not spread widely, and only a few pioneers persevered.

Both the residential home for the aged and the hospital initiatives fell into the prevailing pattern of specialization and ended up adding to our specialization complex: special apartments for the elderly without support services; homes much like nursing homes and even chronic hospitals; acute hospitals separate from chronic disease hospitals; and an array of nursing homes at several levels of complexity, ranging from custodial or residential care something like an enlarged boarding home to skilled nursing facilities akin to a chronic hospital. And among the latter, a few specialize in caring mainly for mentally disturbed patients, while others serve the most complex physically handicapped. To this list of specialty agencies we can add: home health agencies, nutrition agencies, transportation services, adult day care, social day care, and homemaker or home help agencies.

To further emphasize this epidemic of specialization, a new layer of specialist agencies evolved solely to give information about and to steer users through the maze of specialty agencies. The Boston metropolitan area, for example, has between two hundred and four hundred different information and referral agencies to help citizens locate services to match needs.[6] These include city and town nonprofit general information services, similar services offered by specialized service agencies (family service, mental health, and the various voluntary health agencies), and state and town official agencies, such as home-care corporations and the attorney general's office. In addition, almost every service agency of any size offers some information for those applicants whom it decides it cannot accept. But their information is seldom consistent, comprehensive, or up-to-date. They often list what agencies profess to do, not what they do.

These successive innovations were accompanied each by their specialized means for control, organization, and financing. The entitlement or eligibilities of each evolved independently. The result has been a crazy quilt of organization, so complex that it baffles most citizens who try to work their way through it to find services needed. Even professional experts have to grope their way through a maze of services that is constantly changing. This only reflects a modern world of rapid change.

There has been a system response to this complexity: a growing succession of coordination and integrating arrangements, which are not limited to giving information. Each calls for its own organization, so that the proliferation of organization continues in an attempt to reduce complexity. Many years ago, this device was called a social service information exchange. Later, interagency case committees evolved to help agency staffs, which were all involved in a case, to learn who was doing what, to share information, and to allocate responsibility. Hospitals and social agencies began to hire social work and discharge staff, or expanded their admissions staffs, or later, employed case managers.[7] Scores of national and local demonstrations were funded to try to organize home-care services—a new and chaotically growing field. A national channeling project was launched to test various ways for funneling resources to specified needs.[8] Case management was built into home care and home health corporations to help citizens find their way through the maze.

Health maintenance organizations (HMOs) were another attempt to introduce rationality into medical care, and much later the Social HMO concept sought to integrate both financing and delivery of social support and medical services in one administration.[9,10] Here and there, enterprising social workers set up private fee-for-service counseling to help paying clients put together and secure appropriate services out of the complex available in any community. Life care at home is the latest entry to the coordinating arena: insurance with some management to package whatever is needed to remain at home when enfeeblement or disability require more than ambulatory medical care.[11]

These efforts, although not wholly successful, serve various ends. They do help individuals, and even professionals, learn what services are available in any community (and these vary from area to area), what their costs and eligibilities are, and even whether there are long waiting periods.

They also provide a way for specialized agencies to protect their specialties, that is, to deny access to anyone who does not fit into the often narrow slot of specialization each seeks to maintain for itself. They do not deal with the numerous situations that fall between the cracks of the current system. They provide an easy excuse for refusing to accept troublesome cases—those whose behavior is abusive, aggressive, very confused, or difficult to treat by medical means. Still, these are all honorable efforts to bring some order into a complex of specialization.

This then, in brief, is a background to evolution of current efforts to organize our social provision to meet the ends of a population whose wants have become almost as infinitely varied as science, expectations, and economic means have grown. I hope it is not an exaggeration to conclude that life care is the latest in this line of evolution. It proposes, at least, these advantages:

- One organization for security and ready access for independent-living accommodation, easy maintenance of housing, food, laundry, cleaning, exercise if wanted, entertainment (within limits), opportunity for socialization, personal and physical care when required, some nursing care, and medical attention as needed, covered in most situations by specialized group insurance.

- All this is provided with a unique blend of individual freedom and transfer of responsibility for action to a paid staff. Individuals are relieved of many of the decisions and actions required to live in a complex society.
- Numerous services, provided in the wider community on a specialized agency basis, are here brought together in one organization and financed through one fee.
- Living, for those who can afford it, is promised as an ideal, carefree, and liberating way of life, hard to match in any other way. It conjures up the lifestyles of the wealthy of the past.

As such, life care is not so much a new invention as it is the latest adaptation in a long line of social inventions. It differs from the public and professional past in the following ways:

- It now addresses the wants of an economically well-to-do population, not the poor, but hopes to spread to a broad middle-income population;
- It promises integrated service organizations, not specialization, although there is specialization within the structure; and
- It promises a better carefree life.

Looking Ahead: Some Cautionary Notes About Progress

What can be said about the future of this evolution? Are the promises realizable? Prediction is risky, that is well known, but a few elements can be identified.

Some factors are not only uncontrollable, but they also are not very predictable. But other factors can be identified. These open alternative paths into the future, where new choices may lie within human control. They also suggest problems that life care should anticipate:

1. From a practical point of view, the financial viability of life care probably depends on much better data than we now have about demands and needs for various types of care. Will the prolongation of healthy life continue, or the prolongation of life with severe disability, or both at once as has been true in recent years? Will morbidity be compressed or not? Better estimates of this kind are crucial if the financing of comprehensive-

care packages is to continue. It is disastrous for an organization to budget for three years of heavy-duty health in the final life course, when the actual duration may be six years with new technology. The risk of bankruptcy due to inadequate estimates is serious. If it remains serious, we can imagine that life care will slowly erode as the most costly trends limit organizations to small privileged enclaves, something like luxury hotels and apartment dwellings with a few added, less costly service features.

The present ideology suggests that government will be expected to either subsidize private insurance for the large percentage of the population who cannot afford to buy even limited insurance today; or, more likely, that insurers will expect government to also protect them by some reinsurance mechanism against losses of any kind in the total insurance package. This is probable if public policy relies on private enterprise to provide private insurance for retirement and for health care and life care as our major policy vehicle. How far will the public go to insure the profits of a major private industry? The answer is not clear.

A good long-term data base can help us plan better to meet such issues. Unfortunately, current efforts to develop better, comprehensive, long-term data bases have met substantial indifference when it comes to financing. Means to accumulate data to track population experience into and out of numerous specialized agencies are simply lacking.

2. How much control over life events do people want to transfer to professional or managerial (or bureaucratic) others, for this is what life care involves. In a few years, application and withdrawal rates should give some answers, but the flexible responsiveness of managers and professionals will play a major part in the outcome. Currently we still ride on public confidence in professional judgment and decision making, especially regarding the more complex and ambiguous aspects of contemporary living. Despite the growing volume of criticism about medicine and social welfare, and about bureaucrats generally, our confidence rate about expert management is still higher than our rejection rate.

   There is a separate philosophical argument that may someday be advanced: that as citizens transfer more and more choice making to others, their capacity to govern themselves will be eroded. But this lies in the realm of speculation now.

3. For whom is life care intended and to whom is it limited? As of now, most of the action is addressed to the well-to-do. As long as most citizens are so favored, we may be able to ignore the demands for equity for all, but at some point we will face a challenge to make a better life available to all, or to proceed with self-centered greed. We saw this before in nineteenth century England and the United States, where the excesses of industrialism generated a strong middle-class sense of obligation to see that

the needs of the less-favored were attended to by an affluent society (so long as it remains affluent).[12]

Life care, as now defined, is clearly not for everyone. Depending on how the numbers are handled, perhaps one-fourth, or at a more generous estimate, one-half of the elderly could be accommodated if they chose. A rural New Hampshire developer is offering a one bedroom retirement apartment for one, with meals and some maintenance, for $14,000 a year. If extra care is needed, the cost rises to anywhere from $22,000 to $36,000 a year. If we assume that the average older individual owns a home with convertible equity of $55,000 and has other assets in savings totaling $75,000, one could project usable income of $9,000 a year plus social security benefits that might average $6,000. On this basis, one-half of the aged could afford such a plan, provided they were not too sick and did not need too many services.[13] This is an optimistic projection, since it is more likely that the average figures reflect much higher holdings by the upper 20 percent of the aged income range. Social Security Administration reports for 1984 show that median income from all sources for those over the age of 65 to be about $12,000.[14]

Median asset income from elderly couples was $1,700.[15] Social Security average benefit payments total about $6,000 a year and represent an average of 57 percent of all income of those in the middle quintile of income distribution. At best, approximately 24 percent of the retired have private pension retirement incomes. By other estimates, as many as 15 million elderly could afford to pay a $35,000 entrance fee plus a $600 monthly fee.

Whatever figures are used, it is clear that the future will raise serious issues of equity among the aged as well as with other age groups—ethical questions that go to the heart of the kind of society we are: one of major class divisions and self-centeredness, or one willing to share national income to reduce disparities, although with some differentiation in position and comfort.

Perhaps more compelling in the long-term is the likelihood that the proportion of future retired people with such resources will decline, especially if our economy continues to add more new low-paying jobs and shrinks the proportion of higher-paying jobs. The result will be that future retirees will not have built up the kind of retirement reserves just mentioned. The pressure for life care for all will join the shrinkage in the demand for present models as personal incomes decline relatively.

Short of a major economic change, we can still ask whether the basic concept can be adapted to meet the needs of people with modest means. One suggestion has been advanced, for example, at Cushing Hospital in Framingham, Massachusetts, which already has linkage with nearby public housing and its population.[16] Can such public hospitals develop a lower-cost counterpart of life care with public dollars and modest client payments, something that lies between a new luxury life-care campus and life care at home initiatives? That depends on public support of initiatives, which up to now seem reserved for the well-to-do.

4. Will human nature and professional preoccupation with specialization ever permit a different mixing together in dwelling of the very disabled and the active able elderly? There are already clues that life-care community residents who are active are uncomfortable seeing too many very handicapped and sick people in their midst. This, conceivably, could push life care back toward something akin to the previous homes for aged, but at a level of comparative luxury rather than on a charity level: refuge for the well aged. It remains to be tested whether physical design to separate the well and the sick plus social pressure or professional persuasiveness can maintain an acceptable balance for both sick and well. The experience in independent-living apartments for the elderly suggest that this will be anything but easy.

5. Finally, there is serious question about manpower in the future. Today we still operate on a few simple premises: that it may be more cost effective to deliver services in a congregate setting; and that there will always be available manpower to perform both the professional tasks and the menial physical, attendant, and housekeeping chores. If there is a shortage, paying more money will suffice, at least for the more wealthy.

   But for a larger population there are clues that this will not be true much longer. There are ample signs that acceptably qualified or trained staff for lower-level tasks are hard to find. A severe economic decline could reverse this, but in the meantime, less-skilled workers are showing reluctance to take and to stay with the demeaning, wearing, low-paying tasks on which the more professional cares depends, as well as on which paying customers depend for their comforts.[17] The alternatives seem to be, much higher pay and greatly increased cost, leading to buyer resistance or reducing the pool of able buyers; continued rapid turnover in personnel, eroding quality of care; or increased open migration for low-skilled émigrés, not skilled émigrés as prevails today.

   It is possible that a depression could solve all that. Or if current patterns continue, then major restructuring of tasks conceivably could make many jobs more acceptable. Here, the very troublesome problem of racial antipathies, which are still widespread, needs to be faced. Will the now unemployed of minority youth accept such employment, and will residents accept them?

   These questions about the future are troubling and lie beyond straightforward technical solutions. They involve thoughtful and sensitive examination of the dynamics by which our social institutions grow and decline; understanding that permits us to better combine entrepreneurial, fiscally driven energy, and adaptation of our inventions to the more difficult psychological and social forces that determine consumer and professional behaviors.

Some Uncontrolled Trends

Identifying such trends in the relevant (to life-care communities) aging area can give a spurious sense of confidence at best, like ancient reading of entrails. We do fairly well in identifying what has happened; but straight-line projection from that past cannot anticipate how forces of which we are aware, and those we do not even sense yet, will alter the shape of the future. The imponderables are daunting: Will the present tendency to extend life for more elderly continue? Will heroic measure at high cost or miraculous discovery do more to compress morbidity? Will there be an economic recession? Will political tides favor a return to government leadership, or will disillusionment lead to even more reliance on the market and more division between the "haves" and "have nots"? Will family ties be tightened or further relaxed?

The most likely future is one of tension, searching for ways to reconcile conflicting desires; for example:

1. Families will continue to be a first line of protection, but working adult family members will resist a reduction in their life comforts to sacrifice for the major support costs of their independently living elders. As they become dependent, nonfamily means will be sought. Even more stressful will be sharing the costs for the increased proportion of aged with no close relatives or surviving children or with broken family ties on which we rely in time of need.
2. The search for nonfamily means for ensuring security as we grow old will increase the proliferation of diverse and specialized services, which, in turn, will outpace our capacity to systematically integrate them.
3. Public policy will continue to create a two-tier system of services: one for those with some independent means to add to basic public programs like Medicare or Social Security, and one for those who lack such means. The latter will possibly increase proportionately, as our economy generates many more part-time and lower-paying jobs than high-paying jobs. The conflict between tax benefits for one group and direct tax transfers for the other will continue.
4. There will be some form of protection for long-term health-needs, but it will, for the foreseeable future, be most limited, probably to be the more medically related aspects, which will relieve the medical system at rather

high cost and will likely benefit life-care communities substantially. The relative ease with which catastrophic protection for in-hospital care only was passed in Washington as compared with the failure to mount, to date, any long-term protection is suggestive. So is the bitter struggle to enact universal health protection in Massachusetts, which was won only for minimal acute hospital care. And yet both have had troubles. The catastrophic health protection program was subsequently repealed by Congress, and Massachusetts is currently experiencing funding problems.

The struggle to find a better balance between high-cost, high-technology medical provision and social support systems will continue with the odds favoring medicine, since the aged favor medical care, and professional interests are more strongly entrenched in medicine.

5. The current flurry of interest in private insurance will continue to benefit those in better-paying jobs. If, and it is a big "if," the workforce is more organized, and if new as well as old industries find it to their advantage, there can be a boost to private insurance.

However, industry may find it to be a competitive disadvantage to load its wage bill with new social benefits. There are signs that major industries find this not to be an advantage in international competition, and they may turn to support some form of government health insurance to replace their benefits, which would exaggerate the conflict over tax levels.

It is also uncertain whether consumers will choose tailor-made protection that is not comprehensive, since really comprehensive insurance would exceed private insurance capacities and consumer readiness to pay very large premiums. Or will consumers be willing to start saving for older years when they are forty? That is doubtful as long as the current tide of high consumer spending and low saving rates persist.

At best, it is sensible to conclude that the next few years will be years of uncertainty as American society tries to re-establish some foundation for its public responsibility for all and decides how much it will pay for such a foundation, in preference to a market-oriented, private, ability-to-pay system of support in which age, health, or economic misfortune produce dependency. In other words, more of the same tensions and struggles to satisfy conflicting citizen want will prevail, until either a national crisis forces, or our search produces, a consensus about public obligation.

> The preceeding chapter ends with important questions: the viability of the data we rely upon for planning; the retention of individual choice; future availability of personnel; mixing of disability levels; the potential of using public properties and dollars to create broadly affordable versions of life care, and so on. They are the reflections of a distinguished leader in this field. Each deserves in-depth attention in order for us to adequately address our future retirement housing and health-care needs.
>
> —Editors

Notes

1. Thompson, John D. and Goldin, Grace. *The Hospital: A Social and Architectural History.* New Haven, CT: Yale University Press, 1975.

2. Vives, Juan Luis. *Concerning the Relief of the Poor.* Translated by Margaret Sherwood. New York School of Philanthropy (Now the Columbia University School of Social Work), 1917.

3. Rothman, David. *Discovery of the Asylum.* Boston: Little, Brown, 1971.

4. Morris, Robert. *Rethinking Social Welfare.* White Plains, NY: Longman, 1986.

5. Morris, Robert. *A Social Policy of the American Welfare State.* New York: Harper & Row, 1979.

6. Morris, Robert. Personal Communication, 1987.

7. National Association of Social Workers. *Encyclopedia of Social Work,* New York: N.A.S.W., 1971.

8. Kemper, Peter, et al. "The evaluation of the national long term care demonstration: Final report." Princeton, NJ: *Mathematic Policy Research,* May 1986.

9. Leutz, Walter, et al. "Targetting expanded care to the aged: Early S/HMO experience." *The Gerontologist, 28(1),* February 1988, pp. 4–17.

10. Diamond, Larry and Berman, David. "The social health maintenance organization." In Maddox, George and Lawton, Powell (eds.). *Reforming the Long Term Care System.* Lexington, MA: Lexington Books, 1981.

11. Tell, Eileen J., et al. "New directions in life care." *Milbank Quarterly, 65(4),* 1987, pp. 551–574.

12. Morris, Robert. Ibid. 1986.

13. U.S. Bureau of Census. Current Population Reports: Household Wealth and Asset Ownership. Washington, D.C.: Government Printing Office, 1984, Series P 70.

14. U.S. Social Security Administration. Annual Statistical Report. Washington, D.C.: Government Printing Office, 1984.

15. Chen, Yung-Ping, "Better Options for Work and Retirement: Some Suggestions for Improving Economic Security Mechanisms for Old Age." In Maddox, George and Lawton, M. Powell (eds.). *Varieties of Aging-An Annual Review of Gerontology and Geriatrics.* New York: Springer, vol. 8, 1988, pp. 189–216.

16. Morris, Robert. Ibid 1986.

17. Wilner, Mary Ann. *Who Will Care? A Study of Employee Shortages in Massachusetts Nursing and Rest Homes.* Dedham, MA: Massachusetts Federation of Nursing Homes, 1987.

19
Summary and Trends in Life Care

Robert D. Chellis, M.P.H. and
Paul John Grayson, M.Arch., A.I.A.

If the preceding chapters stimulate interest, answer questions, and encourage action to further implement the life-care concept or other helpful forms of appropriate housing and services for the nation's elders, as editors and contributors to this volume, we shall be well pleased.

There is no one perfect solution for all our citizens; indeed, there are many options. But for those older Americans with adequate resources, particularly with built-up equity in a home, who are willing to consider giving up that home for more convenient circumstances, entering a fully insured life-care faculty will allow them to access many benefits, including housing, social and supporting services, and a valuable protective cover for potential long-term illness within a continuum of care, all guaranteed for life.

For those electing residence, for their families, and less obviously but in a number of ways, for our evolving society, life care can be a great comfort. It helps to offset problems caused by the increasing dispersion of families in our society and the difficulty in finding either volunteer or paid support personnel, as well as the problems faced by the various government agencies already concerned with the cost, care, and service implications of the graying of America.

To opt for residence in a life-care facility is in a sense an aspect of the "American Way." It requires a sense of entrepreneurship, a willingness to invest in something new. It requires an openness to change and the acceptance of an altered lifestyle, new associations, and the decision to enter a new form of community environment. Although the notion of life care will never be adopted by everyone, it appears to be the most effective way in the United States to secure the form and style of one's own life in retirement. It permits one to maintain independence, dignity, and self-esteem, to know there is a support system in place to meet every need, which has been voluntarily preplannned and is covered financially. Privately developed life-care facilities, whether nonprofit or for-profit, do not require any new form of government support.

As we well know, Medicaid is already the largest item in many state budgets, and it is rapidly growing. Some feel that Medicaid has become an out-of-control burden on the federal budget. Cities and towns are increasingly concerned with finding and maintaining appropriate local service options that do not further burden their citizens beyond an already tight and almost untenable financial strain. To the extent that individuals and, even better, whole groups can finance and insure their own retirement and future health care, their personal independence and emotional well-being is enhanced, families are protected from financial catastrophe, and society as a whole is unburdened. Further, the whole movement can be largely financed by the private sector, by the beneficiaries themselves, and not by government. This can be done by unlocking and more aggressively investing the equity most older Americans have in their homes.

Shortages of affordable housing and of appropriate housing—increasing problems in this country—will be somewhat relieved every time an older person, finding a viable and attractive alternative, returns their large family-size home to the market in exchange for a new, purpose-built, efficient, smaller, service-rich retirement apartment.

Equity Conversion

Nationally, nearly 75 percent of people over age sixty-five own their own home, and roughly 80 percent of those homes are mortgage-free. This is the leverage that must be utilized to insure a worry-free, independent, financially secure retirement for older people, requiring a minimum of government investment or interference. There are several variations on this, including various reverse annuity mortgage plans, but clearly the life-care model is the most complete solution. Homes are sold, equity freed by the sale is converted to an entrance fee or deposit, and those deposits, plus monthly maintenance charges, can pay all development and operating costs of life-care centers, combining housing, common areas, health-care facilities, support services, social, educational, and recreational programs, health care, and long-term care health insurance—a highly attractive reinvestment of assets for the security-minded planner.

When an older person's house, often increasingly hard to maintain, can be exchanged for such a complete package and preclude a catastrophically expensive illness, it seems we have a winning solution! Add to that the feature of refundability with newer life-care programs—often 90 percent or more of the entry free—and the program becomes even more clearly a form of estate preservation. Heirs are not only relieved of responsibility, but ensured an inheritance. What could do more to promote positive family feeling, while preserving the retiree's independence?

Government Cooperation and Benefits

Already, some cities and towns are wisely using their approval-granting powers to force a broadening of the concept, usually by combining encouragement of the life-care concept with a demand that at least a few of the living units be offered at below-market rates. In two proposals, towns are even offering town-owned land, as well as helping to expedite and simplify the approvals process, in exchange for varying but significant numbers of mixed-income units. In one exciting proposal, in a wealthy town where home values are significantly higher than entry fees need to be, refundable life-use fees can be high enough to finance the extras. In addition, the town can offer a parcel of their attractive parkland and project approvals in return for a broad package of local benefits: elderly housing; subsidized elderly units; additional local nursing beds; affordable townhouses for young families; a new senior center; a day-care program for children; and, most interesting of all, a life care at home program, packaged with a local home-care agency to serve elders throughout the community who wish to stay in their homes at least in the near future. Such a proposal turns the life-care center into a major, privately financed, community-wide resource and hub for elder services. Not only can a good life-care center provide specialized housing, nursing, support services, full-time and part-time jobs, and potentially much more, but it generally, even if nonprofit, pays taxes, while filling gaps in area services.

Creative Sponsorship, Creative Focus

There is great and largely unexplored scope for varied sponsorship of unique special-interest retirement centers, just as children's summer camps have evolved from an all-purpose model into a spectrum where emphasis ranges from single sports to computers to languages to diet-oriented programs. While one may abhor child/elderly comparisons, and would never suggest a narrow-focus for a life-care center where several hundred people will each spend twelve to fourteen years or more, there is nevertheless great scope for specially focused retirement centers, which would enhance the excitement and interest of the people they attracted.

If one feels that the average life-care center is too dull, despite its long list of activities and amenities, they should consider some of these current ideas drawn from projects under development, specifically, life-care campuses that:

- Collaborate with a college campus or school for a cultural, educational emphasis;

- Cater to retired military and their interests or lifestyle;
- Cater to retired missionary and church workers, or other affinity group;
- Are in a wildlife setting abounding in deer and unusual birds, plus a menagerie of unusual animals;
- Are built to share the extensive health and fitness facilities of a YMCA;
- Are built into a golf course setting and feature golf, tennis, swimming, and clubhouse activities;
- Are planned for an urban setting near schools, shops, and theaters;
- Are built in a resort setting, famous for its beauty, cultural events, music, and theater programs; or
- Are built on a beach, with waterfront and harbor activities in view.

The possibilities are endless, and the field is still wide open. Every college has its dedicated following, as do cultural, religious, recreational, wildlife, ethnic, and special interest groups or areas. Why not, for instance, a center in Mexico for adventurous retirees who appreciate a fine climate, cultural interests, lively food and low prices? Or close ties and exchanges between, say, northern and southern facilities, or rural and urban facilities? In many cases, the host area or entity might find itself revivified by the influx of energy and funds from the life-care center and the new people and interests it generates. There is great scope for some creativity and imagination to be brought to bear on the retirement years. Instead of being "gotten through," they really should be viewed as an earned reward for years of hard work, which people are prepared to maximize and enjoy through interesting, lively, and productive activity.

Size of Market and Benefits to Economy

Estimates vary, but in 1988, there were possibly 1,000 variously defined life-care or continuing-care retirement centers, catering to some 250,000 to 300,000 elderly. Given an over-sixty-five population of roughly 30,000,000 in 1988, that is less than 1 percent coverage. Estimates of the number of elderly who can afford life-care range from 10 to 50 percent, with our estimate being 30 to 40 percent. However, knowing the difficulty in effecting major changes in people's lifestyles, expectations, or preferences, suppose that at a maximum of 5 percent more of our 30,000,000 elderly decided to move into a life-care center. That would locate 1.5 million elderly into some 5,000 new life-care centers. But to achieve this number would mean the construction and opening of ten facilities per week from January 1, 1990, to the end of this century. No mean task! If we look at the jobs this undertaking would ensure and the financing that would be generated, assuming that in current dollars a 300-unit facility could be developed for approximately $50,000,000, it would over the next ten years generate approximately $250 billion in project financing and would create 500,000 to 700,000 permanent jobs.

Life care can generate considerably more benefits, many of which have been touched on in other chapters. Life-care retirement centers are programs that can be set in motion by local, individual, sponsoring, and development groups, like President Bush's "one thousand points of light." All can put their special imprint on their local project and can move ahead completely at private expense, if only local, state, and federal government agencies will develop policies that encourage rather than stifle these much-needed programs. Some localities, and some states, are already doing so, but too few and too slowly.

Increasing growth, variety, and prosperity are anticipated for these programs, even without many regulatory changes. They have the potential to give millions of elderly almost literally a new lease on life, one which includes an expanding rather than contracting range of social and activity options, and otherwise unavailable health, financial, and physical security and support services. They also offer manifold benefits to our increasingly hard-pressed society by allowing growing segments of the private sector to secure their own future, never becoming a burden on government, their children, or others. Surely it is a traditional and worthwhile American impulse to encourage as many older people as possible to secure for themselves their own long-term happiness and independence.

A Scenario for the Future: To Make Life Care A Long-Term Solution

The Proposal

In the nineteenth century, a particularly large number of utopian communities were planned in the United States by idealists striving to establish their own vision of a collective living plan, a model and ideal community. The critical problem for most of these visions was financial, and lack of funds triggered all the other problems that brought them down, often with discouraging rapidity. In a sense, life-care communities are small utopias, which are built from the entrance fees of residents, and resident monthly fees pay for operations, offering all the housing, health, social, and other programs most residents need. There are infinite variations on the life-care theme, but a particularly exciting one is outlined below because it is replicable and, if emulated often enough, could make an impact nationally. It would solve retirement housing and health needs, while enhancing the quality of life for its residents and for many others as well, at little or no cost to government.

This scenario proposes a specific type of mutually beneficial private and public cooperation. The suggestion is that *land and/or approvals* from a government body and *home equity* converted to *refundable entrance fees* by inmoving residents combine to achieve a number of housing, service provision, and health-care goals, all paid for by the private sector: the residents. This has already been initiated in two towns in New England. Community services are provided on a fee-for-service basis and are maintained at no expense to the taxpayer. The deposits made by life-care residents in effect allow them to secure their own retirement and preserve their estate, while at the same time leveraging some local "good works."

To sketch out possible steps to achieve this utopian goal:

- Organize a local nonprofit sponsor to develop a community life-care center. A nonprofit organization will be more acceptable to the community than a for-profit organization and will be able to more easily negotiate for government land and successfully market units to seniors at a lower cost.
- Arrange for board members to meet with consultants and specialists in the field to conceptualize an ideal program of facilities and services. The program should meet specific elderly housing and service needs in the area, using a refundable life-use fees (RLUF) arrangement to cover all development costs. Identify character and size of dwelling units, amenities and services to be offered. Develop a financial model.
- Review concept with local officials, service providers, and the community, including potential residents, to refine details.
- Following negotiations, the municipality (or county, state, or federal agency) should offer to lease, donate, or sell to the local sponsor an attractive publicly owned land parcel and to provide all necessary approvals.

Advantages

For the sponsor include:

- Secures a good site and reduces costs, risks, and the time required to go through the approvals process; and
- Cost savings can be translated into substantial subsidies for some residents, and provide other local benefits.

For the community or town include:

- Needed services will be provided by the private sector at no cost to the taxpayers;
- Local quality of life will be enhanced; and
- Property that has been off the tax rolls will be making a voluntary payment in lieu of taxes (assuming they are a nonprofit).

For state and federal governments include:

- All the life-care residents, and affiliated life care at home subscribers, will never be put on Medicaid, resulting in great long-term savings to the community.

Once conceptual agreement is reached, the sponsor develops detailed plans, refines the financial model, and keeps all appropriate agencies informed.

Proposed Program of Facilities and Services for a Typical Community Life-Care Center

- Elderly housing (life care) units, possibly 150 to 250 units, or less.
- Subsidized elderly housing units, possibly 10, 15 or 20 percent of the elderly units.
- A nursing facility, accepting Medicaid and Medicare, serving the life-care community and the local area.
- Affordable family housing units, in a ratio of 10 to 12 percent of life-care units.
- Life care at home, allowing elders throughout the town to subscribe to the health programs and health insurance and other service and social activities of the life-care center while remaining in their homes.
- Space for local social service agencies, possibly also elderly day care, child day care, transportation for area seniors, meals on wheels, periodic health screening clinics, exercise, wellness, and educational programs, depending on local needs and desires.
- Additional possibilities may be suggested by a local community survey of needs, and the sponsor may apply its own market research for ideas or refinements.

Finances

While the first steps can be done economically, with money raised from local foundations, organizations, supporters, or even the trustees themselves, once a conceptual agreement is reached as to the site and approvals, it is time to commission a demographic study, market research, and architectual concept, obtain legal advice, and further develop the financial model. Significant funds, say, over $100,000 the first year, may be needed, with more needed as the project moves through approvals, design, marketing, and financing stages. A project manager will have to be hired by the board of directors to focus control and to deal with the paperwork, meetings, and scheduling. The further the sponsor can take it with money it has raised itself the more control it will have. The ideal is to solicit grant money from foundations or to find a moneyed local nonprofit organization as cosponsor or angel.

Should grants, donations, and other funds be insufficient, and assuming a good site has been identified, it should be possible to bring in a for-profit developer as a joint venture partner. The developer will put his or her money and expertise to work for the project. The nonprofit sponsor can often write the contract so that the developer takes out a fair fee, but the nonprofit is named as sponsor throughout and ultimately takes over ownership as well as management responsibility from the for-profit. Obviously, the greater the contribution of the originator of the project, the more control they can retain.

Results

1. Solve the housing and health needs of a broad spectrum of elderly without government funds.
2. Remove a large number of elders from future Medicaid rolls.
3. Add to local tax base.
4. Provide for every life-care center to be a resource and hub for local senior services and support.
5. Free up existing housing stock for younger families and others.
6. Create construction jobs.
7. Establish many new permanent service-provider jobs.
8. Stimulate the local economy.
9. Stimulate development of local service businesses.
10. Facilitate elders staying close to their families and friends and in their community.
11. Help to improve the quality of life for all.

Conclusion

The above scenario offers a viable option, enabling citizens to provide for their old age with community backing and without need for costly government funding. With this approach, community members can prudently plan for their retirement and old age—be it at a life-care center or in the life care at home program, and in the event of need, know that they are fully covered for all contingencies, such as a catastrophic illness or a long-term health care need. Without fear of future requirements being unmet, the elderly can remain more independent, promote their happiness and wellness, improve their quality of life, and truly enjoy their golden years.

With a good concept, lots of hard work, and some luck, it may be possible to form a whole series of unique and locally based life-care centers, utopias for the twenty-first century.

Appendixes: Life-Care Symposium Workshops

A. Marketing Workshop

A market research/marketing workshop associated with the Symposium featured a panel, moderated by Anne L. Connolly, marketing director of Fox Hill Village, Westwood, MA, and including Ann Hambrook, president of Hamlyn Associates, Philadelphia, PA; Steven Meister, vice president and principal of Roche, Meister & Associates, Wilbraham, MA; Maria Dwight, president of Gerontological Services, Inc., Santa Monica, CA; and Karen Miller, director of Marketing at Brookhaven, a life-care facility in Lexington, MA.

Discussion included the following points:

- Marketing of older established facilities (ten to thirty years old) to prospective residents sometimes brings mention of past problems. When this arises, it requires an awareness on the part of marketing people of how difficulties have been resolved.
- Older facilities may lack the amenities provided by newer ones. In upgrading older facilities it is important to compare older to newer products and upgrade to be competitive.
- Potential residents investigating older facilities appear at presentations with more preconceived notions and concerns than prospects at new facilities. The greatest concern is that of cost. Newer facility fees are costlier than older ones. By stressing the wide range of amenities in the newer life-care centers, a marketing person can help justify cost.
- Most frequent comment from potential residents to a sales office or focus group meeting is, "I'm not ready yet." Best response is to ask "not ready for what?" and to stress that taking residence at a life-care center is not intended to cause a major change in one's lifestyle, but to enhance it by sound planning for security in the years ahead, relieved of the time-consuming "burdens of home ownership."
- One profile of an ideal retirement counselor or salesperson is an MSW with an average age of thirty-one years. He or she listens, knows the product and the marketplace, is sensitive and patient, *does not* give a

close-ended, one-sided stock presentation, and fosters and delivers the presentation around the potential resident's individual needs.

- An ideal counselor will respond to any question or objection that may arise and will be diligent, persistent, organized, disciplined, and well-documented. For example, the counselor may have talked to a lead several months earlier, and if everything was documented, will know those things that are important to that prospective resident, such as their birthday, vacation trips, and the like. In this way he or she becomes a friend and counselor, not just a sales person.
- Because MSWs are wonderful listeners and are comfortable gaining the confidence of prospective residents, it may be hard for them to close a sale. In this situation, a "closer" salesperson or sales manager may be called in to help. This permits the counsellor to remain a friend by being less involved in the negotiation and money end of the sale. This is greatly facilitated by having salary-based remuneration—possibly with modest bonuses for goals met by the whole office—rather than a heavily commission-based payment program.
- Patience is a virtue. One example involves a "be-back" situation, in which a prospective resident came back twenty-one times. Everyone on the sales staff thought the customer would grow old and die before she could possibly move in. But when the sale was closed, she brought in seven of her friends. It is hard to make a judgement. Had someone on the sales staff turned the screws, early on, this prospect would have walked, and a whole lot of people would have walked with her.
- Showing respect and being sensitive can pay off. Take the example of the woman who had just purchased a $329,000 unit, with her daughter present. The elderly lady said, "I'm eighty-two years old and I have bought three things in the last ten years. You are the first person who has looked at me and not my daughter. You understand that I am over eighty, but I know what I am doing." This salesperson knew the buyer and how to treat that buyer appropriately.
- Knowing when not to sell to someone who may not want to buy is important as selling. If somebody moves in who has been pressured, they will be unhappy and move out. This will be bad for the community. The sales staff should develop "win-win" situations, and even provide other alternatives if the facility is really not right for them. In real estate sales, a good salesperson does not pressure anybody. A good salesperson interprets the customer's needs and desires.
- Respect for the market is paramount to success. There are many people out there who do not respect either the product or the older person. Before you hire anyone for a marketing or sales position, look at the phi-

losophy and motivations of the individual candidates and make sure they are in tune with yours.

- Is there an urban constituency for an urban life-care or CCRC product? There is, but to date most urban sites have been renewal sites and older people are not pioneers, they are not thrill seekers and they do mind walking in these neighborhoods at night. They want security.
- Why have there been so few life-care projects in urban areas? One reason is the high cost of land. Most projects are built in the suburbs because of the lower cost of land. There is a market in cities, but land costs are incredible. Another factor is that developers have not been innovative about the use of air rights. A multi-use approach with commercial, retail, and office space on the lower levels could mingle with a life-care housing community on the upper levels and result in a viable working model.
- Co-op models have negatives and positives. The sponsor loses a lot of control but residents can roll over their capital and shelter their gains from the sale of their former residence. Other big features are the real estate write-offs every year and the long-term unit appreciation. If the co-op is a nonprofit, then income from amenities such as the convenience store, the barber shop, and coffee shop, all return rent and income back into the co-op, thereby reducing overhead expenses and resident fees. Co-ops as opposed to condominiums are a matter of perception. In Denver, co-ops are considered a communist plot, and in New York they are very exclusive and keep the riffraff out. Another problem is that the resident-owners are voting their self-interest and may be overly conservative or narrow in their vision. Condominium associations can be narrow in their vision too. But regardless, both forms of ownership offer various advantages and disadvantages, which can be sorted out only on an individual basis.

B. Design Workshop

A design, interiors, and innovative technologies workshop associated with the Symposium featured a panel moderated by Earl R. Lindgren, AIA, principal, Earl R. Lindgren Architects, Naugatuck, CT, and including Barbara Adner, interior designer and principal, Adner/Woodman Associates, Newton, MA; Pamela Cluff, FRAIC, FRIBA, president of Associated Planning Consultants, Inc., Toronto, Ontario, Canada; George Cochrane, M.D., medical director of the Mary Marlborough Lodge at the Nuffield Orthopaedic Centre, Oxford, England, and Paul John Grayson, M.Arch., AIA, president, Environments for Living, Winchester, MA.

The workshop generated informal discussion with questions from the audience. The following are some of the highlights of the proceedings:

- Question: Has anyone had any success in the United States with the use of, or acceptance by public authorities of, flexible or movable partitions in retirement housing projects?
- Comments: Neither the panel nor the audience were aware of any major installation in the United States of movable partitions used between rooms or living units in retirement housing.

  Carleton-Willard Village, Bedford, MA, uses accordian-folding partitions to privatize semi-private nursing rooms, and some studio apartments use wardrobe units as dividers.

  In Canada, an attempt had been made, in a hotel-like setting, to divide a large room into two single bedrooms with the use of an accordian-type folding partition. But this application was not acoustically adequate and was discontinued.

  There could be benefit from the application of flexible partitions in the living unit, but such flexibility would run at a premium, and currently may not be cost effective. There has been research in Japan in the study of space flexibility as an efficient method for adapting the living unit to the users needs, as needs change. This is particularly appropriate in units where the elderly are aging in place, and as they develop special needs, such as adapting existing spaces for wheelchair accessibility in such rooms as a bedroom, bathroom, or kitchen.

Prefabricated products designed for commercial application, such as the Domtar Demountable Partition System, can quickly meet and satisfy tenant requirements for interior space remodeling with acoustical privacy, or the servicing of inside wall utilities. Such systems could be applied to retirement housing, and operators of retirement housing may find them cost-effective in the long-term. These systems have met local building authority approvals, but may not as yet have been used in housing for the elderly.

Flexible office partition systems have been successfully used throughout the United States. Functional analysis, cost benefit, regulatory issues, and the application for various life-care housing models could all be evaluated to determine the benefit of flexible partitions in retirement housing.

- Question: Has anyone asked users or marketing teams what they think about movable partitions?
- Comments: You can get good information from a potential user, but the marketing team takes the position that if a resident is given too many choices, there would be no control. Marketing people say things must be similar and that it is difficult and even a nightmare trying to individualize units. If a resident could pick and choose their color scheme, carpet, wall and door finishes, without controls, or without using a preselected range of finishes and materials, buildings would never be completed, and units would be difficult to resell. There must be controls. One market team suggested that the six different unit layouts proposed by an architect for a project be reduced to four in order to simplify choice, reduce potential confusion, and improve the potential for a resale.

There are projects that permit the tenant to select from a range of finishes, floor materials, and even appliances. This works and gives the resident some control over the unit. After all, it is their home. They want the freedom and opportunity to make personal choices.

Sure it is complex when things are different, but to be safe, we end up with "oatmeal" if each unit is too similar and bland. Everything will look like Pabulum. Let's see what we can do to allow for individualism in our design of retirement housing. Seniors don't want to be put out to pasture. You would be surprised at their response if given new approaches and choice.

- Question: On "siting" retirement housing, what are some of the considerations we should have?
- Comments: Seniors love to see the sun but not be in it if it is too hot. Seniors love to sit outside as long as it is not too windy. Don't put an entrance on a northeast corner in temperate or colder climates where there will be problems from winter snows, ice, and wind.

Views are an interesting subject. Diversity is a benefit and we should allow for it. Seniors are the most diverse group in our population. Everyone looks for something different. Variety in views will be a marketing enhancement and architects should be encouraged to achieve as many different types of views as possible. Some seniors want to be on a garden, or a wooded area, but others want to overview the parking lot so they can see their car. Others want to be over or near an entrance, and it could even be a service area and face the dumpster or service road with the accompanying noise and activity. If on an urban street, the opportunity to view the activities of the community can be very satisfying.

Exposure to potential intergenerational contact can also be beneficial to seniors. This could include the ability to see children on their way to and from school, in a playground, or even to have the children stop by for some activity.

- Question: Some homes have provided beautiful garden areas believing this is what seniors want. Later it is observed that most seniors flock to the front entry porch. What went wrong?
- Comments: Most people, young or old, prefer activity and want to be part of a community. But to achieve the right solutions requires a clear understanding of the needs and wants of the elderly. Being creative and providing diversity for residents includes not only getting the right architect but also the right board of directors. The board needs to be vital and open-minded. Perhaps buildings should not be finished when they are opened to residents. Watch how residents react, then make major decisions to finish off the public and private spaces.

The same approach is helpful when planning a living unit. There should be flexibility built in because needs change. If a resident enters the unit at age seventy and lives in the unit for fifteen years, there are apt to be changes needed in the environment to encourage independent living. If we design and premarket to a younger group without consideration for the changes that will occur as one ages in place, we really are not adequately serving our market. We must preplan for change and build in flexibility.

- Question: We really do need grab bars in our bathrooms, and certainly it would be beneficial if more were provided in living and public spaces, but why do grab bars have to look so institutional?
- Comments: There are ways to design grab bars so that they don't look like grab bars and serve just as well. There are a number of options. For example, we could develop a continuous wall recess, at about elbow height, that provides a lip one can rest the hand over, providing a safety grip. This option doesn't protrude into the room or corridor. It can be a design element in the space, much like a chair rail in traditional interiors. In other words, it is integrated with the design and is not an afterthought. There are some attempts to deinstitutionalize grab bars. In fact, there now *are* some colored "designer" grab bars, which take away the institutional look.

New product designs of moulded bath and shower units are on the market that provide wall recesses, and within the recess, a separate grab bar that doesn't protrude into the space.

But to come up with something new, improved, and different, to accommodate the unsteadiness of frail elders, be it in the corridor, living room, or bathroom, requires research-oriented and open-minded designers who are encouraged by their clients to be creative and innovative. Such undertakings require additional time and expense that most developers or owners are unwilling to incur at this time, even though the consumer may be willing to pay additional cost for better, safer, more supportive, and attractive environments.

It is well-known that our present approach in the United States to bathroom design is to place the appliances in as small an area as possible. Yet these minimal-size bathrooms are not always usable or comfortable for a resident with mobility or transfer problems. To provide a transfer seat at the end of a tub that could have a multi-use function takes up more floor area, and this translates into more cost to the developer. To develop and provide a "plug-in" bathtub, which could be removed and replaced with a room-type shower (that is, the entire room is waterproof and permits a resident in a wheelchair, access and self-help or provides room for assistance in showering), takes a different longer-range investment attitude than most American developers are willing to provide.

It is true that good warm baths help therapeutically to relieve the aches and pains of arthritis and other ailments. Perhaps we should consider what the Japanese MITI research house had provided. A soaking tub in a shower room so that one has an option, and if one needs assistance with bathing, the room is large enough to accommodate the resident, a wheelchair, and an aide.

In the United States it seems that we stick to what has been done in the past. We are concerned about not being different from the Joneses, and we're hesitant in using special products that help with a disability, even though they may benefit us and prove to be an improvement over what is currently available. We consider it a stigma to be old or disabled. We try to hide from such conditions.

Most architects and marketing people take a negative attitude toward the room shower, even though it may mean an elderly persons can remain more independent. Are we not doing a disservice to the elderly if all we focus on is satisfying the needs of today's elderly? When we claim that elders prefer a bathtub to a shower, it is the seniors of today from whom we gathered research and marketing data. What about the seniors of tomorrow?

Marketers claim they have a hard time selling a unit without a bathtub. There is a cultural difference between the United States and Europe, where a shower room would be acceptable. Anyway, here in the United States, the public, and particularly the elderly, just don't want to move into a unit designed for the disabled or for the elderly.

If we were to rethink how we approach our design tasks and how we prioritize the development process, perhaps we would come up with a "win-win" method that satisfies all: the developer, the architect, the service provider, and most important, the user. We need to focus on the purpose of our effort, which is to improve the quality of life and to enable the elderly to remain as independent as possible, maintaining their dignity and self-esteem. If we spend more time understanding what the environmental problems of aging are, we can then solve for the need.

We should turn our minds to the future, and plan for our buildings to accommodate the needs of users by providing for flexibility in design. Tomorrow's elderly will be better-educated, more accustomed to electronic technology, and more receptive to innovative ideas. If we're going to meet the growing elderly market, we should be planning for the twenty-first century today.

C. Development Workshop

The development workshop featured a panel moderated by John Zeisel, Ph.D., president of Building Diagnostics Inc., Cambridge, MA, and including Mel Gamzon, president, Senior Housing Investment Advisors, Inc., Cambridge, MA; Bjarne Hastrup, executive director of EGV Foundation and director of DaneAge, Copenhagen, Denmark; Antony Herrey, president, Newport Management Corporation, Cambridge, MA; and Gardner Van Scoyoc, president, Van Scoyoc Associates, Inc., Alexandria, VA.

Panel members each presented a view of life-care development that focused on a particular aspect of approach, attitude, and process. The following are some of the points emphasized by the panelists in their presentations:

John Zeisel opened the panel with the following comments.

- Life care provides an infrastructure which includes shelter, health care, social and financial security systems.
- Initially, life care provided for both independent living and nursing care. As the model developed, the assisted living unit (ALU) was introduced. Now, some projects are providing two forms of ALUs in addition to independent living and skilled nursing care. They are the residential unit, where assistance is provided with activities of daily living, and the home health care unit, which provides some nursing assistance within the residential setting. This is one approach to aging in place and brings needed services to the resident rather than bringing the resident to the service area.
- Life-care programs are now investing more heavily in health supports that emphasize wellness and service supports that provide unbundled service options, allowing residents to pay for what they use as a method for keeping fees and unnecessary utilization as low as possible.
- Long-term care insurance is a major issue in developing a complete life-care package. Developers must offer clear information to potential resi-

dents on the amount of coverage their group policies will provide. Residents should ask if such policies will provide 100, 50, or 25 percent coverage. The prospective resident needs to understand up-front what their exposure will be.

- In developing life care, one important aspect involves coordination. Putting a team together is a major part of the process. A life-care project requires many specialists from marketing to design, from legal to accounting, from real estate to project management, from construction to interior design, from public relations to agency and community approvals, and so on. All this requires a skilled Seniors Specialist who can help orchestrate and coordinate the process.
- Life care development requires deep pockets, a local presence, and a focus on appropriate design. But most important, the work effort must be responsive to the ultimate resident. It is the resident who will help keep the project viable. If the project is responsive to the resident, then the resident will be an ongoing force who will keep selling the life-care facility to future residents.

Mel Gamzon reported on a national survey he recently completed with Multi-Housing News. The purpose was to determine where the senior housing industry has been and where it is headed. Interviewed were business leaders from the health care, marketing, management and development sectors of the industry. Highlights of his findings, covering six important areas, are indicated below:

1. *Absorption.* Most developers have developed pro formas with absorption rates that have been unrealistic; have been finance-driven, rather than market-driven; and have not understood the needs of the elderly market nor the issue of aging in place. With an industry that is still very young and in a transition phase, developers need to develop a knowledge base and move forward carefully.
2. *Credibility.* Developers need to gain credibility. All the dollars being spent on advertising and marketing material, brochures, and mailers can be wasted unless sufficient ground work (research, financial analysis, and market evaluation) is done up-front. One of the best ways for a developer to gain credibility in the seniors housing industry is through local affiliation with service providers, health providers, local institutions, and community organizations.
3. *Competition.* Significant and heavy competition exists in many parts of the country, with developers vying for the senior's market attention. As a result, this consumer is overloaded and overwhelmed with similar messages for slightly different products. To meet competition, developers need

to understand how to effectively reach the consumer. Market research should be done by professionals who know the field. Developers need to work with gerontologists and others who understand the aging process. For the traditional life-care model to work, it needs to be tied in with some form of long-term care insurance to protect against actuarial risk. Future life-care center projects will be heavily impacted by competing products that offer ownership options, rentals, or shared appreciation.

4. *Housing and Services.* Housing alone will not solve the needs of the elderly. Service programs need to be provided and be carefully integrated. Many developers have been building products that people either don't want or can't afford. The luxury life-care or CCRC facility serves an important market. This traditional model will continue to proliferate for the up-scale market. But for the majority of elders, the upscale "cruise ship" model will need to be modified, with more cost-effective housing and service options. The senior consumer is concerned with monthly affordability, maximum flexibility, and independence. Consumers are indicating a strong interest in a la carte services. Developers should be aware of this trend.
5. *Design.* In understanding the elderly consumer's needs and the aging process, developers will recognize the value of providing for adaptability and flexibility in the living unit to meet the changing needs of the resident.
6. *New Models.* Developers must be concerned with the needs and wants of the senior consumer. They must listen and learn. Life care offers many benefits, and the market is capable of supporting many forms of product. For a large number of seniors with moderate income and limited assets, one model, the rental or congregate model without on-site health services, can become a viable option and an area to watch.

Bjarne Hastrup reviewed the Danish approach to life care and how his organization goes about developing projects. Two points were emphasized, as noted in the following comments:

- Considerable emphasis is given to up-front research when developing appropriate solutions for the housing and care of the elderly in Denmark. Much time is taken in surveying and analyzing the needs and wants of Danish citizens. For example, the EGV organization will interview the elderly, those sixty-five years and older; younger age groups, such as a forty- to forty-five-year-old group; a fifty- to fifty-five-year-old group; and a sixty- to sixty-five-year-old group. The goal is to anticipate demands and therefore provide each age group with a living environment that will support their own unique lifestyle when they retire. By understanding these needs, it is believed a happier and healthier society will be realized and at a lower long-term cost.

- EGV goes beyond its country's boundaries, to research worldwide trends in housing and services. They collect material from everywhere to study and understand different approaches and attitudes as a means of improving their own process. To find out what is going on throughout the world, the EGV organization gathers together a group of elderly retired professionals, such as former professors, linguists, and others, to read, translate, and summarize what is being done in other countries and being said in other languages.
- In developing an actual project for a particular community in northern Denmark, the following example of the EGV preliminary planning approach is worth noting. To prepare for the programming of a project, the EGV development team gathered some fifty active community elders, and brought them together with engineers, site planners, architects, service providers, and social workers to do a great deal of talking with each other so the team could find out what it is the elderly want in their local retirement housing. In another project in southern Denmark, a community decided to hold a design competition, which was judged not only by the future residents, but by service providers, builders, and even bankers.
- In Denmark, development solutions come from the people, from future residents, not from industry and not from the government.

The highlights of comments by Antony Herrey covered the need for carefully managed property acquisition and community relations during the development process. He described a process used some years ago, while he was at the Massachusetts Institute of Technology (MIT), in developing 700 units of elderly housing for the benefit of the residents of Cambridge, MA.

- The concept was to construct 700 units of low-income, subsidized housing for the elderly on three separate sites in the city of Cambridge. It was to be a turn-key project, which would be turned over to the Cambridge Housing Authority (CHA) to manage and to select the tenants. But prior to disclosing their concept and "going public," MIT had to secretly acquire many small sites to create parcels of adequate size. Land acquisition and assembly in urban areas is very difficult process.
- When the sites were assembled, MIT went to the city and advised what they wanted to do for the community. The CHA accepted the concept and worked with MIT to obtain the support of the neighborhoods and zoning approval to permit high-rise construction of greater density than existing regulations permitted.
- Elapsed time for the total program was five years. The projects were well-received and are being well-maintained.

Gardner Van Scoyoc's remarks centered on the difficulty of predicting the utilization of nursing care. He said that average individual utilization runs somewhat over 400 nursing days. Unless managers of life-care facilities provide some form of long-term care insurance for residents, projects will be exposed to downstream financial risk.

During the question and comment period following the panelists remarks, some interesting questions were raised.

- Question: Urban land is scarce and unless we get together with each other, it will be next to impossible to assemble sites of appropriate size. Does the panel have any thoughts on this issue?
- Comments: Institutions and local governments can use surplus land holdings, and some are already doing so. But it is very tough to get neighbors to work together for land assembly, and in the long run, as has occurred on public projects, it may take the power of "eminent domain" to pull sites together. Zoning is still a big concern for all developers, and once the zoning hurdle is achieved, absorption becomes a concern, as many real estate markets seem overbuilt.

  Opportunities exist with properties that are not on the tax rolls. Some great opportunities exist in the current real estate climate, and particularly in the northeast.

  Right now we are being faced with a challenge. Most life-care and CCRC facilities are being built in suburban areas. Most people want to be close to where their homes were. They want to be part of the community. We need to find ways to fit the elderly back into the community.

- Question: Flexibility in design, what does it imply?
- Comment: It implies having the ability to convert a unit design from one form of use to another. For example, let's say we've designed an assisted living unit with 600–650 square feet, and that in time the demand increases for nursing units. Can we conveniently modify the building to become a nursing facility without major construction and renovation? Another example: let's say the assisted living unit demand has changed where larger-sized units are in favor. Can we reasonably convert two smaller assisted-living units into one larger unit? If we can do all of this economically, then, that is flexibility!
- Question: How can one make a deal work even if the town is resisting?
- Comments: One example of a successful approach is the experience in Lexington, MA of GHM. To get the town planning committee and the townspeople to vote favorably for their proposed life-care facility, they

offered to give the town a one-time contribution to be used for affordable housing. This linkage approach was acceptable to the town, permitting the Brookhaven project to move ahead.

Another example is the Fuller Trust project in Milton, MA. The Trust offered to work with the town as they both wish to achieve appropriate and affordable housing. The town also was anxious to have a variety of options to allow elders to remain in town with appropriate housing and services. Both parties worked together: the Trust will subsidize a certain number of units, and the town will obtain affordable housing. On this basis, the town meeting had a unanimous vote to permit the project to proceed.

- Question: Are we saturating some markets with too many and costly types of retirement housing?
- Comment: Affordability is a key concern of seniors. Retirees are consumers as we all are, and they are saying they won't let themselves get into a situation where they have to pay more than is necessary. They are beginning to see retirement centers looking like country clubs, with amenities and services like those of a cruise ship. This is not what the majority of seniors are willing to pay for. So, if we keep our focus on the local marketplace, we will note the following caution signals and trends:

1. Don't overbuild product. This means be careful not to build in too many costly and marginal features. Put in basic needs. Offer value. Listen to the consumer. They will advise what they are willing to pay for.
2. Try to get for-profit developers to work with nonprofit developers. This helps develop credibility, and the synergism can result in a better product.
3. Look for opportunities to work with public-held land of municipalities or with universities and hospitals. There are tremendous opportunities out there, but flexibility is a key.
4. Be cautious about loading development fees. The consumer is beginning to question front-end costs. It is not going to be as easy to load profits as in the past.
5. Public funds are limited. There have been abuses. By putting quality and value into projects, public acceptance of the life-care concept will grow.

D. Insurance Workshop

A long-term insurance workshop associated with the Symposium featured a panel, moderated by Larry M. Diamond, Ph.D., president of Senior Health Systems, Inc., Cambridge, MA; Nancy Bern, vice president of the John Hancock Mutual Life Insurance Company; and Jarvis Farley, an actuary, former board president, and a resident at North Hill, a life-care facility in Needham, MA.

Discussion of this very important topic included the following issues:

- Life-care and continuing-care retirement communities are an ideal way for one part of the population to address the need for long-term care. Many elderly people, however, prefer to stay in their own homes, and they require a way to protect themselves from the potentially catastrophic expense of a nursing home stay.
- The need for financial and insurance protection against a catastrophic illness is strong in both institutional and residential settings.
- Long-term care insurance can help control the fluctuations of health-care costs and spread the risk for those who prefer to remain at home or to live at a life-care center.
- Currently, one-half of the total annual nursing home care costs of about $40 billion is paid out-of-pocket by the elderly, and insurance covers only 1 percent of this total cost.
- The elderly are becoming more aware that Medicare will not cover their needs, and they are interested in additional forms of protection.
- There are relatively few insurance policies available because there has been very little actuarial data, and therefore the available policies have been both restrictive and costly.
- As the younger generation realizes, through the experience of their parents and grandparents, that major changes are needed in the way we address health-care and housing issues of the elderly, new health-care

programs, new housing models, and additional forms of protection through a variety of insurance policies will be offered.

- The new generation of policies will be more affordable, with less focus on institutional care and more on the functional capabilities of the elderly who need the care, in whatever setting.
- One recently offered policy covers skilled, custodial, and home health care. The policy is guaranteed renewable, has level premiums, inflation protection, and provides benefits of between $40 and $200 per day. The premiums for an $80-per-day, six-year benefit period, for the most comprehensive coverage, for a person age fifty-five, would be $290 per year. For a person age sixty-five, it would be $700 per year. Such a policy can be a preretirement planning tool for the target market that are age fifty to sixty-five. If bought at an early age, the cost is affordable.
- Many younger people, average age of forty-two years, say they are signing up for a group long-term product offered by a major employer because of the experiences their parents or grandparents have had, which they would like to avoid.
- A new group product that will come to the market soon will provide nursing-home coverage for CCRC seniors who do not have available nursing-care facilities on-premise. This will be a step between the full life-care community, which provides both housing and health care, and the opposite extreme, where an elderly person remains at home and will have available an individual policy purchased to preplan for the need.
- For those life-care communities and CCRCs that maintain their own coverage, it is vital to adequately provide for the discharging of all obligations for the full term of a resident's contract, including provision for refundable entrance fees and long-term health care. The application of actuarial methods to define and handle risk is a prudent and necessary procedure. Group long-term care insurance can be employed to help carry that risk.
- It should be noted that the generally accepted accounting principles (GAAP), as applied to ordinary business entities, do not adequately cope with the peculiar characteristics of the CCRC, especially the life-care community. Financial statements based on GAAP as presently applied may give a misleading and unduly negative picture of life-care community or a CCRCs financial status and progress.
- There is a close precedent in the development of specialized and generally accepted accounting principles for life insurance companies, with which CCRCs and life-care communities share many of the same special characteristics. Actuary and accounting organization committees are currently engaged in a study to identify how customary GAAP should be

modified to cope with the special needs of life-care communities and CCRCs. The specialized GAAP principles developed for the life insurance industry are being used as a model for the long-term industry study.

- Life-care communities and CRRCs must be viewed as ongoing business organizations. In addition to health-care concerns, they have continuing obligations to meet regarding the housing and services components, and they can't simply terminate operations at some convenient time. Vacancies will occur, and if those vacancies are not filled in a timely fashion, unit costs will become intolerably high. But to fill vacancies and to meet competition, the physical plant must be kept attractive as it wears out, by proper maintenance of roofs, elevators, plumbing, heating, ventilating and air conditioning. Effective financial planning for such maintenance, upgrading, and replacement requires that depreciation accounting be based on the expected costs and that the depreciation be funded.
- When planning the present value of future obligations, one must make assumptions about inflation and interest rates, which are judgements. Two most important points: the assumption made for inflation must be appropriately related to the assumption made for interest, and the assumption made for increase in periodic fees has to be appropriately related to the assumption made for inflation. On the point about interest, it is the *real* interest that must be considered. Real interest is the difference between the nominal interest rate and the nominal inflation rate, which will affect the results. One can have a very high inflation rate corresponding to a very high interest rate and get about the same result.
- Occasionally long-term care insurance products appear to be something they are not. There are efforts underway both in the private and public sector to make sure that customers understand policies. We need to plan for long-term care protection, and the insurance approach is a reasonable solution that can prefund and share the long-term care risk.

E. Financing Workshop

The financing workshop included: Sarah Wilcox, vice president, Institutional Group, Bank of New England, Boston, MA, Moderator; Robert B. Haldeman, president, Coventry Resources, Linthicum, MD, Donald L. Moon, president, FRC Management Inc., Gwynedd, PA, and Roderic Rolett, vice president, Herbert J. Sims & Co. Inc., Westport CT.

Important points made during the workshop included reiteration of the lending and underwriting criteria typically applied to life-care projects, including:

- Working capital, and commitment, must be sufficient to see the project through.
- Experience is critical, both for the development team and for the future management team.
- Demographic study and an analysis of the competition are important. There must be enough people who can afford it, and the project must be able to compete against both existing and future competition.
- Marketing survey is critical, and they have certain things they look for.
- An additional feasibility study by the lenders choice of CPA firm, will be required to confirm the developers figures.
- Real estate market must be strong enough not to hinder the marketing.
- Resident contracts must be reviewed carefully to see that commitments being made are manageable.
- Co-op and condominium models have increasing interest, since the more traditional refundable endowment model is, increasingly, the regulated end of the business, and because they offer residents an equity investment. However, the sponsor loses valuable control.
- A well-thought-out proposal, one that really seems to work, is the critical starting point.

- Recourse, or project guarantees, are a vital subject. Each project is different, and different criteria may apply. For instance, although, unlike a for-profit developer, nonprofit volunteer boards make decisions in which they have no personal financial stake, the nonprofit sponsor is definitely in for the long haul. A for-profit developer may be reviewed more for experience and financial commitment. And the banks always look for more than the borrowers thinks they can come up with. The bank may ask for a security interest in the property.
- Evolving regulations must be monitored and evaluated, and existing regulations must of course be complied with, scrupulously.
- Nursing facilities, even when integrated into a life-care complex, are evaluated separately.
- Refundability of deposits may be a source of concern, in that a sudden significant exodus and loss of equity could destabilize the project. The best structure is to have the entrance fee refunded only after the unit has been resold (subject to state regulations on refundability).
- AICPA standards forbid a projection of more than five years. But life-care centers realize they need a full-blown actuarial study, going out fifteen, twenty-five, or thirty years, even if this can't be published as part of the accountant's report. Actuarial data is especially critical for unit turnover projections.

It was noted that although it may often be quicker to get approval for a bond underwriting, this may not be the case when a bank specializes in a particular type of project.

In states with strong consumer protection laws, where law suits might be most easily pursued, banks have some worry that they may be the deepest pocket in sight. This is another reason why the sponsor or developer must educate a bank to this business, because if the banker doesn't understand the business and the project, there will be no loan.

Among the services banks may offer are construction financing, working capital financing, standby letters of credit, backup relief funds, escrow account services, and permanent financing.

Bond underwriters go through a somewhat different process with somewhat different criteria. Decisions involve fewer people and can be fairly quick. Among the items they focus on are:

- Presales requirements
- Market penetration requirements, and the general acceptance of the life-care concept in the area.

- Site (its amazing how many developers will see the good points of a site and overlook the bad ones).
- Track record of the developer. This is important, but can always be enhanced by purchasing appropriate expertise in the form of management or consulting contracts. The key is to put together a confident team with relevant experience in all critical areas.
- The ability of nonprofits, but not for-profits, to use tax-exempt bonds generates quite a bit of business in this area. Historically and traditionally market acceptance of nonprofits has been high, and that is important for marketing.
- Balance sheets, income statements, and cash flow statements are all important. Underwriters also like to see sensitivity analyses testing worst-case alternatives.
- Personal or corporate guarantees are not required for these bond offerings, and instead the underwriters look to projected cash flows and the ability to make debt service payments.
- Sponsor-developers are not required to keep equity in the project, although they must come up with money up-front to get to the point of underwriting.
- Underwriting fees for tax-exempt bonds have come down in recent years from possibly 6 to 3 or 4 percent, and even as low as 1 ¼ or 1 ½ percent if the bonds are rated and credit enhanced, for example by a bank letter of credit.
- Underwriters generally believe that full life care sells better than modified life care because people want the security that it guarantees, so if a developer is offering only modified life care, the underwriter wants to know why!

F. Management Workshop

A management workshop associated with the Harvard-Farnsworth Life Care Symposium yielded some disparate but potentially useful comments, and a summary is included here.

Panelists included: Barbara A. Doyle, executive director, Carleton-Willard Village, Moderator; Gail Cohn, executive director, Collington Episcopal Life Care Community; Stephen Roizin, executive director, The Willows at Westborough; Martin Trueblood, executive director, Williamsburg Landing.

Among the more interesting points were the following:

Accreditation and the self-examination it forces staff, trustees, and residents to go through can have a revitalizing effect on a life-care community.

Aging in place presents a sequence of varying problems, as to individual residents, and as to the whole resident population. It requires sequential adjustments over the years, which management must be open to and prepared for.

Resident input is important, for many reasons, during the design and development phases, and is too often overlooked.

Resident participation in operations is critically important. Opinion divides on whether residents should serve on the governing board, or send nonvoting representatives. All agree on the importance of volunteer efforts by residents. Opinion is split on whether residents should be hired in paying jobs. Some feel they should be able to apply as any candidate would, and can be hired if they meet all objective criteria and are the best qualified. If hired they should receive full pay, but have no access to confidential resident information. Others feel that this nevertheless may create problems with confidentiality regarding the records of other residents; that it becomes a problem to discharge them when they become too frail to do the work; or that it discourages other residents from making volunteer efforts.

Resident committees should be encouraged, and all agreed that they should be utilized wherever possible. They can undertake the research and evaluation of possible new services or pieces of equipment, or prepare budgets for specific programs, and this can be a big help to board and staff.

Retail services can be handled in many ways. Some can rely on resident or other volunteer help. But all licensed or professional services (banks, beauty parlors) should be handled by appropriate entities.

Banks can often be pressed into paying fairly high space rental fees, and these should be escalated as deposits grow. *Safe deposit boxes* should be included (military style units hold eighty boxes in a unit taking only 3′ × 3′), as should *coupon cutting rooms* and a desk for financial counselling. *ATM's* may be helpful for the staff, but most older residents vastly prefer face to face contact with a teller, so that the volume to justify an ATM may not be there.

Beauty shop operation can be offered for space rental, but a payment formula giving a percentage of the gross to the facility may be equitable for all concerned until usage patterns are established. Usually the facility pays for the appropriate finishing and equipping of the space. Some facilities hire their own beauticians directly to maximize income. One facility claims it pays to have a direct line to the gossip of residents!

Gift shops and convenience stores can be run by volunteer residents if there is enough manpower and it is properly encouraged even before move-in. If this operation is farmed out to a local pharmacy or other store, make sure the contract can be modified or cancelled.

Home care sent into apartments is important from the start. In one case, an RN and one nursing assistant efficiently handle up to twenty-five cases per day. Some large communities build up home-care teams of eight to ten or more over time.

Transfer policies must be clear from the first day. Consensus was that there should be some sort of mediation process, involving both residents and staff; that every step should be precisely documented; and that the final decision should depend heavily on the opinion of the medical director and the health-care staff. Basic conditions requiring transfer should be clear. Two typical conditions cited were incontinence and mental impairment, although many facilities find they can often deal with these conditions outside their licensed units.

Bed utilization is greatly affected by the type of health-care contract. A contract that pays only for the first ten, thirty, or sixty days per year may unintentionally encourage use of at least that many days for nonessential care, whereas contracts that have the patient paying for the first days, not the last, discourage premature scheduling of operations or special care. Contracts that cover all care from first to last are best at minimizing artificial usage patterns. Bed utilization should be tracked at least weekly through meetings of a multidisciplinary health-care team. Resident progress to or from apartments, hospital, and nursing beds should be monitored and planned for in advance.

Spousal care should be encouraged. One survey suggests that the care of one spouse by the other has avoided more patient days than all the allowed patient days, but that this was less likely to happen with second or recent marriages!

Manpower shortages are a problem everywhere. Many strategies were suggested, including the stressing of in-service training combined with a career-ladder approach. Child care, good pay, good benefits, attractive working conditions, flexible schedules, job sharing, efforts to attract nurses or others out of retirement, catering to foreign-speaking workers, hiring the handicapped or the elderly, and many other possibilities exist.

Laundry services have actually been dropped at a few facilities, to keep monthly fees down, with remarkably little protest.

Housekeeping, when rescheduled from weekly to twice monthly for savings and efficiency, generated only minor protest.

Locks on apartments should be changed within ten days after transfer to nursing, and immediately after death. All lock and key management can be greatly facilitated by the new card-key lock systems.

Companions and the policies to control them are a constant question for management. One solution is to require that all companions be employees of the facility, so the facility may bill the resident for their services, and then maintain some control over otherwise ungovernable on-site quasi-staff people.

Life care, as a relatively new concept, should *not* be considered a fixed formula, but should be experimented with and encouraged to evolve in different ways for different groups.

G. Resident Workshop

A resident panel was organized for the Symposium made up of current residents of continuing-care (The Willows, Westborough, MA) and life-care retirement communities (North Hill, Needham, MA, and Carleton-Willard Village, Bedford, MA).

Panelists included: James F. Seagle, executive director, Rogerson House, Moderator; Catherine Elberfeld and Henry Hersey, The Willows; Betty Nutter and Bea Carlson, North Hill; and Marion Pierson and Mary van Etten from Carleton-Willard.

This panel offered symposium participants a chance to review the motivations and reactions of residents who chose the life-care or continuing-care option, and what they do or do not like or recommend about it. The following discussion summarizes comments made by members of the panel.

All panelists professed to be highly pleased with their way of life. They appreciated having no further responsibility for a house and were pleased that their children will not need to worry about their social activities, housing situation, or health-care support system. They felt that there is the chance to have a great deal of fun in a well set-up communal environment, while stressing that you can be as private as you wish. Favored activities include concerts, trips and tours, such as museum visits, and regularly scheduled movies to which outsiders are welcomed.

"I can't say enough for this way of life." "I've never been happier, and I'm so glad I didn't have to move out of state." "Go in while you're young enough to make friends, don't wait till you *have* to go!" "It's important to have the nursing home near the apartments so your friends can visit you, especially if they don't drive."

One described making her decision when she and her husband were having increasing trouble maintaining their house, and opted for a facility more than fifteen miles and half-an-hour's drive away because they knew some of the life care trustees and had heard of it through them. She felt that it was close enough to keep up with old friends. They liked the campus-like setting, with its surrounding woods, meadows, and chances to go birding, or watch the sheep. She liked the area shopping, as well as the convenient on-site shops, her apartment with full kitchen, and the fact that apartments are interconnected with other facilities. "Carleton-Willard is a wonderful haven, with all our needs taken care of and no more household worries . . . and there are so many opportunities at your fingertips." When her husband died, the support, thoughtfulness, and concern from the staff was heartwarming. Residents as well as staff were a great support, and even though she was "on the young side," she has never regretted staying on.

Another panelist agreed with all the above remarks, and "can't say enough about the philosophy." He first heard of the concept when he was a selectman reviewing a local proposal. He liked the concept, and now likes the friendly people, all the varied things to do, and the available services. He wanted to enter such a facility to "take away his worries." After living two years at North Hill, he remarried and, although he would have preferred to stay in his original community, moved with his new wife and her Himalayan cat to The Willows because they allow pets. They have been very happy there. He feels pet policies are good because many people are so much more happy and contented when they can keep their pet with them. At The Willows, pets are a great hit when taken into the nursing center to visit patients. Conversely, a North Hill resident suggested that in such a large community pets might "overrun" the place.

Still, another resident of The Willows first heard of the life-care/continuing-care concept when serving on the local Council on Aging. She asked for the material for a friend, and later realized it would meet many of her needs. Her children were very supportive.

A North Hill resident had visited friends at Foulkeways near Philadelphia, where she and husband were struck with the attractiveness of the concept. Later, when her husband heard about the new North Hill at a Rotary meeting, they visited the marketing office the next day and had no trouble deciding to move a half-hour drive from their home. "Nothing is worse for an adult child than putting a parent in a nursing home—deciding the fate of the parent, and then closing up the house of many years." That was not the only motivating factor, but they did want to save their children from the dilemma. "The nicest thing you can do for the kids is to relieve them of all worry about you, and those hard decisions." It has worked out well. They have a marvellous time, and particularly enjoy never having to eat alone. They are among the large group enjoying a swim every morning. "None of the residents consider themselves old!" They would never go back to their former way of life, pleasant though it was, and their children are delighted.

Another North Hill resident remembered visiting her own mother in a California life-care center in La Jolla, which she compared to a resort hotel. She and her husband were in turn urged to move from Minnesota to Massachusetts so they could enjoy the advantages of North Hill while they were still active. Her husband, a former corporate comptroller, and very aware of costs, studied the financial implications, with positive results. She cited, from Art Linkletter's book on coping with old age, *Old Age Is Not for Sissies,* his advice, including "don't be alone, and plan something every day," and that the two greatest concerns of elders are for their health and for their independence. "And (at North Hill) we are independent—it's like a condo, with full health care attached, and we pinch ourselves every day that we are there." "It's like a continual cruise, or living at a first-class resort hotel." "We are not unhappy to be among the youngest residents." Their daughter and her husband, both medical doctors, plan to get on a waiting list when they are in their fifties, to have the option open for themselves whenever they are ready.

It was noted that most life-care residents seem to have heard of the idea directly through family or friends, that the word is passed along, more effectively than any conventional advertising.

It is very positive that residents can visit a spouse or friends in the nursing home easily, and that nursing patients can visit apartments or the main dining room. "It's not what people think of as a nursing home—it's beautifully decorated, they don't just sit in the halls, they have activities, volunteers, ambiance, a special dining room, they swim, they have cookouts, they have their own social director."

Questioned about specifics, recommendations from these residents included the following:

- Be sure the acoustics are good, between units, in the Dining rooms, everywhere!
- The new auditorium and classrooms at Carleton-Willard have been an exciting and much used addition.
- While it is painful to see friends failing in health, it is reassuring to see the various preventive measures, like physical therapy, available and being applied.
- There should be more resident storage area, and walk-in closets are a must.
- It is attractive to have options for families and friends visiting overnight, such as guest rooms, staying in one's own apartment. Some facilities make extra cots available from the housekeeping department. One resident was able to have her family stay in a friend's vacant apartment for two weeks. "Sometimes it seems as though there are more guests than residents."
- The on-site convenience store is a highly rated amenity.
- One resident thought highly of the bowling alleys projected for the Southgate-at-Shrewsbury CCRC.

- One resident felt that most units, even the typical two bedrooms, were too small.

To the question, "How would you advise friends to prepare for the move to a life-care center?", one resident responded:

1. Organize your belongings, and select what to bring with you.
2. Give children what they want, or should have.
3. Offer things to friends.
4. Offer your "don't know what to do withs" to an antiques dealer.
5. Call the Morgan Memorial to pick up what's left.

A concluding comment was that although their lives naturally tended to revolve around the life-care center, many residents were out as often as they were in, many travelled extensively, held volunteer or paying jobs, served on boards of trustees, and in general felt the life-care lifestyle was a liberating one and the ideal for them.

Bibliography

Action for Boston Community Development. *Planning and Developing a Shared Living Project*. Boston: Action for Boston Community Development, Inc. 1979.

Actuarial Standards of Practice Relating to Continuing Care Retirement Communities. Interim Actuarial Standards Board Exposure Draft developed by the Committee on Continuing Care Retirement Communities for the Specialty Committee of the IASB, American Academy of Actuaries, May 1986.

Adams, Eli. "The graying of America: New Builder Opportunity in a Growing Demographic Market." *Professional Builder,* August 1984, pp. 135–151.

Adams, Eli (ed.) "The graying of America." *Professional Builder,* September 1985, pp. 66–83.

———. "The graying of America.." *Professional Builder,* April 1986, pp. 68–83.

———. "Havens for retirees and empty nesters." *Professional Builder,* February 1983, pp. 104–110.

Aldrich, D. and Mendkoff, E. "Relocation of the aged and disabled: A mortality study." *Journal of American Geriatric Society, 11,* 1963, pp. 185–194.

Alexander, C., Ishikawa, S., and Silverstein, M. *A Pattern Language Which Generates Multi-Service Centers.* California: Center for Environmental Structure, 1968.

Altman, I. *The Environment and Social Behavior*. Monterey, California: Brooks/Cole, 1975.

American Association of Homes for the Aging. *Continuing Care Homes: A Guidebook for Consumers*. Washington, D.C.: AAHA, 1977.

———. *Continuing Care Issues for Nonprofit Providers*. Washington, D.C.: AAHA, 1980.

———. *Model Continuing Care Provider Registration and Disclosure Act,* Washington, D.C.: AAHA, 1980.

———. *Obtaining Capital for Housing and Services for the Elderly.* Washington, D.C.: AAHA and Real Estate Financial Services, 1984.

———. *Market and Economic Feasibility Studies: Guidelines for Continuing Care Retirement Communities*. Washington, D.C.: AAHA, 1984.

American Association of Retired Persons. *Housing Options for Older Americans*. Washington, D.C., AARP, 1984.

American Foundation for the Blind. *An Introduction to Working With the Aging Person Who Is Visually Handicapped*. New York: American Foundation for the Blind, 1972.

———. *Products for People With Vision Problems.* New York: American Foundation for the Blind, 1982.
American Health Care Association. *Trends and Strategies in Long Term Care.* Washington, D.C.: American Health Care Association, 1985.
American Institute of Architects. *Compensation Guidelines for Architectural and Engineering Services.* Washington, D.C.: AIA, 1978.
American National Standards Institute. *Specification for Making Buildings and Facilities Accessible to and Usable by Physically Handicapped People, A117.1.* New York: American National Standards Institute, 1980.
Anchor Housing Association. *Staying Put.* Oxford, England: Anchor Housing Trust, 1980.
Aranyi, L. and Goldman, L.L. *Design of Long-Term Care Facilities.* New York: Van Nostrand Reinhold Company, 1980.
Archea, J., Collins, B., and Stahl, F. "Guidelines for stair safety." *National Bureau of Standards, BSS 120,* Washington, D.C., 1979.
Backett, E.M. *Domestic Accidents.* Geneva, Switzerland: World Health Organization, 1965.
Banton, Jonathan R. and Anthony Luzzi. "Financing the CCRC." *Contemporary LTC,* June 1985, pp. 23–29.
Barbaro, Ellen L. and Lin E. Noyes. "A wellness program for a life care community." *The Gerontologist, 24,* 1984, pp. 568–663.
Barnes, R.D. "Perceived freedom and control in the built environment." In J. Harvey (ed.). *Cognition, Social Behavior and the Environment.* Hillsdale, NJ: Lawrence Erlbaum Associates, 1981.
Bechtel, R.B. "Perception of environmental quality: Some new wineskins for old wine." In K.H. Craik and E.H. Zube (eds.). *Perceiving Environmental Quality.* New York: Plenum Press, 1976.
Becker, Helmut A. "CCRC development needs team approach." *Contemporary Long-Term Care,* February 1986, pp. 52–64.
Beckerman, David S. "Bright prospects for rental retirement housing." *Urban Land,* November 1986, pp. 6–9.
Bell, W.G. "Community care for the elderly: An alternative to institutionalization." *The Gerontologist, 13(3),* 1973, pp. 349–354.
Berman, Phyllis. "The Methodists and Mammon." *Forbes,* December 25, 1978, pp. 25–27.
Best, G. "Direction finding in large buildings." In D. Canter (ed.). *Architectural Psychology.* London: RIBA Publications, 1970.
Beyer, G.H. and Nierstrasz, F.H.J. *Housing the Aged in Western Countries.* New York: Elsevier, 1967.
Birenbaum, A. "Aging and housing: A note on how housing expresses social status." *Journal of Housing for the Elderly, 2(1),* 1984, pp. 33–40.
Birkner, Edward C. "Adult community with all the extras." *Professional Builder,* September 1984, p. 66.
Bisbee, Gerald E. and Lattin, Clark P. "What's hot, what's not in long-term care: An investment banker's perspective." *Contemporary LTC, 9,* December 1986, pp. 26–31.

Blasch, B. and Hiatt, L.G. *Orientation and Wayfinding*. Washington, D.C.: U.S. Architectural and Transportation Barriers Compliance Board, 1983.

Bley, N., Goodman, M., Dye, D. and Harel, B. "Characteristics of aged participants in an age-segregated leisure program." *The Gerontologist, 12(4),* 1972, pp. 368–370.

Boldy, D., Abel, P., and Carter, K. *The Elderly in Grouped Dwellings: A Profile*. Devon: University of Exeter, Institute of Biometry and Community Medicine, 1973.

Bourestom, N. and Pastalan, L. "The effects of relocation on the elderly." *The Gerontologist, 21(1),* 1981.

Boyce, P. "The relationship between the performance of visual tasks and lighting conditions." In R. Greenhalgh (ed.). *Light for Low Vision*. Proceedings of a Symposium, University College, London, April 1978. Sussex: Hove, 1980.

Branch, Laurence G. "Continuing care retirement communities: Self-insuring for long-term care." *The Gerontologist, 27,* February 1987, pp. 4–8.

Brazener, Robert A. "Annotation: Validity and construction of contract under which applicant for admission to home for aged or infirm turns over his property to institution in return for lifetime care." *American Law Reports: Cases and Annotations,* 3rd Series, Vol. 44. Rochester, New York: The Lawyer's Cooperative Publishing Company, 1972, pp. 1174–1195.

Bresnick, Peggy S. "5 levels of congregate care succeed for elderly rentals." *Multi-Housing News,* October 1984, pp. 1, 52.

———. "Extensive rec, open unit design suit active retirement market." *Multi-Housing News,* March 1984, pp. 16, 21.

———. "Projects suited to 50-plus market range from subsidized to luxury." *Multi-Housing News,* March 1984, pp. 1, 16.

Brieff, R., Horwitz, J., and Hiatt, L. *Self-Help and Mutual Aid for the Elderly: A Literature Review*. Grant Report. New York: American Foundation for the Blind, 1981.

Brill, M. "Evaluating buildings on a performance basis." In J. Lang, C. Burnette, W. Moleski, and D. Vachon (eds.). *Designing for Human Behavior.* Stroudsburg, PA: Dowden, Hutchinson and Ross, Inc., 1974.

Brotman, H. *New Facts About Older Americans*. Department of Health, Education and Welfare Publication No. SRS 73–2007. Washington, D.C.: U.S. Government Printing Office, 1973.

Brotman, H.B. "Population projections, part 1: Tomorrow's older population (to 2000)." *The Gerontologist, 17,* 1977, pp. 203–209.

Brown, A.S. "Satisfying relationships for the elderly and their patterns of disengagement." *The Gerontologist, 14,* 1974, pp. 258–262.

Buffalo Organization for Social and Technological Innovation, Inc. *Accidents & Aging*. A Final Report prepared for the Administration on Aging, Grant 90AR0035. Buffalo, New York, December 1982.

Bultena, G.L. and Wood, V. "The American retirement community: Bane or blessing?" *Journal of Gerontology, 24,* 1969, pp. 209–217.

Butler, N.G. "Optimal long-term health care for the elderly: An acute care hospital's perspective." *Topics in Health Care Financing,* Fall 1984, pp. 57–65.

Butler, R.N. *Why Survive? Being Old in America.* New York: Harper and Row, 1973.
Carp, F. "Effects of improved housing on the lives of older people." In Neugarten, B. (ed.). *Middle Age and Aging.* Chicago: University of Chicago Press, 1968.
Carp, F.M. "Impact of improved housing on morale and life satisfaction." *The Gerontologist, 15,* 1975, pp. 511–515.
———. "Long-range satisfaction with housing." *The Gerontologist, 15,* 1975, pp. 68–72.
———. "Housing and living environments of older people." In Binstock, R.H. and Shanas, E. (eds.). *Handbook of Aging and the Social Sciences.* New York: Van Nostrand Reinhold, 1976.
———. "User evaluation of housing for the elderly." *The Gerontologist, 16(2),* 1976, pp. 102–111.
Carp, F. "Impact of improved living environment on health and life expectancy." *The Gerontologist, 17,* 1977, pp. 242–249.
Carp, F.M. "Effects of the living environment on activity and use of time." *International Journal of Aging and Human Development, 9,* 1978, pp. 75–91.
Carp, F. and Carp, A. "Person-environment congruence and sociability." *Research on Aging, 2,* 1980, pp. 395–415.
Carstens, Diane Y. *Site Planning and Design for the Elderly.* New York: Van Nostrand Reinhold, 1985.
Cavan, R.S., Burgess, E.W., Havighurst, R.J., and Goldhamer, H. *Personal Adjustment in Old Age.* Chicago: Science Research Associates, Inc., 1949.
Chellis, Robert D., Seagle, James F. Jr., and Seagle, Barbara Mackey. *Congregate Housing for Older People.* Lexington, MA: Lexington Books, 1985.
Clark, M.C. *Assistance with Activities of Daily Living for the Older Adult.* Miami: Stein Gerontological Institute, 1989.
Cochrane, G.M. and Wilshere, E.R. (eds.). *Equipment for the Disabled.* Volumes 1–13, Oxford, England: Oxfordshire Health Authority, c/o Mary Marlborough Lodge, 1981–89.
Cole, Richard A. and Marr, John A. "Life care retirement centers: The importance of the entry fee fund." *Healthcare Financial Management,* July 1984, pp. 84–90.
"Continuing care communities for graying americans." *Aide Magazine, 16,* Fall 1985, pp. 10–15.
"Continuing care communities for the elderly: Potential pitfalls and proposed regulation." *University of Pennsylvania Law Review, 128,* April 1980, pp. 883–936.
Cranz, G. and Schumacher, T.L. *Open Space for Housing for the Elderly, Working Paper 19.* Princeton, NJ: Princeton University Research Center for Urban and Environmental Planning, School of Architecture and Urban Planning, 1975.
———. "The impact of high-rise housing on older residents." In Conway, D. (ed.). *Human Response to Tall Buildings.* Stroudsburg, PA: Dowden, Hutchinson and Ross, 1977.
Cullinan, T.R. "Low vision in elderly people." In Greenhalgh, R. (ed.). *Light for Low Vision.* Proceedings of a symposium, University College, London, April 1980. Sussex: Hove, 1980, pp. 65–70.
Cumming, E. and Henry, W. *Growing Old. The Process of Disengagement.* New York: Basic Books, 1961.

Curran, Stroud and Brecht, Susan. "A perspective on risks for lifecare projects." *Real Estate Financial Journal, 1,* Summer 1985, pp. 64–69.

Davis, E. and Fine-Davis, M. "Predictors of satisfaction with housing and neighborhood: A nationwide study in the Republic of Ireland." *Social Indicators Research, 9,* 1981, pp. 477–494.

DeJong, Gerben. *Independent Living and Disability Policy in the Netherlands: Three Models of Residential Care and Independent Living.* New York: World Rehabilitation Fund, Spring 1984.

Department of Health and Social Security. *A Happier Old Age.* London: Her Majesty Stationary Office, 1979.

Dickman, I. *Making Life More Livable.* New York: American Foundation for the Blind, 1983.

Donahue, W. "Impact of living arrangement on ego development in the elderly." In Carp, F.M. (ed.). *Patterns of Living and Housing of Middle-Aged and Older People.* Washington, D.C.: U.S. Government Printing Office, 1966.

Faye, E.E. and Hood, C.M. "Visual rehabilitation in the geriatric population." In Hood, C.M. and Faye, E.E. (eds.). *Clinical Low Vision.* Boston: Little Brown, 1976.

Finkelstein, Victor. *Attitudes and Disabled Persons.* New York: World Rehabilitation Fund 1980.

Fisher, Anne B. "The new game in health care: Who will profit?" *Fortune,* March 4, 1985, pp. 138–143.

Flood, J.T. "Special problems of the aged deaf person." *Journal of Rehabilitation of the Deaf, 12(4),* 1979, pp. 34–35.

Fox, T.C., Frum, A.P., Resende, J.E., and Colborn, C. *Real Estate Development: Long-Term Care and Retirement Facilities.* New York: Matthew Bender & Company, 1989.

Gelwicks, L.E. and Newcomer, R.J. *Planning Housing Environments for the Elderly.* Washington, D.C.: National Council on the Aging, 1974.

Genensky, S. "Architectural barriers to the partially sighted—and solutions." *Architectural Record, 167(5),* 1980, pp. 65–67.

Gillmon, Rita. "Pacific homes: Implications for church-state separation." *The Christian Century,* September 27, 1978, pp. 886–888.

Gimmy, A.E. and Boehm, M.G. "Elderly housing—A guide to appraisal, market analysis, development and financing." Chicago: American Institute of Real Estate Appraisers, 1988.

Gold, Margaret. *Guide to Housing Alternatives for Older Citizens.* Mount Vernon, NY: Consumers Union, 1985.

Gordon, Paul A. "What counsel should know about full service retirement communities." *The Practical Real Estate Lawyer, 2(2),* March 1986, pp. 7–18.

———. *Developing Retirement Facilities.* New York: John Wiley & Sons, 1988.

Grayson, Paul. "Taking care of their own: a perspective on international approaches to life care." *Spectrum,* March/April 1988, pp. 22–23.

———. "Technology and aging—the newest business is: home automation." *Aging Network News,* January 1989, pp. 1, 6–7.

———. "Universal Design: Products serve all regardless of age." *Aging Network News.* April 1989, pp. 1, 16.

———. "From Barrier Free to Safe Environments: The New Zealand Experience." Commentary on WRF-IEEIR Monograph 44: *Interchange,* Summer 1989, p. 7.

———. *International Trends and Applications of New Technology in the Design of Housing for Older People.* Presentation at the Canadian Mortgage & Housing Corporation's Conference, Options—Housing Older Canadians. Halifax, Nova Scotia: October 17–20, 1988.

Green, I., Fedewa, B.E., Johnston, C.A., Jackson, W.M., and Deardorff, H.L. *Housing for the Elderly: The Development and Design Process.* New York: Van Nostrand Reinhold Company, 1975.

Gubrium, J.F. "Environmental effects on morale in old age and the resources of health and solvency." *The Gerontologist, 10(4),* 1970, pp. 294–297.

Gutman, G. "Issues and findings relating to multilevel accommodation for seniors." *Journal of Gerontology, 33,* 1978, pp. 592–600.

Gutman, R. and Westergaard, B. "Building evaluation, user satisfaction and design." In Lang, J., Burnette, C., Moleski, W., and Vachon, D. (eds.). *Designing for Human Behavior.* Stroudsburg, PA: Dowden, Hutchinson and Ross, 1974.

Haber, Paul A.L. "Technology in aging." *The Gerontologist,* 26 (4), 1986, pp. 350–357.

Hamovitch, M.B. "Social and psychological factors in adjustment in a retirement village." In Carp, F.M., (ed). *The Retirement Process.* Washington, D.C.: U.S. Government Printing Office, 1968.

Hamovitch, M.B. and Peterson, J.E. "Housing needs and satisfactions of the elderly." *Journal of Gerontology, 35,* 1969, pp. 232–240.

Hancock, Judith Ann (ed.). *Housing the Elderly.* Piscataway, NJ: Center for Urban Policy Research, Rutgers University, 1987.

Hare, P.H. "Carving up the American dream." *Planning, 47(7),* 1981, pp. 14–17.

———. "The empty nest as a golden egg: Using the unused space in single family neighborhoods." *Perspectives on Aging,* 1981.

Harel, Z. and Harel, B.B. "On-site coordinated services in age-segregated and age-integrated public housing." *The Gerontologist, 18(2),* 1978, pp. 153–158.

Harris, C.S. *Fact book on aging: A profile of America's older population.* Washington, D.C.: National Council on the Aging, 1978.

Hartman, C., Horovitz, J., and Herman, R. "Designing with the elderly." *The Gerontologist, 16(4),* 1976, pp. 303–311.

Havighurst, R.J. "Successful aging." In Williams, R.H., Tibbits, C., and Donahue, W. (eds.). *Process of Aging,* Vol. 1. New York: Atherton Press, 1963.

Havighurst, R.J. "A report of a special committee on the gerontological society. Research and development goals in social gerontology." *The Gerontologist, 9,* Part 2, 1969.

Hayden, D. *Seven American Utopias: The Architecture of Communitarian Socialism, 1790–1975.* Cambridge, MA: The MIT Press, 1976.

Heumann, L.F. and Boldy, D. *Housing for the Elderly: Policy Formulation in Europe and North America.* London: St. Martins Press, 1982.

Hiatt, L.G. "Environmental considerations in understanding and designing for mentally impaired older people." In McBride, H. (ed.). *Mentally Impaired Aging: Bridging the Gap.* Washington, D.C.: American Association of Homes for the Aging, 1979.

———. "Disorientation is more than a state of mind." *Nursing Homes, 29(4),* 1980, pp. 30–36.

Hiatt, L. "Care and design: The color and use of color in environments for older people." *Nursing Homes, 30(3),* 1981, pp. 18–22.

———. "A self-administered checklist: Renovation for innovation." *Nursing Homes, 30(1),* 1981, pp. 33–39.

———. "Grouping older people of different abilities." In Chellis, R.D. and Seagle, J.F. Jr. (eds.). *Congregate Housing for Older People: A New Solution.* Lexington, MA: Lexington Books, 1982.

Horn, Dennis M. "Developing and financing retirement center housing." *Real Estate Finance,* Summer 1985, pp. 26–37.

Horowitz, Judith, and Ryan, J. Bruce. "Structuring the life-care contract to minimize financial risk." *Topics in Health Care Financing,* Fall 1984, pp. 66–76.

Horsnell, Tim and Kidd, Brian J. *Changing the Image of Nursing Homes.* Presentation at the International Conference on Housing and Services for the Aging. Jerusalem, Israel, February 8–12, 1987.

Houghton, Rodney N., Batchelor, Dick J., Haldeman, Robert B., and Neff, Robert C. "Life care contract—Haven or heartache. *Real Property Probate and Trust Journal, 16,* Winter 1981, pp. 819–834.

Howell, S. *Designing for Aging: Patterns for Use.* Cambridge, MA: MIT Press, 1980.

Hughes, P.C. and Neer, R.M. "Lighting for the elderly: A psychobiological approach to lighting." *Human Factors, 23(1),* 1980, pp. 65–86.

Hull, Jon D. "Insurance for the twilight years." *Time,* April 6, 1987, p. 53.

Hunt, M.E. *Simulated Site Visits: Preparation for Relocation.* Final report to the U.S. Department of Health and Human Services. Ann Arbor: University of Michigan Press, Institute of Gerontology, 1981.

Hunt, M.E., Feldt, Allan G., Marans, Robert W., Pastalan, Leon A., and Vakalo, Kathleen L. "Retirement communities: An american original." Special issue of *Journal of Housing for the Elderly,* Winter 1983, pp. 1–278.

Jeck, Allister M. and Carlson, June E. "Retirement housing: Exploring the gray area of housing's gray market." *Real Estate Finance,* Winter 1986, pp. 57–68.

Jenkins, T. "Life care contract—A viable option." *Concern,* December 1975–January 1976, p. 35.

———. "Life Care Contracts—Problems?" *Concern,* February–March 1976, p. 27.

J.G. Furniture Systems. *G.P.F. Geriatric Personal Furnishings Planning Manual.* Quakertown, PA, 1980.

Jordan, J.J. *Senior Center Design: An Architect's Discussion of Facility Planning.* Washington, D.C.: National Council on the Aging, 1979.

Kaplan, R. "Predictors of environmental preference: Designers and clients." *Environmental Design Research, 1,* Stroudsburg, PA: Dowden, Hutchinson and Ross, 1973.

Kaplan, S. "Participation in the design process: A cognitive approach." In Stokols, D. (ed.). *Perspectives on Environment and Behavior: Theory, Research and Applications.* New York: Plenum Press, 1977.

Kira, A. *The Bathroom: Criteria for Design.* New York: Cornell University Press, 1966.

Knapp, M.R.J. "Predicting services in the context of the housing environment." *The Gerontologist, 9(1),* 1976, pp. 15–19.

Koncelik, J.A. *Designing the Open Nursing Home.* Stroudsburg, PA: Dowden, Hutchinson and Ross, 1976.

———. "Human factors and environmental design for the aging: Physiological change and sensory loss as design criteria." In Byerts, T.O., Howell, S.C., and Pastalan, L.A. (eds.). *Environmental Context of Aging.* New York: Garland, 1979.

———. *Aging and the Product Environment.* New York: Hutchinson Ross, 1982.

Koncelik, J.A. and Bonner, D. *Environmental Survey: First Community Village.* Columbus: Ohio State University, Department of Industrial Design, 1974.

Koncelik, J.A. and Kropet, R. *Product Survey, Aging and the Product Environment.* Columbus, OH: Final Report to the National Endowment for the Arts, 1981.

Kovner, A.R. and Neuhauser, D. (eds.). *Health Services Management.* Ann Arbor: University of Michigan, Health Administration Press, 1978.

Kozmo, A. and Stones, M.J. "Predictors of happiness." *Journal of Gerontology, 38(5),* 1983, pp. 626–628.

Lake, W.S. "Housing preferences and social patterns." In Tibbits, C. and Donahue, W. (eds.). *Social and Psychological Aspects of Aging.* New York: Columbia University Press, 1962.

Lanahan, Michael B. "Life care retirement centers: A concept in development." *Pride Institute Journal of Long Term Home Health Care, 2,* 1983, pp. 41–42.

Lane, T.S. and Feins, J.D. "Are the elderly overhoused? Definitions of space utilization and policy implication." *The Gerontologist, 25(3),* 1985, pp. 243–251.

Langer, E., and Rodin, J. "The effects of choice and enhanced personal responsibility for the aged: A field experiment in an institutional setting." *Journal of Personality and Social Psychology, 34,* 1976, pp. 191–198.

Laughlin, J.L. and Moseley, S.K. (eds.). *Retirement Housing.* New York: John Wiley and Sons, 1989.

Laventhol & Horwath. *Life Care Retirement Center Industry.* Philadelphia, 1985.

———. *The Senior Living Industry.* Philadelphia, 1986.

———. *The Nursing Home Industry, 1986: A Capsule View.* Philadelphia, 1986. *(Laventhol and Horwath (Certified Public Accountants) publish a series of annual reports on the life-care industry in the United States. Their address: 1845 Walnut Street, Philadelphia, PA 19103 (215–299–1600))*

Lawton, M.P. "Supportive services in the context of the housing environment." *The Gerontologist, 9(1),* 1969, pp. 15–19.

———. *Planning and Managing Housing for the Elderly.* New York: John Wiley and Sons, 1975.

———. "The impact of environment on aging and behavior." In Birren, J.E. and Schaie, K.W. (eds.). *Handbook of the Psychology of Aging.* New York: Van Nostrand Reinhold Company, 1977.

———. *Environment and Aging.* Monterey, CA: Brooks/Cole Publishing Co., 1980.

———. "Environment and other determinants of well-being in older people." *The Gerontologist, 23(4),* 1983, pp. 349–357.

Lawton, M.P., Brody, E. and Turner-Massey, P. "The relationship of environmental factors to changes in well-being." *The Gerontologist, 18,* 1978, pp. 133–137.

Lawton, M.P., Greenbaum, M. and Liebowitz, B. "The lifespan of housing environments for the aging." *The Gerontologist, 20(1),* 1980, pp. 56–64.

Lawton, M.P. and Hoover, S. *Community Housing and Choices for Older Americans.* New York: Springer, 1981.

Lawton, M.P., Moss, M. and Grimes, M. "The changing services needs of older tenants in planning housing." *The Gerontologist, 25(3),* 1985, pp. 258–265.

Lawton, M.P. and Nahemow, L. "Social science methods for evaluating the quality of housing for the elderly." *Journal of Architectural Research, 7(1),* 1979, pp. 5–11.

Lawton, M., Newcomer, R.J. and Byerts, T.O. *Community Planning for an Aging Society.* Stroudsburg, PA: Dowden, Hutchinson and Ross, 1976.

Lefitt, J. "Lighting for the elderly: An optician's view." In Greenhalgh, R. (ed). *Light for Low Vision.* Proceedings of a Symposium, University College, London, April 1978. Sussex: Hove, 1980, pp. 55–61.

Lemke, S. and Moos, R. "Assessing the institutional policies of sheltered care settings." *Journal of Gerontology, 35,* 1980, pp. 96–107.

———. "Coping with an intra-institutional relocation: Behavioral change as a function of residents' personal resources." Palo Alto: VA and Stanford University Medical Center, *Journal of Environmental Psychology, 4,* 1984, pp. 137–151.

Leonard, Lawrence, R. "The tie that binds: Life care contracts and nursing homes." *American Journal of Law and Medicine, 8,* Summer 1982, pp. 153–173.

Lerup, L., Cronrath, D. and Lu, J. "Fires in nursing facilities." In Cantor, D. (ed.). *Fires and Human Behavior.* London: John Wiley and Sons, 1980.

Liebowitz, B., Lawton, M.P. and Waldman, A. "Evaluation: Designing for confused elderly people." *American Institute of Architects Journal, 68,* 1979, pp. 59-61.

"Life care retirement homes—What they're like, what they cost." *Changing Times, 28,* 1982, pp. 28–32.

Linn, M.W., Gurel, L. and Linn, B.S. "Patient outcome as a measure of quality of nursing home care." *American Journal of Public Health, 67,* 1977, pp. 337–344.

"Long term care alternatives: Continuing care retirement communities." *Alpha Centerpiece: A Report on Health Policy Issues,* January 1984, pp. 2–6.

Longino, Charles F. and Lipman, Aaron. "Married and spouseless men and woman in planned retirement communities: Support network differentials." *Journal of Marriage and the Family,* February 1981, pp. 169–177.

———. "The married, the formerly married and the never married: Support system differentials of older women in planned retirement communities." *International Journal of Aging and Human Development,* 1982, pp. 285–297.

Lublin, Joann S. "Costly retirement home market booms, raising concern for aged." *The Wall Street Journal,* October 22, 1986.

Ludington, John P. "Annotation: Enforceability of contract to make will in return for services, by one who continues performance after death of person originally undertaking to serve." *American Law Reports ALR3d Cases and Annotations,* Vol. 84. Rochester, NY: The Lawyer's Cooperative Publishing Company, 1978, pp. 930–937.

Lundgren-Lindquist, Birgitta. *Activities of Daily Living Analysis Among Elderly in Sweden*. Presentation at the International Conference on Housing and Services for the Aging, Jerusalem, Israel, February 8–12, 1987.

Lyles, Jean Caffey. "Methodist litigations and public relations." *The Christian Century,* December 19, 1979, pp. 1256–1257.

McCullough, H.E. and Farnham, M.B. "Kitchens for women in wheelchairs." *Circular 841*. Urbana, IL: College of Agriculture Extension Service, 1961.

McGillivray, R. (ed.). "Aids for elderly persons with impaired vision." *Aids and Appliances Review, 13*. Newton, MA: Carroll Center for the Blind, 1984.

McGuire, M. "Preventive measures to minimize accidents among the elderly." *Occupational Health Nursing, 19,* 1971, pp. 13–16.

McGuire, M.C. *Design of Housing for the Elderly: A Checklist*. Washington, D.C.: National Association of Housing & Redevelopment Officials, 1972.

McMullin, DeWayne, "Hospitals and CCRC's: A growing alternative." *Contemporary LTC,* November 1985, pp. 44–48.

Messer, M. "The possibility of an age concentrated environment becoming a normative system." *The Gerontologist, 7(4),* 1967, pp. 247–251.

Midwinter, Eric. *New Design for Old Function, Style and Older People*. London, England: Centre for Policy and Ageing, 1988.

Miller, D. and Lieberman, M. "The relationships of affect state and adaptive capacity to reactions to stress." *Journal of Gerontology, 20,* 1965, pp. 492–497.

Ministry of Housing and Local Government. *Grouped Flatlets for Old People: A Sociological Study, Design Bulletin 2*. London: Her Majesty Stationary Office, 1962.

Moen, E. "The reluctance of the elderly to seek help." *Social Problems, 25(3),* 1978, pp. 293–303.

Moore, Jim. *Retirement Housing Market Feasibility*. Fort Worth: Moore Diversified Services, 1986.

Moos, R. *The Human Context: Environmental Determinants of Behavior*. New York: John Wiley and Sons, 1976.

———. "Environmental choice and control in community care settings for older people." *Journal of Applied Social Psychology, 11,* 1981, pp. 23–43.

Moos, R. and Lemke, S. "Evaluating specialized living environments for older people." In Birren, J.E. and Schaie, K.W. (eds.). *Handbook of the Psychology of Aging*. 2nd ed. New York: Van Nostrand Reinhold, 1985.

Morrison, I.A., Bennett, R., Frisch, S. and Garland, B.J. (eds.). *Continuing Care Retirement Communities: Political Social and Financial Issues*. New York: The Haworth Press, 1986.

Mulvihill, R. "The relative importance of elements of low-rise housing estates." *Planning division working paper 1*. Ireland: An Foras Forbartha, 1977.

Nahemow, L., Lawton, M.P. and Howell, S. "Elderly people in tall buildings: A nationwide survey." In Conway, D.J. (ed.). *Human Response to Tall Buildings*. Stroudsburg, PA: Dowden, Hutchinson, and Ross, 1977.

National Association for Senior Living Industries. *The Directory of Senior Living Industries*. Annapolis, MD: NASLI, 1986.

National Commission on Architectural Barriers to Rehabilitation of the Handicapped. *Design for All Americans*. Washington, D.C.: U.S. Government Printing Office, 1968.

National Advisory Council on Aging. *Housing an Aging Population: Guidelines for Development and Design.* Ottawa, Canada: Government of Canada, 1987.

National Council on the Aging. *The Myth and Reality of Aging in America.* Washington, D.C.: National Council on the Aging, 1975.

———. *Aging in the Eighties: American in Transition.* Washington, D.C.: National Council on the Aging, 1981.

National Safety Council. *Accident Facts.* Chicago: National Safety Council, 1980 Edition.

Neugarten, B.L., Havighurst, R.J. and Robin, S.S. "The measurement of life satisfaction." *Journal of Gerontology, 16(2),* 1961, pp. 134–143.

Newman, O. *Design Guidelines for Creating Defensible Space.* Washington, D.C.: LEAA, National Institute of Law Enforcement and Criminal Justice, 1976.

Noam, E. *Homes for the Aged: Supervision and Standards.* United States Department of Health Education and Welfare, Washington, D.C.: National Clearinghouse on Aging, 1975.

Noam, E. and Donahue, W. *Assisted Independent Living in Group Housing for Older People: A Report on the Situation in European Countries.* Washington, D.C.: International Center for Social Gerontology, 1976.

Ohta, R.J., Carlin, M.F. and Harmon, B.M. "Auditory acuity and performance on the mental status questionnaire in the elderly." *American Geriatric Society, 29(10),* 1981, pp. 476–478.

Osterberg, A.E. *A Post Construction Evaluation of Westside Retirement Home: The Impact of Design and the Physical Environment on Building Users.* Ann Arbor, MI: University Microfilms, 1980.

Otten, Alan L. "U.S. agencies awaken to the need for more data on nation's elderly." *The Wall Street Journal,* December 9, 1986, p. 36.

Pan American Health Organization. *Toward in Well-being of the Elderly* Washington, D.C.: PAHO Scientific Publication 492, 1985.

Parker, Rosetta E. *Housing for the Elderly: The Handbook for Managers.* Chicago: Institute of Real Estate Management, 1984.

Pastalan, L.A. "Privacy as an expression of human territoriality." In Pastalan, L.A. and Carson, D.H. (eds.). *Spacial Behavior of Older People.* Ann Arbor: University of Michigan Press, 1970.

———. "The emphatic model. A methodological bridge between research and design." *Journal of Architecture Education, 31(1),* 1977, pp. 14–15.

———. "Sensory changes and environmental behavior." In Byerts, T.O., Howell, S.C. and Pastalan, L.A. (eds.). *Environmental Context of Aging.* New York: Garland, 1979.

Philips, R.H. and Salmen, J.P.S. "Building for accessibility: Design and product specification." *The Construction Specifier,* 1983, pp. 20–34.

Pifer, Alan, and Bronte, Lydia. *Our Aging Society.* New York: W.W. Norton, 1986.

Pirkl, James and Babic, Anna. *Guidelines and Strategies for Designing Transgenerational Products.* New York: Copley, 1988.

President's Commission on Housing. *Report of the President's Commission on Housing.* Washington, D.C., 1982.

Pynoos, J. "Continuum of care retirement communities: Option for mid-upper-income elders." *Generations,* 1985, pp. 31–33.

Pynoos, Jon, Regnier, Victor and O'Brien, Terence K. *Continuum of Care Retirement Community Project: Final Report.* Los Angeles, CA: Institute for Policy and Program Development, Andrus Gerontology Center, University of Southern California, April 1983, revised October 1984.

Pynoos, J. and Salend, E. "The delivery of long term care services to the elderly: Services to people or people to services." In *Aging Households, Long Term Care and Environments for the Elderly.* Occasional Papers No. 20. Vancouver: University of British Columbia, Center for Human Settlements, 1982, pp. 3–21.

Raper, A.T. *National Continuing Care Directory.* Glenview, IL: Scott, Foresman & Co., published for the American Association of Retired Persons, (AARP Books, 400 S. Edward Street, Mount Prospect, IL 60056), 1984.

Raschko, Bettyann. *Housing Interiors for the Disabled and Elderly.* New York: Van Nostrand Reinhold, 1982.

Ratzka, Adolph D. *Independent Living and Attendant Care in Sweden: A Consumer Perspective.* New York: World Rehabilitation Fund, 1986.

Rausch, Erwin and Perper, Maria M. *Resident Care Management System.* Boston: CBI Publishing Company, Inc., 1980.

Regnier, V. "Congregate housing for the elderly: An integrative and participatory planning model." In Vonier, T. (ed.). *Proceedings of the Research and Design '85 Conference.* Washington, D.C.: American Institute of Architects, 1985.

———. "Design criteria for outdoor space surrounding housing the elderly." In Vonier, T. (ed.). *Proceedings of the Research and Design '85 Conference.* Washington, D.C.: American Institute of Architects, 1985.

Regnier, V. and Gelwicks, L. "Preferred supportive services for middle to higher income retirement housing." *The Gerontologist, 20(1),* 1981.

Regnier, V. and Pynoos, J. *Housing the Aged: Design Directives and Policy Considerations.* New York: Elsevier Science Publishing Co., 1987.

Reinius, Karen, (ed.). *The Elderly and their Environment-Research in Sweden.* Stockholm, Sweden: Swedish Council for Building Research, 1984.

Rodin, J. and Langer, E.J. "Long-term effects of a controlled relevant intervention with the institutionalized aged." *Journal of Personality and Social Psychology, 35,* 1977, pp. 897–902.

Rogers, Rowena. "Explore life care possibilities." *Journal of Gerontological Nursing, 12,* 1986, pp. 12–21.

Rohrer, Robert L. and Bibb, Robert. "Marketing: The CCRC challenge." *Contemporary Long-Term Care,* May 1986, pp. 41–58.

Rose, Aaron M. "Continuing care retirement centers: An expansion opportunity." *American Health Care Association Journal,* May 1983, pp. 36–39.

———. "Entrepreneurs reshaping lifecare." *Modern Healthcare,* July 1984, pp. 148–153.

Rudnitsky, Howard and Konrad, Walecia. "Trouble in the Elysian fields." *Forbes,* August 29, 1983, pp. 58–59.

Schoenstein, Ralph. *Every Day is Sunday—Lighthearted Search for America's Best Retirement Village.* Boston: Little, Brown & Co., 1986.

Schroeder, S. and Steinfeld, E. *The Estimated Cost of Accessible Buildings.* Washington, D.C.: U.S. Government Printing Office, 1978.

Seiler, Stephen R. "How to develop retirement communities for profit." *Real Estate Review,* Fall 1986, pp. 70–75.

Seip, David E. "Doing it over again." *Contemporary Long Term Care,* May 1987, pp. 28–29.

"Seniors reduce space needs, accept high densities." *Multi-Housing News,* July 1986, pp. 21–24.

Sherwood, S., Greer, D. S., Morris, J. N. and Mor, V. *An Alternative to Institutionalization: The Highland Heights Experiment.* Cambridge, MA: Ballinger, 1981.

Sicurella, V. "Color contrast as an aid for visually impaired persons." *Journal of Visual Impairment and Blindness, 71,* 1977, 252–257.

Sims, William B. "Financing strategies for long-term care facilities." *Health-Care Financial Management,* March 1984, pp. 42–54.

Small, Norma R. and Walsh, Mary B. *Teaching Nursing Homes, The Nursing Perspective.* Owings Mills, MD: National Health Publishing, 1988.

Söderstrom, Bengt and Viklund, Elisabet. *Housing Care and Service for Elderly and Old People—The Situation in Sweden.* Stockholm, Sweden: Swedish Government Printing, 1986.

Spivack, M. "Archetypal places." In Preiser, W.F.E. (ed.). *Environmental Design Research.* Stroudsburg, PA: Dowden, Hutchinson and Ross, 1973.

Steinfeld, E. *Barrier Free Design for the Elderly and the Disabled.* New York: Syracuse University, All University Gerontology Center, 1975.

Steinfeld, E. *Access to the Built Environment: A Review of Literature.* Washington, D.C.: U.S. Government Printing Office, 1979.

Steinfeld, E., Duncan, J. and Cardell, P. "Towards a responsive environment: The psychosocial effects of inaccessibility." In Bednar, M. (ed.). *Barrier-Free Environments.* Stroudsburg, PA: Dowden, Hutchinson and Ross, 1977.

Steinfeld, E., Schroeder, S. and Bishop, M. *Accessible Buildings for People With Walking and Reaching Limitations.* Washington, D.C.: U.S. Department of Housing and Urban Development, 1979.

Thrope, Norman. "Communities for retirees on rise again." *The Wall Street Journal, 13,* September 2, 1983, p. 27.

Tiven, Marjorie and Ryther, Barbara. *State Initiatives in Elderly Housing: What's New, What's Tried and True?* Washington, D.C.: Council of State Housing Agencies and National Association of State Units on Aging, December 1986.

Tolman, E. "Cognitive maps in rats and men." *Psychological Review, 55,* 1984, pp. 189–208.

Topolnicki, Denise M. "The broken promise of life-care communities." *Money,* April 1985, pp. 150–157.

Toseland, R. and Rasch, J. "Factors contributing to older persons' satisfaction with their communities." *The Gerontologist, 18,* 1978, pp. 395–402.

United States Senate, Special Committee on Aging. *Aging America: Trends and Projections.* 1985–86 Edition. Prepared in conjunction with the American Association of Retired Persons, the Federal Council on the Aging, and the Administration on Aging. Washington, D.C.: U.S. Department of Health and Human Services, 1985.

United States Department of Education, Office of Special Education and Rehabilitative Services. "Improving the deaf person's environment." *American Rehabilitation, 5(5),* 1980, pp. 12–13.

United States Department of Housing and Urban Development. *Barrier Free Design.* Washington, D.C.: U.S. Government Printing Office, 1979.

Urban Institute. *Report of the Comprehensive Service Needs Study.* Washington, D.C.: The Urban Institute, 1975.

Urban Land Institute. *Housing for a Maturing Population.* Washington, D.C.: ULI, 1983.

Urban Systems Research and Engineering. *Evaluation of the Effectiveness of Congregate Housing for the Elderly.* Washington, D.C.: United States Department of Housing and Urban Development, 1976.

Vladeck, Bruce C. *Unloving Care—The Nursing Home Tragedy.* New York: Basic Books, Inc., 1980.

Wasser, L. and Cloud, D. (eds.). *Continuing Care Issues for Nonprofit Providers.* Washington, D.C.: American Association of Homes for the Aged, 1980.

Wasser, L. (ed.). *Continuing Care Homes: A Guidebook for Consumers.* Washington, D.C.: American Association of Homes for the Aged, 1976.

Weiner, B. "Industrial designers response to corridor disorientation and the geriatric walker." In Bednar, M., et al. (eds.). *Environment and Aging: Concepts and Issues.* Washington, D.C.: Gerontological Society, 1975.

Weisman, G. "Evaluating architectural legibility: Wayfinding in the built environment." *Environment and Behavior, 13,* 1981, pp. 189–204.

———. "Developing man-environment models." In Lawton, M.P., Windley, P. and Byerts, T. (eds.). *Aging and the environment: Theoretical approaches.* New York: Springer, 1982.

Weiss, J.D. *Better Buildings for the Aged.* New York: McGaw-Hill Book Company, 1969.

Weissert, W.G. *Long-Term Care: Current Policy and Directions for the 80's.* Paper presented at the 1981 White House Conference on Aging. Washington, D.C.: The Urban Institute, 1981.

Welch, P., Parker, V. and Zeisel, J. *Independence through Interdependence.* Boston: Building Diagnostics, 1984.

Welsh, R.L. and Blasch, B.B. (eds.) *Foundations of Orientation and Mobility.* New York: American Foundation for the Blind, 1980.

Wener, R. and Kaminoff, R. "Environmental clarity and perceived crowding." In Seidel, A. and Danford, S. (eds.). *Environmental Design: Research, Theory and Application.* Washington, D.C.: Environmental Design Research Association, 1979.

Winklevoss, Howard E. and Powell, Alwyn V. *Continuing Care Retirement Communities: An Empirical, Financial and Legal Analysis.* Homewood, IL: Richard D. Irwin, for Pension Research Council, Wharton School, University of Pennsylvania, 1984.

Worley, H. Wilson. *Retirement Living Alternatives USA—The Inside Story.* Clemson, SC: Columbia House, 1982.

Zeisel, J. *Inquiry by Design. Tools for Environment-Behavior Research.* Monterey, CA: Brooks/Cole, 1981.

Zeisel, J., Epp, G. and Demos, S. *Low-Rise Housing for Older People: Behavioral Criteria for Design*. HUD Publication No. 483. Washington, D.C.: U.S. Government Printing Office, 1977.

Zeisel, J., Welch, P., Epp, G. and Demos, S. *Mid-Rise Elevator Housing for Older People*. Boston: Building Diagnostics, 1983.

Associations

American Association of Homes for the Aging (AAHA)
1050 17th St., N.W.
Washington, D.C. 20036 (202) 296–5960

Represents sponsors and operators of nonprofit nursing and retirement homes for the elderly and related services. AAHA publishes a number of publications on life care, continuing care, and other subjects.

American Association of Retired People (AARP)
1909 K St., N.W.
Washington, D.C. 22049 (202) 872–4700

Largest association for the elderly in the United States. Lobbies for senior-related legislation and provides information, insurance, travel programs, educational programs, and other services to its members.

National Association of Independent Living Centers (NAILC)
1501 Lee Highway, Suite 205
Arlington, VA 22209 (703) 243–9100

Established to promote professionalism and excellence among developers, operators, and consultants of housing for the independent elderly.

National Association of Senior Living Industries (NASLI)
125 Cathedral St.
Annapolis, MD 21401 (301) 263–0991

Established to promote information sharing among for-profit and nonprofit organizations, professionals, and private citizens in the elderly housing field.

The National Council on the Aging (NCOA)
600 Maryland Ave., S.W., West Wing 100
Washington, D.C. 20024 (202) 479–1200

A nonprofit membership organization promoting development, publications, special programs, and training to meet older people's needs.

Index

About the Contributors

Jerry Avorn, M.D., associate professor of social medicine and health policy at Harvard Medical School, is an internist specializing in geriatric medicine, as well as a researcher in clinical epidemiology and health-care delivery. His current work centers on the interplay between geriatric medicine, clinical decision making, and health policy.

Lawrence G. Branch, Ph.D. is a professor at the Boston University School of Medicine. He was formerly on the faculty of Harvard Medical School and has been president of the board at North Hill, a life-care center in Needham, Massachusetts, with 341 independent living units and a sixty-bed nursing facility. Currently, he is a principal with Later Life, a developer of life-care facilities in the Greater Boston area.

Pamela J. Cluff, FRAIC, FRIBA is president of Associated Planning Consultants Inc., Toronto, Canada, and has been active in the planning and design of housing for the elderly and physically disabled for over thirty years. She consults with national, state, and provincial governments, and with developers of private and nonprofit housing.

George Cochrane, M.D., FRCP, medical director of the Mary Marlborough Lodge at the Nuffield Orthopaedic Centre, Oxford, England, is an international expert on technical aids for the elderly and disabled. He also leads the Disabled Living Research Centre, which assesses the residual abilities and needs of people of all ages, especially the elderly, and recommends individual programs, special equipment, and adaptations that make independent living possible.

Larry M. Diamond, Ph.D., managing director of Senior Health Systems Inc., Cambridge, Massachusetts, works extensively with hospitals, retirement communities, health maintenance organizations, and major insurance companies in the design and implementation of managed-care systems for older adults. Dr.

Diamond was principal staff member of the National Social HMO Demonstration project and is currently working with several hospital networks to implement new Medicare supplement and long-term care arrangements.

Maria B. Dwight, M.S.G. is president of Gerontological Services, Inc., of Santa Monica, California, a nationally recognized market research firm specializing in aging. Her clients include hospitals, municipalities, long-term care providers, housing sponsors and developers, and universities. She has been in this field over twenty years and currently serves as a fellow for the UCLA/USC long-term care gerontology center.

Robert B. Haldeman, M.S.S.W., J.D. is founder of Coventry Resources L.P. and president of C.P.S.C., its general partner. He has been involved with the structure and financing of life-care communities since 1975 and has a background in finance, the application of actuarial study to life care, the practice of law, and the administration of social services.

Ann Hambrook is president and founder of Hamlyn Associates, Inc., which targets senior housing, health care, and services. Under her direction, the company has provided marketing services to over one hundred planned or operating retirement communities.

Bjarne Hastrup, M.A. in economics from the University of Copenhagen, managing director of the EGV Foundation, Copenhagen, Denmark, is responsible for the development of health care and housing for elderly people in cooperation with municipalities. The organization has a staff of four thousand and provides services and housing to approximately forty thousand elders. He is also director of DaneAge, a membership organization working for elderly people, with over one hundred eighty thousand members.

Jeffrey M. Kichen, M.S. is director of research with Roche, Meister & Associates, Inc. and has written extensively on the subject of housing and health care.

Gail L. Kohn brought administrative and consulting experience to her job as executive director of the proposed Collington Episcopal Lifecare Community, Inc., in Mitchellville, Maryland.

Mark R. Meiners, Ph.D. is senior research manager at the National Center for Health Services Research, specializing in the areas of aging and health, with emphasis on financial and reimbursement issues. His sixteen years of research on long-term care insurance has been recognized as a catalyst for the development of creative new ways to insure against the financial risk of chronic illness.

Donald Moon, president of FRC Management Inc. of Gwynedd, Pennsylvania has been executive director for eleven years of the Foulkeways Retirement Community, and currently is president of Jeanes/Foulkeways, which offers a life-care-at-home program, he travels extensively consulting on the design and implementation of the life-care-at-home plan nationwide.

Robert Morris, D.S.W. Cardinal Mederios Lecturer at the University of Massachusetts and Kristen Professor Emeritus at Brandeis University, has worked for over thirty-five years on the development of alternative models of meeting diverse social and medical needs in home and community settings including social-health maintenance organizations.

Joseph L. Roche, M.S., is president of Roche, Meister & Associates, Inc. and has had over fifteen years of experience in planning and marketing of retirement housing and health-care facilities.

D. Martin Trueblood is executive director of Williamsburg Landing, Williamsburg, Virginia and director of development and consulting for American Retirement Corporation (ARC), Nashville, Tennessee.

Gardner W. Van Scoyac has spent over twenty-five years in this field of elderly housing and health care, building a national reputation for his expertise in planning, marketing, development, and management. He has been the CEO of a facility in transition and has gone on to develop a major consulting firm, assisting dozens of project sponsors.

About the Editors

Robert D. Chellis, M.P.H. is the principal of Chellis Associates, Wellesley, Massachusetts, and has a national practice specializing in program planning of life-care and congregate housing. He programmed and followed to completion the first life-care campus in Massachusetts and has testified before the U.S. Senate Special Committee on Aging. He has appeared on national television with Ted Koppel discussing the potential of home equity conversion, life care and life-care insurance and is a lecturer in planning and development of life care and congregate housing at Harvard University Graduate School of Design. He is president of New England Gerontological Association, a former president of National Lifecare Corporation, and has been a trustee of, and consultant to, nonprofit homes for the aging for more than twenty-five years.

Mr. Chellis, a licensed nursing-home administrator and certified housing manager, received his B.A. degree from Princeton University and his M.P.H. from Harvard University in health services administration. A previous publication is Congregate Housing for Older People, published by Lexington Books in 1982 and reprinted in 1984.

Paul John Grayson M.Arch., AIA, president of Environments for Living, Winchester, Massachusetts, is a research and design consultant in the area of barrier-free housing and innovative technology for the elderly and disabled. He lectures extensively here and abroad on retirement housing and promotes the application of products of universal design to serve not only the elderly and disabled, but people of all ages and abilities. As architect of the Elizabeth Seton Residence, he designed an innovative extended-care facility and retirement center for the Sisters of Charity of Saint Vincent de Paul, in Wellesley, Massachusetts. He also provided assistance in the development of the preliminary program, site analysis, and initial feasibility studies on Carleton-Willard Village, the first life-care campus in Massachusetts.

Mr. Grayson has over thirty years of experience in architecture and planning, serving as project architect on major residential and commercial projects throughout the United States. A licensed architect, he received his Master in Architecture degree from Harvard University. Recently, Mr. Grayson was awarded the Arthur W. Wheelwright Traveling Fellowship in Architecture at Harvard, studying how other countries care for and house the elderly and disabled. He is also president of Cooperative Elder Services, Inc., a suburban Boston area provider of adult day care for some one hundred fifty frail elders, and is currently contributing to two other books on the subject of retirement housing.